Company Secretarial Practice

G M Thom
LL B (Hons)
Tutor in Law, The Financial Training Company

Eighth Edition

THE M & E HANDBOOK SERIES

Pitman Publishing
128 Long Acre, London WC2E 9AN

A Division of Longman Group UK Limited

First published in Great Britain 1965
Second edition 1969
Third edition 1974
Fourth edition 1977
Fifth edition 1981
Sixth edition 1984
Seventh edition 1987
Eighth edition 1991

British Library Cataloguing in Publication Data
Thom, G. M.
Company secretarial practice. – 8th. ed. – (The M&E handbook series).
1. Great Britain. Company secretaryship
I. Title
344.106664

ISBN 0 7121 0839 4

Typeset by FDS Ltd, Penarth, South Glamorgan
Printed and bound in Great Britain

Contents

Preface vii
Table of cases ix

1 **Formation of a company** 1
The registered company; Registration; Re-registration; Oversea companies; Memorandum of Association; Matters affecting the Memorandum; Articles of Association; Capital structure; Maintenance of capital

2 **Procedure after incorporation** 62
First board meeting; Raising capital

3 **Application and allotment** 105
Procedure; Restrictions on allotment; Letters of renunciation; Allotment to existing members; Allotment of bonus shares

4 **Calls and instalments** 128
Preliminary considerations; Procedure on making a call; Forfeiture

5 **The common seal** 141
Regulations as to its use and custody; The official seal; Securities seal

6 **The Register of Members** 147
Statutory provisions as to form and contents, location, inspection, etc.; Overseas Branch Register; The Annual Return

7 **Share certificates** 163
Legal effects; Preparation and issue; Share warrants

8 **Transfer and transmission of shares** 179
Transfer of shares; Transmission of shares

9 **Registration of documents** 204
Documents received for registration; Procedure on receipt

10 **Dividends and employees' share schemes** 224
General rules — profits available for distribution; Dividend procedure and documents; Employees' share schemes

11 **Alterations of share capital** 245
Alteration of capital under s.121 CA 1985; Reduction of capital under s.135 CA 1985

12 **Voluntary arrangements; reconstruction; amalgamation;schemes of arrangement; the City Code; Register of interests in shares** 260
Survey of schemes available; Company voluntary arrangements; Schemes of arrangement under s. 425 CA 1985; Reconstruction under s. 110, IA 1986; Other schemes of reconstruction; The City Code; Register of Interests in Shares

13 **Winding-up** 291
Introduction; Winding-up by the court; Voluntary winding-up; Proceedings in a members' voluntary winding-up; Proceedings in a creditors' voluntary winding-up

14 **Directors, secretaries and auditors; directors' report** 312
Directors; The Secretary; Auditors; Directors' report; Insider trading

15 **Borrowing powers; trust deeds; receiverships; administration** 359
Methods of borrowing; Debentures; Procedure on issue of debentures; Trust deeds; Receiverships; Administration orders

Index 387

Preface

The legislative activity commented on in the preface to the seventh edition of this book has continued unabated. In particular, the Companies Act 1989 has altered and supplemented the existing legislation in many ways and, more specifically, has sought to ease the administrative burden placed upon private companies by the introduction of the elective regime.

This activity has called for extensive revision and appropriate re-writing of the original text. In carrying out this process I have sought to keep faith with the intention of the original author and to reduce the subject of company secretarial practice to its bare essentials.

Throughout the text the abbreviation CA is used for Companies Act, the appropriate Act being designated by its date of enactment. Abbreviations used in the text for other Acts are as follows:

Company Securities (Insider Dealing) Act 1985: CS(ID)A 1985
Business Names Act 1985: BNA 1985
Company Directors Disqualification Act 1986: CDDA 1986
Insolvency Act 1986: IA 1986
Financial Services Act 1986: FSA 1986

Likewise references to Table A, B, etc. are to those Tables as published in the Companies (Tables A to F) Regulations 1985.

I trust that this use of abbreviations will not detract from the text and hope it will in fact facilitate the learning process.

The text has been written on the basis that the provisions of all the Acts mentioned above are fully operative.

G M Thom
1990

Table of cases

A-G *v.* Great Eastern Railway Co. (1880) 5 App Cas 473 *26*
Aberdeen Ry. Co. *v.* Blaikie Bros. (1854) 1 Macq. (HL) 461 *328*
Alabaster's Case (1868) L.R. 7 Eq. 504 *152*
Alexander *v.* Automatic Telephone Co. [1900] 2 Ch.56 *130*
Allen *v.* Gold Reefs Ltd. [1900] 1 Ch. 656 *41*
Ashbury Railway Carriage Co. *v.* Riche (1875) L.R. 7 H.L. 653 *26*
Ayre *v.* Skelsey's Adamant Cement Co. Ltd (1904) 29 T.L.R. 587 *40*

Baily *v.* British Equitable Assurance Co. [1906] A.C. 35 *40*
Balkis Consolidated Co. *v.* Tomkinson [1893] A.C. 396 *163*
Barnett, Hoares & Co. *v.* South London Tramways (1887) 18 QBD 815 *340*
Barton *v.* L.N.W. Railway Co. (1889) 24 Q.B.D. 77 *187*
Beeton & Co. Ltd, *Re* (1913) 2 Ch 279 *313*
Bisgood *v.* Henderson's Transvaal Estate [1908] 1 Ch. 743 *277*
Bloomenthal *v.* Ford [1897] A.C. 156 *163*
Bolivia Republic Exploration Syndicate Ltd, *Re* [1914] 1 Ch. 139 *95*
Bradford Banking Co. *v.* Briggs (1886) 12 App. Cas. 29 *154*
Brailey *v.* Rhodesia Consolidated [1910] 2 Ch. 95 *276*
Bridgewater Navigation Co., *Re* [1891] 2 Ch. 317 *225*
Brighton Hotel Co., *Re* (1868) L.R. 6 Eq. 339 *294*
Brown *v.* British Abrasive Wheel Co. (1919) 1 Ch 290 *41*
Burns *v.* Siemens Brothers Dynamo Works Ltd. [1919] 1 Ch. 225 *152, 153*
Bushell *v.* Faith [1970] A.C. 1099 *320*

Campbell's Case (1873) 9 Ch. App. 1; 43 L.J. Ch.1 *246*
Cawley & Co., *Re* (1889) 42 Ch. D. 209 *130*
Chapman's Case (1866) L.R. 1 Eq. 346; 14 L.T. 742 *296*
Clarke & Chapman *v.* Hart (1858) 6 H.L.C. 650 *135*

Dafen Tinplate Co. *v.* Llanelly Steel Co. (1907) Ltd (1920) 2 Ch 124 *41*
Davies *v.* Gas Light & Coke Co. [1909] 1 Ch. 248 *151*
Demerara Rubber Co., *Re* [1913] 1 Ch 331 *276*
De Pass's Case (1859) 4 De G. & J. 544 *180*
Dexine Patent Packing Co., *Re* (1903) 88 L.T. 791 *252*

Eley *v.* Positive Government Security Life Assurance (1876) 1 Ex. D. 86 *35*
Esparto Trading Co., *Re* (1879) 12 Ch. D. 708 *135*
Evans' Case [1867] 2 Ch. App. 427 *153*

Fowler *v.* Commercial Timber Co. Ltd 2 KB1 *302*

General Auction Estate Co. *v.* Smith [1891] 3 Ch. 432 *364*
German Date Coffee Co., *Re* (1882) 20 Ch. D. 169 *292*
Greene, *Re* [1949] Ch. 333 *179*
Greenhalg *v.* Arderne Cinemas (1951) Ch 286 *40*

Hampson *v.* Prices Patent Candle Co. (1876) 45 L.J. Ch. 437 *313*
Hickman *v.* Kent or Romney Marsh Sheep-Breeders Association (1915) 1 Ch 881 *34*
Hopkinson *v.* Mortimer Harley & Co. [1917] 1 Ch. 646 *135*
Household Fire Insurance Co. Ltd. *v.* Grant (1879) 4 Ex. D. 216 *108*
Hutton *v.* West Cork Ry. Co. (1883) 23 Ch. D. 654 *313*

Inman *v.* Ackroyd & Best Ltd [1901] 1 Q.B. 613 *324*
International Securities Corpn., *Re* (1908) 24 T.L.R. 837 *293*

Jones *v.* Bellgrove Properties [1949] 2 K.B. 700 *225*

Ladies' Dress Association *v.* Pulbrook [1900] 2 Q.B. 376 *136*
Licensed Victuallers' Association, *Re* (1889) 42 Ch. D. 1 *95*
Loch *v.* John Blackwood Ltd. [1924] A.C. 783 *293*
London County Coal Co., *Re* (1886) L.R. 3 Eq. 355 *292*
Lundy Granite Co., *Re* (Lewis's Case) (1872) 26 L.T. 673 *323*

Mack Trucks (Britain) Ltd., *Re* [1967] 1 W.L.R. 780 *377*
Metropolitan Coal Consumers' Association *v.* Scrimgeour (1885) 2 Q.B. 604 *99*
Midland Counties Bank *v.* Attwood [1905] 1 Ch. 357 *302*

New British Iron Co. *ex p* Beckwith (1898) 1 Ch 324 *35*
Newdigate Colliery Ltd., *Re* [1912] 1 Ch. 468 *378*
Newhart Developments Ltd. *v.* Co-operative Commercial Bank Ltd. [1978] Q.B. 814 *378*
North-West Transportation Co. *v.* Beatty (1887) 12 App. Cas. 589 *329*

Panorama Developments (Guildford) Ltd *v.* Fidelis Furnishing Fabrics Ltd (1971) 2 QB 711 *340*
Parsons *v.* Parsons (Albert J.) & Sons Ltd. [1979] 1 C.R. 271 *313*
Patent File Co., *Re, ex parte* Birmingham Co. (1870) 6 Ch. D. 83 *364*
Patent Invert Sugar Co., *Re* (1885) 31 Ch. D. 166 *254*
Penrose *v.* Martyr (1858) E.B. & E. 499 *341*
Percival *v.* Wright [1902] 2 Ch. 421 *312*

Rayfield *v.* Hands (1960) Ch 1 *35*
Roberts & Cooper Ltd., *Re* [1929] 2 Ch. 383 *44*
Rowell *v.* John Rowell & Son [1912] 2 Ch. 609 *139*
Ruben *v.* Great Fingall Consolidated [1906] A.C. 439 *164*

Scottish Insurance Corporation *v.* Wilson's and Clyde Coal Co. [1949] A.C. 462 *44*

Shuttleworth *v.* Cox Bros. & Co. (Maidenhead) Ltd (1927) 2 KB 9 *41*

Smith *v.* Fawcett Ltd. [1942] Ch. 304 *180*

Smith *v.* Lord Advocate (1978) SC 259 *302*

South London Greyhound Racecourses *v.* Wake [1931] 1 Ch. 496 *164*

Sykes' Case (1872) LR 13 Eq. 255 *130*

Trevor *v.* Whitworth (1887) 12 App. Cas. 409 *49*

Webb *v.* Earle (1875) LR 20 Eq. 556 *43*

Will *v.* United Lankat Plantation Co. [1914] A.C. 11 *43*

Yenidje Tobacco Co. Ltd., *Re* [1916] 2 Ch. 426 *292*

1 Formation of a company

The registered company

1. Nature

The registered company is a form of body corporate and as such has a distinct legal identity from the persons of which it is composed. It acquires its corporate status by registration under the Companies Act 1985. This provides administrative procedures whereby groups of people may create corporations by registering documents at a public registry. The official administering registration is the Registrar of Companies and the company comes into existence when he issues it with a certificate of incorporation. Each company has to pay a registration fee and an annual fee when it registers its annual return with the Registrar.

2. Types of registered company

(a) In forming a company, the promoters must first decide which type of registered company they wish to form.
(b) They must choose between *limited* and *unlimited* liability. In practice, companies formed to engage in trade or industry are invariably formed as limited companies. Unlimited companies are rare, although certain professional bodies will only permit their members to practice through companies if the liability of the members of the company is to be unlimited. The fact that an unlimited company enjoys the privilege of not filing copies of its annual accounts with the Registrar of Companies, has been

undermined by the introduction of accounting exemptions for small and medium-sized companies (s. 246 CA 1985), and restricted by the requirement that an unlimited company is required to file accounts if it is either a subsidiary or a parent undertaking of an undertaking which is limited: s. 254 CA 1985.

(c) If they decide upon a limited company, there is still a choice between a company with liability *limited by shares* and one with liability *limited by guarantee*. If the company is to trade for profit, the company should be limited by shares. This will enable the company to limit the liability of its members: to raise funds from its members as working capital; to facilitate the transfer of ownership by the sale of members shares; to provide a return on its members' investment by paying dividends out of profits; and to distribute capital and reserves amongst members, on liquidation or otherwise. In the case of companies formed for non-profit-making purposes, a company limited by guarantee should be formed. In fact this is a necessity if the company is to claim charitable status, for the Charity Commission will not approve a company for registration as a charity unless it is limited by guarantee.

(d) Finally, is the company to be a public company or a private company? The implications of this decision are examined immediately below (**3**).

3. Classification of companies

(a) *A public company* is defined by s. 1(3) CA 1985 as a company limited by shares or limited by guarantee and having a share capital, being a company

(*i*) the Memorandum of which states that it is to be a public company, and

(*ii*) which has been registered or re-registered as a public company in accordance with the requirements of the Companies Act 1985 or the former Companies Acts.

A *private company* is a company that is not a public company.

(b) The fundamental difference between public and private companies is that only the securities of public companies may be offered to the public and listed on the Stock Exchange or traded on the Unlisted Securities Market.

(c) Other differences and consequential advantages of private company status will be examined in the text as and where appropriate but for the sake of convenience are listed below.

(*i*) The Memorandum and Articles of Association need not contain a clause indicating the nature of the company: s. 1(3)(a) CA 1985.

(*ii*) There is no minimum capital requirement (at present £50,000 for public companies): s. 117 CA 1985.

(*iii*) In a public company each share allotted must be paid up as to not less than one-quarter of its nominal value plus the whole of any premium payable (s. 101(1) CA 1985); there is no requirement in a private company that shares be paid up on allotment.

(*iv*) The company may commence to trade and borrow immediately upon incorporation and need not obtain the trading certificate required by a public company under s. 117 CA 1985.

(*v*) It may elect to dispense with the holding of annual general meetings: s. 366A CA 1985.

(*vi*) It may elect to dispense with the laying of accounts and reports before the company in general meeting: s. 252 CA 1985.

(*vii*) It may have a sole director: s. 282(3) CA 1985.

(*viii*) The appointment of directors at a general meeting of the shareholders may be effected by a composite, rather than separate, resolution: s. 292 CA 1985.

(*ix*) The age limits for the appointment or re-appointment of directors do not apply unless a private company is a subsidiary of a public company: s. 293 CA 1985.

(*x*) Proxies at a general meeting of a company may not only attend and vote but may also speak at a meeting: s. 372(1) CA 1985.

(*xi*) Only private companies can qualify as small or medium-sized companies which may enjoy exemption from filing full accounts with the Registrar of Companies: ss. 246–249 CA 1985.

(*xii*) While dormant, it may by special resolution make itself exempt from the obligation to appoint auditors: s. 250 CA 1985.

(*xiii*) Provisions relating to insider trading do not apply to private companies: Companies Securities (Insider Dealing) Act 1985 s. 1.

(*xiv*) The directors of a private company may be authorized to allot shares pursuant to s. 80 CA 1985 for an indefinite period: s. 80A CA 1985.

(*xv*) The rights of pre-emption on the allotment of shares conferred upon by members by s. 89(1) CA 1985 may be excluded by the Memorandum and Articles of Association: s. 91 CA 1985.

(*xvi*) Many provisions relating to loans or quasi-loans to directors or transactions involving a company and a director apply only to a public company or to private companies forming part of a public group: ss. 330–342 CA 1985.

(*xvii*) The company may elect to dispense with the obligation to elect auditors annually: s. 386 CA 1985.

(*xviii*) A private company must deliver its accounts to the Registrar of Companies within 10 months of the end of the relevant accounting period; a public company must deliver its accounts within seven months: s. 244(1) CA 1985.

(*xix*) The shares of a private company may be redeemed or purchased out of capital: ss. 171–176 CA 1985.

(*xx*) A private company which is not a member of a group including a public company may, subject to certain provisions, give financial assistance for the acquisition of its own shares: ss. 155–158 CA 1985.

(*xxi*) A private company wishing to allot shares for a consideration other than cash need not obtain an expert's valuation report: s.103(1) CA 1985.

(*xxii*) Only a private company limited by guarantee is capable of exemption from ending its name with 'Limited': s. 30(2) CA 1985.

(*xxiii*) A private company which has lost half or more of its called-up share capital is not obliged to convene an extraordinary general meeting to consider what measures should be taken to deal with the serious loss of capital: s. 142 CA 1985.

(*xxiv*) Anything which may be done by a private company in a general meeting may be done by a written resolution of all the members entitled to attend and vote at such a meeting: s. 381A CA 1985.

(*xxv*) The members of a private company may resolve by elective resolution to reduce the majority required for agreement at short notice to an extraordinary general meeting from 95 per cent to not less than 90 per cent: ss. 369(4) and 378(3) CA 1985.

4. De-regulation of private companies

(a) Part V CA 1989 provides a new flexibility as regards certain procedures in private companies. First, private companies are now able to take decisions by unanimous written resolution of all the shareholders in place of resolutions made at general meetings, provided those resolutions have been approved by the auditors (if they concern the auditors as such) and do not concern the removal of directors or auditors: ss. 113–114 CA 1985. Secondly, a new 'elective regime' designed radically to simplify the management of private companies has been introduced: ss. 115–116 CA 1989. These provisions permit the members unanimously in general meeting or by written resolution to elect to

(*i*) grant directors enduring authority to allot shares;

(*ii*) dispense with laying accounts and reports before the general meeting;

(*iii*) dispense with holding annual general meetings;

(*iv*) authorize short notice of meetings;

(*v*) dispense with annual appointment of auditors.

The provisions outlined above became operative as from 1st April 1990: SI 1990/355.

(b) *Written resolutions of private companies: ss. 113–114 CA 1989*

(*i*) Anything which in the case of a private company may be done by resolution of the company in general meeting, or by resolution of a meeting of any class of members of the company, may be done without a meeting, and without any previous notice being required, by resolution in writing signed by or on behalf of all the members of the company who at the date of the resolution would be entitled to attend and vote at such meetings;

(*ii*) the signatures may appear either on the same document or on several documents in like form;

(*iii*) the resolution is dated when the resolution is signed by or on behalf of the last member to sign;

(*iv*) all resolutions agreed to in writing shall have effect as if passed by the company in general meeting or by meeting of the relevant class of members of the company, as the case may be;

(*v*) any resolution whether ordinary, special, extraordinary or elective may be approved by resolution in writing: s. 381(A) CA 1985.

A copy of any written resolution proposed to be agreed in accordance with s.381(A) must be sent to the company's auditors: s. 381(B) CA 1985. If the resolution concerns the auditors as auditors, they may within seven days from the date on which they receive a copy give notice to the company stating their opinion that the resolution should be considered by the company in general meeting or, as the case may be, by meeting of the relevant class of members of the company.

A written resolution shall not have effect unless the period of seven days elapses without any notice being given by the auditors to the company or within that period the auditors notify the company that in their opinion the resolution does not concern them as auditors, or does concern them but need not be considered by the company in general meeting or, as the case may be, in separate class meeting.

All written resolutions must be in a book, in the same way as minutes of proceedings of a general meeting of a company. Any such record, if purporting to be signed by a director of the company or by the secretary would be evidence of the proceedings in agreeing to the resolution: s. 382(A) CA 1985.

There are two exceptions to the acceptability of written resolutions:

(*i*) the removal of a director under s. 303 CA 1985 before the expiration of his period of office; and

(*ii*) the removal of an auditor under s. 391 CA 1985 before the expiration of his period of office.

In both cases the resolution must be proposed at a general meeting duly convened and held.

The acceptance of written resolutions has necessitated the introduction of various procedural changes relating to the circulation of documents to shareholders. In particular, the following documents must, where a written resolution is to be employed, be circulated to each relevant member at or before the time the resolution is supplied to him for signature

(*i*) The written statement to be given by directors pursuant to a special resolution, waiving rights of pre-emption on the allotment of shares: s. 95(5) CA 1985.

(*ii*) The statutory declaration and auditors report relating to an approval for financial assistance by a company for the purchase of its shares: s. 157(4) CA 1985.

(iii) The copy of the purchase contract or written memorandum of its terms relating to the off-market purchase or contingent purchase by a company of its own shares: s. 164(b) CA 1985.

(iv) The statutory declaration and auditors report relating to the purchase by a company of its own shares from capital: s. 174(4) CA 1986.

(v) A written memorandum setting out the terms of a proposed director's service contract for a term of more than five years: s. 319(5) CA 1985.

(vi) Disclosure of matters relating to the approval of a director's expenditure to enable him to perform his duties properly: s. 337(3) CA 1985.

As regards ss. 164 and 174 (above), in the same way as the votes of a member whose shares are to be purchased by a company are to be disregarded in respect of the particular resolution, it is provided that a member so interested shall not be regarded as a member for the purpose of a written resolution.

(c) *Election by private company to dispense with certain requirements: ss. 115–117 CA 1985*

CA 1989 has introduced what is known as 'the elective regime'. This permits a private company to opt out of certain statutory obligations, thereby easing the burden of legislative requirements. To secure these benefits, the members of a private company must approve 'elective resolutions' by unanimous decision: s. 379A CA 1985; s. 116 CA 1989.

Elective resolutions can be approved to achieve the following concessions:

(i) The grant of authority to directors to allot shares in terms of s. 80 CA 1985 for an indefinite period or for a fixed term greater than five years: s. 80(A) CA 1985.

(ii) Dispensing with the laying of accounts and reports before the company in general meeting: s. 252(1) CA 1985.

(iii) Dispensing with the holding of annual general meetings: ss. 33–66(A) CA 1985.

(*iv*) Reducing the majority required to authorize the holding of general meetings or class meetings upon short notice: ss. 369(4) or 378(3) CA 1985.

(*v*) Dispensing with the requirement to re-appoint auditors each year: s. 386(A) CA 1985.

As regards an elective resolution,

(*i*) it must be approved by unanimous resolution at a general meeting of the company (or by written resolution);

(*ii*) at least 21 clear days' notice in writing must be given of the general meeting;

(*iii*) the notice must state that an elective resolution is to be proposed and state the terms of the resolution;

(*iv*) the resolution must be approved by all the members, in person or by proxy, entitled to attend and vote at the meeting;

(*v*) it may be revoked by an ordinary resolution at any time;

(*vi*) it shall cease to have effect if the company is re-registered as a public company;

(*vii*) a copy must be filed with the Registrar of Companies within 15 days of the date of approval of an elective resolution;

(*viii*) a copy of the resolution revoking an elective resolution must be filed with the Registrar of Companies within 15 days of the date of approval.

Registration

5. Preliminary considerations

Prior to registering a company there will be preliminary discussion by the promoters, particularly concerning the following important matters.

(a) *Type of company* to be formed, taking into consideration the points raised in 2 and 3 above.

(b) *Objects*. What are to be the company's main objects, ancillary objects and borrowing powers (if any)?

(c) *Capital requirements*. This is a vitally important matter and ought to be considered with a view to assessing the required authorized capital with which the company proposes to be registered and the division thereof into shares of a fixed amount — unless, of course, the company is to be limited by guarantee. It must be borne in mind, however, that the 'authorized minimum capital' for a public company is £50,000 (nominal value), or such other sum as may in future be specified by statutory instrument: ss. 11 and 118 CA 1985. In assessing the requirements, the following matters should be taken into account:

(i) purchase price of any business to be acquired if, for example, a partnership is being converted into a limited company;

(ii) preliminary expenses covering the legal and other expenses to be incurred in the formation of the company;

(iii) working capital: after meeting the above items, there must be sufficient capital remaining to enable the company to meet its everyday commitments;

(iv) future requirements: not only immediate requirements but also long-term requirements should be taken into account. The promoters ought to be sufficiently optimistic to anticipate that the company will develop, and development should not be hindered for lack of capital.

(d) *Name*. Consideration might be given at this stage to the choice of a suitable name for the company, but it must be borne in mind that the name chosen must not be contrary to the provisions of the Companies Act 1985 (*see* **24** *below*).

(e) *Registered office*. As the company must have a registered office it might be as well to consider where it is to be situated, bearing in mind that its situation must be stated in the registration documents and that the domicile of the registered office determines the nationality of the company and the law governing its operation: *see* **27** *below*.

(f) *Directors*. Although the first directors cannot be officially appointed at this stage, the constitution of the board may be fixed and the first director(s) named. In the case of a private company one director only would suffice, but two directors constitute the minimum requirement for every public company registered on or after 1st November 1929: s. 282 CA 1985.

(g) *Secretary*. Every company must have a Secretary (s. 283 CA 1985); therefore, a person may be named as such at this stage, although his appointment will have to be ratified later. It should be noted, however, that a sole director cannot also act as Secretary of the company. (*See also* **14:34** as to qualifications required in the case of a Secretary of a public company.)

(h) *Solicitors*. The promoters may now decide to instruct a solicitor to prepare the necessary documents, and it is usually advisable to choose one who specializes in company formation. In practice, the solicitor may well utilize the services of a company formation agent to carry out the formation and registration of the company. If the need for the company is particularly urgent then, to cut down the inevitable two or three week delay in the registration, a 'tailor-made' company may be purchased from the agent and customized to the promoters' particular requirements.

6. Underwriting

If a public company is to be formed, consideration will almost certainly be given to the question of underwriting the issue of any shares to be offered to the public — if that is the immediate intention — but the contacts with firms of underwriters and the drafting of an underwriting agreement are best left to the solicitors.

7. Documents

The solicitors will be instructed to prepare the necessary documents. These will vary according to the decisions already taken, but some or all of the following will be required.

(a) *Documents to be filed* with the Registrar of Companies, including the Memorandum of Association and the Articles of Association. These and the other necessary documents are explained later in this chapter.
(b) *Business purchase agreement* where the company is being formed to acquire an existing business, e.g. where the business of a sole trader or of a partnership is being converted into a company.
(c) *Prospectus* (or equivalent document) where the company is to be a public company and intends to offer its shares (or debentures) to the public.
(d) *Underwriting contract.* This will be required if it is decided to ensure the success of a public issue of shares (or debentures), the underwriters, agreeing in the contract to take up any shares which are not subscribed by the public on payment of underwriting commission.

8. Signing of documents

When the registration and other documents are prepared, those responsible for signing the various documents

(a) *attend the solicitors' office*, where convenient, to examine the documents;
(b) *after approval*, sign the various documents, the only exception being the statutory declaration in prescribed form which the solicitor who has prepared the documents usually signs, although it may be signed by a person named as a director or secretary of the company: s. 12 CA 1985. This declares that all requirements of the Companies Act in respect of registration have been complied with.
(c) *Payment of registration fee*: a cheque to cover the registration fee may be signed at the same time.

9. Documents to be filed with the Registrar

The following are the documents to be lodged with the Registrar of Companies before incorporation of a company with share capital.

(a) *A Memorandum of Association* stating, *inter alia*, the objects of the company and if, as is common, the company is a limited company with a share capital, the amount of share capital with which the company proposes to be registered and its division into shares of a fixed amount.
(b) Usually, printed *Articles of Association* providing for such matters as the transfer of shares in the company, the holding of general meetings, the directors' powers of management and the extent to which they can delegate their powers to a managing director, and dividends.
(c) If the Memorandum states that the registered office is to be situated in Wales and the Memorandum and Articles are in Welsh, a *certified translation* in English.
(d) *A statement in the prescribed form (Form G10)* of the names of the intended first director or directors, and the first secretary or joint secretaries, and the particulars specified in Schedule 1 of CA 1965. Such statement must be signed by or on behalf of the subscribers of the Memorandum and must contain a consent to act signed by each of the persons named in it. Where the Memorandum is delivered for registration by an agent for the subscribers, such statement must specify that fact and the name and address of that person. The statement must also specify the intended situation of the company's registered office.

(e) *A statutory declaration,* by a solicitor engaged in the formation of the company or by a person named as director or secretary of the company in the statement delivered under **(d)** *ante,* of compliance with the requirements of the Acts in respect of registration.

For the purpose of ensuring that documents delivered to the Registrar are of standard size, durable and easily legible, the Secretary of State for Trade and Industry may prescribe such requirements as he considers appropriate. If a document delivered to the Registrar does not, in his opinion, comply with such requirements, he may serve a notice on the person or persons by whom the document was required to be delivered whereupon, for the purposes of any enactment which enables a penalty to be imposed in respect of an omission to deliver a document to the Registrar, the duty to deliver is not discharged but the person subject to the duty has 14 days after the date of service of the notice in which to discharge it.

The Registrar may, if he thinks fit, accept, under any provision of the Companies Acts requiring a document to be delivered to him, any material other than a document which contains the information in question and is of a kind approved by him. Thus, the Registrar has power to accept information on microfilm.

The duty of the Registrar on receiving the above-mentioned documents is to examine them to see whether the statutory requirements have been complied with, but in exercising his duty he has no power to hold a judicial enquiry on evidence. Among the statutory requirements to be observed are:

(a) That the Memorandum is signed by at least two persons, and, if the Memorandum is accompanied by Articles, that the Articles are signed by the same persons.
(b) That the company is being formed for a lawful purpose.
(c) That the other requirements of the Act, e.g. as to the contents of the Memorandum and Articles, are complied with.
(d) That the proposed name is not one which is absolutely or conditionally prohibited.
(e) That the Memorandum and Articles are in the statutory form.

Any person may inspect a copy of the documents or other material kept by the Registrar relative to individual companies on payment of a fee, and may require a copy or extract of them on payment of the current fee.

10. Procedure on filing documents

(a) *Examination of documents.* The person presenting the documents at the Registrar's office (probably the solicitor who prepared the documents, or his clerk) is generally asked to leave them for examination and return at a stated time on the next or subsequent day.

(b) *After examination.* Any defects will be pointed out to the solicitor (or other person presenting the documents) on his return to the Registry. Defects of a trivial character may be corrected on the spot, but it may be necessary to take away any documents requiring material alterations. Such documents ought to be referred back to their respective signatories and any alterations made should be initialled by them.

(c) *After approval.* When the documents are approved, the registration fee will be paid.

11. Certificate of Incorporation

(a) *Issue of certificate.* All registration documents having been approved and the registration fee paid, the Registrar will issue the Certificate of Incorporation, usually within two weeks.

(b) *Effect of the certificate*

(*i*) The certificate provides conclusive evidence that all requirements of the Companies Act 1985 in respect of registration have been complied with, and that the company is duly registered under the 1985 Act as (say) a public company. The certificate also bears the company's registered number and this must be quoted in all formal returns made to the Registrar of Companies. It must also be quoted on all business letters and order forms.

(*ii*) The company comes into existence as a body corporate.

12. The Companies Registry

(a) When a company is formed the Registrar opens a file. The formation documents and a copy of the certificate of incorporation become the first enclosures on the file. As additional documents, such as each year's annual return or a notice of change of directors, are presented to the Registry they are added to the file. The file thus builds up by the addition in chronological order of documents received plus copies of any certificates (change of name, registration of a charge etc.) issued by the Registrar. There is no index except for particulars of registered charges.

(b) Documents required to be delivered to the Registrar in legible form or otherwise must

(*i*) state in a prominent place the registered number of the company to which they relate;

(*ii*) satisfy any requirements prescribed by regulations; and

(*iii*) be forms held in such form and conform to such requirements as the Registrar may specify for the purpose of enabling him to read and copy the documents.

If these requirements are not satisfied the Registrar may serve on the person by whom the document was delivered a notice indicating the respect in which the document does not comply. If the Registrar is not provided with a replacement document satisfying the requirements within 14 days after the service of the notice, the original document shall be deemed not to have been delivered to him.

The information contained in a document delivered to the Registrar may be recorded and kept by him in any form he thinks fit, provided it is possible to inspect the information and to produce a copy of it in legible form. In practice the contents of each file are copied on to microfilm and much of the public inspection is now by means of the microfiche copies. Any person may inspect a copy of the documents or other material kept by the Registrar relative to individual companies on payment of a fee, and may require a copy or extract of them on payment of the prescribed fee.

(c) There is at the Registry an alphabetical index of all companies on the register. Such an index may be purchased from the Registrar and is updated twice weekly.

(d) The principal Registry for companies in England and Wales is now located in Cardiff, though there are public inspection facilities in London also. Companies incorporated under the same Companies Act but in Scotland are similarly recorded and documented at the Companies Registry in Edinburgh.

13. Official notification

(a) On issuing the Certificate of Incorporation and on the receipt of documents of various classes relating to companies the Registrar is required to give official notification of such in the *Gazette*: s. 711 CA 1985. The notice must state the name of the company, the description of documents and the date of issue or receipt by the Registrar.
(b) In the following cases the company may not rely against other persons on the happening of the event unless the notification requirements have been satisfied:

(*i*) the making of a winding up order or the appointment of a liquidator;
(*ii*) an alteration of the memorandum or articles
(*iii*) any change among the company's directors;
(*iv*) (as regards service of any document on the company) any change in the situation of the company's registered office: s. 42 CA 1985.

Even when official notification has taken place there is a period of 15 days' grace during which the company cannot rely on the event against a person who was unavoidably prevented from knowing of the event.

14. Section 117 certificate

A private company can commence business and exercise any borrowing powers immediately it is incorporated. A public company cannot do either of these things unless the Registrar has issued it with a certificate under s. 117 CA 1985.

The certificate will be issued when the Registrar is satisfied that the nominal value of the company's allotted share capital is not less than the authorized minimum (£50,000), and not less than one-quarter of the nominal value of each issued share in the company plus the whole of any premium on such shares have been paid up, though employees' shares may be excluded from this calculation.

In order to obtain such a certificate a statutory declaration in the prescribed form (Form G117) signed by a director or secretary of the company, must be filed with the Registrar. It must state:

(a) that the nominal value of the company's allotted share capital is not less than the authorized minimum;
(b) the amount paid up, at the time of the application, on the allotted share capital of the company;
(c) the amount, or estimated amount, of the preliminary expenses and the persons by whom any of those expenses have been paid or are payable; and
(d) any amount or benefit paid or given or intended to be paid or given to any promoter of the company, and the consideration for the payment or benefit.

If a public company does business or exercises borrowing powers in contravention of s. 117 CA 1985, the company and any officer of the company who is in default shall be liable on conviction on indictment to a fine and on summary conviction to a fine not exceeding the statutory maximum.

Further, if the company fails to comply with its obligations in connection with such a transaction within 21 days of being called upon to do so, the directors become jointly and severally liable to indemnify the other party to the transaction for any resultant loss or damage.

Re-registration

15. Re-registration of companies

The procedure outlined in 9 above refers to a company on its *original* incorporation.

The Companies Act 1985 sets out in some detail the requirements for re-registration in the following cases:

(a) re-registration of a private company as a public company;
(b) re-registration of an unlimited company as a public company;
(c) re-registration of a public company as a private company;
(d) re-registration of an unlimited company as limited;
(e) re-registration of a limited company as unlimited.

The requirements in each case are outlined below.

16. Re-registration of a private company as a public company

A private company with share capital wishing to re-register as a public limited company must comply with the requirements of s. 43 CA 1985:

(a) A special resolution must be passed:

(*i*) that the company be re-registered as a public company;

(*ii*) altering the company's Memorandum of Association so that it states the company is to be a public company;

(*iii*) making such other alterations in the Memorandum of Association as are necessary to conform with requirements of the Companies Act 1985 with respect to the Memorandum of a public company;

(*iv*) altering the Articles of Association as required in the circumstances.

NOTE: A private company cannot be re-registered as a public company unless, at the time the resolution is passed, the nominal value of the company's allotted share capital is not less than the authorized minimum. These additional requirements are set out in s. 45 CA 1985.

(b) An application for re-registration in the prescribed form (Form G43(3)), signed by a director or secretary of the company, must be delivered to the Registrar, together with:

(*i*) a printed copy of the Memorandum of Association and Articles of Association as altered in accordance with the special resolution;

(*ii*) a copy of a written statement by the auditors of the company that, in their opinion, the relevant balance sheet shows that, at the balance sheet date, the amount of the company's net assets was not less than the aggregate of its called-up capital and undistributable reserves;

(*iii*) a copy of the relevant balance sheet, together with a copy of an unqualified report by the company's auditors in relation to that balance sheet;

(*iv*) a copy of any report with respect to the value of the allotment, where shares are allotted by the company between the balance sheet date and the passing of the special resolution;

(*v*) a statutory declaration in the prescribed form (Form G43(3)(*e*)) by a director or secretary of the company that the special resolution (mentioned above) has been passed and that between the balance sheet date and the application of the company for re-registration there has been no change in the financial position of the company that has resulted in the amount of the company's net assets becoming less than the aggregate of its called-up share capital and undistributable reserves.

If the Registrar is satisfied that the application and documents comply with the requirements for re-registration, he will retain the application and other documents and issue to the company a Certificate of Incorporation, stating that the company is a public company.

17. Re-registration of an unlimited company as a public company

The procedure laid down in s. 48 CA 1985 for re-registration of an unlimited company as a public company is the same as that described in **16** above, except that the special resolution must, in addition:

(a) state that the liability of the members is to be limited by shares and what the share capital of the company is to be; and

(b) make such alterations in the company's Memorandum of Association as are necessary to bring it in substance and in form into conformity with the requirements of the Companies Acts with respect to the memorandum of a company limited by shares.

If the Registrar is satisfied that application and documents comply with the requirements for re-registration, he will issue to the company a Certificate of Incorporation, stating that the company has been incorporated as a company limited by shares, and that:

(a) the company shall by virtue of the issue of that certificate become a public company so limited; and

(b) the certificate shall be conclusive evidence of the fact that it is such a public company.

18. Re-registration of a public company as a private company

The requirements in this case, as laid down in s. 53 CA 1985, are as follows:

(a) A special resolution must be passed:

(*i*) that the company be re-registered as a private company;

(*ii*) altering the company's Memorandum of Association so that it no longer states that the company is to be a public company, and making such other alterations in the company's Memorandum and Articles as are required in the circumstances.

NOTE: The Court has power to cancel this resolution on the application of a specified number (or proportion) of members who had not consented to or voted in favour of the resolution, made within 28 days after passing the resolution: s. 54 CA 1985.

(b) An application for re-registration in the prescribed form (Form G53), signed by a director or secretary of the company, must be delivered to the Registrar, together with a printed copy of the Memorandum and Articles of the company as altered by the resolution.

After the period during which an application for the cancellation of the special resolution in accordance with s. 54 CA 1985 has expired without any such application having been made, or, if an application has been made, it has been withdrawn, or the Court has made an order confirming the resolution, and a copy of that order has been delivered to the Registrar, then:

(a) if satisfied that the company has complied with re-registration requirements, the Registrar will retain the application and other documents delivered to him; and
(b) issue to the company a Certificate of Incorporation appropriate to a company that is not a public company.

The effects of the issue of the Certificate of Incorporation to the company are:

(a) the company, by virtue of that certificate becomes a private company;
(b) the alterations in the Memorandum and Articles set out in the special resolution take effect accordingly; and
(c) the company has conclusive evidence that the requirements in respect of re-registration and of matters precedent and incidental thereto have been complied with, and that the company is a private company.

19. Re-registration of an unlimited company as limited

A company which was formed as unlimited (but not one already converted from limited to unlimited (*see* **20** *below*)) can be re-registered as limited under s. 51 CA 1985. In this case there must be filed at the Companies Registry:

(a) an application in the prescribed form (Form G51) signed by a director or by the secretary of the company;
(b) a copy of a special resolution making the necessary amendments of the Memorandum and Articles of Association;
(c) a copy of the Memorandum and Articles as amended.

The Registrar retains the application and other documents lodged with him and issues a new Certificate of Incorporation as a private limited company.

If a company which has so converted its status goes into liquidation within three years of the conversion, any person who was a member at the time of the conversion has unlimited liability to contribute to the payment of outstanding debts incurred while the company was unlimited.

20. Re-registration of a limited company as unlimited

A change in status of this nature requires the following to be filed at the Companies Registry:

(a) an application in the prescribed form (Form G49(1)) signed by a director or the secretary of the company;
(b) a form of assent to the change on Form G 49 (8)(a) signed by all the members;
(c) a statutory declaration by the directors on Form G49(8)(b) that all the members have signed the assent;
(d) a copy of the Memorandum and Articles incorporating the necessary changes: s. 49 CA 1985.

The Registrar then issues a new Certificate of Incorporation of the company as unlimited. Such a change in status does not affect the limited liability of past members of the company. Although a company formed with limited liability can take advantage of s. 49 CA 1985, it cannot having done so be converted back to limited: no public company can apply under the section to be re-registered as an unlimited company.

Oversea companies

21. Establishment in Great Britain

An oversea company is a company incorporated outside Great Britain which establishes a place of business within Great Britain.

Within one month of establishing such a place of business an oversea company must deliver the following documents to the appropriate Registrar: s. 691 CA 1985;

(a) a certified copy of the charter, statutes or Memorandum and Articles of the company or other instrument defining the constitution of the company, and, if the instrument is not written in the English language, a certified translation of it;
(b) a list of the directors and secretary, with similar particulars to those required by s. 289 CA 1985 in the case of an English or Scottish company;
(c) the name and address of a person resident in Great Britain authorized to accept, on behalf of the company, service of process and notices;
(d) a list of the above documents.

The Registrar must be notified of any alterations in the above documents.

Memorandum of Association

22. Main purpose

The Memorandum of Association is often described as a company's charter, since it defines and limits its powers, particularly as regards the company's dealings with the outside world.

Internally, the Memorandum and Articles bind the company and its members to the same extent as if they respectively had been signed and sealed by each member: s. 14 CA 1985.

23. Contents

The Memorandum of Association must contain clauses setting out the following information:

(a) the name of the company;
(b) in the case of a public company the statement 'The company is to be a public company';
(c) whether the registered office is to be situated in England and Wales, or in Scotland;
(d) the objects of the company;
(e) a statement that the liability of the members is limited by shares (or by guarantee) where this is the case;
(f) the amount of the share capital (if any) with which the company proposes to be registered and its division into shares of a fixed amount.

NOTE:

(*i*) As an alternative to **(c)** above, the Memorandum may contain a statement that the company's registered office is to be situated in Wales, in which case both Memorandum and Articles may be in Welsh: if they are they must be accompanied by a certified translation into English: s. 21 CA 1985;

(*ii*) In the case of a company limited by guarantee the Memorandum must state that each member undertakes to contribute to the assets of the company in the event of its being wound up, such amount as may be required, not exceeding a specified amount;

(*iii*) There is no equivalent of the share capital clause (**(f)** above) in the Memorandum of an unlimited company;

(*iv*) In a public company the stated share capital must be at least £50,000;

(*v*) In addition to the matters stated above (**(a)**–**(f)**) the Memorandum may contain other information. The persons drafting the company's constitution having a choice between the Memorandum and Articles in the case of other provisions.

The Memorandum is completed by the association (or subscription) clause in which the subscribers declare their intention to be associated as a company.

The Act requires the Memorandum to be in the form set out

in the Tables contained in the Companies (Tables A–F) Regulations 1985 or as near thereto as possible. Table B is that appropriate for a private company limited by shares and Table F for a public company. In practice however, considerable modifications are made.

A company may not alter its Memorandum except in the cases, in the mode and to the extent, for which express provision is made in the Companies Act 1985.

24. Name of the company: ss. 25–34 CA 1985

By s. 26 CA 1985 a company shall not be registered under that Act by a name:

(a) which includes otherwise than at the end of the name any of the following words and expressions, that is to say, 'limited', 'unlimited' or 'public limited company' or their Welsh equivalents;
(b) which includes otherwise than at the end of the name abbreviations of any of those words or expressions;
(c) which is the same as a name appearing in the Registrar's index of company names (*see below*);
(d) the use of which by the company would in the opinion of the Secretary of State constitute a criminal offence; or
(e) which in the opinion of the Secretary of State is offensive.

Further, except with the approval of the Secretary of State, a company may not be registered under the Companies Act 1985 by a name which:

(a) in the opinion of the Secretary of State would be likely to give the impression that the company is connected in any way with Her Majesty's Government or with any local authority; or
(b) includes any word or expression for the time being specified under regulations made under s. 29 CA 1985 (*see below*).

The index of names referred to above and required to be kept by the Registrar contains the names of all existing companies, incorporated and unincorporated bodies and limited partnerships: s. 714 CA 1985. It is against this index that the promoters of a company check to ensure that the proposed name of the company they intend to form is not the same as that of an existing company. Assuming that such is not the case, that the proposed name ends with the appropriate designation and is not in the opinion of the Secretary of State offensive or one the use of which would be a criminal offence, the proposed name will be accepted by the Registrar. The Registrar's prior approval to a choice of name is only required where the name includes any word specified under s. 29 CA 1985 or gives the impression that the company is connected with Her Majesty's Government or with any local authority. Among the words specified under s. 29 CA 1985 are the words British, Queen's, International, European, Council, Society, Group and Trust: Companies and Business Names Regulations 1981 and the Company and Business Names (Amendments) Regulations 1982.

25. Companies exempt from requirement to use word 'limited', etc.: s. 30 CA 1985

A company is permitted CA 1985 to omit the word 'limited' from its name if it fulfils the following conditions (and submits a statutory declaration to that effect):

(a) it is or is about to be registered as a private company limited by guarantee; or
(b) is a company which on 25th February 1982 was a private company limited by shares with a name which, by virtue of a licence under s. 19 CA 1948, did not include 'limited', and which satisfies the following requirements:

(*i*) its objects are or in the case of a company about to be registered are to be the promotion of commerce, art, science, education, religion, charity or any profession and anything incidental or conducive to any of those objects; and

(*ii*) it is a company the Memorandum or Articles of which:

(1) require its profits, if any, or other income to be applied in promoting its objects;

(2) prohibit the payment of dividends to its members; and

(3) require all the assets which would otherwise be available to its members generally to be transferred on its winding up either to another body with objects similar to its own or to another body the objects of which are the promotion of charity and

anything incidental or conducive thereto (whether or not the body is a member of the company).

A company so exempted from the requirements of the 1985 Act relating to the use of the word 'limited' as any part of its name is also exempted from the requirements of the Act relating to the publishing of its name and the sending of lists of members to the Registrar of Companies.

26. Trading under a misleading name: s. 33 CA 1985

(a) It is an offence for a 'person' who is *not* a public company to carry on any trade, profession or business under a name which includes the words 'Public Limited Company', or their Welsh equivalent.
(b) A public company will be guilty of an offence if, where it is likely to be material, it uses a name which may give the impression that it is a private company.
(c) A company or any officer of the company in default in either of the above cases is liable to a fine.

27. Domicile of the registered office

(a) The Memorandum must state whether the registered office is to be situated in England, Wales, Scotland or England and Wales. Where the registered office is to be situated in England or Wales, the company must be registered in Cardiff and where the registered office is to be in Scotland, registration must be effected in Edinburgh. If the Memorandum states that the company is to be registered in Wales, the Welsh language may be used in the name and in the company documents. Such a company is obliged to maintain its registered office in Wales at all times.
(b) The intended situation of the registered office must be given in a statement in the prescribed form and delivered to the Registrar when the Memorandum is presented for registration (*see* **9** *above*).
(c) Subject to the exception stated in **(d)** below, a company cannot change its domicile, so long as the requisite 14 days' notice is given to the Registrar: s. 287(2) CA 1985.
(d) A company with its registered office in Wales may alter its

Memorandum by *special* resolution so that it provides that its registered office is to be situated in Wales: s. 2(2) CA 1985.

28. Objects of the company

(a) The Memorandum is required to set out the 'objects' for which the company is formed. By s. 3(A) CA 1985, where the company's Memorandum states that the object of the company is to carry on business as a general commercial company it will be deemed to have the power to carry on any trade or business whatsoever and to have the power to do all such things as are incidental or conducive to the carrying on of any trade or business.

(b) The specimen forms of Memorandum contained in the Companies (Tables A–F) Regulations 1985 simply give a brief statement of the company's objects relying on the implication of powers under the doctrine in *A-G* v. *Great Eastern Railway Co.* (1880). In practice, however, the objects clause of the Memorandum will specify all objects a company might ever conceivably wish to follow and any powers necessary to achieve those objects.

(c) At common law a registered company can only do that which it is incorporated to do or is authorized to do by statute: *Ashbury Railway Carriage Co.* v. *Riche* (1875). An act beyond its given powers being *ultra vires*. However, s. 35(1) CA 1985 provides that the validity of an act done by a company shall not be called into question on the ground of lack of capacity by reason of anything in the company's Memorandum; though by s. 35(2) CA 1985 a member of a company may bring proceedings to restrain the doing of an act which but for s. 35(1) CA 1985 would be beyond the company's capacity. No such proceedings shall lie in respect of an act to be done in fulfilment of a legal obligation arising from a previous act of the company.

Further, by s. 35(3) CA 1985 it remains the duty of the directors to observe any limitations on their powers flowing from the company's Memorandum; and action by the directors which but for s. 35(1) CA 1985 would be beyond the company's capacity may only be ratified by the company by special resolution. A resolution ratifying such action shall not affect any liability incurred by the directors or any other person; relief from any such liability must be agreed to separately by special resolution.

29. 'Limitation of liability' clause

(a) This is merely a statement that the liability of members is limited, i.e. limited to the amount (if any) unpaid on their respective shares.
(b) As previously stated, the Memorandum of an *unlimited* company does not include this clause, nor does it require a capital clause. (*See* specimen Memorandum of an unlimited company in Table E, The Companies (Tables A–F) Regulations 1985.)
(c) In the case of a company limited by guarantee, it can no longer be formed as or become a company limited by guarantee with a share capital: s. 1(4) CA 1985.

An *additional* clause is, however, required in such a company, stating that every member of the company guarantees to contribute to the assets of the company in the event of its being wound up — subject to various conditions — but not exceeding the sum guaranteed.

> NOTE: A member's right to limitation may be lost if a company carries on business without having at least two members and does so for more than six months. In such circumstances a person who, for the whole or any part of the period that it carries on business after those six months, is a member of the company and knows that it is carrying on business with only one member, becomes liable (jointly and severally with the company) for payment of the debts of the company contracted during (i.e. after) the period or part of it: s. 24 CA 1985.

30. Capital clause
This sets out the authorized capital of the company, and states the number and denomination of its shares. Types of shares are not usually stated in the Memorandum; they are generally named and described (where necessary) in the company's Articles of Association.

31. Association (or subscription) clause

(a) This is a statement by the subscribers to the Memorandum that they desire to be formed into a company, and agree to take up one or more shares in the company.

(b) It must be subscribed by at least *two* persons, irrespective of whether it is a public or private company.
(c) Their signature must be attested (one witness is sufficient to all signatures) and the document dated.
(d) Subsequently, it will bear the registration fee stamp at the prescribed rate.

Matters affecting the Memorandum

32. Alteration of the Memorandum

(a) *When permissible*. Subject to certain expressions (*see below*), any condition in the Memorandum which could lawfully have been contained in the Articles of Association instead of in the Memorandum may be altered by *special resolution*: s. 17 CA 1985. If, however, the specified proportion of shareholders object to the alteration, it will have no effect unless it is confirmed by the court (s. 17(1),(3) CA 1985).
(b) *Exceptions*. The right to alter a condition in the Memorandum does *not* apply:

(*i*) where the Memorandum itself provides for, or prohibits, the alteration of its conditions;

(*ii*) where alteration of the Memorandum would vary or abrogate the special rights of any class of members;

(*iii*) where alteration of the Memorandum would compel a member to take up more shares, or increase liability, unless the member agrees in writing, either before or after the alteration, to be bound by it: s. 16 CA 1985.

(*iv*) where an order under Part XVII (court order protecting minority) requires a company not to make any, or any specified alteration in the Memorandum, unless the Court gives leave to make an alteration in breach of such a requirement: s. 461(3) CA 1985.

33. Alteration of the 'objects' clause

(a) *When permissible*. Section 4 CA 1985 permits alteration of the objects clause of the memorandum by *special* resolution.

A company to which s. 30 CA 1985 applies (*see* **25** *above*) and the name of which does not include 'limited' cannot alter its

Memorandum or Articles of Association so that it ceases to be a company to which s. 30 applies.

(b) *Procedure.*

(*i*) *Board meeting.* The directors should resolve to convene a general meeting of the company to consider the terms of the required special resolution and to approve an explanatory circular to be sent to all members of the company.

(*ii*) *Convene a general meeting.* A general meeting of the company must be convened, giving at least 21 days' notice. The notice must state that it is proposed to pass a *special* resolution, and should be sent to:

(1) all members of the company; and

(2) all debenture holders (if any) who are entitled to object to the alteration.

(*iii*) *Special resolution.* At the general meeting a *special* resolution is passed, i.e. by a majority of not less than three-quarters of the members voting in person or (where proxies are allowed) by proxy: s. 378 CA 1985.

(*iv*) *File a copy* of the special resolution with the Registrar within 15 days of its being passed: s. 380 CA 1985.

(c) *Objections to the alteration.*

(*i*) Any applications for cancellation of the special resolution must be made to the court within 21 days after the resolution was passed, by those entitled to object, namely:

(1) the holders of not less in the aggregate than 15 per cent in nominal value of the company's issued share capital, or any class thereof; or

(2) not less than 15 per cent of the company's members, if the company is not limited by shares; or

(3) the holders of not less than 15 per cent of the company's debentures secured by a floating charge created prior to 1st December 1947.

NOTE: An application cannot be made for cancellation of the alteration by any person (in any of the above cases) who has consented to, or voted in favour of, the alteration.

(*ii*) If application is made by objectors (who are entitled to do so) within 21 days after the passing of the resolution:

(1) they must notify the Registrar on Form G6 forthwith that such an application has been made;

(2) the Court has power to confirm the alteration wholly or in part, to cancel the alteration, to postpone the matter, or to require alteration of the company's name so as to indicate the changed objects;

(3) the objectors must file an office copy of the court order within 15 days of the date of the order; and

(4) if the order confirms the alteration, the objectors must deliver to the Registrar, at the same time, a printed copy of the Memorandum in its altered form.

(iii) If no application is made by objectors within 21 days after passing the resolution:

(1) the alteration cannot be questioned;

(2) the company must, within a further 15 days (after expiration of the 21 day period) deliver to the Registrar a printed copy of the Memorandum in its altered form.

(d) *Subsequent issues of the Memorandum.* Every copy of the Memorandum issued after the date of the alteration must embody the alteration. The company and every officer of the company in default are liable to fines: s. 20 CA 1985.

> NOTE: If the company concerned was listed, the procedure outlined above would have to be modified and the documentation drafted to take account of the Continuing Obligations imposed upon such a company by the Stock Exchange. The Continuing Obligations are set out in Chapter 2 and reference should be made thereto.

34. Change of name

(a) *Conditions.* A company is permitted by s. 28 CA 1985 to change its name by special resolution.

(b) *Procedure.*

(i) Ensure that the proposed new name complies with the requirements of s. 26 CA 1985.

(ii) The directors should resolve to call a general meeting of the company to consider the required special resolution and to approve an explanatory circular to be sent to members.

(iii) *Convene a general meeting* of the company giving not less than 21 days' notice.

(iv) *Pass a special resolution* at the meeting, sanctioning the change of name. A three-quarters majority of those actually voting

in person (or, where permitted, by proxy) is required for this purpose.

(*v*) *File a copy* of the special resolution with the Registrar, within 15 days after the passing of the resolution, together with a copy of the Memorandum as altered and the appropriate fee.

(*vi*) The Registrar shall, subject to s. 26 CA 1985, enter the new name on the register in place of the company's former name, and shall issue a Certificate of Incorporation altered to meet the circumstances of the case.

(*vii*) *Subsequent procedure.* The change of name having become official:

(1) ensure that every copy of the Memorandum issued after the date of the alteration embodies the alteration, otherwise the company and every officer of the company in default are liable to fines: s. 20 CA 1985.

(2) arrange for the alteration of the company's name on the common seal, nameplates, stationery, etc.;

(3) as it is unlikely that the company will call in share and debenture certificates, alterations or replacements are usually made as and when the documents are submitted for registration in connection with transfers;

(4) advertise the name in the *Gazette* and, where appropriate, in one or more provincial papers.

(c) The Secretary of State has power under s. 28 CA 1985 to direct a company to change its name within 12 months of registration in the index of company names if the name is the same as one already on the index: s. 28(2) CA 1985.

(d) Where it appears to the Secretary of State that a company has provided misleading information for the purposes of its registration by a particular name or has given undertakings or assurances for that purpose which have not been fulfilled, the Secretary of State may within five years of the date of its registration by that name in writing direct the company to change its name within such period as he may specify: s. 28(3) CA 1985.

(e) *Power of the Secretary of State* to require a company to abandon a misleading name.

(*i*) Section 32 CA 1985 gives the Secretary of State power to direct a company to change its name where it has been registered with a name which is so misleading as to be likely to cause harm to the public.

(*ii*) The company is, however, permitted to apply to the Court to set the direction aside.

(f) *Trading under a misleading name.*

(*i*) Section 33 CA 1985 makes it an offence to trade under a name that is misleading as to a person's status or, in the case of a company, its classification; where, for example, a person or company that is *not* a public company trades under a name that includes the words 'Public Limited Company' or an abbreviation, or their Welsh equivalent or its abbreviation.

(*ii*) Any person or, if the 'person' is a company, any officer of the company in default will be liable to a fine.

35. Publication of a company's name: ss. 348–351 CA 1985

(a) The Act requires every company:

(*i*) to have its name painted or affixed on the outside of every office or place of business, in a conspicuous position and in letters easily legible;

(*ii*) to have its name engraven in legible characters on its seal, if it has a seal;

(*iii*) to have its name mentioned in legible characters in all business letters, on notices and other official publications, on bills of exchange, promissory notes, endorsements, cheques and orders for money or goods, and in all bills of parcels, invoices, receipts and letters of credit of the company.

(b) Failure to comply with the above requirements renders the company and every officer in default liable to fines. Moreover, any officer of the company may be held *personally* liable on documents such as cheques, bills of exchange etc. from which the company's name has been omitted: s. 349(4) CA 1985.

(c) Where a limited company with a registered office in Wales has adopted 'Cyfyngedig' as the last word of its name, the fact that the company is a limited company must be stated in English in all prospectuses, bill heads, letter paper, notices and other official publications of the company; and in a notice conspicuously displayed in every place in which the company's business is carried on: s. 351(4) CA 1985. Section 351(3) CA 1985 makes a similar provision where the name of a *public* limited company includes, as its last part, the equivalent in Welsh of the words 'Public Limited

Company'. In both cases failure to comply renders the company and every officer in default liable to fines.

36. Business names

Sections 1 and 2 BNA 1985 provide that any company which has a place of business in Great Britain under a name which in the case of a company, being a company which is capable of being wound up under CA 1985, does not consist of its corporate name without any addition shall not, without the written approval of the Secretary of State, carry on a business in Great Britain under a name which:

(a) would be likely to give the impression that the business is connected with Her Majesty's Government or with any local authority; or
(b) includes any word or expression for the time being specified under regulations made under the BNA 1985.

Where a company falls within the scope of the BNA 1985, s. 4 of that Act requires that company to state in legible characters on all business letters, invoices and receipts issued in the course of business and written demands for payment of debts arising in the course of the business its corporate name and an address within Great Britain at which service of any document relating in any way to the business will be effective; and, in any premises where the business is carried on and to which the customers of the business or suppliers of any goods or services to the business have access, to display in a prominent position, so that it may easily be read by such customers or suppliers, a notice containing such name and address.

Further, a company falling within the scope of the BNA 1985 must provide the name and address specified by s. 4 of that Act immediately, in writing, to any person with whom anything is done or discussed in the course of the business and who asks for such name and address.

Articles of Association

37. Articles of Association

A company limited by shares *may*, and a company limited by

guarantee or unlimited *must*, register Articles of Association along with its Memorandum of Association: s. 7 CA 1985.

38. Purpose

The Articles contain regulations for management of the internal affairs of the company, e.g.:

(a) rights of the various classes of shareholder;
(b) rules governing meetings;
(c) appointment and powers of directors;
(d) common seal, its custody and use;
(e) alteration of share capital;
(f) procedure for making calls;
(g) forfeiture of shares etc.

In a private company, although no longer a legal necessity, the Articles will usually contain a restriction on the right to transfer the company's shares.

39. Legal effects

(a) The Memorandum and the Articles, when registered, bind the company and its members to the same extent as if they respectively had been signed and sealed by each member, and contained covenants on the part of each member to observe all the provisions: s. 14(1) CA 1985.
(b) All money payable by any member to the company under the Memorandum or Articles is in the nature of a speciality debt: s. 14(2) CA 1985.
(c) The nature of the statutory contract created by s. 14(1) CA 1985 has been the subject of much discussion. It appears that:

(*i*) This statutory contract has some rather odd characteristics. First, s. 14 provides that it is subject to the provisions of the Act and accordingly can under s. 9 CA 1985 be altered unilaterally by the company (*see* **43** *below*). Secondly, the normal remedies for breach of contract do not necessarily apply and the remedies of a member for external redress appear to be limited to an injunction or a declaration.

(*ii*) The articles bind members *qua* (in their capacity as) members: *Hickman* v. *Kent or Romney Marsh Sheep-Breeders Association* (1915).

(iii) The articles bind the company to members *qua* members: *Pender* v. *Lushington* (1877).

(iv) The articles bind members to members: *Rayfield* v. *Hands* (1960).

(v) The articles do not *per se* constitute an enforceable contract between a company and an outsider, i.e. a person who is not a member or a member acting in a capacity other than that of a member: *Eley* v. *The Positive Government Security Life Assurance Co. Ltd* (1876), though they may be used as a reference document to determine the terms of an implied contract outside the articles: *Re New British Iron Co. ex p Beckwith* (1898).

(d) Articles are inoperative if they conflict with statutory requirements, e.g. the right of shareholders to present a winding-up petition cannot be abolished by the articles. Likewise, if the provisions of the articles conflict with those of the memorandum, the provision of the latter prevail.

40. Table A

(a) This is a model set of Articles of Association, setting out regulations for the management of a company limited by shares. It is set out in the Companies (Tables A–F) Regulations 1985. Specimen articles prescribed by the Companies Act are as follows.

(i) Table A — A company limited by shares.

(ii) Table C — A company limited by guarantee and not having a share capital.

(iii) Table D — A company limited by guarantee and having a share capital.

(iv) Table E — An unlimited company having a share capital.

(v) Table G — A partnership company, i.e. a company limited by shares whose shares are intended to be held to a substantial extent by or on behalf of its employees (to be introduced by regulations pursuant to s. 8(A) CA 1985; s. 128 CA 1989).

(b) Section 8 CA 1985 provides that a company may for its articles adopt the whole or any part of Table A. In the case of a company limited by shares, if articles are not registered, or if articles are registered, in so far as they do not exclude or modify Table A, that Table constitutes the company's Articles.

Small private companies, through considerations of cost and

convenience, generally adopt Table A with amendments and additions. It is unusual to adopt Table A in full as further powers and regulations are often required. Larger private companies and public companies generally exclude Table A entirely and adopt individual articles tailored to their own specific requirements.

41. Form of Articles

If a company registers its own Articles, they must be:

(a) in printed form (typewriting is not admissible);
(b) divided into paragraphs, consecutively numbered;
(c) signed by each subscriber of the Memorandum in the presence of at least one witness who must attest the signature;
(d) dated.

If the Memorandum states that the registered office is to be situated in Wales, the Memorandum and Articles to be delivered for registration under s. 10 CA 1985 may be in Welsh but, if they are, they must be accompanied by a certified translation into English: s. 21 CA 1985.

42. Stock Exchange requirements of the Articles

In the case of a company listed on the Stock Exchange the Articles will have to comply with the requirements of the Stock Exchange. These require that the Articles must provide:

(a) *As regards transfer and registration,*

(*i*) that transfers and other documents relating to or affecting the title to any shares will be registered without payment of any fee;

(*ii*) that fully-paid shares be free from any restriction on the right of transfer and from all lien;

(*iii*) that where power is taken to limit the number of shareholders in a joint account, such limit will not prevent the registration of a maximum of four persons;

(*iv*) that the closing of the registers will be discretionary.

(b) *As regards definitive certificates,*

(*i*) that all certificates for capital will be under the common seal, which may only be affixed with the authority of the directors;

(*ii*) that a new certificate issued to replace one that has been worn out, lost or destroyed will be issued without charge (other than exceptional out-of-pocket expenses) and that where the holder has sold part of his holding, he will be entitled to a certificate for the balance without charge;

(*iii*) where power is taken to issue warrants to bearer, that no new share warrant will be issued to replace one that has been lost unless the company is satisfied beyond reasonable doubt that the original has been destroyed.

(c) *As regards dividends,*

(*i*) that any amount paid up in advance of calls on any share may carry interest but will not entitle the holder of the share to participate in respect of such amount in any dividend;

(*ii*) where power is taken to forfeit unclaimed dividends, that power will not be exercised until 12 years or more after the date of the declaration of the dividend.

(d) *As regards directors,*

(*i*) that, subject to such exceptions specified in the Articles of Association as the committee may approve, a director will not vote on any contract or arrangement or any other proposal in which he has a material interest;

(*ii*) that any person appointed by the directors to fill a casual vacancy on or as an addition to the board will hold office only until the next following annual general meeting of the company, and will then be eligible for re-election;

(*iii*) that, where not otherwise provided by law, the companuy in general meeting will have power by ordinary resolution to remove any director (including a managing or other executive director, but without prejudice to any claim for damages under any contract) before the expiration of his period of office;

(*iv*) that the minimum length of the period during which notice to the company of the intention to propose a person for election as a director, and during which notice to the company by such person of his willingness to be elcted may be given, will be at least seven days;

(*v*) that the latest date for lodgement of the notices referred to immediately above will be not more that seven days prior to the date of the meeting appointed for such election;

(*vi*) that where power is taken to delegate the powers of directors to a committee, which includes co-opted persons not being directors, the number of such co-opted persons will be less than one-half of the total number of the committee and no resolution of the committee shall be effective unless a majority of the members of the committee present at the meeting are directors.

(e) *As regards accounts,*

(*i*) that a printed copy of the directors' report, accompanied by the balance sheet (including every document required by law to be annexed thereto) and profit and loss account or income and expenditure account, will, at least 21 days previous to the general meeting, be delivered or sent by post to every member.

(f) *As regards rights,*

(*i*) that adequate voting rights will, in appropriate circumstances, be secured to preference shareholders;

(*ii*) that a quorum for a separate class meeting (other than an adjourned meeting) to consider a variation of the rights of any class of shares will be the holders of at least one-third of the issued shares of the class.

(g) *As regards companies to be included in the 'Investment Trusts' section of the Official List,*

(*i*) that all moneys realized on the sale or other realization of any capital assets in excess of book value and all other moneys in the nature of accretion to capital will not be treated as profits available for dividend.

(h) *As regards notices,*

(*i*) That where power is taken to give notice by advertisement such advertisement will be inserted in at least one national daily newspaper;

(*ii*) that where it is provided that notices will be given only to those members whose registered addresses are within the United Kingdom, any members whose registered address is not within the United Kingdom, may supply an address within the United Kingdom which, for the purpose of notices, will be considered as his address.

(i) *As regards redeemable shares,*

(*i*) that, where power is reserved to purchase for redemption a redeemable share,

(1) purchases will be limited to a maximum price which, in the case of purchases through the market or by tender, will not exceed the average of the middle market quotations taken from the Stock Exchange Official List for the 10 business days before the purchase

is made or in the case of a purchase through the market, at the market price, provided that it is not more than 5 per cent above such average; and

(2) if purchases are by tender, tenders will be available to all shareholders alike.

(j) *As regards capital structure,*

(*i*) that the structure of the share capital of the company will be stated and where the capital consists of more than one class of share it must also be stated how the various classes will rank for any distribution by way of dividend or otherwise.

(k) *As regards non-voting or restricted-voting shares,*

(*i*) that, where the capital of the company includes shares which do not carry voting rights, the words 'non-voting' will appear in the designation of such shares;

(*ii*) that, where the equity capital includes shares with different voting rights, the designation of each class of shares, other than those with the most favourable voting rights, will include the words 'restricted voting' or 'limited voting'.

(l) *As regards proxies,*

(*i*) that where provision is made in the Articles as to the form of proxy, this will be so worded as not to preclude the use of the two-way form.

(*ii*) that a corporation may execute a form of proxy under the hand of a duly authorized officer.

(m) *As regards purchases of own shares,*

(*i*) that no purchase by the company of its own shares will take place unless it has been sanctioned by an extraordinary resolution passed at a separate class meeting of the holders of any class of convertible shares.

(n) *As regards votes of members,*

(*i*) that, where provision is made in the article to disenfranchise members in cases where there is default in supplying information in compliance with a notice served under Section 212 of the Companies Act 1985, disenfranchisement will not take effect earlier than 28 days after the service of the notice.

(o) *As regards untraceable members,*

(*i*) that where power is taken to cease sending dividend warrants by post, if such warrants have been returned undelivered or left uncashed, it will not be exercised until such warrants have been so returned or so left uncashed or two consecutive occasions.

(*ii*) that where power is taken to sell the shares of a member who is untraceable it will not be exercised unless

(1) during a period of 12 years at least three dividends in respect of the shares in question have become payable and no dividend during that period has been claimed; and

(2) on expiry of the 12 years the company gives notice by advertisement in two national daily newspapers of its intention to sell the shares and notifies the Department of such intention.

Where necessary a certified copy of a resolution of the board of directors undertaking to comply with the provisions must be lodged with the Quotations Department of the Exchange.

43. Alteration of Articles of Association

(a) Section 9 CA1985 permits alteration of the Articles:

(*i*) subject to the provisions of that Act and the conditions contained in its Memorandum of Association;

(*ii*) by *special* resolution of the company.

(b) Other restrictions of the power to alter the Articles have arisen out of various cases decided in the courts, namely

(*i*) any alteration in the Articles must be legal; thus the introduction of an article requiring a four-fifths majority on resolutions altering certain articles was held to be illegal: *Ayre* v. *Skelsey's Adamant Cement Co. Ltd* (1904);

(*ii*) a company cannot justify a breach of contract by altering its Articles: *Baily* v. *British Equitable Assurance Co.* (1906);

(*iii*) any alteration of the Articles must be made in good faith for the benefit of the company as a whole.

This test includes two elements (good faith/benefit) but it is a single principle. In *Greenhalgh* v. *Arderne Cinemas* (1950) the benefit to the company as a whole was held to be a benefit which any individual hypothetical member of the company could enjoy directly or through the company and not merely a benefit to the majority of members only. The test of good faith did not require proof of actual benefit but merely the honest belief on reasonable grounds that benefit could follow from the alteration. In several cases the court has held that actual and foreseen detriment to a minority affected by the alteration was not in itself a sufficient ground of objection if the benefit to the company test was satisfied.

In Greenhalgh's case the issue was the removal from the articles of the members' right of first refusal of any shares which a member might wish to transfer; the majority wished to make the change in order to admit an outsider to membership in the interests of the company. In *Shuttleworth* v. *Cox Bros. & Co. (Maidenhead) Ltd* (1927) the purpose of the alteration was to remove from office a director who repeatedly failed to account to the company for its money in his hands. He was permitted to allege malice as well as discrimination but failed in his objections. In both cases the alteration was upheld as *id*.

Several cases relate to alterations conferring a power on the company to enforce a transfer by a member of his shares, thereby in effect expelling him from membership. In *Sidebottom* v. *Kershaw Leese & Co.* (1920) the new power could only be exercised against a member who carried on a business competing with the company; this was upheld. In *Dafen Tinplate Co.* v. *Llanelly Steel Co. (1907) Ltd* (1920) the power was not so restricted and was overruled; so also in *Brown* v. *British Abrasive Wheel Co.* (1919) where the holders of 98 per cent of the shares wished to be rid of the small minority as a pre-condition for subscribing additional capital which the company badly needed. A bare power of expropriation without obvious benefit to the company is unlikely to be valid since it can only benefit the majority which promotes it.

An alteration, which is otherwise valid, may be made with retrospective effect: *Allen* v. *Gold Reefs of West Africa* (1900). But it cannot deprive members or directors of accrued rights, e.g. to dividend or to remuneration.

(c) The necessary procedure is as follows.

(*i*) *Board meeting*. The directors will resolve to recommend to the members that the Articles of Association be amended and shall instruct the secretary to sign and issue a notice on behalf of the board, convening an extraordinary general meeting for the purpose of approving a special resolution. If the alteration varies the rights attaching to a particular class of shares or if the terms of issue of a share provide for that particular class to be enfranchised, the terms of the particular debenture issue require such notice to be given.

(*ii*) *Extraordinary general meeting*. The meeting should be held and the special resolution approved. The chairman or secretary should sign a copy of the resolution in the form required by the Registrar of Companies.

(*iii*) *Registrar of Companies* — the signed copy of the special resolution should be delivered to the Registrar of Companies within 15 days of the meeting. If new articles have been adopted a copy, initialled by the chairman for identification, should be forwarded with the resolution.

(*iv*) *Articles of Association* — a printed copy of the Articles of Association as amended must be delivered to the Registrar of Companies. In addition, it is recommended that the Memorandum and Articles of Association be reprinted and copies passed to those persons having need of an up-to-date copy.

NOTE: If the company concerned was listed, the procedure outlined above would have to be modified and the documentation drafted to take account of the Continuing Obligations imposed upon such a company by the Stock Exchange. The Continuing Obligations are set out in Chapter 2 and reference should be made thereto.

Capital structure

44. Authorized, nominal or registered capital

(a) *Various considerations*. As already indicated (*see* **5**) capital requirements are determined by taking into account:

(*i*) the *purchase price* of any business to be acquired, or assets to be taken over;

(*ii*) *preliminary expenses*;

(*iii*) *working capital*;

(*iv*) *future requirements* arising out of anticipated development of the business.

(b) *Classes of shares*. Although shares need not be classified it is usually advantageous to do so in order to give the investors a wider choice of investment. Basically shares may be divided into three classes:

(*i*) preference shares;

(*ii*) ordinary shares;

(*iii*) deferred shares.

45. Preference shares

(a) The common feature of preference shares is that they confer upon their holder some form of preference as compared with the ordinary shareholder. This preference invariably relates to the payment of dividend, the holder of the share being entitled to a fixed rate of dividend out of the profits of the company, to be paid in priority to other classes of shareholder.

(b) The preference enjoyed by any particular preference shareholder may take a number of forms. In particular:

(*i*) *Cumulative preference shares.* All preference shares are presumed to be cumulative: *Webb* v. *Earle* (1875); unless otherwise described. That is, arrears of dividend are to be made up in subsequent years, when profits are available. No dividend will be paid to other classes of shareholder until preference dividends (including arrears) are paid to date.

(*ii*) *Non-cumulative preference shares.* The holders of such shares are entitled to a specified rate of dividend, but only out of profits in the current year. If the profits do not warrant payment of a dividend, the arrears are *not* carried forward to subsequent years.

(*iii*) *Participating preference shares.* Such shares entitle the holder to preferential dividend at a fixed rate and to participate further in any profit remaining after the ordinary shareholders have received, say, 10 per cent dividend. In the absence of express provisions, preference shares are deemed to be non-participating: *Will* v. *United Lankat Plantation Co.* (1914).

(*iv*) *Preference as to repayment of capital.* This is a right which may be given in addition to, or instead of, some of those already mentioned. It gives the preference shareholders the right to repayment of their capital in full in priority to the ordinary shareholders in the event of a winding-up. Unless this right is expressly given in the Articles or conditions of issue, preference shareholders rank equally with other shareholders as to return of capital.

(*v*) *Participation in surplus assets.* The preference shareholders may be entitled to participate with the ordinary shareholders in any surplus assets, but this is a right that must be expressly conferred by the company's Articles, Memorandum or conditions of issue: *Scottish Insurance Corporation* v. *Wilson's & Clyde Coal Co.* (1949).

(*vi*) *Entitlement to arrears of dividend on winding-up.* The right to arrears of preference dividend may be provided for in the company's Articles; even so, however, it does not necessarily entitle the holders to payment of their arrears before the repayment of capital to other classes of shareholder. If, for example, the Articles provide for payment of arrears of preference dividend 'due' at the date of the winding-up, no arrears will be payable unless a dividend has been declared, because a dividend is not due until it has been declared: *Re Roberts & Cooper Ltd.* (1929)

46. Ordinary shares

(a) The holders of these shares are the main risk-bearers of a company, since ordinary shares confer no special dividend rights apart from an implied right to participate in the profits, if any.
(b) In most companies the ordinary shares constitute the equity share capital, i.e. the holders are entitled to the 'equity' or residue of profits after payment of dividends on prior-ranking shares and of any surplus assets in a winding-up.
(c) In recent years some companies have issued *non-voting* ordinary shares, sometimes described as 'A' shares. Such shares apart, however, the ordinary shareholders carry the bulk of the voting power in most companies. Preference shareholders, on the other hand, are often without any voting power, or are entitled to a vote only when their dividends are in arrears.

47. Deferred shares

(a) These are sometimes issued to the vendors in full or partial settlement of the purchase price of the business acquired by the company. If, for example, A. Brown Ltd. is formed to acquire the business of A. Brown, he may be allotted deferred (or founder's) shares in consideration of the purchase price.
(b) They are usually valuable shares, as they may have the right to all profits remaining after payment of prior dividends and to all surplus assets on winding up the company. In that event the deferred shares, and not the ordinary shares, will form the 'equity' of the company.
(c) Deferred shares, although they are sometimes of small

denomination, usually give the holder heavy voting power, e.g. on a poll vote, where each share is worth one vote, £5000 worth of 5p deferred shares might well out-vote the ordinary shares. Thus the deferred shareholders can retain control of the business, and it is for this reason that deferred shares are sometimes referred to as management shares.

48. Redeemable shares

(a) Section 159 CA 1985 enables a company limited by shares or limited by guarantee and having a share capital, if authorized by its articles, to issue shares which are, or at the option of the company or a shareholder are liable, to be redeemed.

However, no such shares may be issued at any time when there are no issued shares of the company which are not redeemable; redeemable shares may not be redeemed unless they are fully paid; and the terms of the redemption must provide for payment on redemption.

(b) By s. 159(A) CA 1985 redeemable shares may not be issued unless the following conditions are satisfied as regard the terms and manner of redemption:

(*i*) the date on or by which, or dates between which, the shares are to be or may be redeemed must be specified in the company's articles or, if the articles so provide, fixed by the directors, and in the latter case the date or dates must be fixed before the shares are issued;

(*ii*) any other circumstances in which the shares are to be or may be redeemed must be specified in the company's Articles;

(*iii*) the amount payable on redemption must be specified in, or determined in accordance with, the company Articles, and in the latter case the Articles must not provide for the amount to be determined by reference to any person's discretion or opinion;

(*iv*) any other terms and conditions of redemption shall be specified in the company's Articles.

(c) In general redemption may only take place by utilizing distributable profits or the proceeds of a fresh issue; and any premium payable on redemption must be paid out of the company's distributable profits.

(d) On redemption out of the profits of the company, the company is required to establish a capital redemption reserve equivalent to the amount by which the company's issued share capital is thereby reduced. Such a fund is a capital fund, though it may be used to pay up unissued shares for the purpose of a bonus issue: s. 170 CA 1985.

(e) Shares so redeemed are treated as cancelled on redemption, but although the company's issued share capital is reduced thereby a redemption of shares under the provision is not treated as reducing the amount of the company's authorized share capital. A company which has issued shares up to its maximum nominal capital is permitted to issue fresh shares for the purpose of redeeming an existing issue of redeemable shares.

(f) Section 171 CA 1985 extends the power provided by s. 159 of the Act in that it enables a private company limited by shares or limited by guarantee and having a share capital, if authorized to do so by its Articles, to redeem its own shares out of capital. The procedure to be followed on redemption of such shares out of capital is the same as that entailed when a private company purchases its shares out of capital (*see* **61** *below*).

49. Stock

(a) A company cannot make an original issue of stock, i.e. stock can only be created out of fully paid up shares:

(*i*) if authorized by the Articles; and

(*ii*) by resolution of the company in general meeting. An ordinary resolution is adequate unless the Articles require some other form of resolution: s. 121 CA 1985.

(b) There is only one real advantage in converting shares into stock; the requirement of CA 1985 that shares shall bear distinctive numbers does not apply to stock. Thus the conversion will be expected to lead to some simplification of work in the company's registration department.

> NOTE: Even this advantage has been nullified to some extent, as s. 182(2) CA 1985 permits a company to dispense with the numbering of all its issued shares (or all the issued shares of a particular class) so long as they are fully paid up and rank *pari passu* for all purposes.

(c) Theoretically, there is a further advantage, in that the stock created is transferable in fractional amounts. In fact, however, this would create more work for the registration department, and the Articles invariably provide for the transfer of stock in units or multiples of fixed amount.

50. Debentures

(a) Strictly, debentures do not form part of a company's true capital; they may, however, be described as 'borrowed' or 'loan' capital and are included in this section for that reason. They are dealt with in greater detail in Chapter 15.

(b) The term 'debenture' is usually applied to any form of long-term borrowing, but technically it describes the document which acknowledges the indebtedness. In most cases, such a document is under seal and sets out the conditions for securing repayment of the loan, date of repayment, and payment of interest.

51. Determination of capital structure

(a) *Various considerations*. If capital is to be raised in various forms, some or all of the following points ought to be considered.

(*i*) *Redeemability*. Share capital is essentially *permanent*, i.e. it cannot be reduced except with the sanction of the Court under s. 135 CA 1985 or redeemed or purchased in accordance with the provisions of Chapter 7 of Part V of that Act. Debentures are a *redeemable* security and might, therefore, be preferred to satisfy a long-term (but not permanent) need of financial assistance.

(*ii*) *Cost*. Debentures are usually more economical than preference shares. Provided adequate security is offered to the debenture-holders, they are usually prepared to accept a comparatively low rate of interest, i.e. when compared with the dividend that would have to be offered to make preference shares attractive.

(*iii*) *Capital gearing*, i.e. the ratio of fixed interest capital to 'equity' capital, ought to be considered very carefully. If, for example, a large issue of debentures (or preference shares) is contemplated, it might be well to consider the effect upon the capital gearing. If the capital gearing is high (where the proportion of fixed interest bearing capital is high in relation to 'equity' capital), the company's ordinary shares might appear less attractive to prospective investors, who realize that both debenture-holders and preference shareholders must be satisfied before they would earn any dividend on their ordinary shares.

(b) *Under-capitalization.* In calculating capital requirements, the aim must be neither too much nor too little. Under-capitalization is almost certain to result in all kinds of difficulties, in particular:

(*i*) lack of working capital;
(*ii*) inability to meet present commitments;
(*iii*) inability to obtain credit;
(*iv*) failure to work to optimum capacity.

(c) *Over-capitalization* must also be avoided, for the following reasons.

(*i*) The excess capital must be invested outside the business, probably at a low rate of interest.

(*ii*) As a result, dividends paid on the company's capital may be reduced or, in the case of preference shares, fall into arrears.

(*iii*) Failure to maintain dividends will soon have an adverse effect upon the market value of the company's shares.

(d) *Taxation.* Debenture interest is charged against profits, whereas dividend on shares is regarded as a distribution of profits — a very important consideration as regards taxation.

Maintenance of capital

52. Maintenance of capital

The Companies Act 1985 consolidates various provisions introduced by the Companies Acts 1980 and 1981 designed to ensure that a company maintains its capital. These provisions constitute the subject matter of 53–61 below.

53. Serious loss of capital: s. 142 CA 1985

(a) If a serious loss of capital occurs, i.e. if the assets of a public company fall to half or less of the amount of the company's called-up capital, the directors of the company must convene an extraordinary general meeting of the company to consider whether any, and if so what, measures should be taken to deal with the situation. (The object is, of course, to give the shareholders an opportunity to consider the position of the company before it becomes insolvent and is compelled to cease trading.)

(b) The meeting must be convened not later than 28 days after the earliest date on which the situation became known to a director of the company, for a date not later than 56 days from that date.
(c) The notice of the meeting must comply with the requirements of s. 369 CA 1985 for convening an extraordinary general meeting, i.e. not less than 14 days' notice in writing — unless it is intended to pass a special resolution at the meeting for any reason, in which case not less than 21 days' notice in writing is required.
(d) Failure on the part of any director of the company who knowingly and wilfully authorizes or permits the failure to convene an extraordinary general meeting — or permits the failure to continue after expiry of the 28-day period — will be liable to a fine.

54. Acquisition of a company of its own shares: s. 143 CA 1985

Except as permitted by the Companies Act, the courts have consistently refused to allow a company to reduce its capital, however attempted. This principle was established in *Trevor* v. *Whitworth* (1887) which held that a company could not purchase its own shares, even though there was express power to do so in its Memorandum of Association.

This important basic principle is reinforced in the following terms.

(a) No company limited by shares or limited by guarantee and having a share capital shall acquire its own shares, whether by purchase, subscription or otherwise: s. 143(1) CA 1985.
(b) If a company acts in contravention, it becomes liable to a fine, and any officers of the company in default are liable to a fine or imprisonment or both, and the purported acquisition is *void*: s. 143(2) CA 1985.

However, s. 143(3) CA 1985 provides that the basic prohibition in s. 143(1) does not apply in relation to:

(a) the redemption or purchase of any shares in accordance with Chapter 7 of Part V of the Act;
(b) the acquisition of any shares in a reduction of capital, duly made;
(c) the purchase of shares in pursuance of an order of the court under s. 5, s. 54 or Part XVII of the Act;

(d) the forfeiture of shares or the acceptance of shares, surrendered in lieu of forfeiture, in accordance with its Articles of Association, for non-payment of any sum due in respect of those shares.

Under s. 143(3) CA 1985 a company limited by shares may also acquire its own fully paid shares 'otherwise than for valuable consideration' (e.g. by way of gift). This means that shares so acquired need no longer be put into the name of a nominee.

55. Acquisition of shares in a company by company's nominees: s. 144 CA 1985

(a) Section 144 CA 1985 provides that a limited company (whether public or private) is regarded as having no beneficial interest in any shares it has issued to a nominee of the company, nor in any partly paid shares acquired by a nominee of such company for a third person; that is, for all purposes, the shares will be treated as being held by the nominee on his own account.

(b) If, in the case of partly paid shares, a nominee fails to pay the amount of any call in respect of the nominal value or premium on such shares within 21 days of his being called upon to do so, then

(*i*) if the shares were issued to him as a subscriber to the Memorandum of Association, the other subscribers to the Memorandum, or

(*ii*) if the shares were otherwise issued to him, or acquired by him, the directors of the company at the time of the issue or acquisition,

will be jointly and severally liable with him to pay that amount.

(c) A subscriber or director who believes that a claim will, or might, be made against him in **(b)** above may apply to the court for relief. The court has power to grant such relief either before or in the course of any proceedings for recovery of any amount due, if it appears that the person or persons concerned acted honestly and reasonably and, in the circumstances of the case, he ought to be excused from liability, either wholly or partly.

(d) By s. 145 CA 1985 the above provisions do not apply

(*i*) to shares issued or transferred in consequence of an application or agreement made before 22nd December 1980; or

(*ii*) to shares acquired by a nominee of a company when the company has no beneficial interest in the shares (other than any rights the company may have as trustee, whether as personal representative or otherwise); or

(*iii*) to shares acquired otherwise than by subscription by a nominee of a public company with the financial assistance of the company, and where the company has a beneficial interest in those shares — *see* **56 (a)**(*iv*).

56. Treatment of shares held by or on behalf of a public company: s. 146 CA 1985

(a) *Cases affected.* Section 146 of the Act provides for the treatment of forfeited and surrendered shares, and shares held by a nominee of a public company in the following cases:

(*i*) where shares in the company are forfeited or are surrendered to the company in lieu of forfeiture, in accordance with the Articles of Association, for failure to pay any sum due on the shares;

(*ii*) where the nominee of a public company acquires shares of the company from a third person without financial assistance by the company for the purpose, and the company has a beneficial interest in the shares;

(*iii*) where shares in the company are acquired by the company otherwise than by any of the methods mentioned in s. 143(3)(*a*)–(*d*) (*see* **55**), and the company has a beneficial interest;

(*iv*) where any person acquires shares in the company without financial assistance being provided by the company for the purpose, and the company has a beneficial interest in those shares.

NOTE: In determining whether a company has a beneficial interest in any shares, any rights the company has as trustee or personal representative to recover expenses, or to be remunerated out of the trust property, must be disregarded.

(b) *Treatment* of shares held in the above cases.

(*i*) Unless the shares (or any interest of the company in them) are previously disposed of, the company must not later than the end of the 'relevant period' (*see* **(c)** *below*) from the date of their forfeiture, surrender or acquisition, as the case may be,

(1) cancel them and diminish the amount of the share capital by the nominal value of the shares; and

(2) if the effect of the cancellation is to reduce the nominal value of the company's allotted share capital below the authorized minimum, the company must apply for re-registration as a private company, stating the effect of the cancellation.

NOTE: The directors of the company may take such steps as are necessary to comply with the above requirements, and the usual procedures for reduction of capital under ss. 135 and 136 CA 1985 can be dispensed with for this purpose.

(*ii*) The company, the company's nominee, or, as the case may be, the other shareholder, must not exercise any voting rights in respect of the shares involved, and any purported exercise of such rights is void.

(c) The *'relevant period'* referred to in **(b)**(*i*) above means:

(*i*) *three years*, in the case of shares forfeited or surrendered to the company (case **(a)**(*i*)) or acquired, as in cases **(a)**(*ii*) and **(a)**(*iii*) above.

(*ii*) *one year*, in the case of shares acquired, as in case **(a)**(*iv*) above.

(d) *Penalties*. Failure to cancel shares or to apply for re-registration, as required in **(b)**(*i*) above, renders the company, and every officer of the company, in default liable to fines.

57. Charges taken by a public company on its own shares: s. 150 CA 1985

A lien or other charge that a public company holds on its own shares is generally *void*, but s. 150 permits the following exceptions:

(a) in a company of every description, a charge on its own partly paid shares for any amount remaining unpaid on them;
(b) in the case of a company whose ordinary business includes the lending of money or providing hire-purchase (or both), a charge of the company on its own shares (whether fully or partly paid) in connection with any transaction which the company enters into in the ordinary courses of its business;
(c) in the case of a company (other than a company referred to in **(d)** below) which is re-registered or registered as a public company, a charge on its own shares held immediately before it applies for re-registration or, as the case may be, registration;

(d) in the case of any company which after the end of the re-registration period remains or remained an old public company and did not apply to be re-registered before the end of that period as a public company, any charge in its own shares which was in existence immediately before the end of that period.

> NOTE: A lien or charge taken by a company which is a trustee, and where the trust property includes its own shares, is not specifically excepted.

58. Financial assistance for acquisition of shares: ss. 151–158 CA 1985

(a) Section 151 provides that:

(*i*) where a person is acquiring or is proposing to acquire any shares in a company it shall not be lawful for the company or any of its subsidiaries to give financial assistance directly or indirectly for the purpose of that acquisition before or at the same time as the acquisition takes place; and

(*ii*) where a person has acquired any shares in a company and any liability has been incurred (by that or any other person) for the purpose of that acquisition it shall not be lawful for the company or any of its subsidiaries to give any financial assistance directly or indirectly for the purpose of reducing or discharging the liability so incurred.

(b) Neither of the prohibitions stated in **(a)**, however, prohibit a company from giving any financial assistance for the purpose of any acquisition of shares in the company or its holding company or from giving financial assistance to reduce or discharge any liability incurred by a person for the purpose of the acquisition of any shares in the company or its holding company if:

(*i*) such is not the principal purpose of the assistance, but is an incidental part of some larger purpose of the company; and

(*ii*) the assistance is given in good faith in the interests of the company.

Nor do they prevent:

(*i*) any distribution of a company's assets by way of dividend lawfully made or any distribution made in the course of the winding-up of the company;

(*ii*) the allotment of any bonus shares;

(*iii*) anything done in pursuance of an order of the court made under s. 425 CA 1985;

(*iv*) anything done under an arrangement made between a company and its creditors which is binding on the creditors by virtue of Part IIA 1986;

(*v*) anything done under an arrangement made in pursuance of s. 110 IA 1986;

(*vi*) any reduction of capital confirmed by order of the court under s. 137 CA 1985;

(*vii*) a redemption or purchase of any shares made in accordance with Chapter 7 of Part V CA 1985 .

(c) Further, neither of the general prohibitions is declared to prohibit:

(*i*) where the lending of money is part of the ordinary business of the company, the lending of money by the company in the ordinary course of its business;

(*ii*) the provision by a company, in good faith in the interests of the company, of financial assistance for the purposes of an employee share scheme;

(*iii*) without prejudice to (*ii*) above, the provision of financial assistance by a company or any of its subsidiaries for the purposes of or in connection with anything done by the company (or a company connected with it) for the purpose of enabling or facilitating transactions in shares in the first-mentioned company between, and involving the acquisition of beneficial ownership of those shares by, any of the following persons:

(1) the bona fide employees or former employees of that company or of another company in the same group; or

(2) the wives, husbands, widows, widowers, children or step-children under the age of 18 of any such employees or former employees;

(*iv*) the making by a company of loans to persons, other than directors, employed in good faith by the company with a view to enabling those persons to acquire fully paid shares in the company to be held by themselves by way of beneficial ownership.

In the case of a public company these four exceptions only operate if the company has net assets which are not thereby reduced or, to the extent that those assets are thereby reduced, if the financial assistance is provided out of distributable profits.

(d) If a company acts in contravention of s. 151 CA 1985 the company and any officer who is in default commits a criminal offence.

(e) Section 155 CA 1985 provides a further exception to the general prohibitions established in s. 151 in that it provides that they do not prohibit a private company from giving financial assistance in any case where the acquisition of the shares in question is or was an acquisition of shares in the company or if it is a subsidiary of another private company, in that other company, provided that the following conditions are satisfied:

(*i*) The company must have net assets which are not thereby reduced or, to the extent that they are reduced, the financial assistance must be provided out of distributable profits.

(*ii*) The assistance must be approved by a special resolution.

(*iii*) The directors are required to make a statutory declaration giving details of the assistance and certifying that in their opinion the company can pay its debts and will continue to be able to do so during the ensuing 12 months. This must be supported by a report made by the auditors confirming that the directors' conclusions are reasonable.

(*iv*) The holders of 10 per cent of the company's issued share capital or any class thereof may apply to the court to cancel the resolution authorizing the assistance.

59. Procedure for financial assistance upon the acquisition of own shares

Assuming the company concerned to be a private company, the procedure would be as follows:

(a) Check the Memorandum and Articles of Association to ensure that the company is properly authorized to provide financial assistance.

(b) In determining whether net assets are reduced, consideration must be given to the form of financial assistance to be provided.

(c) A statutory declaration on Form G155(6)(a) must be made by the directors of the company proposing to give financial assistance. Annexed to the statutory declaration there must be a report by the auditors of the company addressed to the directors stating that:

(*i*) they have enquired into the state of affairs of the company; and

(*ii*) they are not aware of anything to indicate that the

opinion expressed by the directors in the declaration is unreasonable in all the circumstances: s.156(4) CA 1985.

(d) An extraordinary general meeting of the shareholders of the company must be convened to approve a special resolution of the company authorizing the giving of financial assistance.

The special resolution must be approved on the same day as or within one week of the making of the statutory declaration. The statutory declaration and the auditors' report must be available for inspection at the extraordinary general meeting: s. 157 CA 1985.

(e) A copy of the special resolution, the statutory declaration and the auditors' report must be filed with the Registrar of Companies within 15 days of the date of the resolution.

(f) Unless all the members of the company voted unanimously in favour of the resolution or resolutions, the financial assistance may not be given until after the expiry of four weeks from the date of the resolution or the last resolution where more than one was necessary (s. 158(2) CA 1985). This waiting period is to allow any members who did not vote in respect of the resolution, and holding at least 10 per cent in aggregate in nominal value of the company's issued share capital or any class thereof, to apply to court for cancellation of the resolution. If no application is made for cancellation, the financial assistance may be made at any time after the expiry of the four-week period but no later than eight weeks from the date of the statutory declaration, or the earliest of the declarations where there is more than one.

60. Purchase by a company of its own shares: ss. 162–169 CA 1985

(a) Section 162 provides that a company limited by shares or limited by guarantee and having a share capital may, if authorized by its Articles, purchase its own shares (including any redeemable shares). However, a company may not purchase any of its shares if as a result of such purchase there would no longer be any member of the company holding shares; and any such purchase must be in accordance with the procedures set out in the Act.

(b) The procedure prescribed for the purchase of shares varies according to whether or not the purchase takes place through a recognized investment exchange.

(i) *Off-market purchase.* Such must be in pursuance of an interim contract of purchase, approved in advance by a special resolution of the company. The contract, or a memorandum thereof, must have been available for inspection by members for 15 days before the meeting and at the meeting at which it is approved.

(*ii*) *Market purchase.* Such a purchase must have been authorized by an ordinary resolution of the company, specifying the maximum number of shares that may be purchased, the maximum and minimum prices to be paid and the date the authority expires.

In either case, within 28 days of the transfer to the company of the shares concerned, the company must deliver to the Registrar a return stating with respect to shares of each class purchased the number and nominal value of the shares and the date on which they were transferred to the company. Further, in the case of a public company this return must also state the aggregate amount paid by the company for the shares and the maximum and minimum price paid in respect of each class purchased.

Details of the purchase must be disclosed in the directors' report.

(c) The provisions of s. 170 CA 1985 apply to the exercise of the power to purchase own shares, in the same way as they apply to the exercise by the company of the power to issue redeemable shares.

61. Redemption or purchase of own shares out of capital: ss. 171–178 CA 1985

Section 171 extends the powers provided by ss. 159 and 162 CA 1985 (**48** and **60** above respectively) in that it enables a private company limited by shares or limited by guarantee and having a share capital, if authorized to do so by its Articles, to redeem or purchase its own shares out of capital.

A payment out of capital to redeem or purchase the company's own shares will not be lawful, however, unless:

(a) The directors of the company make a statutory declaration specifying the amount of capital required and stating that having made full inquiry into the affairs and prospects of the company it will not thereby become insolvent, and will still be able to continue to carry on business as a going concern. Such declaration must be supported by, and have annexed to it, an auditors' report.

(b) A special resolution approving the payment out of capital is passed within the week immediately following the date on which the directors make the statutory declaration.
(c) Within the week immediately following the date of the resolution for payment out of capital, and having delivered a copy of the statutory declaration and the auditors' report to the Registrar, the company must cause to be published in the *Gazette* and in an appropriate newspaper (or give notice in writing to that effect to each of its creditors) a notice detailing its intention and actions and bringing to the attention of creditors the statutory rights of objection.
(d) The payment out of capital must be made not earlier than five or more than seven weeks after the date of the resolution.

The right of objection referred to in (c) above is exercisable within five weeks of the date on which the resolution was passed and is exercised by:

(a) any member of the company other than one who consented to or voted in favour of the resolution; or
(b) any creditor of the company who may apply to the Court for the cancellation of the resolution.

On the hearing of such application the Court may make such order as it thinks fit.

Progress test 1

1. The company of which you are secretary has recently been changed from private to public. The directors are contemplating further expansion and you are asked to prepare a memorandum for consideration by the Board setting out the advantages and disadvantages, from the point of view of the company, in having an official quotation. (3)

2. Tabulate the documents to be lodged with the Registrar before incorporation of a company with a share capital can be effected. (9)

3. (*a*) Set out the procedure for forming a private company, and (*b*) specify the matters which you would expect to be dealt with at the first board meeting. *ICSA* **(9–10: 2:2)**

4. What is a Certificate of Incorporation? What is its effect in regard to (*a*) the existence of a company; (*b*) the legal rights to trade? Write fully. *CCS* **(11)**

5. As a practising secretary, you are approached by Messrs Smith and Robinson to convert their firm into a private limited company. Report to them, outlining the procedure and indicating the principal advantages and disadvantages of such a conversion. **(9–11)**

6. You are asked by your directors to arrange for the formation of a wholly owned subsidiary company, which is to be a private company with a nominal capital of £100. The suggested name for the company is Exe Limited. In numbered paragraphs, explain the action you would take up to the time of delivery to the Registrar of Companies of the documents necessary to obtain a Certificate of Incorporation. (NOTE: It should be assumed that you are expected to undertake all the work involved.) **(5, 7–11)**

7. You are asked to apply for the registration of a private company limited by shares. List the items of information about the proposed company which you would require to enable you to draft the memorandum and articles of association. *ICSA* **(9, 23, 30)**

8. For what purposes are companies limited by guarantee usually formed? What are the advantages of using this type of company, rather than other possible methods of organization, for such purposes? What is the nature of the 'guarantee'? *ICSA* **(2, 3, 27)**

9. What are the statutory requirements for publishing a company's name and the names of its directors? *ICSA* **(35, 14:2)**

10. Set out in numbered paragraphs the procedure to be

followed by a company which desires to alter the objects clause of its Memorandum of Association. Who, apart from members, may object to such an alteration, and what steps may objectors take? **(33)**

11. Your directors wish to change the objects of the company. In a memorandum advise them how this may be achieved. *ICSA* **(33)**

12. Your company wishes to change its name, and also to trade under a different name from its registered name. Set out in detail the steps that are required for these purposes. *ICSA* **(34)**

13. Where would you expect to find the rights attaching to different classes of your company's shares, and how may these be varied? *ICSA* **(44)**

14. Your directors would like to issue preference shares. In the form of a memorandum to them, summarize the rights attaching to such shares, and explain how they may be repaid. *ICSA* **(45, 48)**

15. Your company is considering raising further capital. Consider the relative advantages and disadvantages to the company and the investor of raising capital by means of shares and convertible loan stock. *ICSA* **(41, 51)**

16. Comment briefly on the usual rights of holders of preference shares as to dividends, return of capital and participation in the distribution of surplus assets. **(45)**

17. The directors of a company seek your advice as to the relative merits of preference and ordinary shares as a means of raising capital. What are the general considerations involved? **(45–46)**

18. The issued shares of your company are now fully paid up and the board considers it desirable to de-number them. The articles require that the shares be numbered. What is the appropriate procedure? **(49)**

19. Write a letter to the directors of your company, explaining the significance of redeemable shares. Indicate briefly in your letter a comparison with an issue of debentures as a means of raising money. *ICSA* **(48, 50, 51)**

20. Examine the power of a company to purchase its own shares. **(60–61)**

21. As a chartered secretary in public practice you have been engaged by the promoters to form a company. For the guidance of the promoters set out in detail the requirements and procedure relating to the choice of a company's name. *ICSA* **(24)**

22. (*a*) Explain in detail the formation of private and public companies.
(*b*) Define public and private companies. *ICSA* **(3, 9)**

2
Procedure after incorporation

First board meeting

1. Appointment of first directors

Section 10 CA 1985 provides that a Memorandum delivered for registration must be accompanied by a statement in prescribed form (Form G10), signed by the subscribers to the Memorandum, giving particulars of the first directors (and secretary or joint secretaries) and containing a consent signed by each person named in it as a director or as secretary, to act in the relevant capacity. On incorporation, the persons named shall be deemed to have been appointed as first directors (and secretary or secretaries).

2. The first board meeting

This should be held as soon as possible, i.e. after the first directors have been appointed and following receipt of the Certificate of Incorporation. Some or all of the following items are likely to be included in the agenda, but it should be borne in mind that certain items might not be relevant in the case of a private company.

(a) Record receipt of the *Certificate of Incorporation,* etc. The Certificate of Incorporation will be produced by the secretary together with a copy of the Memorandum and Articles of Association as registered.

(b) Record appointment of the *first directors*. The first directors having already been appointed, this is merely a question of producing formal evidence of their appointment so that it can be recorded in the minutes. If registration agents have been employed and their staff appointed as first directors (and secretary) this item of business will have to accommodate this fact and the change in the directorate that will occur.

(c) Appoint the *chairman of the board*. The person appointed will usually also take the chair at general meetings of the company.

(d) Record the appointment of the first secretary. As stated above, the person named as secretary is deemed to be appointed on incorporation of the company in a Memorandum delivered for registration, accompanied by a statement signed by the subscribers to the Memorandum, and containing the signed consent of the person appointed first secretary.

As with item **(b)** if registration agents have been employed and one of them appointed as first secretary, the item of business will have to accommodate this fact and the change in office holder that will occur.

(e) Record the address of the *registered office* of the company. This item may, if registration agents have been used, take the form of a resolution changing the address and establishing a new one.

(f) Appoint the company's *solicitors*.

(g) Appoint the company's *brokers*. This item would not normally appear on the agenda of a private company. In the case of a public company, the appointment would be necessary in order to obtain permission to deal in the company's shares on the Stock Exchange.

(h) Appoint the company's *bankers*. The resolution passed for this purpose will usually be in the form required by the bank concerned; in fact the London clearing bankers have adopted a standard form which requires the signatures of all persons authorized to sign cheques, bills of exchange, etc., on behalf of the company.

(i) Appoint the company's *auditors*. Although it is not essential to make such an appointment at this stage, a public company intending to offer shares to the public would, no doubt, consider it advisable to include the name of a well-established and reliable firm of auditors. The company's accounting reference date would be established and the secretary instructed to file the prescribed form (Form G224) with the Registrar of Companies.

(j) Submit and adopt a design for the common seal if the company is to have one. At the same time it will be necessary to lay down rules for the use and custody of the seal, unless these have been included in the company's Articles. An impression of the company's seal would be made in the minute book.

(k) *Allotment of shares*. Note applications form and resolve upon the allotment of shares. The secretary should be instructed to file the prescribed form (Form G88(2)) with the Registrar of Companies.

(l) Determine the method (or methods) to be adopted for obtaining capital. In the case of a public company intending to offer shares and/or debentures to the public, the principal methods available are a direct public offer for sale and Stock Exchange placing.

(m) Arising out of the previous item:

(*i*) prepare and/or consider draft issue documents submitted by the secretary;

(*ii*) consider the terms of draft underwriting contract, submitted by the secretary.

(n) Execute any purchase agreement, e.g. for purchase of the business from the vendor.

NOTE: Even after a Certificate of Incorporation has been received, a *public* company is still not entitled to do business until it has received a certificate to commence business from the Registrar. If such a company does business or exercises its borrowing powers in contravention of these requirements, the company and any officer of the company in default will be liable to a fine; moreover, the validity of any purported transaction is not affected and, if the company fails to comply with its obligations in connection with the transaction within 21 days of being called upon to do so, the directors become jointly and severally liable to indemnify the other party to the transaction for any resultant loss or damage (*see* **1:14**).

(o) Instruct the secretary to:

(*i*) submit the following forms to the Registrar of Companies:

(1) Form G288 detailing the appointment, if appropriate, of any new directors or secretary.

(2) Form G287 detailing the new registered office if any.

(3) Form G88(2) detailing shares allotted and the

names and addresses of those persons to whom the shares are issued.

(4) Form G224 notifying the accounting reference date of the company. If this form is not submitted within nine months of incorporation, the company's accounting reference date will automatically be the last day of the month in which the anniversary of its incorporation falls: s. 224(2) CA 1985.

(5) Forms G325, G353 and G190 notifying the Registrar of the location of the Register of Directors' Interests in Shares or Debentures, the Register of members and the Register of Charges respectively if they are kept at an address other than the registered office. In a public company the Register of Interests in Shares required by s. 211 CA 1985 must be kept at the same place as the Register of Directors' Interests in Shares or Debentures.

(*ii*) submit an application to the Stock Exchange for permission to deal;

(*iii*) deal with the appointment of bankers;

(*iv*) purchase the necessary books and stationery;

(*v*) arrange for the engagement of staff;

(*vi*) register the company with HM Customs and Excise for the purpose of VAT and supply particulars to the Inland Revenue for tax purposes.

3. After the first board meeting

Apart from drafting minutes of the meeting and submitting the appropriate forms to the Registrar, the secretary will have the following business to attend to:

(a) Forward to the bank appointed under a covering letter:

(*i*) one copy of the resolution of appointment, signed by the chairman and all authorized signatories;

(*ii*) a copy of the company's Memorandum of Association, and of the Articles of Association, if required;

(*iii*) the company's Certificate of Incorporation, for inspection only.

NOTE: Later, in the case of a *public* company, the bank will also wish to inspect the certificate to commence business when it is obtained.

(b) Notify the brokers of their formal appointment and, in due course, submit formal application for admission to listing to the Stock Exchange.

NOTE: The application must be in the form prescribed by the Stock Exchange. Various documents must be lodged at the same time, together with a cheque for the appropriate Stock Exchange charges.

(c) Purchase the necessary books and stationery, if this has not already been dealt with. In particular, the secretary must ensure that all books required by the Act (usually referred to as statutory books) are provided, namely:

(*i*) Register of Members: s. 352 CA 1985;
(*ii*) Register of Directors and Secretaries: s. 288 CA 1985;
(*iii*) Register of Directors' Interests: s. 325 CA 1985;
(*iv*) Register of Charges: s. 397 CA 1985;
(*v*) Minute Books: s. 382 CA 1985;
(*vi*) Accounting records: s. 221 CA 1985;
(*vii*) Register of Interests in Shares: s. 211 CA 1985.

(d) Also various *non-statutory* books may be purchased, such as:

(*i*) Register of Debenture Holders.

NOTE: If the company issues debentures, the conditions of issue may require the keeping of such a register; in that event, the Act provides for its location, inspection, etc.: s. 190 CA 1985.

(*ii*) Minute Book for board meetings.

NOTE: Although the Act provides for the keeping of minutes of both general directors' and managers' meetings, only the minutes of general meetings are required to be kept open for inspection by shareholders; therefore, it is usually considered advisable to have separate minute books.

(*iii*) Register of Documents Sealed (or Seal Book). Most companies find this useful for recording particulars of documents issued under the company's seal.

(*iv*) Register of Transfers (or Transfer Register). Although this is no longer a statutory requirement, many companies still find it a useful medium for the posting of transfer particulars from transfer forms to the Register of Members.

(*v*) Register of Important Documents. To record receipt of various documents lodged with the company for purpose of registration, a comprehensive register of this kind may suffice, but large public companies usually prefer to have separate registers, such as Register of Power of Attorney, Register of Probates and Letters of Administration, etc.

Raising capital

4. Principal methods

If the founders themselves are unable to raise the necessary capital, then the balance may be raised by one or more of the following methods:

(a) *Offer for subscription.* This term is used to describe an offer by or on behalf of a company to persons who will subscribe directly for the shares or debentures of the company, without the intervention of another contracting party such as a merchant bank or other financial intermediary. A merchant bank may nevertheless still underwrite the issue (in which case it will probably be involved in the preparation of the listing particulars or prospectus). However, the significant distinction from an offer for sale is that the merchant bank will not act as principal in relation to any contracts concluded under applications made pursuant to the listing particulars or prospectus

(b) *Offer for sale.* An offer for sale is an offer to sell shares (or the right to the allotment of shares) rather than an offer of shares for direct subscription. It is often made by a merchant bank or stockbroking firm which immediately prior to such offer has agreed to purchase the shares from one or more existing shareholders or to subscribe for the shares. The expression is, however, equally applicable to a sale by a substantial shareholder who has held some or all of the shares over a period.

Most significant public offers of shares which are to be listed on the Stock Exchange are offers for sale rather than offers for subscription. Typically such offers are made by merchant banks. The arrangements between the issuing company and the merchant bank are contained in some form of agreement, probably called an offer for sale agreement or perhaps, if only new shares are involved, a subscription agreement. This agreement will provide for the shares to be allotted to the merchant bank provided that certain conditions are satisfied. If existing shares are involved, the vendor or vendors of those shares will be parties to the agreement, agreeing to sell the shares subject to similar conditions. Other parties, such as directors of the issuing company, may be added to give warranties or indemnities.

As has been indicated, those who successfully apply for the shares will enter into a contract with the merchant bank (or other person making the offer), rather than with the issuing company. As a result the merchant bank is seen to put its name more emphatically behind the offer.

> NOTE: Whichever method is used, the price at which the shares are sold may either be that fixed by the seller (a fixed price offer) or that fixed by a system of tendering by interested buyers (a tender offer). The problem with a fixed price offer is judging the appropriate price.

It is not unknown for the market value of shares, when dealings in them begin, to be at a considerable premium to the fixed offer price. To try and curtail this, a tender offer may be used. under a tender offer system the seller invites prospective purchasers to tender whatever price they wish for the shares, provided it is above a minimum or reserve figure indicated by the seller. The price at which the shares will actually be sold (known as 'the striking price' will be the highest price at which all the shares on offer will have been applied for and thus will be sold.

(c) *Placings*. A placing may take various forms. A company wishing to raise capital for an expansion programme (or any other commercially sound purpose) may seek investment by a venture capital fund or other financial institution. The company places the shares directly with the investor which retains them and becomes an equity partner in the company. The advantages of a direct placing are that no prospectus or listing particulars need be published, keeping the cost of the exercise to a minimum, and it enables private limited companies (which are generally prohibited from making public offers of their shares) to tap the financial resources of the big financial institutions without the expense of 'going public' together with the potential loss of control which that may entail.

(d) *Selective marketing.* A selective marketing is, as its name suggests, not an offer to the public generally but to a selected number of persons, e.g. pension funds or other financial institutions. If the shares are to be admitted to listing, the approval in principle of the Committee on Quotations must be obtained. Approval will not be given in the case of a newcomer to listing if the expected market value of the securities exceeds the limit set from time to time (currently £15,000,000). If the anticipated market value exceeds £2,000,000, at least 25 per cent of the shares must either be made available to the general public by the sponsoring firm or taken firm (i.e. acquired unconditionally) and distributed by another Stock Exchange member firm which is independent of the sponsoring member firm.

> NOTE: It will be appreciated that *all* the above methods are available to a public company, whereas a private company cannot make an application for a listing in respect of its securities or issue or cause to be issued in the UK any advertisement offering securities to be issued by the company: ss. 143(3) and 170(1) FSA 1986.

5. The regulation of public offers

(a) Public offers of securities are now regulated by the Financial Services Act 1986.
(b) This provides in Part IV rules governing offers of listed securities. No investment can be admitted to the Official List of the Stock Exchange unless Part IV of the Act is complied with. Investments include shares, debentures, instruments entitling the holders to subscribe for shares and certificates which represent property rights or contractual rights in shares. The Council of the Stock Exchange is specified under the Act as the 'competent authority' for the purpose of establishing the requirements for admission to listing.
(c) Part V of the Act controls the public advertisement of shares and other securities for which an official listing on the Stock Exchange is not being sought. An advertisement offers securities and is accordingly regulated by the provision of the Act if:

(*i*) it invites a person to enter into an agreement for or with a view to subscribing for or otherwise acquiring or underwriting any securities; or (*ii*) it contains information calculated to lead directly or indirectly to a person entering into such an agreement: s. 158(4) FSA 1986.

(d) Part V applies in different ways to advertisements involving securities which are to be admitted to dealings on an approved exchange and to other offers.

(*i*) An approved exchange is a recognized investment exchange (i.e. one designated as such by the Secretary of State under s. 207 FSA 1986) which has been approved for this purpose by the Secretary of State: s. 158(6) FSA 1986.

(*ii*) Where no dealings on an approved exchange are sought, s. 160 FSA 1986 applies. This includes all 'primary' and 'secondary' offers except those specifically exempted, e.g. those of a private character.

No advertisement offering securities which amounts to a primary or secondary offer can be made unless a prospectus has been delivered to the Registrar or no agreement can be entered into as a result of the advertisement until such delivery: s. 160(1) FSA 1986.

A primary offer is an advertisement (not connected with an approved exchange) directly or indirectly inviting persons to subscribe for or to underwrite the securities involved: s. 160(2) FSA 1986.

A secondary offer is an advertisement (not connected with an approved exchange) directly or indirectly inviting persons to acquire the securities involved (i.e. not direct from the issuer). In such a case the offeror must either have acquired the securities from the issuer with a view to making such an offer, or have acquired them otherwise than from the issuer with a view to making an offer, provided that they have never been dealt with on an exchange or held by a person purely as an investment, or be a controller of the issuer who is acting with the issuer's consent in making the offer: s. 160(3) FSA 1986.

For this purpose an offeror is presumed to have acquired the securities with a view to making an offer if he makes it either within six months of the issue of the securities or before he has paid the issuer: s. 160(4) FSA 1986.

6. Official listing of securities

(a) Section 142 of FSA 1986 provides that no securities shall be admitted to the Official List of the Stock Exchange, unless:

(*i*) an application for listing has been made to the Stock Exchange in such manner as the listing rules require;

(*ii*) the consent of the issuer of the securities has been given; and

(*iii*) the Stock Exchange is satisfied that:

(1) the requirements of the listing rules made by the Stock Exchange for these purposes and in force when the application was made; and

(2) any other requirements imposed by the Stock Exchange in relation to that application, have been complied with.

(b) The rules referred to in (a)(*iii*)(1) may, in particular, require as a condition of the admission of any securities to the Official List:

(*i*) the submission to, and approval by, the Stock Exchange of listing particulars in such form and containing such information as may be specified in the rules; and

(*ii*) the publication of that document.

(c) Further, in addition to the information specified by listing rules or required by the Stock Exchange as a condition of the admission of any securities to the Official List s. 146 FSA 1986 provides that any listing particulars submitted to the Stock Exchange must contain all such information as investors and their professional advisers would reasonably require, and reasonably expect to find there, for the purpose of making an informed assessment of:

(*i*) the assets and liabilities, financial position, profits and losses and prospects of the issuer of the securities; and

(*ii*) the rights attaching to those securities.

(d) On or before the date on which listing particulars are published as required by listing rules, a copy of the particulars shall be delivered for registration to the Registrar of Companies and a statement that a copy has been so delivered must be included in the particulars: s. 149 FSA 1986.

(e) Where listing particulars are or are to be published in connection with an application for the listing of any securities, no advertisement or other information of a kind specified by listing rules shall be issued in the UK unless the contents of the advertisement or other information have been submitted to the Stock Exchange and it has either:

(*i*) approved those contents; or

(*ii*) authorized the issue of the advertisement without such approval.

7. Basic conditions for official listing

Any company which wishes to apply to the Stock Exchange for its securities to be admitted to the Official List is expected to comply with the following basic conditions as set out in the formal book *Admission of Securities to Listing*, known as the Yellow Book.

(a) The issuer must be duly incorporated or otherwise established under the law of the place where it is incorporated and it must be in conformity with that law and its Memorandum and Articles of Association or equivalent documents. In particular it must not be a private company.

(b) The securities for which listing is sought must be issued in conformity with the law of the place where the issuer is incorporated and in conformity with the issuer's Memorandum and Articles of Association and all authorizations needed for their creation and issue under such law or documents must have been duly given.

(c) The expected market value of securities for which listing is sought must be at least £700,000 in the case of shares, and £200,000 in the case of debt securities, other than tap issues.

(d) The securities for which listing is sought must be freely transferable.

(e) A company must have published or filed accounts in accordance with its national law covering the three years preceding application for listing.

(f) Where a company has a relationship with a corporate substantial shareholder which could result in a conflict of interest between its obligations towards that shareholder and its duties to the general body of shareholders, the conflict could render the company unsuitable for listing.

(g) Where any fee or other remuneration or consideration is to be paid or given to any director, officer, technical adviser or promoter otherwise than in cash, the Council reserve the right to reject any application for listing of the company's securities.
(h) At least 25 per cent of any class of shares must, not later than the time of admission, be in the hands of the public (i.e. persons who are not associated with the directors or major shareholders), in one or more member states.
(i) Where application for admission to listing is made in respect of any class of security:

(i) if none of the securities of that class is already listed, the application must relate to all securities of that class issued or proposed to be issued;

(ii) if some of the securities of that class are already listed, the application must relate to all further securities of that class issued or proposed to be issued.

(j) If shares issued by a company incorporated in a non-member state are not listed either in its country of incorporation or in the country in which a majority of its shares are held, they will not generally be admitted to listing.
(k) All applicants for listing must follow the prescribed application procedure. In particular, listing particulars or equivalent offering documents and supporting documents must be lodged in final form at least 48 hours before hearing of the application by the Committee.
(l) Listing particulars or equivalent offering documents must not be published until they have received the formal approval of the Department in their final form.
(m) All new applicants are required to publish listing particulars or equivalent offering documents in accordance with the regulations of the Exchange.
(n) Issues for cash of securities having an equity element must, in the absence of exceptional circumstances, be offered in the first place to the existing equity shareholders in proportion to their holdings unless the shareholders have approved other specific proposals.
(o) In the absence of exceptional circumstances, the issue of options or warrants to subscribe equity capital must be limited to an amount equal to 10 per cent of the issued equity capital at the time the warrants or options are issued.

(p) Securities convertible or exchangeable into another class of securities, or options or warrants to subscribe or purchase such other class, may be admitted to listing only if that other class of securities is (or will become at the same time)

(*i*) a class of listed securities, or

(*ii*) a class of securities listed or traded on another regulated, regularly operating, recognized open market.

8. The Continuing Obligations

The Continuing Obligations of the Stock Exchange may be broken down under the following headings:

(a) *General.*

(*i*) Generally and apart from compliance with all specific requirements which follow, any information necessary to enable holders of the company's listed securities and the public to appraise the position of the company and to avoid the establishment of a false market in its listed securities must be notified.

(*ii*) When further securities are allotted of the same class as securities already listed, application for listing such further securities must be made not more than one month after allotment.

(*iii*) A company whose securities are also listed on other stock exchanges must ensure that equivalent information is made available to the market at the Stock Exchange and each of such other exchanges.

(*iv*) (1) A company having listed shares in issue must ensure equality of treatment for all holders of such shares who are in the same position.

(2) A company having listed debt securities in issue must ensure equality of treatment for all holders of such securities of the same class in respect of all rights attaching to such securities.

(b) *Public announcements.*

(*i*) The company must notify any major new developments in its sphere of activity which are not public knowledge and which:

(1) in the case of a company having listed shares in issue may, by virtue of their effect on its assets and liabilities or financial position or on the general course of its business, lead to substantial movements in the price of its shares; or

(2) in the case of a company having listed debt securities in issue may significantly affect its ability to meet its

commitments.

(*ii*) The date fixed for any board meeting at which the declaration or recommendation or payment of a dividend on listed shares is expected to be decided, or at which any announcement of the profits or losses in respect of any year, half-year, or other period is to be approved for publication must be notified in advance.

(*iii*) Any decision to pay or make any dividend or other distribution on listed securities or to pass any dividend or interest payment on listed securities must be notified after board approval.

(*iv*) A preliminary announcement of profits or losses for any year, half-year or other period must be notified after board approval.

(*v*) A company having listed debt securities in issue must notify any new issues of debt securities and, in particular, any guarantee or security in respect thereof.

(*vi*) Any proposed change in capital structure, including that of the company's listed debt securities must be notified after board approval.

(*vii*) Any drawing or redemption of listed securities must be notified immediately after board approval.

(*viii*) Any change in rights attaching to any class of listed securities (including any change in the rate of interest carried by a debt security) and any change in the rights attaching to any shares into which any listed debt securities are convertible or exchangeable must be notified.

(*ix*) The basis of allotment of securities offered generally to the public for cash and of open offers to shareholders must be notified and appear in the press before dealings commence.

(*x*) Details of acquisitions or realizations of assets as specified in Chapter 1 of Section 6 of 'Admission of Securities to Listing' must be notified.

(*xi*) Any information required to be disclosed to the Stock Exchange under the provisions of the City Code on Take-overs and Mergers for the time being in force must be notified.

(*xii*) (1) In the case of a United Kingdom company, any information notified to the company under Part VI of the Companies Act 1985 must be notified.

(2) As regards directors' interests, any matter which relates to securities which are or will be listed and which

(*A*) is notified to the company pursuant to ss. 324 or 328 of the Companies Act 1985, or

(*B*) is required pursuant to ss. 325(3) and (4) of that Act to be entered in the register referred to therein,

must be notified immediately to the Company Announcements Office.

(3) In the case of companies not subject to the Companies Acts, equivalent information to that required under (1) and (2) above in respect of the interests, including options, whether or not held through another party (corporate or otherwise) of each director, including his spouse and children under the age of 18 years in, and so far as is known to the company, of each holder of 5 per cent or more of the share capital of the company, must be notified.

(4) Any decision by the board to submit to the company's shareholders a proposal for the company to be authorized to purchase its own shares must be notified immediately. An indication must be given as to whether the proposal relates to specific purchases, or to a general authorization to make purchases. The outcome of the shareholders' meeting must also be notified immediately, and four copies of the relevant resolutions forwarded to the Stock Exchange as soon as possible.

(*xiii*) Any purchase by the company, or the group of which the company is part, of its listed securities must be notified.

(*xiv*) Any board decision to change the general character or nature of the business of the company or of the group must be notified.

(*xv*) Any change in the status of the company for taxation purposes under the statutory provisions relating to chose companies or to approved investment trusts must be notified.

(c) *Annual accounts.*

(*i*) The company must issue an annual report and accounts within six months of the end of the financial period to which they relate. If the company has subsidiaries, the accounts must be in consolidated form. The company's own accounts must be published in addition if they contain significant additional information. If the relevant annual accounts do not give a true and fair view of the state of affairs and profit or loss of the company or group, more detailed and/or additional information must be provided.

(*ii*) The company must include in its annual report and accounts:

(1) In the case of domestic companies, a statement by the directors as to the reasons for any significant departure from applicable standard accounting practices.

(2) An explanation in the event of trading results shown by the accounts for the period under review differing materially from any published forecast made by the company.

(3) A geographical analysis of both net turnover and contribution to trading results of those trading operations carried on by the company (or group) outside the United Kingdom and the Republic of Ireland.

(4) The name of the principal country in which each subsidiary operates.

(5) The following particulars regarding each company (not being a subsidiary) in which the group interest in the equity capital amounts to 20 per cent or more as follows:

(*A*) the principal country of operation;

(*B*) particulars of its issued capital and debt securities; and

(*C*) the percentage of each class of debt securities attributable to the company's interest (direct or indirect).

(6) A statement as at the end of the financial year showing as regards (*a*) bank loans and overdrafts and (*b*) other borrowings of the company (or group) the aggregate amounts repayable:

(*A*) in one year or less, or on demand;

(*B*) between one and two years;

(*C*) between two and five years; and

(*D*) in five years or more.

(7) In respect of the financial year, a statement of the amount of interest capitalized by the company (or group) during the year, with an indication of the amount and treatment of any related tax relief.

(8) In the case of a United Kingdom company a statement as at the end of the financial year, showing the interests of each director in the capital of any member of the group appearing in the register maintained under the provisions of s. 325 CA 1985, together with any options in respect of such capital, distinguishing between beneficial or non-beneficial

interests. Such statement should include by way of note any change in those interests or options occurring between the end of the financial year and a date not more than one month prior to the date of the notice of meeting or, if there has been no such change, disclosure of that fact.

(9) In the case of a United Kingdom company a statement showing particulars, as at a date not more than one month prior to the date of the notice of meeting, of an interest of any person other than a director in any substantial part of the share capital of the company appearing in a register maintained under the provisions of s. 211 CA 1985 and the amount of the interest in question or, if there is no such interest, a statement of that fact.

(10) In the case of a United Kingdom company, a statement showing whether, so far as the directors are aware, the company is a close company for taxation purposes and whether there has been any change in that respect since the end of the financial year.

(11) Particulars of any contract of significance (as defined in (12) below) subsisting during or at the end of the financial year in which a director of the company is or was materially interested, or, if there has been no such contract, a statement of that fact.

(12) Particulars of any contract of significance between the company, or one of its subsidiary companies, and a corporate substantial shareholder. Where a company has subsidiaries, comparison will be made with the purchases, sales, payments, receipts or net assets of the group on a consolidated basis.

(13) Particulars of any contract for the provision of services to the company or any of its subsidiaries by a corporate substantial shareholder. Exceptionally, such a contract need not be disclosed, if it is a contract for the provision of services which it is the principal business of the shareholder to provide and it is not a contract of significance, for the purposes of paragraph (12) above.

(14) Particulars of any arrangement under which a director has waived or agreed to waive any emoluments.

(15) Particulars of any arrangement under which a shareholder has waived or agreed to waive any dividends.

(16) In the case of a United Kingdom company, particulars of any shareholders' authority for the purchase by the

company of its own shares existing at the end of the year and, in the case of such purchases made otherwise than through the market or by tender or partial offer to all shareholders, particulars of the names of the sellers of such shares purchased, or proposed to be purchased, by the company during the year. In the case of any such purchases or options or contracts to make such purchases, entered into since the end of the year covered by the report, equivalent information to that required under Schedule 7 Part II of the Companies Act 1985 should be given.

(17) In the case of any issue for cash of securities having an equity element made otherwise than to the company's equity shareholders in proportion to their equity shareholdings and which has not been specifically authorized by the company's shareholders, in addition to the particulars required by Paragraph 39 of Schedule 4 to the Companies Act 1985:

(*A*) the names of the allottees, if less than six in number, and in the case of six or more allottees a brief generic description of them; and

(*B*) the market price of the securities concerned on a named date, being the date on which the terms of the issue were fixed.

(18) In the case of an investment trust as defined in Chapter 3 of Section 10 of 'Admission of Securities to Listing':

(*A*) a statement confirming, in the case of a United Kingdom company, that the Inland Revenue has approved the company as an investment trust for the purpose of s. 359 of the Income and Corporation Taxes Act 1970, specifying the last accounting period in respect of which such approval has been given (or, in the case of a newly listed company, a statement that it has announced that it will direct its affairs to enable it to seek approval) and also that the company has subsequently directed its affairs so as to enable it to be so approved;

(*B*) a broad geographical analysis based on country of incorporation of the companies whose securities are held in the portfolio;

(*C*) an analysis of the portfolio by broad industrial or commercial sectors;

(*D*) a list of the largest investments by market value, such value being stated in the case of each such investment;

(*E*) an analysis of the portfolio between equity

capital securities having an equity element and fixed-income securities.

(*F*) an analysis of income between dividends, interest, and other forms of income, distinguishing, where significant, between underwriting income and the results of dealing by subsidiaries;

(*G*) an analysis, where material, to an appreciation of the investment trust's financial position, of realized and unrealized profits and losses as between listed and unlisted investments (taking the definition of 'listed' applicable to investment trusts set out in Section 10 of 'Admission of Securities to Listing'); and

(*H*) the name of the group or company which manages the investments, together with an indication of the terms and duration of their appointment and the basis for their remuneration.

(19) In the case of an investment company (as defined in Chapter 3 of Section 10 of 'Admission of Securities to Listing'):

(*A*) a list of all investments with a value greater than 5 per cent of the company's assets, and at least the 10 largest investments stating, with comparative figures where relevant: (*a*) a brief description of the business, (*b*) proportion of share capital owned, (*c*) cost, (*d*) directors' valuation, (*e*) dividends received during the year (indicating any abnormal dividends), (*f*) dividend cover or underlying earnings, (*g*) any extraordinary items, and (*h*) net assets attributable to investment;

(*B*) an analysis of any provision for diminution in the value of investments, naming the investments against which provision has been made and stating for each investment: (*a*) cost, (*b*) provision made, and (c) book value;

(*C*) an analysis of realized and unrealized surpluses, stating separately profits and losses as between listed and unlisted investments (taking the definition of 'listed' applicable to investment trusts set out in Section 10 of 'Admission of Securities to Listing').

(20) The identity of independent non-executive directors together with a short biographical note on each.

(21) Where a company issues summary financial statements as permitted by the Companies Act, earnings per share should be disclosed in addition to the required contents for

summary financial statements set out in Statutory Instrument No. 515.

(*iii*) Where the company has listed shares in issue, is a subsidiary of another company and has received notification from its parent company of the parent company's proposal to participate in future issues of shares by the company not made on a *pro rata* basis to existing shareholders, in order that the parent company may maintain its stake in the company, the proposal must be given the authority of a resolution of the company passed at a general meeting. Such authority must be renewed annually and the parent company must abstain from voting. Particulars of the participation by the parent company in any vendor consideration placing made during the year under review must be set out in the annual accounts.

(d) *Half-yearly reports and preliminary profits statements for the full year.*

(*i*) A company must prepare a report (a 'half-yearly report') on the group's activities and profit or loss during the first six months of each financial year. The half-yearly report must be either sent to the holders of listed securities or inserted as a paid advertisement in two national daily newspapers not later than four months after the end of the period to which it relates. In exceptional circumstances, the Committee may extend the time limit for publication. If the report is not advertised as referred to above, copies must be made available to the public at the registered office of the company in the United Kingdom (if any) and at the office of the company's paying agent in the United Kingdom (if any).

A copy of the report (in English) must be sent simultaneously to the Company Announcements Office and to the competent authority of each other member state in which the company's shares are listed, not later than the time when the half-yearly report is published for the first time in a member state.

(*ii*)(1) The half-yearly report or preliminary profits statement for the full year must consist of figures and, in the case of the half-yearly report, an explanatory statement relating to the group's activities and profit or loss during the relevant period.

(2) The figures, in table form, must state at least the following:

(*A*) net turnover;

(*B*) profit or loss before taxation and extraordinary items;

(*C*) taxation on profits (United Kingdom taxation and, if material, oversea and share of associated companies to be shown separately);

(*D*) minority interests;

(*E*) profit or loss attributable to shareholders, before extraordinary items;

(*F*) extraordinary items (net of taxation);

(*G*) profit or loss attributable to shareholders;

(*H*) rates of dividend(s) paid and proposed and amount absorbed thereby;

(*I*) earnings per share expressed as pence per share (computed on the figures shown for profits after taxation as defined in SSAP 3); and

(*J*) comparative figures in respect of (*A*)–(*I*) inclusive for the corresponding previous period.

(3) The explanatory statement in the half-yearly report must include any significant information enabling investors to make an informed assessment of the trend of the group's activities and profit or loss together with an indication of any special factor which has influenced those activities and the profit or loss during the period in question, and enable a comparison to be made with the corresponding period of the preceding financial year. It must also, as far as possible, refer to the group's prospects in the current financial year.

(4) Where the accounting information given in a half-yearly report has not been audited that fact must be stated. Reference should also be made to s. 255 of the Companies Act 1985. If the accounting information contained in a half-yearly report has been audited by the company's auditor, his report thereon including any qualifications must be set out in the half-yearly report.

(5) A company listed as an investment trust or investment company must disclose in any half-yearly report or preliminary profits statement for a financial year a division of its income between (*a*) dividend and interest received and (*b*) other forms of income (which may be income of associated companies), distinguishing where significant between underwriting income

and the result of dealing by subsidiaries. Additional disclosures may be required in special circumstances.

(e) *Settlement.*

(*i*) The company must arrange for transfers to be certified against certificates or temporary documents and to be returned on the day of receipt or, should that not be a business day, on the first business day following their receipt, and to split and return renounceable documents within the same period.

(*ii*) Transfers and other documents must be registered without payment of any fee.

(*iii*) Certificates must be issued without charge within:

(1) one month of the date of expiration of any right of renunciation; or

(2) 14 days of the lodgement of transfers.

(*iv*) Designated accounts must be arranged if requested by holders of securities.

(*v*) Where warrants to bearer have been issued or are available for issue, (1) certificates must be exchanged for warrants (and vice versa), if permitted, within 14 days of the deposit of the warrants or certificates) and (2) transfers must be certified against the deposit of warrants on the day of deposit or, if that is not a business day, on the first business day following deposit.

(f) *Communications with holders of listed securities.*

(*i*) Where required in accordance with Chapter 1 of Section 6 of Admission of Securities to Listing on Acquisitions and Realizations, the company must send a circular to shareholders of listed securities relating to acquisitions, disposals, take-overs, mergers and offers.

All circulars to holders of listed securities together with notices of meetings, proxy forms and notices by advertisement to holders of listed bearer securities must be submitted to the Department in draft form for approval before they are published. Drafts of any proposed amendment to the company's memorandum and Articles of Association or equivalent documents must be submitted to the Department; in the case of listed debt securities, this is only required where the amendment would affect the rights of the holders of such securities.

(*ii*) Whenever shareholders are sent a notice of meeting which includes any business other than routine business at an annual general meeting, an explanatory circular must accompany the notice or, if the business is to be considered at or on the same day as an annual general meeting, an explanation must be incorporated in the directors' report. an explanatory circular must also accompany any notice of meeting sent to holders of listed debt securities.

(*iii*) Where an increase in authorized capital is proposed, the directors must state in the explanatory circular or other document accompanying the notice of meeting whether they have any present intention of issuing any part of that capital.

(*iv*) Where an increase of authorized capital is proposed and 10 per cent or more of the voting capital will remain unissued, the explanatory circular or other document accompanying the notice of meeting must state that no issue will be made which would effectively alter the control of the company without prior approval of its shareholders in general meeting.

(*v*) The company must forward to the Company Announcements Office six copies of all circulars, notices, reports, announcements or other documents at the same time as they are issued and four copies of all resolutions passed by the company other than resolutions concerning routine business at an annual general meeting.

(*vi*) The company must ensure that, at least in each member state in which its securities are listed, all the necessary facilities and information are available to enable holders of such securities to exercise their rights. In particular, it must inform holders of the holding of meetings which they are entitled to attend, enable them to exercise their right to vote, where applicable, and publish notices or distribute circulars giving details of the allocation and payment of dividends or interest in respect of such securities, the issue of new securities (including arrangements for the allotment, subscription, renunciation, conversion or exchange of such securities) and repayment of securities. The company must appoint a registrar and/or, where appropriate, a paying agent in the UK, unless the company itself performs these functions.

(*vii*) The company must send proxy forms, with provision for two-way voting on all resolutions intended to be proposed, with the notice convening a meeting of holders of listed securities to all persons entitled to vote at the meeting.

(*viii*) (1) Unless shareholders otherwise permit, a company proposing to issue securities having an equity element for cash must offer those securities to existing equity shareholders (and where appropriate, to holders of other securities having an equity element of the company entitled to be offered them) in proportion to their existing holdings, and only to the extent that the securities to be issued are not taken up by such persons may they be issued to others or otherwise than in proportion as mentioned above.

(2) Similarly, unless shareholders otherwise permit, a company must obtain the consent of shareholders before any major subsidiary of the company makes any issue for cash of securities having an equity element so as materially to dilute the percentage equity interest of the company and its shareholders in that subsidiary.

(*ix*) In the event of a circular being issued to the holders of any particular class of security, the company must issue a copy or summary of such circular to the holders of all other listed securities unless the contents of such circular are irrelevant to such other holders.

(*x*) Air mail must always be used when communicating with oversea holders of listed securities.

(*xi*) When a foreign company sends a circular to holders of a listed security at an address in the United Kingdom or the Republic of Ireland, it must be in the English language.

(g) *Directors, etc.*

(*i*) Any change in the directorate, and any important change in the holding of an executive office, must be notified immediately.

(*ii*) (1) Copies of all directors' service contracts of more than one year's duration or, where any such contract is not reduced to writing, a memorandum of the terms thereof, must be made available for inspection at the registered office or transfer office during usual business hours on any weekday (Saturdays and public holidays excluded) from the date of the notice convening the annual general meeting until the date of the meeting and made available for inspection at the place of meeting for at least 15 minutes prior to the meeting and at the meeting.

(2) The company must state in a note to the notice convening the annual general meeting the place and time to which copies or, as the case may be, memoranda of all such service contracts will be available for inspection or, if so, that there are no such contracts.

(3) The company must state in the directors' report the

period unexpired of any service contract of any director proposed for re-election at the forthcoming annual general meeting, where the service contract or a memorandum of its terms is required to be made available under (1) above, or, if he does not have a service contract of more than one year's duration, the directors' report must contain an appropriate negative statement.

(iii) Investment companies whose investment policy is principally to subscribe for shares in another company or fund which itself invests in a portfolio of securities must ensure that at all times its directors will comprise a majority of the directors of the company, or fund, in which its assets are or are proposed to be principally invested, so as to control the policy of the underlying company or fund.

(iv) The company must adopt rules governing dealings by directors in the listed securities of the company in terms no less exacting than those of the model code issued by the Stock Exchange.

9. The listing particulars

(a) Listing particulars are the 'prospectus' required by the Stock Exchange. Section 144 FSA 1986 provides that one of the main requirements of the listing rules is the prior approval of listing particulars by the Stock Exchange and their publication.

(i) Publication. Section 154 FSA 1986 provides that where an application for listing has been made and listing particulars either have been or are to be published, no advertisement or any other information relating to that application shall be issued, unless the Stock Exchange has either seen and approved its contents or authorized its publication.

Any breach is a criminal offence. There is a defence for anyone who can prove that, acting in the ordinary course of non-investment business, he believed on reasonable grounds that its issue had been approved or authorized.

Where the advertisement or other document has been approved or authorized for publication, neither the publisher nor the person responsible for the listing particulars shall be liable in tort or contract by reason of any mis-statement or omission if the document and the listing particulars, taken together, would not be likely to mislead persons of the kind likely to consider the acquisition of the securities in question.

(ii) Form and content — general duty. Section 146 FSA 1986 contains a general duty of disclosure. The listing particulars must contain such information as is necessary to enable investors and their advisers to make an informed assessment of the assets and liabilities, profits and losses, the prospects of the company and the rights attaching to the securities. The general duty covers all information possessed by the persons responsible for the issue of the particulars and information they could reasonably have obtained by making enquiries.

The section sets out four criteria to assist in determining what information is required:

(1) the nature of the securities and the issuer;

(2) The nature of the prospective buyers (e.g. the general public or professional investment managers);

(3) that professional advisers, who may reasonably be expected to have been consulted, will have professional knowledge of certain matters; and

(4) any information provided by the interim reports required of listed companies or under any other statutory provision or that required by recognized exchanges (including the Stock Exchange) to determine the value of the securities.

Under s. 148 FSA 1986 the Stock Exchange may grant an exemption from the general duty of disclosure for any information if disclosure of that information would be contrary to the public interest, seriously detrimental to the issuer of the securities, or, in the case of certain specialized debt securities, unnecessary.

The Secretary of State or the Treasury may certify that the disclosure of information would not be in the public interest.

Information detrimental to the issuer must still be published, however, if non-disclosure would be likely to mislead a potential buyer as to any knowledge which would be essential for him to have in order to make an informed decision.

(iii) Content of listing particulars. The contents requirements are set out in detail in *Admission of Securities to Listing*. This requires that the listing particulars provide:

(1) Details of the issuer, the persons responsible for the listing particulars, the auditors and other advisers.

(2) Details of the securities for which application for listing is being made.

(*A*) a statement that an application has been or will be made for the admission of shares to the Official List;

(*B*) a statement that, in the opinion of the directors, the working capital available to the company and its subsidiaries is sufficient and, if it is not, how it is proposed to provide the necessary additional working capital;

(*C*) the date on which the shares will be admitted to listing and the date on which dealings will commence, if it is known;

(*D*) details of any public take-over offers either for or by the company in the financial year in which listing is sought or the previous financial year;

(*E*) if the issue is being made simultaneously on the markets of two or more countries, and if a tranche has been reserved for any one or more of them, an indication of any such tranche;

(*F*) the period after publication of the particulars during which the issue will remain open;

(*G*) an estimate of the charges payable by the company in relation to the issue and the total remuneration of the financial intermediaries;

(*H*) the size of the issue and the issue price or offer or marketing price—as these figures may not be determined until a late stage, they may be entered in manuscript in the copies submitted for approval;

(*I*) details must be given of any payment or benefit made or given to a promoter of the company to the extent that disclosure is required by law.

(3) General information about the issuer and its capital.

(4) Information about the activities of the group and its subsidiaries.

(5) Financial information concerning the issuer or group. This includes the following.

(*A*) The accountants' report. The report must deal with the profits, losses, assets, liabilities and financial record and position of the company or group (i.e. the company and its subsidiaries) for each of the preceding three financial years.

(*B*) If the date of the listing particulars is more than nine months after the end of the last financial year in respect of which annual accounts have been published, an interim financial statement must be included covering at least the first six months of the current financial year.

(6) Details relating to the management. This part provides for disclosure of information about the persons having the management control of the company and in particular, the following.

(*A*) An indication of the main activities of the directors outside the company or group where such activities are significant with respect to the company or group, together with a description of any other relevant business interests or activities they may have.

(*B*) Details of directors' remuneration and benefits in the last financial year.

(*C*) Details of directors' service contracts.

(*D*) Particulars of the interests of any director in transactions which were either unusual in their nature or condition or significant to the business of the group and were effected by the company in the current or preceding financial year or remain in any respect outstanding or unperformed. If there have been no such transactions, there must be a statement to that effect.

(*E*) Details of the beneficial and non-beneficial interests of any directors in the shares or debentures, or in rights to subscribe for shares or debentures, in the company, any subsidiary or holding company and any subsidiary of any holding company (including in the case of interests in the shares or debentures themselves, the interests of the spouse and children of the director).

(*F*) Details of any employees' share or share option schemes.

(7) Recent development and prospects of the group. The particulars must include information about trends in the company's business since the end of the last financial year in respect of which accounts have been published, and on the company's prospects for at least the current financial year.

(*iv*) Supplementary particulars: s. 147 FSA 1986. Where in the time between the submission of the original listing particulars and the commencement of dealings on the Stock Exchange:

(1) there is a significant change in any matter which was required to be disclosed in the listing particulars, either under the rules or other general duty of disclosure, or

(2) a significant new matter arises which would have had to have been disclosed if it had arisen at the time of application,

the issuer of the securities must, under the listing rules, submit supplementary listing particulars to the Stock Exchange for its approval and, if they are approved, must publish them.

If the issuer is unaware of the change or new matter he is under no duty to submit supplementary listing particulars. However, any person responsible for the listing particulars who is aware of such a matter is under a duty to notify the issuer of it. Failure to comply with these requirements renders the appropriate person liable to compensate any person who has acquired the securities and suffered loss as a result.

(*v*) Registration of listing particulars. The listing particulars must be registered with the registrar on or before the date of publication. A statement that a copy has been delivered to him must appear in the particulars. There is a criminal sanction if this provision is not complied with: s. 149 FSA 1986.

10. Offers of unlisted securities

(a) *Offers of securities on admission to approved exchange.* By s. 159(1) FSA 1986 no person may issue or cause to be issued in the UK an advertisement offering any securities on the occasion of their admission to dealings on an approved exchange (i.e. a recognized investment exchange approved by the Secretary of State for these purposes) or on terms that they will be issued if admitted to such dealings unless:

(*i*) a prospectus containing information about the securities has been submitted to and approved by the exchange and delivered for registration to the Registrar of Companies; or

(*ii*) the advertisement is such that no agreement can be entered into in pursuance of it until such a prospectus has been submitted, approved and delivered.

This requirement does not apply however, if a prospectus relating to the securities has been delivered for registration in the previous 12 months and the approved exchange certifies that it is satisfied that persons likely to consider acquiring the securities will have sufficient information to enable them to decide whether to do so from that prospectus and any information published in connection with the admission of the securities.

(b) *Other offers of securities.* Section 160(1) FSA 1986 provides that no person may issue or cause to be issued in the UK an advertisement offering any securities which is a primary or secondary offer unless:

(*i*) he has delivered for registration to the Registrar of Companies a prospectus relating to the securities and expressed to be in respect of the offer; or

(*ii*) the advertisement is such that no agreement can be entered into in pursuance of it until such a prospectus has been delivered to the Registrar as provided in s. 159(*a*) above.

(c) Section 160(1) FSA 1986 does not apply:

(*i*) to a secondary offer if a prospectus has been delivered in respect of the same securities made in the previous six months by a person making a primary offer or a previous secondary offer;

(*ii*) to an advertisement issued in such circumstances as may be specified by an order made by the Secretary of State for the purpose of exemption:

(1) advertisements appearing to him to have a private character whether by reason of a connection between the person issuing them and those to whom they are addressed or otherwise;

(2) advertisements appearing to him to deal with investments only incidentally;

(3) advertisements issued to persons appearing to him to be sufficiently expert to understand any risks involved; or

(4) such other class of advertisement as he thinks fit.

(d) Sections 159 and 160 FSA 1986 do not apply:

(*i*) to any advertisement offering securities if the offer is conditional on their admission to official listing on the Stock Exchange and s. 159 does not apply to any advertisement offering securities if they have been officially listed on the Stock Exchange in the previous 12 months and the approved exchange concerned certifies that persons likely to consider acquiring them will have sufficient information to enable them to decide whether to do so;

(*ii*) to an advertisement inviting persons to subscribe in cash for any securities if the advertisement is issued or caused to be issued by the person by whom the investments are to be issued and either the advertisement consists of a registered prospectus or the following matters (and no others that would make it an investment advertisement) are contained in the advertisement:

(1) the name of that person and his address or particulars of other means of communicating with him;

(2) the nature of the investments, the number offered for subscription and their nominal value and price;

(3) a statement that a prospectus for the purposes of ss. 159 and 160 FSA 1986 is or will be available and, if it is not yet available, when it will be; and

(4) instructions for obtaining a copy of the prospectus.

(*iii*) if other securities issued by the same person (whether or not securities of the same class as those to which the offer relates) are already dealt in or on an approved exchange and the exchange certifies that persons likely to consider acquiring the securities to which the offer relates will have sufficient information to enable them to decide whether to do so having regard to the steps that have been taken to comply in respect of those other securities with the requirements imposed by the exchange for the purpose of affording to persons dealing in the securities proper information for determining their current value, to the nature of the securities to which the offer relates, to the circumstances of their issue and to the information about the issuer which is available to investors by virtue of any enactment.

(e) *Form and content of a prospectus.* If a prospectus is required under ss. 159 and 160 FSA 1986 it must contain such information and comply with such other requirements as may be prescribed by rules made by the Secretary of State. If it appears to the Secretary of State that an approved exchange has rules in respect of prospectuses relating to securities dealt in on the exchange, and practices in exercising any powers conferred by the rules, which provide investors with protection at least equivalent to that provided by the rules made by the Secretary of State, he may direct that any such prospectus shall be subject to the rules of the exchange instead of the rules made by him: s. 162 FSA 1986. In addition to the information required to be included in a prospectus by virtue of s. 162 FSA 1986 a prospectus issued under s. 159 or 160 FSA 1986 must comply with the general duty of disclosure referred to in relation to listed securities in 9(**a**)(*ii*) above.

(f) *Supplementary prospectus.* Section 164 FSA 1986 requires the registration of a supplementary prospectus in exactly the same circumstances as s. 147 FSA 1986 applies to supplementary listing particulars, i.e. to note a significant change or where a significant new matter has arisen which affects the original prospectus and the disclosure requirements.

11. The Unlisted Securities Market

(a) The Unlisted Securities (USM) was launched in late 1980 to provide a formal, regulated market designed to meet the needs of those smaller, less mature companies unlikely to apply for listing.
(b) A company may enter the USM by a placing, by means of an introduction or, where neither of these methods is appropriate, through an offer for sale.
(c) The following contrasts with fully listed securities may be noted:

(*i*) There is *no* minimum market capitalization for USM companies. For listed companies the minimum is £700,000 per security.

(*ii*) Companies will normally be required to have been trading for at least two years. Newer companies requiring capital for fully researched projects may be acceptable. For full listing a period of at least five years would be expected.

(*iii*) 10 per cent of the share must be in the hands of the public. For fully listed securities 25 per cent is required.

(*iv*) Under the FSA 1986, *all* marketing operations, i.e. fund-raising exercises, require a full prospectus to be prepared. The Stock Exchange, as the competent authority under that Act and under its authority, has expanded this requirement so that a company which wishes to apply for full listing must prepare listing particulars even if it is coming to the market by way of an Introduction.

This Stock Exchange requirement has been relaxed for applicants for an introduction to the USM, who may produce for the public far more limited information. In particular they can present their last three years' figures (or less if company not in existence for three years) in the form of a *table of financial statistics*, without the need for an *auditors' report* on these figures.

(*v*) A second major point concerning the prospectus is the amount of advertising that must be given to it. The Stock

Exchange has laid down the following *minimum* advertising requirements:

	Full listing	USM securities
Offer for sale	Listing particulars in two newspapers	Small box in one newspaper
Placing	Listing particulars in one newspaper and one small box	Small box in one newspaper
Introduction	Small box in two newspapers	Small box in one newspaper

On the assumption that full listing particulars would take up to three full pages of a newspaper and an abridged version something in the region of 5 per cent of a page, the saving to USM companies is considerable.

(*vi*) All companies are required to provide a statement by the directors that the working capital of the company is adequate. For companies applying for listing, an additional supporting letter to the Stock Exchange must be submitted by the sponsoring agency broker (the broker responsible for bringing the company to the market). This is not required for a USM company.

(*vii*) No initial fee, compared with a scale for listed companies reaching a maximum of £17,000 at monetary value of £500 million.

(*viii*) They will *not* comply with the Continuing Obligations contained in the Yellow Book. However, they are obliged to sign a *general undertaking*, the details of which are almost identical to the Continuing Obligations.

12. Underwriting

(a) *Underwriting* is merely a form of insurance against the risk of a poor public response to an issue of shares or debentures.

(b) *An underwriting contract* is, therefore, one between the company offering the shares to the public and the underwriter who relieves the company of the risk. Such a contract has been aptly defined as:

> 'An agreement entered into before the shares are brought before the public that in the event of the public not taking

up the whole of them, or the number mentioned in the agreement, the underwriter will, for an agreed commission, take an allotment of such part of the shares as the public has not applied for': *Re Licensed Victuallers' Association*(1889).

(c) *Advantages of underwriting.* Apart from the obvious advantage, i.e. of relieving the issuing company of all or a large part of the risk, there is good advertising value in the fact that a firm of underwriters has been prepared to accept the risk — particularly if it has done so at a comparatively low rate of commission.

(d) *Statutory provisions affecting underwriting commission.* Section 97 CA 1985 permits both public and private companies to pay underwriting commission, subject to the following provisions.

(*i*) The company's Articles must permit such payment.

NOTE: At common law, authority in the Memorandum alone is apparently not sufficient: *Re Bolivia Republic Exploration Syndicate Ltd* (1914).

(*ii*) The commission must not exceed 10 per cent of the issue price of the shares, or the amount or rate authorized by the Articles, whichever is less.

(*iii*) Any conditions which apply in respect thereof under the FSA 1986 are complied with.

NOTE: It is also provided (in Schedule 4 CA 1985) that the amount of commission must be disclosed in every balance sheet, so far as it has not been written off.

(e) *Underwriting of debentures.* Section 97 CA 1985 does not apply to debentures; therefore, they may be underwritten at *any* rate of commission, unless the company's Articles impose a limit (where debentures are concerned, there is no restriction on their issue at what amounts, in effect, to a discount, as debentures (unlike shares) do not, of course, form part of a company's capital).

Examples:

(1) Exe Ltd agree to underwrite an entire issue of 100,000 shares of £1 each, offered to the public by Zed Plc. If the *whole* issue is subscribed, Exe Ltd are under no obligation to take up any of the shares. If, however, the public subscription is for only (say) 80,000 shares, Exe Ltd will be liable to take up the whole of the 20,000 balance.

(2) If, in the above example, Exe Ltd had underwritten only 75,000 of the 1000,000 offered, they would then be liable *rateably* for the balance, i.e.

$$\frac{75{,}000}{100{,}000} \times 20{,}000 = 15{,}000$$

13. Sub-underwriting

(a) *Method.* In most cases (and particularly when the whole of a large issue is underwritten by one underwriter), underwriters 'spread' their risk by sub-underwriting, i.e. the main underwriter makes separate contracts with various sub-underwriters, each of them agreeing to take a specified share of the risk.

(b) *Over-riding commission.* If the main underwriter agrees to procure sub-underwriters, the commission he receives for that service is known as 'over-riding commission' (that commission is, of course, additional to the one paid to the sub-underwriters). It must be emphasized that, where the main contract takes the form just described, the primary underwriters' service to the company is to ensure that the issue is fully and reliably underwritten.

NOTE: The term 'over-riding commission' is also sometimes used in a different context, i.e. it may be applied to the *difference* between the underwriting commission paid to the principal underwriter and the slightly lower commission he pays to the sub-underwriters.

(c) *Statutory provisions.* The provisions of s. 97 CA 1985 apply equally to both underwriting and over-riding commission, i.e. in any form of underwriting contract to which the issuing company is a party.

Example:

Wye Ltd agreed to underwrite 80,000 shares of an issue of 100,000 shares of £1 each and subsequently procured sub-underwriting contracts with Jay and Ess for 30,000 and 10,000 respectively. The public response was poor, as only 60,000 of the shares were subscribed — an under-subscription of 40,000, of which the *total liability of underwriters* is 80,000/100,000 x 40,000 = 32,000 shares.

Wye Ltd: $\frac{40,000}{80,000}$ x 32,000 = 16,000 shares

Jay Ltd: $\frac{30,000}{80,000}$ x 32,000 = 12,000 shares

Ess Ltd: $\frac{10,000}{80,000}$ x 32,000 = 4,000 shares

Total liability of underwriters 32,000 shares

NOTE: In such a contract, the principal underwriters, Wye Ltd, are *primarily* liable to take up the whole of the 32,000 shares; if either Jay or Ess fail to take up any of the shares they have underwritten, then Wye Ltd must make up their deficiency.

14. 'Firm' underwriting

(a) An underwriter may agree to *take firm* all or part of the shares he agrees to underwrite.
(b) He will then be allotted whatever number of shares he has agreed to take 'firm' no matter whether the issue is under-subscribed or over-subscribed, but any other shares underwritten will be dealt with by the usual method, i.e. in the case of an under-subscription, the total liability of the underwriters is apportioned amongst them rateably.
(c) The effect of the 'firm' underwriting upon all the underwriters will depend upon the terms of the contract; that is, whether the 'firm' subscriptions are to be applied:

(*i*) exclusively in relieving the liability of those who have underwritten 'firm'; or

(*ii*) to reduce the respective liabilities of *all* underwriters proportionately.

Example:

A public company issues 250,000 shares. The issue is underwritten as follows: X, 100,000 shares (including 25,000 firm); Y, 50,000 shares (including 25,000 firm); and Z, 100,000 shares. The public subscription totalled only 150,000 shares. The following table shows the alternative methods of dealing with the 'firm' underwriting.

Shares offered to public	250,000			
Public subscription	150,000			
		X, 4/10	Y, 2/10	Z, 4/10
Gross liability of underwriters	100,000	40,000	20,000	40,000
Less relief for 'firm' subscriptions	50,000	25,000	25,000	—
	50,000	15,000	5,000	40,000
Allocation of Y's excess (X, 4/8; Z, 4/8)		*2,500*	5,000	*2,500*
(*i*) *Final liability* of underwriters where 'firm' subscriptions are used to reduce liability of those underwriting 'firm'	50,000	12,500	—	37,500
(*ii*) *Final liability* of underwriters where 'firm' subscriptions are used to reduce respective liabilities of all underwriters proportionately	50,000	20,000	10,000	20,000

SUMMARY

	Method (*i*)		Method (*ii*)	
X: Final liability	12,500		20,000	
Add 'firm' subscription	25,000	37,500	25,000	45,000
Y: Final liability	—		10,000	
Add 'firm' subscription	25,000	25,000	25,000	35,000
Z: Final liability	37,500		20,000	
Add 'firm' subscription	—	37,500	—	20,000
		100,000		100,000
Public subscription		150,000		150,000
Total issue		250,000		250,000

15. Brokerage

(a) Brokerage might be defined as a payment to a person who in some way carries on the business of a broker for 'placing' shares.
(b) It must not be confused with underwriting commission. The placing of shares does not involve the broker in any risk of having to take up the shares, whereas risk-taking is the main feature of an underwriting contract.
(c) Brokerage can, in fact, be paid in addition to underwriting commission and s. 98(3) CA 1985 clearly indicates that a company has the right to pay such brokerage as was previously lawful. In *Metropolitan Coal Consumers' Association* v. *Scrimgeour* (1885) it had previously been held that the payment of brokerage was legal, as long as it was 'reasonable' and payable in the ordinary course of business.

16. Prohibition on issue of shares at a discount: s. 100 CA 1985

(a) Section 100(1) CA 1985 specifically prohibits the allotment of shares at a discount.

(b) Shares allotted in breach of s. 100(1) CA 1985 shall be treated as paid up by the payment to the company of the amount of the nominal value of the shares less the amount of the discount, but the allottee shall be liable to pay the company the latter amount and shall be liable to pay interest thereon at the appropriate rate: s. 100(2) CA 1985.
(c) The prohibition in s. 100(1) CA 1985 does not apply to debentures. These can be issued at a discount, as they do not form part of a company's capital.

17. Issue of shares at a premium: ss. 130–134 CA 1985

(a) There are no restrictions imposed upon the issue of shares or debentures at a premium, i.e. at more than the nominal value of the security; for example, a £1 share may be issued for 125p, giving the company a capital profit of 25p per share.
(b) However, there are restrictions as to the use which the company can make of a share premium, as s. 130 CA 1985 provides that a sum equal to the aggregate amount or value of the premiums must be transferred to a 'share premium account', which is to be treated as though it were paid-up shares capital of the company and subject to provisions of the Act relating to reduction of capital.
(c) Although the company cannot use the premium as it thinks fit — as, for example, to pay a dividend — it is permitted by s. 130 CA 1985 to apply the balance in the following ways:

(*i*) to allot fully paid bonus shares to its members;
(*ii*) to write off preliminary expenses of the company;
(*iii*) to write off expenses of, or commission paid or discount allowed on, any issue of shares or debentures;
(*iv*) to provide for any premium payable on redemption of debentures.

In addition, by virtue of s. 171(5) CA 1985, the share premium account may be used by private companies to pay off any premium on a redemption or purchase by such companies of their own shares.
(d) The balance (if any) of a company's share premium account must be shown in any balance sheet subsequently issued, until such time as it may be written off by reason of its having been used in any of the ways permitted under s. 130 CA 1985.

(e) The provisions of s. 130 CA 1985 do *not* apply to debentures. If, therefore, a company issues debentures at a premium, the company is not legally bound to transfer the amount of the premium to a debenture premium account (although it is common practice to do so). Nor are there any restrictions placed upon the use to which the company can put the debenture premium.

(f) Further, ss. 131–132 CA 1985, in order to facilitate the concept of merger and acquisition accounting, seek to provide relief from s. 130 in certain defined situations.

(*i*) *Merger relief.* If a company makes an arrangement to acquire equity share capital of another company in exchange for an allotment by it of equity shares in itself and as a result of the arrangement acquires nine-tenths or more of the other company's equity capital, any excess value received over the nominal value of the shares it allots need not be credited to the share premium account.

If the bid is for non-equity shares as well as equity shares, the non-equity shares may be held as to less than nine-tenths. If a company has more than one class of equity share capital the bidder will qualify for relief only if it acquires nine-tenths of each class of equity shares.

(*ii*) *Group reconstructions.* Where a wholly owned subsidiary company acquires shares in another subsidiary in return for an allotment of its shares to its holding company (or to another wholly owned subsidiary company) only the minimum premium value has to be transferred to the share premium account. The minimum premium value is the difference between the nominal value of the shares issued and the lower of the cost of the shares being transferred or their book value.

These exceptions cannot both be applied in relation to the same share issue.

The Secretary of State can by regulations modify the above rules.

18. Arrangements for a public issue

If the issue is to be a large one, a great deal of the office work entailed can be passed on to firms specializing in new issue work. It has been assumed, therefore, that the work of underwriting and publishing the required documentation is being dealt with by such a firm, leaving further arrangements to be handled as follows.

(a) *Arrangements with the company's bankers.* Most banks, and certainly all the large banks, have specialist departments for handling share issue work. The following arrangements will be made with one of these banks:

(*i*) to receive application forms and application moneys;

(*ii*) to credit all application moneys received to a separate 'Application Account', or 'Application and Allotment Account', if that method is preferred;

(*iii*) to number serially all applications received;

(*iv*) to keep a progressive total of the number of shares applied for;

(*v*) to return direct to applicants any applications (and accompanying remittances) received after the closing of the subscription lists.

(b) *Office staff and stationery.* Finally, even before the actual issue of the offer documents, the following matters ought to be arranged, to ensure that the application and allotment procedure is handled with speed, accuracy and efficiency.

(*i*) Available office staff must be well organized to handle the work, so that each section is responsible for a particular aspect of the work, and the whole of the work to be under the supervision of either the secretary himself, or his registrar.

(*ii*) If necessary (and it might well be necessary if the issue is a large one), engage temporary office staff preferably with experience of share issue work. Practising secretaries may be able to help in this direction by hiring out temporary staff.

(*iii*) Ensure that all necessary documents, such as allotment sheets, allotment letters, letters of regret, share certificates, etc., will be available when required.

(*iv*) Stock Exchange requirements must be borne in mind, if 'admission to listing' has been applied for, e.g. as regards the form of certificate, which must have Stock Exchange approval, and allotment letters, which must be accompanied by a 'letter of renunciation'.

(*v*) If more than one class of share is being offered to the public (or where both shares and debentures are being offered simultaneously) the task of sorting and filing can be eased considerably by the use of application forms in different colours or (in the case of newspaper application forms) by coding. Similar methods can also be adopted to simplify identification of existing shareholders, if it is intended to give preference to their applications.

Progress test 2

1. **(a)** What formal business should be considered at the first meeting of the directors of the company?
(b) Describe the procedure for opening a bank account for a company which has just received its certificate of incorporation. ICSA **(2, 3)**

2. You are secretary of A Plc., which has recently been changed from a private to a public company. Business continues to expand, and your directors decide to consider the advisability of seeking a Stock Exchange official listing for the company's shares. They ask you to prepare a memorandum setting out the advantages and disadvantages, from the point of view of the company, in having an official listing. *ICSA* **(5, 6)**

3. A company sometimes issues capital by means of a 'placing'. In certain circumstances, a company's shares are said to be 'placed' or 'introduced' on a stock exchange. Explain fully what is meant by the terms 'placing' and 'introduction'. **(4)**

4. Draft a memorandum for the board of your company, explaining from the legal aspect, the various ways of raising capital. *ICSA* **(4)**

5. The directors of your company are considering making an offer of its shares to the public. Write a memorandum to them explaining what is meant by underwriting. Indicate any relevant statutory requirements. *ICSA* **(12)**

6. Set out in a memorandum to your board the main statutory requirements regarding the contents of a prospectus. *ICSA* **(10)**

7. Explain in detail what is meant by underwriting. *ICSA* **(12)**

8. Write full notes on (*a*) placing of shares and (*b*) share warrants. *ICSA* **(4, 7:9–13)**

9. You are secretary of a private company. The shareholders would like to realize some of their holdings and at the same time raise some money for the company. It appears to you that the Unlisted Securities Market is the solution and you are asked to write a memorandum on the matter explaining:

(a) The advantages of 'going public', and
(b) The advantages of proceeding via the Unlisted Securities Market compared with obtaining a full listing. *ICSA* **(4–11)**

3

Application and allotment

Procedure

1. Maintain contact with the bank

As from the time of opening the subscription lists, regular contact should be maintained with the bank, which (it has been assumed) had been authorized to receive applications, and arrangements made for the collection from the bank of applications and application lists at frequent intervals, to enable the office staff to proceed with the work.

NOTE: There is usually a sense of urgency in handling applications and it is likely to be even more acute if there is a poor or rather lukewarm public response to the issue. In such a case, the aim will be to get the allotment letters posted before any of the applicants (suspecting failure, perhaps) withdraw their applications.

2. Check each batch of applications

Each batch of applications should be checked with the bank's application lists, prior to sorting the applications for distribution to various sections of the staff.

3. Recording applications

After applications have been sorted and distributed amongst the available staff, they are entered on Application and Allotment Sheets which, being loose sheets, are usually arranged either:

(a) alphabetically, i.e. according to applicants' names; or
(b) according to number of shares applied for.

4. Particulars entered on Application and Allotment Sheets

As the result of the issue may not yet be known at this stage (and no allotment having been made), only the following particulars can, so far, be entered on the Application and Allotment Sheets:

(a) Serial no. of application.
(b) Name of applicant.
(c) Address.
(d) Occupation of applicant.
(e) Number of shares applied for.
(f) Amount paid on application.

NOTE: Subscribers to the Memorandum and (where applicable) 'firm' underwriters are usually entered first in the appropriate sheets.

5. Totals to a Summary Sheet

When all applications have been entered, totals of the appropriate columns so far completed are carried to a Summary Sheet, on which all information as to 'number of shares applied for' and 'amount paid on application' is aggregated.

6. The Summary Sheet is placed before the board

The Summary Sheet, having been totalled and thoroughly checked, can now be placed before a meeting of the board of directors (or allotment committee), to enable them to ascertain the final result of the issue.

7. Decisions of the board (or allotment committee) at this stage

Having considered the results of the issue, the decisions they must now make will depend upon whether the issue was over-subscribed or under-subscribed.

(a) *If over-subscribed,* they must decide upon a suitable basis for allotment of the shares, e.g. they may favour the 'small' applicant, those applying for 100 shares or less being allotted in full; those from 100 upwards to be allotted on a reducing scale down to (say) 10 per cent of the number of shares applied for.
(b) *If under-subscribed,* it may reasonably be assumed that the deficiency will be taken up by underwriters; therefore, it will be merely a question of calculating rateably their respective liabilities. Even this is often unnecessary, as the company's

contract is, more often than not, with the principal underwriter only, and the liabilities of sub-underwriters are his, not the company's, concern.

8. Further entries on Application and Allotment Sheets

Arising out of decisions made at the board (or allotment committee) meeting, the following further information can be added to the Application and Allotment Sheets:

(a) number of shares allotted, if any;
(b) total amount received in respect of shares allotted;
(c) total amount due on allotment.

9. Summary Sheet again placed before the board

Further totals can now be carried from the Application and Allotment Sheets to the Summary Sheet. The Summary Sheet is totalled and checked, and again placed before the board (or allotment committee) meeting.

10. Allotment procedure

At the board (or allotment committee) meeting, the following procedure may be followed.

(a) The chairman of the board (or allotment committee) signs or initials each Application and Allotment Sheet, for the purpose of identification.

(b) A resolution of allotment is put to the meeting and carried, for example:

> RESOLVED: THAT 200,000 ordinary shares of £1 each, numbered 1 to 200,000 inclusive, be and they are hereby allotted to the applicants whose names and addresses are set out in the .... Application and Allotment Sheets now produced to the Board (or Committee) and initialled by the Chairman for the purpose of identification.

(c) The Secretary is then entrusted to prepare and issue, with the least possible delay, letters of allotment and, where applicable, letters of regret. The latter must be sent to any applicants to whom no allotment has been made, together with their returned application moneys.

> NOTE: Section 80 CA 1980 requires the authority of the company in general meeting or in the Articles of the company to give the directors the power to allot 'relevant securities', i.e. shares in the company other than shares shown in the Memorandum to have been taken by the subscribers thereto or shares allotted in relation to an employees' share scheme, and any right to subscribe for, or to convert any security into, shares in the company other than shares so allotted. If such power is already contained in the company's Articles and expressed in general terms, the authority must be renewed every five years.

A private company may elect, by elective resolution, to disapply the provisions of s. 80 so that an authority given by the shareholders may be conferred for an indefinite period or for a period in excess of five years: s. 80 CA 1985. The authority must however state the maximum amount of relevant securities to be allotted.

A copy of the elective resolution must be forwarded to the Registrar.

An elective resolution under s. 80(A) CA 1985 may be revoked or varied by an ordinary resolution.

11. Dealing with letters of allotment and letters of regret

In order to ensure that the instructions he received at the board (or allotment committee) meeting are efficiently and expeditiously carried out, the secretary must organize the work of allotment with as much care as was given to the handling of applications, bearing in mind that (unless there is any contrary arrangement) the posting of the letter of allotment is deemed to be valid acceptance of the application: *Household Fire Insurance Co. Ltd.* v. *Grant* (1879). He must, therefore, divide the staff into sections and put a responsible official in charge of each section.

Special arrangements must also be made, and the staff briefed, on the following important matters.

(a) *Stock Exchange requirements.* If application has been, or will be made, for listing on a stock exchange, the following requirements must be met.

(*i*) The document of title, if renounceable, must show as a heading, that the document is of value and negotiable and that in all cases of doubt, or if prior to receipt the addressee has sold (other than ex rights or ex capitalization) all or part of his registered holding of the existing securities, a stockbroker, bank manager, or other professional adviser should be consulted immediately.

(*ii*) Temporary documents of title must be serially numbered and printed on good-quality paper. The name and address of the first holder and names of joint holders (if any) must be stated and, in the case of fixed-income securities, a statement as to the amount of the next payment of interest or dividend must be included.

(*iii*) The documents of title must state the *pro rata* entitlement, the last date on which transfers were or will be accepted for registration for participation in the issue, how the securities rank for dividend or interest, the nature of the document of title and proposed date of issue and how fractions (if any) are to be treated. In the case of a rights issue the documents of title must state how securities not taken up will be dealt with and the time, being not less than 21 days, in which the offer may be accepted.

(*iv*) When a security is offered on conversion of another security and is also offered for subscription in cash, allotment letters must be marked 'conversion' and 'cash' respectively.

(*v*) Letters of regret should preferably be issued simultaneously with, but in any event not later than three business days after, the issue of letters of allotment. In the event of it being impossible to issue letters of regret at the same time as the letters of allotment, notice to that effect must be inserted in the press and appear on the morning after the allotment letters have been posted.

(*vi*) In the absence of contrary instructions from the shareholder all letters of right to shareholders with addresses outside the United Kingdom and the Republic of Ireland must be despatched by air mail.

(b) *Organize a thorough system of checking* at each stage of the work.

(c) *Organize a final check* by responsible persons — preferably persons who have done none of the earlier work — of the sealed envelopes with the Application and Allotment Sheets, to avoid misposting.

(d) *Obtain a certificate of posting* and ensure that a record of the posting is made on the final Application and Allotment Sheet, the entry being signed and dated by the person who was responsible for the posting.

12. Deal with letters of renunciation and split letters of renunciation

It may be assumed that allottees have been given facilities for renouncing the whole or part of their allotments of shares during a specified 'renunciation period'. If that is the case, the order of procedure must be changed, as the preparation of share certificates and the work of writing up the Register of Members must be delayed until the end of the renunciation period. The next stage is, therefore:

(a) to deal with letters of renunciation; and
(b) to attend to requests for split letters of renunciation.

The procedure for dealing with renunciation is dealt with later in this chapter (*see* **21**).

13. Preparation of share certificates

As already stated, this work must be delayed until the end of the renunciation period, after which the certificates are prepared from the Application and Allotment Sheets and from the separate sheets on which renunciations have been recorded. If, however, the amount payable on the shares goes beyond the allotment stage, the certificates may not be prepared until the shares are fully paid.

14. Write up the Register of Members

As soon as possible after the end of the renunciation period, i.e. when the names of the final allottees are known, their names must be entered in a Register of Members.

15. Return of Allotments

In compliance with s. 88 CA 1985, *within one month* after the allotment of the shares, deliver to the Registrar a Return of Allotments in the prescribed form, Form G88(2), showing the following.

(a) In respect of shares allotted for cash:

(*i*) number and nominal amount of the shares allotted;

(*ii*) names, addresses and descriptions of the allottees;

(*iii*) amount, if any, paid or due and payable on each share whether on account of the nominal value of the share or by way of premium.

(b) In respect of shares allotted for consideration *other than* cash:

(*i*) a written contract constituting the titles of the allottees, duly stamped;

(*ii*) any contract of sale (or for services or other consideration for the allotment) duly stamped; and

(*iii*) a return stating the number and nominal amount of shares allotted for consideration other than cash, the extent to which they are treated as paid up, and the consideration for which they have been allotted.

NOTE: If the contrast referred to in **(b)**(*i*) above is *not* reduced to writing, particulars of the contract, stamped as though it had been a contract in writing, must be filed with the Registrar on Form G88(3) within one month after allotment.

(c) Section 103 CA 1985 provides that a public company shall not allot shares as fully or partly paid up (as to their nominal value or any premium payable on them) otherwise than in cash unless, *inter alia,* a report with respect to its value has been made to the company by an expert appointed by the company during the six months immediately preceding the allotment of the shares. Where such a report has been delivered to the company it shall deliver a copy of the report to the Registrar for registration at the same time that it files the return of allotment of these shares under s. 88.

(d) The capital duty payable on an allotment is paid as follows:

(*i*) where shares are issued for a cash consideration — on a return of allotments (Form G88(2)), delivered to the Registrar of Companies pursuant to s. 88(2) CA 1985;

(*ii*) where shares are issued wholly or partly for a consideration other than cash — on a return of allotments (Form G88(3)) delivered to the Registrar of Companies pursuant to s. 88(2) CA 1985.

Restrictions on allotment

16. Allotment where issue not fully subscribed

(a) Section 84 CA 1985 provides that no allotment shall be made of any share capital of a public company offered for subscription unless:

(*i*) that capital is subscribed for in full; or

(*ii*) the offer states that, even if the capital is not subscribed for in full, the amount of that capital subscribed for may be allotted in any event or in the event of the conditions specified in the offer being satisfied;

and, where conditions are so specified, no allotment of the capital may be made by virtue of (*ii*) unless conditions are satisfied.

(b) If the above conditions are not fulfilled within 40 days after the first issue of the prospectus:

(*i*) all application money must be repaid 'forthwith', without interest; and

(*ii*) *if not repaid within a further eight days*, i.e. within 48 days after the first issue of the prospectus, the directors become jointly and severally liable to repay with interest at 5 per cent per annum after expiration of the 48th day.

(c) Any waiver of this requirement is *void*.

(d) Section 101 CA 1985 provides that shares in a public company cannot be allotted unless at least one-quarter of the nominal value of the share and the whole of any premium on it have been received by the company.

17. Effect of irregular allotment: s. 85 CA 1985

If shares *are* allotted in contravention of s. 84 CA 1985:

(a) the allotment is *voidable* at the instance of the applicant and may be set aside within one month after the date of the allotment and not later;

(b) any director who knowingly permits the allotment is liable to compensate the company and the applicant respectively for any loss, provided that proceedings are commenced within two years after the date of the allotment.

Letters of renunciation

18. Renunciation

is an important facility which is almost invariably given to allottees, whereby they are permitted to renounce shares allotted to them by completing a *letter of renunciation* (which accompanies the letter of allotment) in favour of another person, who is usually referred to as the 'nominee'.

19. Stock Exchange regulations

Stock Exchange regulations concerning letters of allotment require that, where the right of renunciation is given:

(a) a form of renunciation must appear on the back of the allotment letter, or be attached to it;
(b) facilities must be given to allottees for 'splitting', i.e. by providing split letters of allotment, where an allottee wishes to renounce his allotment in favour of more than one nominee, or to retain part of his allotment and renounce the balance;
(c) when, at the same time as an allotment is made of shares issued for cash, shares of the same class are also allotted, credited as fully paid, to vendors or others, the period for renunciation may be the same as, but not longer than, that provided for in the case of shares issued for cash.

Further, the company must arrange to split and return renounceable documents on the day of receipt or, should that not be a business day, on the first business day following their receipt.

20. Advantages of facilities for renouncing and 'splitting' allotments

There are particular advantages both for the company and for the allottees.

(a) For the company, it reduces the amount of work in its registration department in the two following ways.

(*i*) The original allottees can renounce all or part of the shares allotted to them without going through all the usual formalities of registering their transfers, so long as the renunciations take place during the renunciation period.

(*ii*) None of the original allottees will be recorded in the Register of Members until the end of the renunciation period; if during that period any of them have renounced their shares, the nominees' names will be recorded, and not the names of the original allottees. Thus, the number of entries in the Register of Members is cut down considerably.

(b) For the allottee the main advantage is that he may renounce during the renunciation period, making a profit if the issue is a successful one. It is this feature which attracts the 'stag' operator, who applies for shares with the intention of renouncing them if he can do so at a profit.

21. Procedure for dealing with letters of renunciation and 'split' letters

(a) *Renunciation by allottee.* Assuming that stock exchange regulations have been complied with, i.e. that the allotment letters included a form of renunciation and an undertaking to 'split' letters of allotment:

(*i*) the allottee has the right to renounce in favour of a third party, by completing the form of renunciation and returning it to the company along with the Registration Application Form, completed by the nominee; or

(*ii*) he may renounce to several nominees, or retain some of the shares for himself and renounce the balance, in which case he may return his allotment letter to the company and ask for two or more 'splits' (i.e. split letters of allotment, or split letters of renunciation, to give them their alternative names) in whatever denominations he may require them to be 'split'.

(b) *Procedure on receiving letters of renunciation.*

(*i*) Number the completed letters of renunciation as they are received and check that both renunciation form and Registration Application Form have been signed and dated.

(*ii*) Record particulars or renunciations either on the Application and Allotment Sheets (if additional columns have been provided for that purpose) or on a separate List of Renunciations.

(*iii*) Send a receipt to each nominee, acknowledging receipt of his completed Registration Application Form.

NOTE: This receipt is important to the nominee, since it is usually accepted as 'good delivery' on the Stock Exchange; in fact stock exchanges require that companies whose shares are 'listed' shall certify transfers against the evidence of such a receipt, pending the issue of a share certificate.

(*iv*) Mark the Application and Allotment Sheets to indicate that renunciations have been received, e.g. a letter R may be made in red ink in a column provided for the purpose, against the name of any allottee who has renounced his allotment.

NOTE: At this stage it is *not* usual to cancel out the names of those who have renounced their allotments.

(*v*) Refuse to accept any letter of renunciation received after the closing date of the renunciation period, even if it had been signed before the closing date, as that is the last day for dealing free of transfer duty.

(c) *Procedure on receiving requests for split letters of allotment.*

(*i*) Ensure that the request is accompanied by the letter of allotment and a remittance for the appropriate fee for 'splitting'.

(*ii*) Send the required number of split letters to the original allottee. These will be in whatever denominations he requires, and they are usually numbered in such a way as to facilitate cross-reference with the original letter of allotment.

(*iii*) Cancel the original allotment letter, e.g. by rubber stamp; and carefully file it, bearing in mind that it is the company's acceptance of the allottee's offer for shares.

(*iv*) Record the issue of the split letters. This can be done by marking the original entry in the Application and Allotment Sheet with a letter S in red ink and adding the serial numbers of the split letters in a column provided for this purpose. If, for example, the original letter of allotment is no. 100, the split letters may be numbered 100/1, 100/2, 100/3, etc., to simplify cross-reference.

NOTE: At this stage it is too early to cancel any of the original entries in the Application and Allotment Sheets.

(*v*) When the split letters are received, bearing the signatures of the nominees, signifying that they agree to accept the shares renounced in their favour:

(1) send a receipt to each nominee, acknowledging lodgment of his acceptance; and

(2) record particulars of the split letters received, either on the List of Renunciations (already being used for

renunciations in full) or on a supplementary list, which may be referred to as a 'Split Letters Record Sheet'.

(d) *Procedure after the closing date for renunciations.*

(*i*) Cancel the appropriate entries on the Application and Allotment Sheets (i.e. those marked R or S) but only after ascertaining that the nominees concerned have agreed to accept the shares renounced in their favour.

(*ii*) If any of the shares renounced have not been accepted by the nominees, or if acceptances have been received *after* expiry of the renunciation period, the name of the original allottee will be allowed to remain on the Application and Allotment Sheet in respect of any shares for which he remains responsible.

(*iii*) Check Application and Allotment Sheets and any supplementary lists, such as the List of Renunciations and Split Letters Record Sheets, to ensure that the shares now remaining on all lists together equal the number of shares originally allotted.

(*iv*) The Register of Members can now be written up from particulars on the Application and Allotment Sheets and where applicable, supplementary lists of renunciations.

(*v*) Share certificates may be prepared at this stage in favour of the original allottees and accepting nominees. It must be borne in mind that they are to be ready *within two months* after allotment of the shares (s. 185) except where conditions of issue provide otherwise, e.g. where the shares are to be paid for in full over a short period of, say, three months.

NOTE: In the case of 'listed' shares, when the Stock Exchange regulations will apply, share certificates must be ready *within one month*; in the case of a new issue, that means within one month of the date of expiration of any right of renunciation. However, as already indicated above, the conditions under which the shares are issued now alter the case, as it is not usual to issue share certificates until the shares concerned are fully-paid, and that may be several months or even years after the shares are first allotted. This point is dealt with more fully in Chapter 7.

22. Consolidation listing forms

(a) In practice it is usually found that many of the original allottees renounce in favour of the same nominee.

(b) In order to save the nominee the trouble of completing several forms, the wording of the registration application form (or acceptance form, where that is used as an alternative) can be slightly altered and a consolidation listing form is added, for example:

We accept the shares...comprised in the within allotment letter and in the attached allotment letters, the definitive numbers whereof and the number of shares comprised wherein are tabulated below:

No. of allotment letter	No. of shares	No. of allotment letter	No. of shares

(c) The nominee is required to complete only one of the allotment letters in the above manner; the other allotment letters renounced in his favour are stamped by the broker to link them up with the 'parent' allotment letter bearing the signed acceptance form.

(d) Finally, the broker will return all the allotment letters to the company, where, having gone through the normal renunciation procedure, the nominee's name will be recorded in the Register of Members after expiration of the renunciation period, and a *single* share certificate will be prepared for *all* the shares renounced in his favour.

Allotment to existing members

23. When a company wishes to make a subsequent issue of its authorized capital

A company may decide, or be required by CA 1985 or its Articles to offer the shares of the new issue in the first place to existing shareholders (*see* **31** as regards the statutory pre-emption rights provided by CA 1985) — usually on terms advantageous to the shareholders, e.g. £1 shares may be offered at 120p whereas the market price of the same class of shares at that time is 130p.

24. The number of shares offered to each of the existing shareholders

As a rule, *pro rata* to their present holdings, e.g. one new share may be offered for every five shares now held. This usually results in entitlement to fractions of shares, with consequent complications for the company. For that reason, fractions are frequently ignored.

25. Offers made to existing shareholders are known as 'rights' issues

They may be made:

(a) *by provisional allotment letter,* in which the shareholder is informed that a certain number of shares have been 'provisionally allotted' to him; or
(b) *by letter of rights,* in which a certain number of shares are offered to him.

26. Underwriting

As the existing shareholders are not bound to take up the shares offered to them, it is usual to underwrite a 'rights' issue.

27. Procedure on a 'rights' issue, using provisional allotment letters

(a) Convene a board meeting to decide whether to make a 'rights' issue and, having decided that it would be advisable to do so, to discuss the following important matters:

(*i*) the amount and terms of the proposed issue;
(*ii*) whether to underwrite the issue; and
(*iii*) if not, how to deal with any excess shares not taken up.

(b) Prepare lists, showing the number of shares to be offered to each shareholder, based upon his holding at a stipulated date.
(c) Convene another board meeting for the purpose of passing a resolution authorizing the 'rights' issue, and instructing the secretary to:

(*i*) arrange for the preparation and printing of the necessary documents, e.g. provisional allotment letters, letters of renunciation, applications for excess shares, Allotment Sheets, share certificates, etc.;

(*ii*) arrange for the underwriting of the issue, unless other arrangements are being made for dealing with excess shares;

(*iii*) submit an application to the Stock Exchange, through the company's brokers, for a listing for the new shares.

NOTE: It has been assumed that a *board* meeting would be adequate to authorize the 'rights' issue, and that the authority required by s. 80 CA 1985 (*see* **10** *above*) and/or any specific regulation in the Articles has been obtained.

(d) Approach underwriters and arrange for an underwriting contract after its terms have been approved by the board.

(e) Prepare all necessary documents referred to above.

(f) Arrange for the closing of Register of Members (and Transfer Register, if any) and give notice of the proposed closing in the press.

NOTE: If this course is not adopted, it will be announced that the holders on a stipulated date will be entitled to the 'rights' issue.

(g) Send a provisional allotment letter to each shareholder so entitled, and obtain a certificate of posting.

(h) Deal with letters of renunciation and requests for 'split letters'.

(i) Record acceptances on provisional allotment lists. If, however, payment of the first instalment (or the full amount, if that is required) is not made to the company's bankers by the shareholder or his nominee(s) on or before the due date, the offer is deemed to have been declined.

(j) Applications for excess shares may be used to make up any deficiency. If there is still a deficiency, the shares under-subscribed will be taken up by the underwriters.

(k) Subsequent procedure will follow closely the usual allotment procedure already described in detail, briefly as follows.

(*i*) Board (or allotment committee) passes a resolution, authorizing the allotment. Notify Stock Exchange.

(*ii*) After expiry of the renunciation period, write up the Register of Members and (if the shares are then fully paid) prepare and issue share certificates.

(*iii*) File a Return of Allotments in the prescribed form (Form G88(2)) with the Registrar, in compliance with s. 88 CA 1985.

NOTE: If the company concerned was listed, the procedure outlined above would have to be modified and the documentation drafted to take account of the regulations of the Stock Exchange.

28. Procedure on a 'rights' issue, using a letter of rights

(a) A letter of rights may be used as an alternative to a provisional allotment letter, and neither appears to have any important advantage over the other.
(b) The principal difference lies in the wording of the documents, i.e. the letter of rights invites the member to *apply* for a specified number of shares, whereas the provisional allotment letter informs him that a specified number of shares have been 'provisionally allotted' to him and requests him to *accept* them by a certain date.
(c) Whichever document is used, the shareholder usually has the right to renounce the shares offered to him. In that case the document is of value, for even if the shareholder does not wish to take up the new shares he can sell his 'rights' to do so on the market.

29. 'Rights' not taken up by existing shareholders

Various ways have been suggested for dealing with excess shares, although several of them are wide open to criticism.
(a) Underwriting the issue is the most obvious method to adopt, but it may prove unpopular with those shareholders who would like the opportunity to apply for any excess shares.
(b) Excess shares may be offered to the remaining shareholders, or forms of 'Application for Excess Shares' issued to shareholders along with the provisional allotment letter, any balance of shares still remaining to be taken up by the underwriters.
(c) Excess shares may be offered to the company's employees. This may be encouraged by those who favour the idea of employees entering into the field of investment, but might not have the support of those who contribute the bulk of the company's capital.
(d) Excess shares may be allotted to a trustee for those who failed to apply, who sells the shares for their benefit and distributes the proceeds (less expenses) to them. This method might lead to even greater apathy on the part of the shareholders; if they felt certain

that the company would look after their interests in this way, they might be encouraged to ignore any future offers of shares.

(e) Excess shares may be sold, and the net proceeds utilized by the company to reduce the issue expenses.

(f) Excess shares may be offered as an alternative to commission for underwriting the issue. It would, of course, be necessary to ensure that this did not amount to an excessive rate or amount of commission, having regard to the provisions of. s. 97 CA 1985.

(g) Excess shares may be disposed of by the directors, usually amongst themselves. This method might be far from popular with the shareholders, unless they had already been given the opportunity to apply for the excess shares.

30. Allotment letters which are not surrendered in exchange for a new share certificate

When shares are offered, either in a direct offer or on a 'rights' issue and the shares are payable on application and allotment, e.g. 25p per share on application and the 75p balance on allotment, it is still the usual practice of many companies to require the surrender of the allotment letter in exchange for the new share certificate. If, however, a shareholder *fails* to surrender his letter of allotment, the course to be adopted by the company will depend upon whether the letter of allotment is of the 'returnable' or 'non-returnable' type.

(a) If it is of the *non-returnable* type, the company will, after a stipulated date, issue a share certificate to the allottee in any case, without any need for him to submit the letter of allotment, which then becomes valueless.

(b) If it is a *returnable* letter of allotment, the allottee's failure to surrender it may be due to inadvertence or to his failure to pay the allotment money; therefore, the company might adopt either or both the following courses.

(*i*) Write to the shareholder, requesting surrender of the letter of allotment. If this has no effect, record the fact in the Register of Members, so as to prevent any attempt to transfer the shares concerned against the letter of allotment, which is a valuable document and 'good delivery' on the Stock Exchange.

(*ii*) Forfeiture of the shares may be carried out in accordance with the company's Articles, or, if applicable, Table A.

31. Pre-emption rights: ss. 89–96 CA 1985

(a) Section 89(1) CA 1985 provides that no new shares may be issued by a company unless existing shareholders are given an opportunity to subscribe for such shares *pro rata* to existing holdings. Whereas a public company cannot exclude the provisions of s. 89(1) (except by special resolution in the manner set out in s. 95 CA 1985), a private company may exclude the requirements in their entirety by provisions contained in the Articles, and either substitute amended rights of pre-emption or exclude rights of pre-emption completely.

(b) Section 89(1) applies only to 'equity securities'. Accordingly, the rights of pre-emption prescribed by s. 89(1) do not apply to the following.

(*i*) The issue of any shares carrying a fixed dividend. Non-participating preference shares may therefore be issued without reference to s. 89(1).

(*ii*) the issue of shares under an employees' share scheme.

(*iii*) the issue of shares for a non-cash consideration.

(c) In practice, it is normal for the articles of a private company to exclude the provisions of s. 89(1) and to provide for a non-statutory pre-emption right, over-riding the statutory provisions. Non-statutory provisions will normally be drafted in broader terms than s. 89(1).

(d) Where s. 89(1) does apply, the provisions may be excluded by special resolution of the shareholders whether the company is public or private: s. 95 CA 1985. The power of exclusion is, like s. 80 CA 1985, limited to a period of five years, but is normally only applied to a particular issue or for a particular period.

(e) Where the disapplication is for a specific allotment rather than a general allotment, a statement by the directors must be circulated with the Notice incorporating a resolution to disapply the provisions of s. 89(1) and s. 95(5). This statement must set out the reasons for the directors recommending a disapplication, the amount to be paid for the shares to be allotted and the directors' justification of that amount. If in the case of a private company it is proposed to pass the resolution by written resolution of the shareholders pursuant to s. 381(A) CA 1985, the statement must be sent to each shareholder at or before the time of supplying the resolution for signature.

(f) In the case of public companies and in particular listed companies, it is the practice to link a resolution for the disapplication of pre-emption rights to a resolution authorizing the directors to allot shares in terms of s. 80 CA 1985. In such cases, the disapplication will normally be for a period expiring upon the date of the next annual general meeting.

(g) The Stock Exchange requires listed companies to obtain shareholders' approval annually for a special resolution to disapply pre-emptive rights and to observe cumulative limits to the extent to which it uses its disapplication entitlement in any rolling three-year period.

Allotment of bonus shares

32. Authority to allot bonus shares

If the Articles permit, a company may allot fully paid bonus shares to its members:

(a) *out of undistributed profits,* in which case it amounts to a capitalization of its reserves; or

(b) *out of a Share Premium Account balance,* i.e. out of the account created on allotting shares at more than their nominal value; or

(c) *out of a Capital Redemption Reserve,* created in connection with the redemption or purchase of its own shares.

33. Procedure

The procedure for making a bonus issue is similar in some respects to that for a rights issue, but there are many points of difference. A bonus issue procedure may be carried out in the following stages.

(a) Before attempting to carry out any of the necessary procedures, the following preliminaries must be dealt with.

(*i*) Ensure that the Articles permit the issue of bonus shares. If not, they must be altered by special resolution. (In this case, it has been assumed that the Articles give the necessary permission.)

(*ii*) Consult the Articles, also, to ensure that authority to make the issue will be given by the appropriate meeting. In this case, it has been assumed that the directors have power to recommend the issue but the company in general meeting must adopt the recommendation before it becomes effective. This is typical of most cases.

(*iii*) Ascertain that the company has sufficient unissued capital to cover the intended amount of the bonus issue. If not, an ordinary resolution must be passed to increase the company's authorized capital, and capital duty paid on the increased capital and a copy of the resolution would be filed with the Registrar within 15 days.

(b) Convene a board meeting, where, after discussion, the following business is carried out:

(*i*) a formal resolution is passed, recommending a bonus issue;

(*ii*) the basis of distribution, method of dealing with fractions and other details are settled;

(*iii*) the secretary is instructed to convene a general meeting and, on the assumption that the directors' recommendation will be adopted, he will no doubt also receive instructions to arrange for the drafting and subsequent printing of the necessary documents;

(c) Arising out of the board meeting, the secretary will:

(*i*) convene an extraordinary general meeting, the notice giving brief particulars of the directors' recommendation;

(*ii*) draft, and obtain the board's approval of, the necessary documents, e.g. fully paid allotment letters, allotment lists, certificates, etc.

(d) An extraordinary general meeting is held, at which an ordinary resolution is passed, adopting the directors' recommendation to issue bonus shares. At that meeting, a trustee may be appointed for the shareholders entitled to participate in the bonus issue, and either then or at a subsequent board meeting a contract will be executed between company and trustee. (*See* **(i)** *below* for reference to the filing of a Return of Allotment.)

(e) A further board meeting will be held soon after the general meeting for the purpose of:

(*i*) passing a resolution allotting the bonus shares to members named in an allotment list produced by the secretary; and

(*ii*) executing the contract between the company and the trustee for the shareholders, constituting the title of the allottees to the shares — unless, as stated above, it has already been executed at the general meeting.

(f) Post fully paid allotment letters, with accompanying letters of renunciation.

NOTE: Alternatively many companies now send renounceable share certificates in lieu of allotment letters.

(g) Deal with letters of renunciation and requests for 'split' letters.

(h) After expiry of the renunciation period:

(*i*) write up the Register of Members;

(*ii*) prepare and issue new share certificates to original allottees and, where applicable, accepting nominees.

(i) File a Return of Allotments (Forms G88(2) and G88(3)) with the Registrar within one month, and, as a bonus issue amounts to an allotment for consideration other than cash, the return must be accompanied by the contract in writing, duly stamped, constituting the title of the allottees to the allotment: s. 88 CA 1985.

NOTE: This is the contract referred to in **(d)** and **(e)**(*ii*) above between the company and a trustee for the shareholders. The contract is in the form of a deed, and bears a 50p impressed stamp. As a rule, the secretary, chairman or one of the largest shareholders is appointed trustee.

34. Methods of dealing with fractional entitlements

Both bonus and rights issues are likely to result in fractional entitlements; for example, where a company makes a bonus issue under which each shareholder is entitled to one new share for every three registered in his name, a member holding 100 shares would be entitled to $33^1/3$ bonus shares. How to deal with these fractional entitlements is a matter which the directors must consider and deal with as fairly as possible to those concerned, since the company cannot allot fractions of shares. Various methods are available. The following are examples.

(a) Shares representing fractional entitlements may be sold, and any shareholder entitled to a fraction of a share will subsequently receive payment for the net proceeds of the sale of that fraction.

(b) All shares representing fractional entitlement may be allotted to a trustee for the shareholders affected, who has power to sell them on the open market for the benefit of the shareholders entitled to fractions.

(c) Fractional certificates may be issued to shareholders entitled to fractions of shares, enabling those who wish to do so to sell them to others who wish to buy sufficient fractional certificates to make up a whole share or shares.

(d) Shareholders may be invited to tender for shares representing fractional entitlements, a trustee for the shareholders affected being responsible for distributing the proceeds.

(e) Fractions may be ignored entirely, a method which would certainly be unpopular if adopted in a bonus issue.

Progress test 3

1. List the various stages in a procedure for receiving and handling application for shares, and for the preparation and despatch of allotment letters. It may be assumed that the issue is oversubscribed. **(1–15)**

2. State briefly the information to be given in a Return of Allotments. Within what period must it be filed? **(15)**

3. What statutory restrictions are imposed upon the allotment of shares by a public company? What is the effect (if any) of irregular allotment in each of the cases you mention? **(16–17)**

4. Briefly outline the procedure followed on receiving letters of renunciation and 'split letters' at the company's office. **(21)**

5. Distinguish between each of the following:

(a) a capitalization issue and a rights issue;
(b) high geared capital and low geared capital;
(c) an offer for sale and an advertised statement.
(1:51, 2: 4, 25)

6. Explain the meaning of the following terms used in connection with the issue of shares:

(a) brokerage;
(b) firm underwriting;
(c) a provisional allotment letter;
(d) a consolidated listing form.
ICSA **(2: 12–15, 22)**

7. A company whose shares are listed on the Stock Exchange is about to make a substantial issue of shares to be offered to existing shareholders with rights of renunciation. Describe the records that should be kept by the company in respect of such an issue. **(27)**

8. What is a rights issue, and how is it effected? *ICSA* **(25–30)**

9. On a new issue of shares to existing ordinary shareholders, what are the possible methods of dealing with:

(*i*) fractional entitlements;
(*ii*) rights not taken up;
(*iii*) allotment letters not surrendered in exchange for new share certificates? **(29–30, 34)**

10. In relation to an issue of shares explain the following:

(a) provisional allotment letter;
(b) fractions;
(c) excess shares. *ICSA* **(27, 29, 34)**

11. Define and explain fully the use of:

(a) a Form of Renunciation;
(b) a Split Allotment Letter. *ICSA* **(1–21)**

12. What are the usual contents of an underwriting letter? What disclosures must be made of underwriting and sub-underwriting agreements? *ICSA* (2: **12–14**)

4

Calls and instalments

Preliminary considerations

1. When shares are payable

When a company makes an issue of shares, they may be payable:

(a) *in full, on application* — although this is comparatively rare in the case of issues to the public;
(b) *on application and allotment,* for example 25p per share on application and the balance of 75p per share on allotment, for a £1 share issued at par; or
(c) *by calls or instalments,* for example, a £1 share issued at par may be payable:

(*i*) 25p per share on application;
(*ii*) 25p per share on allotment; and
(*iii*) the balance of 50p by calls or instalments

NOTE: Section 101 CA 1985 provides that a *public* company shall not allot any shares unless at least one-quarter of the shares' nominal value and the whole of any premium on such shares, has been paid up. *Exception* is made, however, in the case of shares allotted under an employees' share scheme.

2. A call is not an instalment

Any power given in the Articles to forfeit shares for non-payment of calls, or to charge interest on unpaid calls, does not apply to instalments — unless (as in Table A) the Articles provide that amounts due on allotment and instalments are deemed to be calls: Article 16.

3. An instalment differs from a call

(a) *An instalment* is due and payable on a fixed date specified in the conditions of issue; *a call* only becomes due as or if required.
(b) *An instalment* becomes due and payable without the passing of a resolution; *a call* only becomes due on the passing of a resolution to that effect — usually a resolution of the board of directors.
(c) *An instalment* is automatically due on the date fixed, without making any formal demand of the shareholder; *a call* must be made by giving proper notice in compliance with the provisions of the Articles.

4. Table A provisions as regards calls

Provisions and making of calls are as follows.

(a) The directors are authorized to make calls at a properly constituted board meeting: Article 12.
(b) A call is deemed to have been made at the time the directors' resolution was passed, and may be payable by instalments: Article 13.
(c) The resolution must state the amount, time and place of payment.
(d) The time for payment must be not less than one month from the date fixed for payment of the last preceding call: Article 12.
(e) At least 14 days' notice must be given to the member, specifying time and place of payment: Article 12.
(f) A call may be revoked or postponed, as the directors may determine: Article 12.
(g) Joint holders are jointly and severally liable to pay calls: Article 14.
(h) Amounts due on allotment and instalments are deemed to be calls for the purpose of regulations as regards the charging of interest and forfeiture: Article 16.
(i) Interest may be charged on unpaid calls, after the date appointed for payment: Article 18.

(j) Forfeiture of shares is permitted, for failure to pay a call or an instalment: Article 19.
(k) Power is given to differentiate between shareholders as regards the amount and time of payment of calls: Article 17.

NOTE: Section 119(a) CA 1985 permits differentiation, where authorized by the Articles, but the directors must use this power only for the benefit of the company and not of individuals: *Alexander* v. *Automatic Telephone Co.* (1900).

5. If a call is made improperly

A shareholder may be relieved of liability to meet the call, until such time as it is properly made, by application to the Court: *Re Cawley & Co.* (1889), where the call letter omitted the date of payment. It was held that the call was invalid until a resolution was passed fixing the date of payment.

6. Payment in advance of calls

(a) If authorized by the Articles, a company may accept payment from a member of the whole or a part of the amount remaining unpaid on his shares, although no part of this amount has been called up: s. 119(*b*) CA 1985.
(b) When a payment in advance of calls has been made the consequences are:

(*i*) the shareholder's liability to the company is extinguished or reduced, as the case may be;

(*ii*) he becomes a creditor to the extent of the payment in advance, so that interest on it can be paid out of capital, i.e. whether profits are made by the company or not; the company cannot be compelled to repay the payment, except in winding up;

(*iii*) the company cannot repay without the consent of the shareholder;

(*iv*) in a winding up he will rank after the other creditors but will be entitled to repayment of the advance with interest in priority to the other shareholders who have not paid in advance.

(c) The power of receiving payment in advance of calls is a fiduciary power and must be exercised by the directors bona fide for the benefit of the company as a whole: *Sykes' Case* (1872).
(d) Under the regulations of the Stock Exchange the Articles of

a company must provide that any amount paid up in advance of calls on any share may carry interest but will not entitle the holder of the share to participate in respect of such amount in any dividend.

Procedure on making a call

7. Board meeting

The original decision to make a call will be made at a board meeting, after which the secretary will be instructed:

(a) to prepare the necessary documents; and
(b) to arrange for the bank to receive call moneys.

NOTE: The directors *may* have to seek approval of the call by the company in general meeting, although this would be very unusual, as the Articles almost invariably vest the power to make calls in the directors.

8. Reference to the Articles

Before preparing documents or making any arrangements with the company's bankers, the secretary would be well advised to refer to the Articles, to ensure that the call will be strictly correct as regards amount, notice, interval since last call, etc.

9. Preparation of documents

(a) The secretary's next step is to draft a form of *call letter,* which usually includes:

(*i*) *a form of receipt,* which the bank returns to the shareholder after he has paid his call money; and

(*ii*) *a detachable voucher,* which the bank returns to the company as advice of call money received.

(b) Other documents that may be drafted at this stage include a Call List and a formal letter of reminder for shareholders who fail to pay by the specified date.

(c) After obtaining board approval of the draft documents — but more particularly of the call letter — an order may be placed for the printing of the call letters, specifying that they must be numbered consecutively.

10. Arrangements with the bank

Arrangements can then be made with the bank, in particular:

(a) to receive payment of call moneys;
(b) to credit amounts received to a special Call Account;
(c) to return receipted call letters to shareholders; and
(d) to submit to the company, in due course, a list of call moneys received together with vouchers detached from call letters, referred to in 9(a) above.

11. Convene a board meeting

Having received the printed call letters, a board meeting may now be convened (unless, as already explained, the Articles should make it necessary to hold a general meeting) to transact the following business.

(a) The call letter will be submitted to the board for approval.
(b) A resolution is passed, authorizing the call, for example:

RESOLVED: THAT a call of 25p per share on the 200,000 ordinary shares of the Company, numbered 1 to 200,000, be and is hereby made; and that the holders of such shares be requested to pay the same on or before the.........day of.............19.....to the Company's bankers, Town and Country Bank Plc, Westcheap, London E.C.5.

(c) The Secretary will be instructed to issue call letters.

12. Preparation of Call Lists

Having ensured that the Register of Members is written up-to-date, Call Lists can now be prepared for the Register, taking care, of course, to exclude any shareholders who may, by arrangement with the company, have paid calls in advance. The Call List may take the following form.

The Blank Company Plc

Call List
Second and final call of 25p per share on 200,000 ordinary shares of £1 each.

Call made............. 19....... Payable on or before............ 19.......

No. of call letter	Folio in reg.	*Shareholder*		No. of shares held	Amount due on call at 25p per share	*Paid*			Out-standing	Remarks
		Name	Address			CB Folio	Date	Amount		

13. Preparation of call letters from Call Lists

After making a thorough check of the Call Lists, and reconciling the total number of shares with the total amount of calls payable, call letters are prepared from particulars on the Call Lists. Care must be taken to ensure that the call letters are strictly in accordance with the Articles, as failure to do so may invalidate the call. The following are the points requiring particular attention:

(a) amount of the call;
(b) interval since making the last call;
(c) length of notice;
(d) date fixed for payment;
(e) to whom cheques, etc., are to be payable;
(f) place of payment.

14. Post the call letters

After completion, the call letters should receive a final check prior to posting. A certificate of posting may be obtained.

15. Checking

Lists of all call moneys received will arrive in due course from the bank. They will be accompanied by the appropriate vouchers, and these should be checked against the list.

16. Completion of Call Lists

The Call Lists can now be completed from the particulars provided by the bank, and the share ledger written up from the Call Lists.

NOTE: The procedure, at this stage, will depend upon whether it has been the company's practice to issue share certificates for partly paid shares, or to issue certificates only after the shares are fully paid.

(1) If a share certificate had already been issued, the shareholder must return it to the company along with his receipted call letter. If it is the *final* call, the 'partly paid' share certificate will be cancelled and a 'fully paid' certificate issued to the shareholder. If it is *not* the final call, the company will merely record the payment in the space provided — usually on the back of the share certificate — and return the endorsed certificate to the shareholder.

(2) If a share certificate is issued only after shares are fully paid no certificate will be issued at this stage, unless the call concerned is the *final* one

17. Reminders

After a short interval, send reminders to shareholders who have failed to pay calls on or before the due date

18. Calls still overdue

If the Articles permit, payment of interest may be demanded on overdue calls and, as a last resort, the necessary steps may be taken to forfeit the shares.

NOTE: If the shares referred to in the above procedure were 'listed', the Stock Exchange would require notification of board decisions, and a specimen (or two advance proofs) of the share certificate would be submitted at the appropriate stage.

Forfeiture

19. Nature of forfeiture

Forfeiture is a step, taken by a company only in the last resort, to expropriate the shares of a member who defaults in paying any part of the moneys due from him in respect of the shares declared forfeit.

It amounts to a reduction of capital, even though it may be only a temporary reduction in those cases where the forfeited shares are subsequently re-issued.

20. Limits imposed on the right of a company to forfeit shares

(a) Acts themselves do not expressly impose any limits, but because forfeiture amounts to a reduction of capital it can be carried out only:

(*i*) *when the Articles permit,* or where Table A applies (Articles 19–22 give the directors power to forfeit); or

(*ii*) *if the Articles are silent* and Table A has been excluded, by obtaining sanction of the Court: *Clarke & Chapman* v. *Hart* (1858).

(b) The directors of a company are not entitled to declare forfeit the shares of a member, unless:

(*i*) express power to do so is given to them in the Articles, or in Table A if their Articles are silent; and

(*ii*) as forfeiture is in the nature of a penalty, it must be carried out strictly in the manner prescribed in the Articles, or Table A where applicable; and

(*iii*) for the benefit of the company and not, for example, to relieve a shareholder of his liability on the shares: *Re Esparto Trading Co.* (1879); and

(*iv*) where the default arose in respect of non-payment of calls or other sums due from the member in respect of his shares, i.e. not for non-payment of *other debts* due to the company: *Hopkinson* v. *Mortimer Harley & Co.* (1917).

21. Summary of the legal effects of forfeiture

(a) It amounts to a cancellation of the shares concerned and, therefore, to a reduction of capital, even though it may be only a temporary reduction.

(b) It cancels the membership of the shareholder concerned.

(c) It discharges the shareholder's liability in respect of the forfeited shares: *Ladies' Dress Association* v. *Pulbrook* (1900). But the Articles usually preserve the liability of the shareholder, as does Table A (Article 21).

22. Forfeiture under Table A

Table A permits forfeiture but sets out the necessary conditions and indicates the procedure to be followed.

(a) The directors may serve notice requiring payment with interest. If a call or instalment is unpaid on the due date, the directors may serve notice on the member in default, requiring payment with interest: Article 18.

> NOTE: Non-payment may refer to default in paying a sum due on account of the nominal value of the share or on any sum due by way of premium: Article 16.

(b) The notice must name a further day (not less than 14 days after service of the notice) by which payment is to be made, failing which the shares concerned are liable to forfeiture: Article 18.

(c) In the event of failure to comply with the notice, the directors may by resolution declare the shares forfeited, for example:

> RESOLVED: THAT the 200 ordinary shares of £1 each, numbered 301 to 500 both inclusive, on which the sum of 50p per share has been paid, and now registered in the name of Mr A. Blank of 15 Chetwynd Grove, Redpoole, Wessex, be and the same are hereby forfeited for non-payment of a second call of 25p per share, served on 1st November 19. . . in accordance with Minute No. 4 of the board meeting held on the 24th October 19. . . and for his failure to comply with the requests for payment sent to him on 8th December 19. . . and 15th December 19. . .

(d) Forfeited shares may then be sold or otherwise disposed of, as the directors decide, but before sale or disposition the forfeiture may be cancelled, on terms decided by the directors: Article 20.

(e) Membership ceases on forfeiture, but liability for calls remains with the original holder until the company receives payment in full of all money due on the shares: Article 21.
(f) A statutory declaration in writing, stating that the declarant is a director or secretary of the company, and that a share (or shares) in the company has been duly forfeited on a given date, is conclusive evidence against all persons claiming to be entitled to the shares: Article 22.

NOTE: This provision is a protection for the company where the original holder refuses to return his share certificate, as the unreturned share certificate can be rendered invalid by production of the statutory declaration.

(g) On re-issuing the forfeited shares: Article 20,

(*i*) the company may receive the consideration (if any) for shares sold or otherwise disposed of;

(*ii*) the company may execute a transfer of the shares in favour of the person to whom the shares are sold or disposed of;

NOTE: In order to comply with s. 183(1) CA 1985 where applicable (which makes it illegal to register a transfer unless a proper instrument of transfer has been delivered to the company) the company will have to nominate some person to execute a transfer to the purchaser of the re-issued forfeited shares. Usually a member of the board will be empowered to do so.

(*iii*) the person to whom the shares are sold shall be registered as the holder of the shares;

(*iv*) he shall not be bound to see to the application of the purchase money, and his title to the shares will not be affected by any irregularity or invalidity of the procedure for forfeiture, sale or disposal of the shares.

23. Notice of forfeiture

(a) It will be observed that Table A does not require the company to send notice to the shareholder to inform him that his shares have been forfeited.
(b) Nevertheless, it is usual to notify the shareholder by

registered post that his shares have been declared forfeited, to prevent any misunderstanding.

(c) At the same time, it is customary to ask the shareholder to return his share certificate. In practice, shareholders seldom comply with such a request.

(d) The secretary should, however, make every attempt to secure the return of the certificate; otherwise, if the shares are re-issued, there will be two share certificates in existence for the same set of shares.

> NOTE: A provision similar to that in Table A, Article 22, referred to in **22(f)** above, will however enable the company to prove the invalidity of an unreturned share certificate.

24. Treatment of forfeited shares

(a) *Re-issue.* If forfeited shares are re-issued, the price for which they are sold plus the amount already paid up by the original holder must not be less than the full nominal value; that is, the shares cannot be re-issued at a price which would, in effect, amount to the issue of the shares at a discount.

(b) *Disposal of shares forfeited* (or surrendered) to a *public* company. Such shares must be disposed of by the company, or cancelled, within three years from the date of forfeiture or surrender. If such cancellation reduces the company's issued share capital below the 'authorized minimum', the company will then be obliged to re-register as a private company: s. 146(2)(*b*) CA 1985.

25. Surrender of shares

(a) In general, it may be said that a *surrender of shares is unlawful* because:

(*i*) it amounts to an unauthorized reduction of capital; and

(*ii*) the company's acceptance of the surrendered shares would make it a member of itself, which is illegal.

(b) But a surrender of shares is not always unlawful; for example:

(*i*) the directors may accept a surrender of shares and thus relieve the company of going through the formalities of forfeiture — if the Articles permit, and where the circumstances would justify forfeiture;

(*ii*) where the surrender does not involve a reduction of capital, e.g. a surrender of existing fully paid shares in exchange for new fully paid shares of the same nominal value: *Rowell & Son* (1912).

(c) In any other circumstances, where a reduction of capital will result from the surrender of shares, application must be made for Court sanction.

(d) The effect of a *public* company's failure to dispose of shares surrendered to it is stated in **24(b)**.

Progress test 4

1. Explain precisely the differences between the following terms:

(a) rights and capitalization issues;
(b) repayment of capital and a capital distribution;
(c) a call and an instalment.
ICSA **(3: 23–25, 33; 4: 2, 3)**

2. When making a call, what are the important matters to be borne in mind? Is it permissible to differentiate between shareholders of the same class as regards the amount and time of payment of calls? If so, in what circumstances? **(4, 7)**

3. Describe an office procedure for making a call, and prepare a call list suitable for the occasion. **(6–13)**

4. 'Forfeiture is a procedure that demands the utmost care.' Explain, and suggest any precautions that ought to be taken in relation to forfeiture of shares and their re-issue. **(18, 20–22)**

5. The directors of your company wish to forfeit the shares of a member. Write a memorandum explaining the procedure. Assume that Table A applies. *ICSA* **(20, 21)**

6. Distinguish between forfeiture and surrender of shares. Is a surrender of shares necessarily unlawful in all cases; if not, what are the exceptional circumstances? **(18–19, 23)**

7. A final call has been made and has remained unpaid by a shareholder. Assuming Table A applies, explain in a memorandum to your board the action the company can take. *ICSA* (18–21)

8. One of the shareholders of a private company has died and by his will bequeathed his holding to his wife. As Company Secretary you receive a letter from the sole executor enquiring:

(a) Whether he can be registered by the company as the holder of the shares;
(b) As to his position, as executor, regarding any calls made on the shares.

Draft a reply giving the advice requested. *ICSA* (4)

5

The common seal

Regulations as to its use and custody

1. Execution of documents: s. 36A CA 1985

(a) A document is executed by a company by the affixing of its common seal.

(b) A company need not have a common seal, however, and whether it does or not:

(*i*) A document signed by a director and the secretary of a company, or by two directors of a company, and expressed (in whatever form of words) to be executed by the company has the same effect as if it was executed under the common seal of the company.

(*ii*) A document executed by a company which makes it clear on its face that it is intended by the person or persons making it to be a deed has effect, upon delivery, as a deed; and it shall be presumed, unless a contrary intention is proved, to be delivered upon it being so executed.

(c) Where a company does have a common seal it must have its name engraved in legible characters on the seal; and if it fails to comply to this requirement it is liable to a fine: s. 350(1) CA 1985.

2. Regulations governing the use and custody of the seal

If a company has a common seal, the regulations governing its use and custody are usually set out in the company's Articles of Association; they may, however, be prescribed by resolution of the board.

3. Table A provisions

The use and custody of the seal are set out in Article 101, as follows.

(a) It is to be used only by the authority of the directors, or of a committee authorized by them.
(b) The instrument sealed must be signed by a director, and countersigned by the secretary, or by a second director or by some other person appointed by the directors for the purpose.

4. Safe custody of the seal

Where a company has a common seal, then to ensure its safe custody and to prevent its misuse, various precautions are usually taken.

(a) The seal is often kept in a suitable safe or in a strong room.
(b) It is often fitted with a double-locking device, with one key in the hands of the secretary, the other with the chairman or one of the other directors. This provides a form of internal check.
(c) Spare key(s) may be deposited with the company's bankers, with instructions to hand them over only to a specified person or against the written request of specified signatories.
(d) The use of an automatic sealing press has various 'built-in' security measures, e.g. the die can be removed and locked away in a very small space, and the machine protected from unauthorized use by removing and locking away the electric plugging-in arrangement.
(e) If a 'sealing committee' is appointed, e.g. to seal share certificates, that any limitations to the committee's power to use the seal should be clearly ascertained.
(f) Supervision of sealing by the company's auditors, or transfer auditors, at regular intervals is an alternative method used in sealing large numbers of share certificates.

5. Form of company contracts

(a) A contract may be made

(*i*) *by a company*, by writing under its common seal, or
(*ii*) *on behalf of a company*, by any person acting under its authority, express or implied;

and any formalities required by law in the case of a contract made by an individual also apply, unless a contrary intention appears, to a contract made by or on behalf of a company.
(b) Subject to the provisions of the Articles even where the law requires a document to be executed under seal such document will only require sealing as such where the company has a seal.

6. Register of Documents Sealed (or Seal Register)

(a) This is not one of the statutory books; however, although there is no statutory obligation to keep such a register, most companies find it an advantage to do so.
(b) The particulars usually recorded are shown in the following suggested ruling for such a register:

Register of Documents Sealed

Minute No.	*Date of Resolution*	*Description of documents sealed*	*Date of sealing*	*Names of persons present*	*Names of persons signing*	*Disposal of documents sealed*

The official seal

7. The official seal

The official seal is a facsimile of the common seal of the company, but with the addition on its face of the territory, district or place where it is to be used.

8. Company's power to have an official seal

According to s. 39 CA 1985, a company which has a common seal *may* have an official seal for use in any district, territory or place not situate in the United Kingdom:

(a) if the company's objects require or comprise the transaction of business in foreign countries; and
(b) if the company's Articles permit.

9. Provision as to use of official seal

If the official seal is used upon any deed or other document, it will have the same effect as the company's common seal, provided that:

(a) the person affixing it had the company's authority in writing under seal;
(b) the deed or other document is one to which the company is party; and
(c) he is carrying out his authority in the territory, district or place in which the official seal was intended to be used: s. 39(2) and (3) CA 1985.

10. Further provisions in the Articles regarding the official seal

In addition to authorizing the use of an official seal, a company's Articles may also include some or all of the following provisions as to its use, security, attestation, etc.:

(a) Authority to use the official seal may be made, under the company's common seal, to a person or persons, e.g. to a sealing committee.
(b) The person or persons appointed are to affix the official seal and, by writing under hand, certify on the deed or other instrument to which the seal is affixed the date on which and the place at which it is affixed.
(c) Limits may be imposed upon the power of the person or persons appointed to use the official seal, as for example in the case of a sealing committee, and for revocation.
(d) Similar provisions may be made for custody and security measures as are made for the company's common seal, e.g. a double-locking device.
(e) Provision for attestation of signatures on documents on which the official seal is affixed.

Securities seal

11. Securities seal

By s. 40 CA 1985, a company which has a common seal may have, for use for sealing securities issued by the company and for sealing documents creating or evidencing securities so issued, an official seal which is a facsimile of its common seal with the addition on its face of the word 'Securities'. The official seal when duly affixed to a document has the same effect as the company's common seal.

12. Authentication of documents

By s. 41 CA 1985 a document or proceeding requiring authentication by a company is sufficiently authenticated for the purposes of the law of England and Wales by the signature of a director, secretary or other authorized officer of the company.

Progress test 5

1. What provisions does the Act make concerning the common seal of a limited company? What steps do you suggest ought to be taken to ensure (*a*) its safe custody, (*b*) that it is not misused? **(1–4)**

2. The chairman of your company wishes to save the time consumed at monthly board meetings by the necessity to execute large numbers of documents under the common seal of the company. Prepare a memorandum, for consideration by him, setting out your proposals to remedy this situation. *ICSA* **(4)**

3. What do you understand by the term 'common seal' as applied to a limited company? The articles of Zed Ltd are silent on the subject of its common seal. What rules must the company apply as to (*a*) use and custody of the seal, (*b*) the signing of documents sealed? **(1–4)**

4. When is a contract effectively sealed? Give examples of documents which must be under the common seal of the company in order to comply with statutory requirements, and of other documents where the necessity for sealing is dependent upon other considerations. **(1, 5)**

5. Give a specimen ruling for a Register of Documents Sealed, and insert at least six different entries. Is there any statutory obligation to keep such a register? **(6)**

6. A company requires in the normal course of its business to execute documents under its common seal almost every day. The board of directors meets only once a month. Describe in detail the arrangements that should be made to deal with this position. **(4, 6)**

7. In order to give authenticity to a document or proceeding, is a company bound to use its common seal? Explain the position, and state your authority. Distinguish between a common seal and an official seal. **(1–3, 5, 7–9)**

8. Your directors have decided to make use of an official seal at one of the company's important overseas branches. You are required to report to them, suggesting any provisions that ought to be made for the effective and safe use of the official seal. **(9, 10)**

9. (a) In relation to the common seal of the company explain:

(*i*) the authority for its use including its use in the issue of share certificates;

(*ii*) how the use of the seal may be authorized where there are infrequent board meetings; and

(b) Explain what is meant by the official seal. *ICSA* **(1–4, 7)**

6 The Register of Members

Statutory provisions as to form and contents, location inspection, etc.

1. Contents: s. 352 CA 1985

Every company must keep a Register of Members, showing:

(a) the name and address of every member;

(b) the date on which he was entered as a member and the eventual date on which he ceased to be a member;

(c) the number (and the distinguishing numbers of the shares if relevant) and, where the company has more than one class of issued shares, the class of shares which he holds (unless the company has no share capital) and the amount paid up on each share. If the shares have been converted into stock corresponding particulars of stock held are entered.

NOTE: Section 355 CA 1985 also requires particulars relating to the issue of any share warrants, where applicable (*see* 7:10).

Any entry relating to a former member of a company may be removed from the company's register of members after the expiration of twenty years from the date on which he ceases to be a member.

2. The form of the register

(a) Section 722 CA 1985 provides that any register, index, minute book or accounting records required by the Companies Acts to be kept by a company may be kept by making entries in bound books or by recording the matters in question in any other manner. By s. 723 of the 1985 Act the power to keep a register or other record by recording the matters in question otherwise than by making entries in bound books, includes power to keep the register or other record by recording the matters in question otherwise than in a legible form, so long as the recording is capable of being reproduced in a legible form. This, in effect, legalizes the use of a computer for the keeping of registers, books of accounts and other records, and it is under the authority of s. 723 CA 1985 that the Company Registrar's Departments of the clearing banks and similar organizations operate their computer-based registers.

The detailed requirements relating to registers and records kept in non-legible form are contained in the Companies (Registers and Other Records) Regulations 1985 (S.I. 1985 No. 724). Special forms are prescribed for notifying the Registrar of Companies of the place where registers kept in non-legible form may be inspected in legible form.

(b) By s. 354 CA 1985 if the membership of the company exceeds 50, there must be an alphabetical index, unless the register itself is in the form of an index. However, this requisite can be dispensed with, in any case, by utilizing the provisions of s. 722 of the 1985 Act and keeping the register in looseleaf form, provided adequate precautions are taken to prevent fraud and falsification.

(c) Failure to take adequate precautions against fraud and falsification renders the company and every officer in default liable to fines; therefore, it is usual to take the necessary security measures, for example:

(*i*) Fitting the register with a suitable locking device, and placing the keys in the custody of a responsible officer of the company.

(*ii*) Keeping the register in a fireproof safe or strongroom, a precaution to be taken whatever form the register may take.

(*iii*) The issue of new sheets to be carefully supervised, preferably by the officer who has custody of the keys.

(*iv*) Duplicate keys may be deposited with the company's bank and instructions given to hand them over only against instructions of authorized signatories.

(*v*) The loose sheets for the register may be specially

watermarked and printed with the company's name, for purposes of identification.

(*vi*) The sheets may also be consecutively numbered, so that closer records can be maintained of sheets issued.

(*vii*) No unauthorized persons will be given access to the register(s) or to the loose sheets for the register.

(*viii*) The microfilming of loose sheets in use at regular intervals is a useful additional safeguard against loss of the records by fire or any other risk.

3. Advantages of using a looseleaf register

Although a bound register may be quite adequate for, say, a small private company with few shareholders and little or no share transfer activity, larger companies will usually derive great advantage from the use of a looseleaf register, apart from being able to dispense with an index.

The principal advantages are as follows.

(a) The register can be split up, for example, when preparing dividend lists or the annual return, to enable the secretary or registrar to distribute the work more evenly among the available staff.
(b) The shareholders' accounts can be kept in strict alphabetical order and are, therefore, more easily located.
(c) Closed accounts can be withdrawn entirely, i.e. after a suitable interval the accounts of any persons who have ceased to be members can be withdrawn and subsequently filed away in a safe place (*see* **1** *above*).
(d) Accounts of new members are easily inserted in their proper alphabetical order.
(e) Inspection is facilitated. If a member or other person demands to inspect the register, the fact that it is in looseleaf form would give greater facility for inspection and, moreover, as it could be inspected in sections, registration work could still proceed on the other sections.
(f) Microfilming of sheets is simplified. If, as indicated above, it is desired to microfilm the particulars in the Register of Members at regular intervals, it is much simpler to do so from loose sheets rather than from a bound book.

4. Location: s. 353(1) CA 1985

(a) It must be kept at the registered office of the company, or at any office of the company (or its agent) at which it is written up.
(b) It must, however, be kept within the company's domicile, i.e. within the country in which the company was registered.
(c) The index (if any) must be kept at the same place as the register.
(d) When the register is not kept at the company's registered office notice specifying the address at which it is kept must be given to the Registrar on Form G353 (*see* **8** *below*).

5. Changes and alterations

(a) All entries and amendments to the registers require the prior approval of the board.
(b) The company must register any changes in the particulars required to be entered in the register as soon as it is made aware of them.
(c) Any alteration to the register must also be made within 14 days in the index, if any: s. 354 CA 1985.
(d) Great care is essential in making alterations in the register; for example:

(*i*) an entry to be cancelled must on no account be erased;

(*ii*) to cancel an item it should be neatly ruled out and the correction typed or written above or alongside the cancelled entry;

(*iii*) any alteration must be initialled by the person who makes the alteration.

6. Inspection

Provisions as to inspection and the taking of copies of the register are set out in s. 356 CA 1985.

(a) The register (and index, if any) must be available:

(*i*) for inspection by any member, free of charge; and

(*ii*) for inspection by any other person, on payment of such fee as may be prescribed.

The obligation imposed on a company by the Companies Act to allow inspection, or to furnish a copy (*see* **(d)** *below*) of any register or other record shall under s. 723(3) (*see* **2** *above*) be treated as a duty to allow inspection of, or to furnish, a reproduction of the recording or of the relevant part of it in legible form.

(b) If, however, the company gives notice of its intention to close the register (by advertisement in a newspaper circulating in the district in which the registered office is situated), the register may be closed for any time or times not exceeding on the whole 30 days in each year: s. 358 CA 1985.

(c) The register may be closed, for example, when dividends are paid, or when bonus or rights issues are made to existing members. On the other hand, some companies prefer not to close the register in such cases and simply declare that the dividend shall be paid (or the bonus shares issued) to members on the register at a specified date.

(d) Any person may demand a copy of the register (or any part of it) on payment of the appropriate fee and the copy must be sent to the person requiring it *within ten days* of receiving the request.

(e) Refusal to grant inspection or default in supplying copies on request: (*i*) renders the company, and every officer in default, liable to fines; and (*ii*) the Court may compel inspection and order that the required copies be sent.

(f) Inspection cannot be refused on the grounds that it is desired for purposes hostile to the company. *Davies* v. *Gas Light & Coke Co.* (1909).

(g) The right of inspection ceases when a company goes into liquidation — but the Court can order inspection by creditors and contributories: s. 155 I.A. 1986.

7. Rectification

(a) Section 359 CA 1985 gives the Court power to order rectification of the Register of Members:

(*i*) if a person who has not agreed to take shares is included in the register, e.g. where he has been induced to take shares by misrepresentation; or

(*ii*) if his name is omitted or wrongfully removed from the register, e.g. by reason of an invalid forfeiture or forged transfer; or

(*iii*) if there has been default or unnecessary delay in

recording the fact that a person has ceased to be a member, e.g. the directors may delay unduly the registration of a transfer which they have no power to reject.

(b) Application to the Court for rectification may be made by the person aggrieved, any member of the company, or the company itself, according to the circumstances.

(c) The Court may refuse the application, or order the rectification and payment of damages by the company to the aggrieved party: *Alabaster's Case* (1868).

(d) The section is not exhaustive of the Court's powers of rectification: *Burns* v. *Siemens Bros. Dynamo Works Ltd.* (1918) (*see* 9 *below*).

> NOTE: The register is only *prima facie* evidence of matters which the Act requires to be entered in it, but those who apply for its rectification must bear in mind that the onus of proof lies with the person who contests its accuracy. If, therefore, a person allows his name to remain in the register, he may be held liable as a member.

8. Notices to the Registrar: s. 353(2) CA 1985

(a) If the Register of Members is kept elsewhere than at the company's registered office, notice in the prescribed form (Form G353) must be sent to the Registrar, stating *where* the register is kept. The notice must be given *within 14 days*; thus notice of its location is not required so long as it is kept at the registered office, but if it is removed to another place the Registrar must be notified within 14 days of the change. Any subsequent change of place must also be notified within 14 days of the change (*see also* 18 *below*).

(b) The company and any officer in default are liable to fines for non-compliance with the above requirements: s. 353(4) CA 1985.

9. Joint holders

(a) The joint holder first named in the Register of Members is, according to the Articles of most companies, entitled to receive payment of dividend and to exercise voting rights of the joint holding. As a rule, notices will be sent to him as the 'senior' joint holder.

(b) For that reason, joint holders have the right to determine in which order their names shall be entered in the register.

(c) Alternatively, they are entitled to require the company to split their holding, so that each joint holder becomes the first named in the register for part of the holding: *Burns* v. *Siemens Bros. Dynamo Works Ltd.* (1918).

(d) A limit may be imposed by the Articles as to the number of persons who may be registered in respect of a joint holding.

10. What constitutes membership?

Entry in the Register of Members is only *prima facie* evidence of membership. A person may become a member in the following ways.

(a) By subscribing to the Memorandum of Association. This, according to s. 22(1) CA 1985, is sufficient to indicate agreement to become a member. Neither allotment nor registration is necessary in this case: *Evans' Case* (1867).

(b) In other cases, a person becomes a member by:

(*i*) *agreement* to become a member;

(*ii*) *entry* of his name in the Register of Members: s. 22(2) CA 1985.

> NOTE: A person improperly entered in the register may *constructively* agree to his name remaining there, by exercising the rights of a member; in that case he may be estopped from denying his membership.

11. Notice of trust

(a) Section 360 CA 1985 provides that: 'No notice of any trust, express, implied or constructive, shall be entered on the register, or be receivable by the Registrar, in the case of companies registered in England.'

(b) A person entered in the Register of Members is the person legally entitled to deal with the shares, but some person or persons may possess an equitable or beneficial interest in them, e.g.:

(*i*) the registered member may have borrowed money from a banker, or other person, on the security of the shares; or

(*ii*) he may be merely a nominee of a person or persons entitled to the beneficial interest in the shares, e.g. the nominee of a limited company; or

(*iii*) he may hold them as a trustee, i.e. in trust for another.

(c) However, by virtue of s. 360 CA 1985, the company is unable to take notice of these outside interests, and is entitled to regard the person named in the register as the beneficial owner of the shares in his name, even if he gives notice that some other person has a lien on, or equitable interest in, the shares concerned.

> NOTE: A company is, nevertheless, bound to accept certain documents, such as probate of a will, as sufficient evidence of a legal representative's powers to deal with shares: s. 187 CA 1985.

(d) On receipt of a 'notice of trust', the usual procedure is as follows.

(*i*) Write a letter in reply, stating that the company is unable to recognize the trust or to act upon it in any way. The notice may be returned with this letter, which ought to be sent by registered post or recorded delivery, to the person submitting the notice.

(*ii*) Keep an unofficial record of the contents of the notice, but not in the Register of Members.

> NOTE: Although s. 360 CA 1985 enables the company to treat the registered holder of shares as the beneficial owner, it cannot ignore the notice as regards fixing priorities in respect of a lien: *Bradford Banking Co.* v. *Briggs* (1886). An unofficial note will warn the company that notice of a lien has been received which will, should the occasion arise, have priority over their own lien on the shares concerned.

12. Stop notice

(a) Although, as stated above, a company cannot recognize notice of a trust, under the Charging Orders Act 1979, s. 5, and the Rules of the Supreme Court, Order 50, Rules 11–14, any person claiming to be beneficially interested in shares of a company who wishes to be notified of any proposed transfer of those shares may serve a stop notice on the company.

(b) To obtain such the person concerned must file with the Central Office of the Supreme Court (or a district registry) an affidavit identifying the shares in question and describing his interest in them, together with the notice being served. The copy of the notice served on the company must be sealed with the seal of the Central Office (or district registry) and must be accompanied by an office copy of the affidavit.

(c) On receipt of such notice, the company is restrained from accepting any transfer of the shares included in the notice for a period of 14 days after giving notice of lodgment of the transfer to the person indicated in the notice as having an interest in the shares.

(d) During the 14-day period, the interested party must take whatever steps are necessary to prevent the company from accepting a transfer of the shares.

(e) If, after 14 days, no further instructions have been received by the company, it can then proceed to register the transfer of the shares affected.

13. Designated accounts

(a) The increasing amount of work done in recent years by banks and insurance companies as executors and trustees has resulted in a corresponding increase in the number of requests which company registrars receive to open 'designated accounts', e.g. a banking company acting as trustees for many persons may ask to have several accounts opened in its name, so that the separate holdings of its clients can be easily distinguished by letter or number.

(b) Some companies refuse to permit designation of accounts, as they consider that in acting upon such instructions they would be taking notice of a trust, contrary to the requirements of s. 360 CA 1985.

(c) It appears to have been unofficially established that the designation or 'earmarking' of accounts does not of itself constitute notice of a trust. Nevertheless, it has been suggested that companies acting upon instructions to designate accounts might protect themselves by:

(*i*) reserving the right to treat all the designated accounts as one account if at any time they should think fit to do so; and

(*ii*) making it clear to the sender of the notice that they are *not* recognizing a trust.

(d) Despite such precautions, the method used to designate accounts in the Register of Members also requires careful consideration.

(e) The Continuing Obligations of the Stock Exchange require listed companies to permit members to have designated accounts.

Overseas Branch Register

14. What companies may keep an Overseas Branch Register?

Section 362 CA 1985 permits the keeping of an Overseas Branch Register by any company:

(a) having a share capital; and

(b) whose objects authorize the transaction of business in any of the countries or territories specified in Part 1 of Schedule 14 CA 1985.

It should be noted that the Act does *not* compel a company to keep an Overseas Branch Register.

15. Provisions

If an Overseas Branch Register is kept, it is subject to the regulations set out in Part 2 of Schedule 14.

This provides, *inter alia,* that:

(a) A company keeping such a register shall give to the Registrar of Companies notice in the prescribed form (Form G362) of the situation of the office where it is kept and of any change in its situation, and, if it is discontinued, of its discontinuance. Such notice must be given within 14 days of the event concerned.

(b) Such a register is deemed to be part of the company's register of members — the latter being known in this context as the principal register.

(c) Essentially the Overseas Branch Register is to be kept in the same manner as the principal register.

(d) A copy of every entry in the register must be sent as soon as possible to the company's registered office for entry in the principal register. A duplicate of the Overseas Branch Register has to be kept along with the principal register.
(e) Shares in the register must be distinguished from those registered in the principal register. Transactions in relation to shares so registered must be recorded in the Overseas Branch Register.
(f) If the Overseas Branch Register is discontinued the entries in that register must be transferred to some other Overseas Branch Register kept by the company in the same country or territory, or to the principal register.

Subject to the above, a company may, by its articles, make such provisions as it thinks fit respecting the keeping of Overseas Branch Registers.

16. The advantages of opening an Overseas Branch Register

(a) Shareholders resident in the country or territory concerned are able to register transfers locally, and thus avoid much of the delay involved if transfers had to sent to the company's registered office in the United Kingdom.
(b) Dividends may also be paid from the overseas branch office, and earlier payment is ensured.
(c) The above factors make the shares more attractive — at least to shareholders in the country or territory concerned — and that is an advantage to the company itself, particularly when it requires more capital.

17. Transfer of shares to an Overseas Branch Register

When a shareholder who is already entered in the principal register wishes to transfer his holding to the company's Overseas Branch Register, the usual procedure is as follows.

(a) A request in writing is usually required by the Articles. This should be lodged at the company's registered office, together with his share certificate(s).
(b) The share certificate(s) are cancelled and carefully filed; a note to this effect is made in the principal register.
(c) A Branch Removal Receipt is then sent to the shareholder

by way of receipt for the certificate(s) he has lodged with the company.
(d) The shareholder will receive a Branch Share Certificate on producing his removal receipt at the branch office in the country or territory.

> NOTE: The share certificate he receives will probably be of distinctive design and (if the Articles permit) may bear the company's official seal. As already indicated, the shares must, in any case, be distinguished from those registered in the principal register.

(e) The necessary entry is made in the Overseas Branch Register from particulars on the removal receipt.
(f) Notice of entry is recorded on a Transmission Sheet containing particulars of all transfers to the Overseas Branch Register over, say, one month. At the end of the month the Transmission Sheet will be sent to the registered office and the transfer particulars recorded in the duplicate register.

The Annual Return

18. Duty to deliver Annual Returns: s. 363 CA 1985

(a) Every company must deliver to the Registrar successive annual returns each of which is made up to a date not later than the date which is from time to time the company's 'return date', i.e.

(*i*) the anniversary of the company's incorporation, or
(*ii*) if the company's last return delivered in accordance with the provisions of the Act was made up to a different date, the anniversary of that date.

(b) Each return must:

(*i*) be in the prescribed form;
(*ii*) contain the information required by or under the Act; and
(*iii*) be signed by a director or the secretary of the company;

and it must be delivered to the Registrar within 28 days after the date to which it is made up.

(c) Failure to deliver an annual return as required by the Act renders the company liable to a fine. Every director or secretary of the company is similarly liable unless he can show that he took all reasonable steps to avoid the commission or continuation of the offence.

19. Contents of Annual Return (general): s. 364 CA 1985

Every annual return must state the date to which it is made up and must contain the following information:

(*i*) the address of the company's registered office;

(*ii*) the type of company it is and its principal business activities;

(*iii*) the name and address of the company secretary;

(*iv*) the name and address of every director of the company;

(*v*) in the case of each individual director —

(1) his nationality, date of birth and business occupation, and

(2) such particulars of other directorships and former names as are required to be contained in the company's Register of Directors;

(*vi*) in the case of any corporate director, such particulars of other directorships as would be required to be contained in that register in the case of an individual;

(*vii*) if the register of members is not kept at the company's registered office, the address of the place where it is kept;

(*viii*) if any register of debenture holders (or a duplicate of any such register or a part of it) is not kept at the company's registered office, the address of the place where it is kept;

(*ix*) if the company has elected —

(1) to dispense under s. 252 CA 1985 with the laying of accounts and reports before the company in general meeting, or

(2) to dispense under s. 366A CA 1985 with the holding of annual general meetings,

a statement to that effect.

20. Contents of Annual Return (particulars of share capital and shareholders): s. 364A CA 1985

(a) The Annual Return of a company having a share capital must contain the following information with respect to its share capital and members:

(*i*) the total number of issued shares of the company at the date to which the return is made up and the aggregate nominal value of those shares;

(*ii*) with respect to each class of shares in the company —

(1) the nature of the class, and

(2) the total number and aggregate nominal value of issued shares of that class at the date to which the return is made up;

(*iii*) a list of the names and addresses of every person who

(1) is a member of the company on the date to which the return is made up, or

(2) has ceased to be a member of the company since the date to which the last return was made up (or, in the case of the first return, since the incorporation of the company);

and if the names are not arranged in alphabetical order the return must have annexed to it an index sufficient to enable the name of any person in the list to be easily found;

(*iv*) the number of shares of each class held by each member of the company as at the date to which the return is made up, and the number of shares of each class transferred since the date to which the last return was made up (or, in the case of the first return, since the incorporation of the company) by each member or person who has ceased to be a member, and the dates of registration of the company.

(b) The return may, if either of the two immediately preceding returns has given the full particulars required by (*iii*) and (*iv*) above, give only such particulars as relate to persons ceasing to be or becoming members since the date of the last return and to shares transferred since that date. Further, they do not require the inclusion of particulars entered in an Overseas Branch Register if copies of those entries have not been received at the company's registered office by the date to which the return is made up. In this latter case, the particulars must be included in the company's next Annual Return after their receipt.

(c) Where the company has converted any of its shares into stock, the return must give the corresponding information in relation to that stock, stating the amount of stock instead of the number or nominal value of shares.

21. Registration fee
The fee payable on registration of an Annual Return is £25.

Progress test 6

1. Enumerate the main requirements of the Act as to the contents of a Register of Members. Is it permissible to use a looseleaf register? If so, what precautions are necessary, and why? **(1,2)**

2. What are the provisions of the Act in regard to the form of the Register of Members? What are the advantages of using a looseleaf register? **(2, 3)**

3. State briefly the Act's requirements concerning **(a)** location of the Register of Members, **(b)** right of inspection and the taking of copies, and **(c)** the company's power to close it. **(4–6)**

4. What practical difficulties might the secretary of a large public company encounter in affording inspection of the Register of Members and providing copies of its contents, in accordance with statutory requirements? **(6)**

5. You have been appointed secretary of a company shortly after incorporation and subsequent to the allotment of 100,000 shares of £1 each. All transactions have been properly carried out and recorded, except that the Register of Members has not been opened. Explain the steps you would take to open the Register and bring the entries up-to-date. **(1–4; 8)**

6. In what different ways can a person become a member of a company, and with what documents is the secretary concerned in each case? **(10)**

7. **The Act states that no notice of any trust shall be entered on the Register of Members. What is the purpose and effect of this statement? As secretary of a company receiving such a notice, what steps would you take, and why? (11)**

8. **Describe the various precautions normally taken in a registrar's office to minimize the risk of a company being affected by notice of a trust. (11–13)**

9. **Draft a report to your board, setting out the advantages to the company and members concerned of opening an Overseas Branch Register, explaining the statutory requirements, and recommending a procedure for satisfying them. (14–17)**

10. **Set out briefly the contents of an annual return. What would you do if the Accounts were not ready by the latest date for holding the annual general meeting?** *ICSA* **(18–21)**

11. **You are the secretary of a company which has issued bearer warrants. The company's Articles of Association permit the holder of a share warrant to have his name entered as a member in the Register of Members upon surrendering the warrant for cancellation. Explain in detail the procedure to be adopted when a holder of bearer shares applies to be registered.** *ICSA* **(7: 10)**

7
Share certificates

Legal effects

1. Definition

A share certificate is a document under the common seal of the company and which, when issued to a member, indicates the extent of his interest in the company's capital.

2. Effect of a certificate

A certificate under the common seal of a company is only *prima facie* evidence of title: s. 186 CA 1985, that is, the holder is *not* given an absolute title to the shares included in the certificate.

Nevertheless, at common law, a company is estopped from denying the validity of a certificate issued under seal both as to the *title* of the holder and as to the *amount paid* on the shares, e.g.:

(a) a company will be liable to any person who, in good faith, suffers loss through relying on the certificate, where the company has denied that he is the registered holder: *Balkis Consolidated Co.* v. *Tomkinson* (1893);
(b) where the company has denied that shares included in a certificate are fully paid: *Bloomenthal* v. *Ford* (1897).

3. Holder's remedies

The holder's remedy in such cases is to sue the company for damages, i.e. for the value of the shares at the date of the breach. He is *not* entitled to the shares, as the true owner cannot be deprived of them; nor can he compel the company to enter his name in the Register of Members.

4. Where estoppel does not operate

The holder's right of estoppel against the company is lost in the following circumstances.

(a) If the certificate upon which the holder relied had been issued fraudulently and without the company's authority: *South London Greyhound Racecourses* v. *Wake* (1931).
(b) Where the certificate issued was a forgery: *Ruben* v. *Great Fingall Consolidated* (1906).
(c) Where it can be shown that the holder knows that the amount stated on the certificate as paid has not in fact been paid.

> NOTE: The right of estoppel is also lost where a person has not relied upon the certificate; if, for example, he had not required the transferor to produce a certificate.

Preparation and issue

5. Preparation

In preparing share certificates, the following matters must be borne in mind as regards their form and contents.

(a) *Form.* The form of the certificate may vary, but approval of the stock exchange must be obtained if the shares are 'listed' (*see* **(f)** *below*).
(b) *Distinguishing types.* Certificates covering different classes of shares are often distinguished by the use of different styles or colours. The form may also vary according to whether the shares are fully or partly paid, the latter usually having space on the back of the certificate in which to record payments of calls.
(c) *Book form or loose?* Certificates printed in book form are still favoured by some companies. When this method is used the certificates are in three parts, comprising the counterfoil (which remains in the book), certificate, and receipt of the certificate. For a small company, this method will probably prove quite

adequate but larger companies — particularly those which are highly mechanized — will probably prefer certificates on loose forms, so that several members of the staff can enter particulars on the certificates simultaneously from the Register of Members or direct from the Allotment Sheets.

(d) *When under seal.* Share certificates must, by implication, be under seal of the company, s. 186 CA 1985 stating that 'a certificate under the common seal of the company is *prima facie* evidence of title'. In the case of listed shares, Stock Exchange regulations expressly provide that share certificates *must* be under seal but a company is permitted to have an official seal for sealing securities issued by the company, and for creating or evidencing securities so issued. This must be a facsimile of the common seal with the addition on its face of the word 'Securities'.

(e) *Contents.* The share certificates of most companies follow a similar pattern, and the following contents are common to most:

(*i*) name of the company;
(*ii*) act under which the company was incorporated;
(*iii*) authorized capital and its division into shares;
(*iv*) class of shares to which the certificate relates;
(*v*) number of shares included in the certificate;
(*vi*) distinctive numbers of shares, unless dispensed with under s. 182(2) CA 1985;
(*vii*) name and address of the holder and a statement that he (or she) holds the shares subject to the company's Memorandum and Articles;
(*viii*) notice to the effect that no transfer of the shares can be registered unless accompanied by the certificate;
(*ix*) signature (as required by the Articles) and seal.

(f) Stock Exchange requirements. In the case of registered securities the definitive document of title must conform to the requirements set out below.

(*i*) The overall size of the certificate should be no larger than 9 inches x 8 inches (22.5 cm x 20 cm).

(*ii*) The following matters must appear on the face of the certificate:

(1) the authority under which the issuer is constituted or the country of incorporation and registered number (if any);

(2) preferably at the top right-hand corner, the

number of shares or amount of stock the certificate represents and if applicable the number and denomination of units;

(3) a footnote stating that no transfer of the security or any portion thereof represented by the certificate can be registered without production of the certificate; and

(4) if applicable, the minimum amount and multiples thereof in which the security is transferable.

(*iii*) Certificates must be dated and (in the absence of statutory authority for issue under signature of appropriate officials) be issued under seal.

(*iv*) Certificates relating to debt securities must state, on the face, the interest payable and the interest payment dates, and include on the back (preferably with reference shown on the face) a statement or summary of the conditions as to redemption or repayment and (where applicable) conversion.

(*v*) If the certificates relate to shares, and there is more than one class in issue, the certificates of the preferential classes must also bear (preferably on the face) a statement of the conditions conferred thereon as to capital and dividends.

(g) *Mechanical signatures on share certificates.* Because of the considerable time involved in autographic signing of share certificates by the directors and secretaries of large companies, many of them use mechanical signatures in place of the autographic signatures of directors; others have dispensed entirely with signatures on share certificates.

(h) In order to facilitate the operation of the TALISMAN settlement system, s. 185(4) CA 1985 provides that a company is exempted from the obligation imposed by s. 185(1) CA 1985 to prepare certificates in consequence of shares, debentures or debenture stock allotted or transferred to a stock nominee.

(i) CA 1989 has introduced provisions for enabling titles to securities to be evidenced and transferred without a written instrument: CA 1989 s. 207. The Secretary of State is empowered to make the appropriate regulations by statutory instrument.

6. Issue of certificates

The preparation and issue of share certificates following a *transfer* of shares is dealt with in 8:**4**, **5** and **6.** At this stage it is intended to deal with matters affecting the issue of certificates by a company following the usual application and allotment procedure already described in 3:1–15.

(a) *The first certificate* is usually given free of charge to every member whose name is entered in the Register of Members. Table A entitles a member to one free certificate for *all* his shares, with the proviso that if he requires more than one, each certificate after the first will cost him such reasonable sum as the directors may so determine: Article 6.

(b) *Time limit for delivery.* It should be borne in mind that certificates must be ready for delivery:

(*i*) *within two months* after the shares have been allotted, unless the conditions of issue otherwise provide: s. 185 CA 1985; or

(*ii*) *within one month* after the expiration of the renunciation period, in the case of certificates covering shares which are listed on the Stock Exchange.

NOTE: For non-compliance with s. 185 CA 1985, the Court may, on application of the person entitled to the certificate, direct the company and any officer of the company to make good the default within a specified time. It may also order that the costs of the application be borne by the company and any officer responsible.

(c) *After the expiration of the renunciation period,* and assuming that allotment letters and bankers' receipts for the allotment money have been received either from the original allottees or their accepting nominees, the Register of Members is written up and, unless the conditions provide to the contrary (e.g. if further calls or instalments are to be paid on the shares, certificates may not be issued until the shares are fully paid) share certificates are prepared.

(d) *Checking the certificates.* After preparation of the certificates, they should be thoroughly checked by the company's auditors, or, if possible, by responsible officials of the company who have played no part in preparing the certificates.

NOTE: As the company is estopped from denying that the person named in a share certificate is the legal owner of the shares to which it refers, and as to the amount paid up on them, great care must be exercised in preparing all share certificates.

(e) *Authorization by the board.* At a board meeting especially convened for the purpose, the share certificates (perhaps supported by a report in which the auditors vouch for the accuracy of the documents) are submitted to the board by the secretary. The board then authorize the signing and sealing of the certificates in the words of a resolution such as the following:

> RESOLVED: THAT share certificates, numbered ...... to ...... both inclusive, in respect of ...... ordinary shares of £1 each, allotted by resolution of the Board dated ...... be sealed under the common seal of the Company and signed by .... and .... and counter-signed by the Secretary.

> NOTE: The wording of the resolution must, of course, depend upon the degree of relaxation permitted by the Stock Exchange (in the case of listed shares) as regards directors' and secretary's signatures.

(f) *Recording the resolution.* After the certificates have been signed and sealed, the resolution is recorded in the minute book of board meetings, and an entry made in the Register of Sealed Documents.

(g) *Final steps.* The certificates can now be prepared for posting and a final check made by a responsible official before posting. When they are posted, it is advisable to send them by registered post or recorded delivery.

> NOTE: In some cases, the company advises the shareholders when certificates are ready, stating that the documents may be collected at the company's registered office in exchange for the allotment letter and receipt for the allotment money.
>
> Another alternative is to write to the shareholders, informing them that their certificates will be posted to them on receipt of their written requests to do so. In that way the company puts the onus upon the shareholder in the event of his certificate going astray after posting.

(h) *Receipts.* Whichever method is used, i.e. whether the certificates are sent through the post or collected by the shareholders, a receipt for the certificate should be asked for, and this should bear the usual signature of the shareholder. In this way the company ensures that it has a specimen of each shareholder's signature.

7. Lost certificates

(a) A duplicate share certificate must not be issued without taking adequate precautions. Companies frequently receive requests for replacement of certificates which have been lost, destroyed or mislaid; therefore, the Articles usually give the directors the necessary power to protect the company against any loss it may incur by reason of its issuing a replacement certificate.

(*i*) The company may require the shareholder to make a *statutory declaration* that he has lost the certificate and the circumstances of the loss.

(*ii*) *A letter of indemnity* may be demanded from the shareholder in which he undertakes to compensate the company for any loss it may suffer as the result of the issue of a duplicate certificate.

(*iii*) *A guarantee* given by a bank or person of sound financial standing may be accepted by the directors as an alternative, or in addition to, a letter of indemnity.

NOTE: Table A permits the directors to require evidence, indemnity and the payment of the company's out-of-pocket expenses: Article 7.

(b) A further precaution that may be taken before issuing a replacement certificate is to examine the Register of Members and ensure that no 'stop notice' has been received in respect of the shares concerned. It has been known for a shareholder to deposit the original share certificate by way of security for a loan, and then to make a fraudulent attempt to obtain a duplicate.

(c) If a duplicate certificate is issued, it should be marked conspicuously with the word DUPLICATE across the face of the certificate, preferably in a distinctive colour or spelt out by perforation.

(d) Note of the loss and issue of a duplicate certificate should then be made against the shareholder's name in the Register of Members. If the member himself, or some unauthorized person, presents the original certificate at some later date, the entry in the Register will draw attention to the loss. In that event, an explanation would be demanded and transfer of the shares permitted only on production of the duplicate certificate.

(e) A charge is usually made for a duplicate certificate. As already stated in this chapter, Table A permits a reasonable charge to be made for renewal of a certificate. Stock Exchange regulations do not permit a charge to be made in such circumstances.

8. Damaged, worn or mutilated certificates

In cases where a certificate has been damaged, badly worn or mutilated, any request for replacement must be accompanied by the original certificate, if possible; if it is not produced when the original request is made, the shareholder must be asked to surrender it, after which the necessary procedure may be followed.

(a) If the certificate is badly damaged or mutilated, it must be thoroughly examined and identified. If it is not identifiable as a share certificate, or if there is any doubt, it may be decided to treat it as though it were a 'lost' certificate and to require a letter of indemnity from the shareholder.

(b) In any case, when a duplicate certificate has been prepared, the original must be clearly marked CANCELLED across its face, and carefully filed.

> NOTE: If the mutilated condition of the 'document' will not permit this treatment, the only alternative is to place what remains of the document in a suitable envelope and (having stated on the outside of the envelope what it contains) keep it in a safe place pending any later developments.

(c) The issue of the duplicate certificate must then be recorded in the Register of Members, and the duplicate sent to the member on receipt of evidence (where necessary), letter of indemnity and/or letter of guarantee, and any charge for the replacement certificate permitted by the Articles.

Share warrants

9. Authority to issue share warrants etc.

(a) A company limited by shares may, if so authorized by its Articles, issue with respect to any fully paid shares a warrant (a 'share warrant') stating that the bearer of the warrant is entitled to the shares specified therein: s. 188(1) CA 1985.

(b) A share warrant issued under the company's common seal entitles the bearer to the shares specified in it; and the shares may be transferred by delivery of the warrant: s. 188(2) CA 1985. A share warrant is a form of negotiable instrument and, accordingly, anyone who takes it in good faith and for value acquires a good title to it, even if he received it from someone who had no title to it.

(c) Stock Exchange requirements. In the case of bearer securities the definitive document of title must conform to the requirements set out below

(*i*) Proofs of securities and coupons must be submitted to the Department for approval at as early a date as possible, preferably in 'sketch' form. It is advisable for proofs to be submitted at least three to four weeks prior to the hearing of the application for listing being considered by the Committee.

(*ii*) The printing of bearer securities must be entrusted to recognized security printers; it is preferable that the same printer should be employed on behalf of a particular company, or borrowing organization, for all its bearer securities.

(*iii*) The paper for securities and coupons must be first-class bond or banknote paper containing a watermark of the printer, borrowing organization or issuer. Accurate records must be kept regarding manufacture and consumption of security paper. The watermark should be repeated at staggered intervals of not more than 8 inches.

(*iv*) The overall size of the security (excluding sheets of coupons) should, if possible, be 9 inches x 8 inches (22.5 cm x 20 cm), but no more than 11¾ inches x 8¼ inches (29.7 cm x 21 cm).

(*v*) The serial number of the security must appear in the top right-hand corner of each security, on the talon and on each coupon and should be printed from a unique typeface and by indestructible ink.

(*vi*) The coupon sheets must be attached to the right-hand side or foot of the security and each coupon must bear the serial number of the security and be numbered consecutively. If a talon or renewal coupon is used it must be so placed as to be the last coupon to be removed. The margin between the coupons must be sufficiently wide to ensure that the text of any coupon is not damaged when coupons are detached.

(*vii*) Securities must have at least one printing by direct engraved steel plate which must include the border. The plates must be produced by the security printer by mechanical or electrolytic means from original steel engravings and must remain in the responsible custody of the security printer. The impression must be perfect, giving uniform sharpness, no interrupted or broken lines and no choking or widening at points of intersection. Background colours must be chosen which cannot easily be distinguished by photographic means.

(*viii*) If the name of the security printer appears it must be placed outside the border at the foot of the security and of each coupon.

(*ix*) The following matters must appear on the face of the security:

(1) the authority under which the issuer is constituted and the country of incorporation and registered number (if any):

(2) the authority under which the security is issued; and

(3) the dates when fixed interest or dividend is due.

In all cases the securities must bear an authenticating signature or signatures which may be in facsimile where permissible. Share warrants to bearer issued by United Kingdom company must be under seal.

(*x*) The following matters must appear on the face or back of the security:

(1) in the case of a debt security, all conditions of issue as to redemption, conversion, meetings and voting rights; and

(2) in the case of shares with preferential rights, a

statement of the conditions conferred thereon as to capital (including redemption), dividends, meetings and voting rights.

(*xi*) A declaration may be required from the security printers that:

(1) the security is being produced in accordance with the requirements of the Committee as set out here;

(2) records will be kept of the production and consumption of the security paper;

(3) the steel engraved plates have been produced by the security printers on their premises and since production they have remained and will remain under their control and will not be used on the securities of any other company or borrowing organization; and

(4) at the request of the issuer all plates used in the preparation of the securities will be destroyed and satisfactory proof of destruction will be produced to the issuer.

10. Issue procedure

(a) If the Articles do not authorize the issue of share warrants, they must be altered by special resolution to give the necessary authority. (It is, of course, being assumed that the company concerned is one permitted to issue share warrants under s. 188 CA 1985 and that the shares to be included are fully paid.)

(b) Printed application forms are made available to all shareholders affected, on which they are entitled to apply for share warrant(s) in exchange for share certificate(s).

(c) On receipt of application forms:

(*i*) ensure that they are fully completed;

(*ii*) see that they are accompanied by the share certificate(s) and a remittance to cover stamp duty plus any small fee charged by the company;

(*iii*) check the particulars against the Register of Members;

(*iv*) issue a carefully worded receipt to the applicant, signifying that the receipt must be produced on or after a specified date in exchange for the 'document(s)' for which he has applied — without specifying the nature of the documents.

(d) Having arranged for the printing of share warrants in fixed denominations of (say) 1, 5, 10, 25, etc.:

(*i*) complete the required warrants, i.e. other than signing and sealing;

(*ii*) cancel the relative share certificate(s);

(*iii*) strike the member's name out of the Register of Members and enter the following particulars:

(1) a statement that the warrant has been issued;

(2) the date of the issue;

(3) particulars of shares included in the warrant, with distinguishing numbers (if any), as required by s. 355 CA 1985;

(*iv*) record the exchange of share warrants for share certificates in a separate register kept for that purpose;

(*v*) write up the Share Warrants Register (or Registers). A separate book, or part of the Register, is usually kept for *each* denomination of share warrant, so that a separate record can be kept of stock and issues of all warrants for (say) five shares; another for ten-share warrants, and so on.

> NOTE: Obviously, great care must be taken in the preparation and issue of the warrants, as they are negotiable instruments; for example, the printers may be required to certify that they have printed only the exact number ordered, and all unused forms ought to be securely locked away and issued only by a responsible official (*see* **9** *above*).

(e) A thorough check of the warrants can now be made and the particulars on the warrants reconciled with entries in the registers already mentioned. If this work is done by the company's own registration department staff, it must obviously be done by persons who had no part in preparing the warrants. In most cases, however, the checking of warrants is done by the company's internal audit staff or by the transfer auditors, in which event they will prepare an audit certificate if they find everything in order.

(f) At a meeting of the board the completed warrants are produced, supported (where applicable) by the audit certificate, and a resolution passed, authorizing the signing, sealing and issue of the share warrants.

(g) The warrants are signed and sealed, and appropriate entries made in the minute book of board meetings and in the Register of Documents Sealed.

(h) Finally, the share warrants are issued in exchange for the appropriate receipts. It must, however, be borne in mind that in the case of a listed company the warrants ought to be ready for issue within 14 days of deposit of the share certificates in order to comply with Stock Exchange requirements.

11. The effects of issuing share warrants

(a) Unless the Articles so provide, the holder of a share warrant is no longer a member of the company, as his name does not appear in the Register of Members: s. 355(5) CA 1985.
(b) In most cases the Articles, supported by the conditions of issue, give him most, if not all, the normal rights of a member; for example:

(*i*) on deposit of his share warrant at the registered office of the company, he may be entitled:

(1) to sign a requisition for calling a meeting or give notice of intention to submit a resolution to the meeting; or

(2) to attend and vote in person or by proxy, and to exercise any other privilege of a member at a meeting;

(*ii*) on delivering up a 'coupon' (detachable from the warrant by perforation) bearing the appropriate serial number, in accordance with instructions published in one or more specified newspapers, he will be entitled to receive the dividend payable on the shares specified in his share warrant:

> NOTE: An additional coupon, usually referred to as a 'talon', can be detached from the warrant and exchanged for a new set of coupons for dividend as and when required.

(*iii*) on surrendering his share warrant to the company for cancellation, to have his name entered as a member in the Register of Members;

> NOTE: He has a statutory right to do this, subject to the Articles: s. 355(2) CA 1985.

(*iv*) on application, he may be able to arrange for the company to furnish him with a copy of the annual reports and accounts at a specified address.
(c) The holding of a share warrant is not sufficient qualification to allow the holder to act as a director, where a share qualification is required by the Articles: s. 291(2) CA 1985.

12. Lost share warrants

(a) The Articles and/or conditions of issue of the warrants usually authorize the directors to issue a new warrant to replace one which has been lost or destroyed, if satisfactory evidence and adequate indemnity are provided.

(b) Some or all of the following precautions are usually taken to safeguard the company:

(*i*) to insist that the applicant advertises his loss and offers a reward;

(*ii*) to demand proof of loss or destruction (this is, in fact, a Stock Exchange requirement);

(*iii*) to require a statutory declaration from the applicant as to the circumstances of the loss (or evidence of destruction) and as to his title to the shares included in the warrant;

(*iv*) to demand a substantial guarantee and/or letter of indemnity.

(c) If a share warrant or dividend coupon is destroyed or defaced, the directors must insist upon surrender of the document for cancellation.

(d) The applicant must pay any fee which the company charges for a replacement.

13. Surrender of share warrants for share certificates

The procedure is as follows:

(a) On receipt of the prescribed form of request for reconversion together with the share warrant and registration fee:

(*i*) issue a transfer receipt to the applicant;

(*ii*) check particulars of the documents against the Register of Share Warrants;

(*iii*) record the exchange of share certificates for share warrants in a separate register kept for that purpose;

(*iv*) write up the Register of Share Warrants, noting the fact that the warrants have been surrendered;

(*v*) cancel the share warrant(s) surrendered and file them;

(*vi*) prepare the new share certificate in favour of the applicant. Check thoroughly.

(b) At a meeting of the board (or transfer committee), the share certificates are produced, supported (where applicable) by an audit certificate, and a resolution passed, authorizing the signing, sealing and issue of the share certificates.

NOTE: The board or transfer committee will deal with the certificates as for ordinary transfer procedure.

(c) The share certificates are signed and sealed, and appropriate entries made in the minute book of board meetings, and in the Register of Documents Sealed.
(d) The Register of Members is amended to restore the applicant's name.
(e) Finally, the share certificate(s) are issued in return for the transfer receipt.

Progress test 7

1. Define a share certificate. Explain its functions, and mention any statutory provisions affecting it. **(1, 2)**

2. Discuss the legal effect of a share certificate and explain the doctrine of estoppel in relation to that document. In what circumstances might the right of estoppel be lost? **(2–4)**

3. What are the usual contents of a share certificate? To what extent might the transferability of the shares be affected by the contents of the certificate? **(5)**

4. The Stock Exchange regulations permit the use of mechanical signatures on share certificates as an alternative to the autographic signatures of directors. Under what conditions is the alternative form of signature permitted? Draft a specimen article authorizing the use of mechanical signatures. **(5)**

5. What particulars must be given on documents of title of a company with Stock Exchange listing? *ICSA* **(5)**

6. Describe the preparation and issue of a share certificate. **(5, 6)**

7. Suggest a procedure to be adopted for dealing with requests

from shareholders for the replacement of lost or damaged share certificates. (7, 8)

8. What are the principal features of a share warrant? In what circumstances, and by what authority, is a company permitted to issue share warrants? (9, 10)

9. Enumerate the advantages and disadvantages of a share warrant. What are the respective purposes of (*a*) a 'coupon' and (*b*) a 'talon', when used in connection with a share warrant? (10, 12)

10. Describe fully the methods by which a person may become a member of a company. Is the holder of a share warrant to bearer a member of the company which has issued it? Give reasons for your answer. (6: **10**; 7: **12**)

11. Write full notes on (*a*) placing of shares, and (*b*) share warrants. *ICSA* (2: **4**, 7: **9–13**)

12. As the registrar of a listed company, you receive a letter from a broker informing you that unfortunately he inserted the name and address of Ocean Nominees Ltd as the transferee on the transfer form, whereas the shares should have been registered in the name and address of Oriental Nominees Ltd. He has received the relevant share certificate for 20,000 Ordinary Shares but in the incorrect name, i.e. Ocean Nominees Ltd. The broker seeks your advice as to how this matter can be corrected. Draft a reply setting out in detail the procedure to be followed. *ICSA* (7)

8

Transfer and transmission of shares

Transfer of shares

1. Form of transfer

(a) Section 182 CA 1985 provides that shares (or any other interest of any member in a company) are personal estate, as distinct from real estate, and transferable in manner provided by the Articles though subject to the Stock Transfer Act 1963.

(b) The Stock Transfer Act 1963 made radical changes in the form and contents of a transfer instrument and over-rides any special provisions contained in the Articles governing the form in which securities subject to the Act are to be transferred, including *(inter alia) fully paid up* registered securities issued 'by any company within the meaning of the Companies Act 1985, except a company limited by guarantee or an unlimited company': s. 1(4), Stock Transfer Act 1963.

(c) It is unlawful to register a transfer of shares (or debentures) unless a proper instrument of transfer is delivered to the company, or the transfer is an exempt transfer within the Stock Transfer Act 1982: *Re Greene* (1949).

(d) Section 6 of the Stock Exchange (Completion of Bargains) Act 1976 extended the powers of the Treasury under s. 3 of the Stock Transfer Act 1963, prescribing alternative stock transfer forms, and thus enabling the Treasury to prescribe transfer forms to meet the requirements of the Stock Exchange TALISMAN settlement system. The 'TALISMAN sold transfer', as it is designated, is based on the usual stock transfer form though in a more computer-orientated format, with the name of the designated Stock Exchange nominee, SEPON Ltd, preprinted as the transferee.

2. Right of transfer

(a) Shareholders have a *prima facie* right to transfer their shares to whomsoever they please, even to a pauper: *De Pass's Case* (1859). But the company's regulations may give the directors the power to restrict a member's right of transfer.
(b) In the case of private companies, the Articles often set out restrictions on the transfer of shares. These generally take the form of pre-emption provisions on transfer, whereby any shareholder wishing to dispose of his shares is initially obliged to offer such shares to existing shareholders for purchase in the same proportions as their current holdings. Only if the shares are not purchased by the members, may they be offered to a third party.
(c) Notice of refusal to register a transfer must be given to the transferee within two months after lodgment of the transfer: s. 183 CA 1985. In the case of listed companies, the Continuing Obligations of the Stock Exchange require share certificates to be issued without charge within 14 days of the lodgment of transfers.
(d) Table A provides that the directors may decline to register a transfer of *partly paid* shares to a person of whom they do not approve. They also have power to decline registration of a transfer of shares on which the company has a lien: Article 24.
(e) In the case of listed shares, i.e. where Stock Exchange regulations apply, the power of refusal to register a transfer must be restricted to *partly paid* shares.
(f) The power of refusal to register a transfer must be exercised by the directors in the interests of the company. Any abuse of this power may justify rectification of the register by the Court, e.g. on proof of bad faith on the part of the directors: *Smith* v. *Fawcett Ltd.* (1942).
(g) The directors' refusal to register a transfer does not affect the contract between transferor and transferee, unless there was agreement between them to that effect. The transferor remains as registered holder of the shares, and will hold them 'in trust' for the transferee.

(h) Power of refusal in the Articles does not extend to letters of renunciation, nor does it apply to letters of request submitted by executors and administrators. These are not 'transfers' within the meaning of the Act; if, therefore, the power of refusal is to be extended to them, there must be special provision to that effect in the company's Articles.

3. Transfer procedure

Although the secretary (or his registrar) is not concerned with transfers of his company's shares until the transfer forms are actually received in the registration department, it might be well to give a brief outline of the procedure which has already taken place on the Stock Exchange and in the brokers' office.

(a) A shareholder wishing to sell instructs a broker — a member of the stock exchange concerned — to get a quotation for his shares, or he may give instructions to sell them so long as he can obtain a specified minimum price.
(b) The broker then acts as 'middleman' between his client and a market-maker who specializes in a particular 'market', such as oil shares or industrial shares. Both broker and market-maker may be members of the same firm.
(c) Having obtained a quotation from the market-maker which appears to be a fair one (and not less than the minimum price which his client may have specified), the broker will either sell or report back to his client for further instructions.
(d) The deal between market-maker and broker having been completed, each makes a brief note of the transaction in his notebook. However, as Stock Exchange transactions are settled at fortnightly intervals — on 'account days' — the shares in the transaction just described may be bought and sold several times between the date of the original purchase and the next account day.
(e) All of these intermediate transactions are processed within the clearing department of the Stock Exchange, using the TALISMAN settlement system which came into operation in 1979, and, finally, the seller's broker is advised of the name and address of the last purchaser.
(f) The seller's broker is then in a position to prepare a form of transfer, ready for his client's signature, if required.

NOTE: The form of transfer required to be completed at this stage is referred to in the Stock Transfer Act 1963, as a *Stock Transfer Form,* although a subsidiary form (a Broker's Transfer Form) may also be required (*see* 7).

(g) After the seller (who will now be referred to as the transferor) has signed the Stock Transfer Form, his broker places his own stamp and date on the form (in a 'box' beside the transferor's signature) and then has it stamped by the Inland Revenue for the appropriate transfer duty.

(h) The Stock Transfer Form, together with the relevant share certificate, is now passed to the purchaser's broker.

NOTE: It is being assumed that the *whole* of the shares included in the certificate are being transferred to a *single* buyer, otherwise a more complicated procedure becomes necessary.

(i) The purchaser's (transferee's) broker places his stamp on the Stock Transfer Form in the place provided and sends the form, now fully completed, together with the share certificate, to the company for registration.

NOTE: It will be noted that the Stock Transfer Act 1963 has removed the need for the transferee's signature on the transfer instrument, i.e. in those cases to which the Act applies.

4. The TALISMAN settlement system

(a) In the mid-1970s the Stock Exchange decided to introduce a computerized settlement system to replace the then-existing ticket system. The new system, termed by the abbreviation TALISMAN, provides for all market transactions in the securities of companies to be executed through the agency of a Stock Exchange 'pool' account. Towards this end a nominee company, Stock Exchange Pool Nominees (SEPON Ltd) was established and an account opened in its name in the register of members and debenture-holders of every company with listed securities.

(b) To facilitate the introduction of the system the Stock Exchange (Completion of Bargains) Act 1976 was passed. It provided that a company need not prepare share or stock certificates in respect of securities allotted or transferred to the Stock Exchange nominee, SEPON Ltd; that a company should have an official seal for use in sealing share or stock certificates; that a company's registers and records could be kept on a computer; and that s. 6 of the Stock Transfer Act 1963 be amended to facilitate the operation of the TALISMAN system.

(c) The TALISMAN system does not, as yet, extend to all Stock Exchange transactions and thus the documentation introduced by the Stock Transfer Act 1963 (the Stock Transfer Form and the Broker's Transfer Form) is still in use, though to a much reduced extent, and the procedure outlined in **3** above is still applicable where the TALISMAN system is not operative. The Stock Transfer Form can, in any case, be used generally for non-listed shares and/or debentures.

(d) A market transaction carried out utilizing the TALISMAN system involves the following.

(*i*) The selling broker concerned and the market-maker involved both report the bargain struck to the Stock Exchange Settlement Centre (SESC) which records and keeps accounts of acquisitions and disposals of securities on behalf of market-makers and brokers.

(*ii*) The SESC will then forward a sale docket to the selling broker.

(*iii*) The selling broker forwards to SESC the certificate relating to the securities involved accompanied by a TALISMAN sold transfer form signed by the seller and made out in favour of SEPON Ltd.

(*iv*) SEPON Ltd, which acts as a depository of securities throughout the settlement period, submits through SESC both documents to the company whose securities are involved.

(*v*) The company will effect a transfer of the holding concerned into the name of SEPON Ltd. There is no need for a share certificate to be made out in favour of SEPON Ltd; and in order that the interposition of transfers paid into and out of the nominee account does not result in double stamp duty being paid, such transfers are exempt from stamp duty.

(*vi*) On account day SESC effects delivery to buyers by debiting the account of sellers and crediting the accounts of the buyers before the commencement of business on account day.

Sellers and buyers are informed what is due to and from them and settlement is made later on account day.

(*vii*) Once credited to his account the market manager is able to deliver them by having his account debited and that of the buyer credited.

(*viii*) The buyer's broker communicates the relevant information concerning a purchase of an amount of shares to SESC.

(*ix*) SESC acting on behalf of SEPON Ltd prepares a TALISMAN Bought Transfer Form and submits it to the company involved.

(*x*) The company will effect a transfer of the shares concerned from SEPON Ltd's account to the buyer and prepare a new share certificate in the buyer's name.

(*xi*) The company will forward the new share certificate to SESC and the latter will pass it on to the buyer's broker.

(*xii*) On account day, the buyer's broker will conclude the transaction by payment of the agreed price for the shares to SESC.

5. Dematerialization (TAURUS)

(a) In November 1988 the Department of Trade and Industry published a consultative paper on the dematerialization of share certificates and share transfers. The stated intention was to make provision so that when both parties to the transfer wish, and the company has agreed, to its shares being transferable in this way:

(*i*) shares held on a recognized computer system may be transferred from one person to another without the need for transfer forms or certificates;

(*ii*) companies should be required not to issue certificates to any shareholder who has chosen to make use of the new arrangements; and

(*iii*) any person shall be free to convert a holding from one system to the other.

The proposals would not alter the legal status of the register of members, nor affect the relationship between the shareholder and the company.

(b) The legal implications of the TAURUS system were also considered in a report of the Securities Industry Steering Committee on TAURUS published in April 1989. It was concluded that the primary legislation was the preferred method of implementation. The basic proposals include an effective 'look through' under which a Central Nominee would be entered on a company register in place of the names of the underlying owners, but that Central Nominee would not possess membership rights and would hold no certificate. It is regarded as vital that companies should both make shareholder information available, and have access to particulars of all underlying investors and their holdings, unless these are held in a conventional nominee.

(c) The framework of the new regime is set out in s. 207 of the Companies Act 1989, subject to regulations to be made by the Secretary of State enabling title to securities to be evidenced and transferred (including a transfer by way of security) without a written instrument.

Apart from procedural matters, the regulations may include provision for the following:

(*i*) safeguards for the protection of investors and for ensuring that competition is not restricted, distorted or prevented;

(*ii*) the preservation of existing rights and obligations of persons in relation to securities so dealt in;

(*iii*) transmission of securities by operation of law;

(*iv*) restrictions on transfer, for example under a court order or agreement; and

(*v*) payment of fees and delegation of the functions of the Secretary of State.

Provisions enabling consequential stamp duty changes to be made were enacted in the Finance Acts 1989 and 1990.

6. Duties of secretary

(a) *Check validity of transfer.* The first duty of the Secretary (or registrar) on receiving transfer form and share certificate at the company's registered office is to check them as regards form of transfer etc. as follows.

(*i*) *Form of transfer.* Ensure that the form of transfer is in accordance with that prescribed for the occasion in the Stock Transfer Act 1963.

(*ii*) *Transferor's name*. Check the name given in the transfer instrument with that on the share certificate and in the Register of Members. Any discrepancy must be referred back to the transferor or his broker.

NOTE: The transferor's address is not essential. If it is not stated, the address shown against his name in the register can be used. If, however, an address is given which *differs* from that in the register, the matter should be investigated.

(*iii*) *Transferor's signature*. Compare the signature of the transferor on the transfer form with his name as stated in the body of the form (e.g. the addition or omission of an initial) and with his specimen signature, if available.

NOTE: Where the transferor is a corporate body having a common seal, execution under seal is necessary.

(*iv*) *Transferee's name and address* should be clearly stated. This must not be left blank.

NOTE: As already stated, the transferee's signature is no longer required on a transfer to which the 1963 Act applies.

(*v*) *Particulars of the shares transferred*, i.e. number, distinctive numbers (if any) and class, as stated in the transfer form, must be checked with those stated in the Register of Members and on the share certificate.

(*vi*) *Transfer fee*. Ascertain that the appropriate transfer fee (if specified in the Articles) has been received.

(*vii*) *Stamps*. The stamps of both transferor's and transferee's brokers should be looked for, in the case of a Stock Exchange transaction. In non-market transactions, the stamp of an agent or other person acting for transferor and transferee, respectively, will replace the brokers' stamps.

(*viii*) *Check the Register of Members* to ensure that there is no legal impediment to the transfer, such as a stop notice.

(*ix*) *Partly paid shares*. If the transfer form relates to partly paid shares, it might be considered advisable to make enquiry concerning the transferee, to prevent the shares passing (for example) to an infant who might be able to repudiate liability either before or within a reasonable time of his coming of age.

(b) *Endorse the transfer form by rubber stamp* or small adhesive label, with a list of the various stages of the registration procedure. As each stage of the procedure is completed, an appropriate entry is made in the space provided on the panel and, in some cases, the person who carried out the work initials the entry and records the date. A specimen panel is shown below:

TRANSFER No.	RECEIPT TO TRANSFEREE
DATE RECEIVED	CHECK
OLD CERT. No.	SELLER'S FOL.
NEW CERT. No.	BUYER'S FOL.

NOTE: Although the transfer register is not a statutory book, some companies use it for the purpose of recording the above particulars.

(c) *Transfer advice.* A transfer advice may be sent to the transferor, in a 'plain, opaque envelope'. This advises him of the lodgment of the transfer and states that, if the company receives no intimation to the contrary by return of post, it will be assumed that the transfer is in order and that the registration of the transfer can be proceeded with.

NOTE: As most companies insure against forged transfers, the practice of sending these advices is becoming comparatively rare. In any case, it has been held that if the transferor fails to reply, he is *not* thereby prevented from denying the validity of the transfer: *Barton* v. *L.N.W. Rly. Co.* (1889).

(d) *Transfer receipt.* As the transfer form and contents appear to be in order, a transfer receipt is prepared and issued to the transferee or his broker. This acknowledges receipt of the transfer documents and (where applicable) transfer fee. If it is of the *returnable* type, it will state that, if the transfer is approved, the new certificate can be obtained on or after a certain date, in exchange for the transfer receipt. If, on the other hand, the *non-returnable* form of transfer receipt is used, it merely acknowledges the transfer form and transfer fee, and informs the transferee that the certificate will be sent to him (or his broker) if or when the transfer is approved, by ordinary post at his risk.

(e) *Cancellation.* Cancel the old share certificate and prepare a new one in favour of the transferee.

(f) *Record* on the back of the old certificate the number of the *new* certificate, then file the old one.

(g) *Preparation for board meeting.* Convene a meeting of the board (or transfer committee), unless meetings are held automatically at (say) weekly or monthly intervals. Prior to the meeting, all transfer forms and new certificates must be given a final check. In some cases this is done by the company's auditors, who prepare an audit certificate. Transfer forms, share certificates, and (where applicable) audit certificate are then placed before the board or transfer committee; if approved, the following resolution will be passed:

> RESOLVED: THAT share transfers nos. .... to .... both inclusive in respect of £1 ordinary shares be and they are hereby approved, and that the corresponding share certificates nos. .... to .... inclusive be signed, sealed and issued.

(h) *Signing and sealing.* The share certificates are then signed and sealed, following the passing of the above resolution.

(i) *Record the sealing of the certificates* in the Register of Sealed Documents.

(j) *Adjust the Register of Members* from particulars on the transfer forms, to show:

(*i*) *in the transferor's account,* the date on which membership ceased (if applicable); the transfer number, number of shares transferred, distinctive numbers of shares, name of transferee, balance (if any) now held;

(*ii*) *in the transferee's account,* date of entry in the register, transfer number, number of shares acquired, name and address, distinctive numbers of shares acquired, and amount paid up.

(k) *The new share certificates are issued* after a thorough check of the certificates and of entries in the Register of Members, i.e. they will be sent by post, and a certificate of posting should be obtained. If, however, a *returnable* transfer receipt had been issued to the transferee, the certificate will be issued on production of the receipt.

NOTE: Care must be taken to ensure that the certificates are ready for delivery within two months of lodgment of the transfer unless the conditions of issue provide to the contrary, s. 185 CA 1985. But the time limit is reduced by the Stock Exchange to *one month* from the date of expiration of any right of renunciation, and to *two weeks* from the date of lodgment of a transfer in the case of a company with listed shares.

(l) *The transfer forms are securely filed.*

(m) *Receipts.* File the signed receipts for the new share certificates, i.e. if the new certificates were issued originally with receipt forms attached. As an alternative, the receipts may be posted, or stapled to their corresponding counterfoils where the certificates had been in book form.

(n) *Notice of refusal.* It has been assumed that all transfers have been approved by the board or allotment committee; if any transfer is *not* approved, notice of refusal must be sent within two months of lodgment of the transfer, unless the conditions of issue provide to the contrary.

7. Certification of transfers

(a) *Certification is necessary*:

(*i*) where the shareholder wishes to split the sale of his shares, e.g. A has a share certificate for 1000 shares, and wishes to transfer (say) 500 to B, 300 to C and 200 to D;

(*ii*) where the shareholder wishes to sell part of his holding and retain the balance, e.g. A, with a share certificate for 1000 shares, wishes to transfer 700 to B and retain the 300 balance;

(*iii*) where the shareholder has not yet received a share

certificate for the shares he wishes to transfer and can produce only a 'temporary' document, such as a transfer receipt (of the returnable type), an allotment letter or a balance receipt.

(b) *Procedure.* In the above circumstances, the seller (or his broker) lodges the transfer form and the relevant share certificate (or a temporary document) with the company for certification. However, if the shares are listed, they may be lodged with the Stock Exchange, which will undertake the work of certification against share certificates, but *not* against temporary documents.

Assuming that certification is to be carried out by the company, the procedure is as follows.

(*i*) On receipt of the transfer form and share certificate (or temporary document), ensure that the shares referred to in the transfer form are in fact those included in the certificate or temporary document.

NOTE: The Stock Transfer Form, introduced by the Stock Transfer Act 1963, is suitable for *all* transactions, whether through the medium of a stock exchange or otherwise, but a separate *Broker's Transfer Form* must also be lodged in favour of each buyer where a holding is being sold to more than one buyer as the result of stock exchange transactions.

(*ii*) Check the transfer form(s) and in particular:

(1) ensure that the appropriate form, or forms, are being used for the occasion — Broker's Transfer Forms must *not* be accepted for 'non-market deals';

(2) where Broker's Transfer Forms are received, they must be linked up with the Stock Transfer Form to which they relate, e.g. as regards name of the transferor, stamp of the selling broker, etc.;

(3) other points to be checked at this stage are the transferor's signature, the name of the transferee(s), consideration money, and particulars of the shares transferred;

NOTE: In the case of 'market' transactions, the Stock Exchange suggests that the name of the transferee need *not* be given to the Registrar at the time of the certification.

(*iii*) If the transfer documents are in order, the transfer forms are endorsed by rubber stamp with the following certificate, which must be signed (not merely initialled) by the secretary:

> Certificate/Documents of title for ....
> shares/stock has/have been lodged at the Company's office.
> Date .... Blank Company Limited
> Moorgate, ... Secretary
> London, E.C.2.

NOTE: Where certification is carried out by the Stock Exchange, the secretary of the Quotations Department of the Stock Exchange concerned sends the certificate(s) to the company and gives advice of certification. The subsequent procedure carried out by the company will then depend upon whether the shareholder is transferring his holding to two or more buyers, or transferring to one buyer and retaining the balance.

(*iv*) After certification, or after advice of certification from the stock exchange concerned, a transfer advice *may* be sent to the transferor (as already indicated in 6(c), this practice has been abandoned by most companies). If this procedure is followed, it will, of course, be unnecessary to send a transfer advice when the transfer is subsequently lodged for registration.

(*v*) Endorse particulars of the certification on the back of the share certificate (or temporary document of title) and file the latter after cancellation.

(*vi*) Return the transfer form to the seller (or his broker) and, if he is selling only *part* of his holding, a balance receipt will be sent at the same time or as soon as possible afterwards.

NOTE: Where certification is effected by a stock exchange, a balance receipt is *not* sent by the stock exchange, but the company is advised of the certification and asked to send a balance certificate to the selling broker — unless any other instruction is included.

(*vii*) A new certificate, or certificates, will be issued to the transferee(s) and, where applicable, to the transferor; i.e.:

(1) on receipt of transfers for registration from the transferees (or their brokers); and/or

(2) on receipt of a balance receipt from the transferor (or his broker).

NOTE: If the Stock Exchange suggestion is followed, and a non-returnable balance receipt is used, the company will send a balance certificate to the transferor (or his broker) without awaiting production of documents.

8. The effects of certification

(a) The buyer (or his broker) accepts the certification as evidence of the seller's title to the shares concerned, and certified transfers are accepted by common custom as 'good delivery' on the stock exchange.
(b) Legally, however, certification is *not* a warranty that the seller has any title to the shares; it is merely a representation by the company that the documents have been produced which purport to give the seller a *prima facie* title to the shares.
(c) If a false certification is made negligently, the company is under the same liability as if it had been made fraudulently: s. 184 CA 1985; thus the company will be liable to compensate any person who acts on the faith of a false certification.
(d) A company is deemed to have certificated an instrument of transfer and is, therefore, liable upon it if:

(*i*) the act of certification is performed by a person duly authorized by the company to do so; and

(*ii*) the certification is signed by a person authorized to certify transfers on the company's behalf, or by any officer or servant, either of the company or of a body corporate so authorized: s. 184(3) CA 1985.
(e) Where the stock exchange undertakes the certification of transfers, the company cannot be held liable on a false certification, as the stock exchange is not authorized by the company to carry out the work.

9. Blank transfers

(a) A blank transfer is frequently given as security for a loan and operates as a mortgage of the shares included in the transfer form.
(b) The borrower completes a transfer form, but leaves the name of the transferee blank. Transfer form and share certificate are then deposited with the lender in return for the loan.
(c) If the borrower fails to repay the loan on the date arranged, the lender may insert his own name as transferee and get the transfer registered in his own favour; or he may sell the shares to a third party, after giving reasonable notice of his intention to the borrower.
(d) As the Stock Transfer Act 1963 provides that registered securities may be transferred by means of an instrument under hand, the position of the lender is strengthened as it is now a comparatively simple matter to enforce his security. Hitherto there had been various legal complications when a transfer was required to be under seal.

10. Forged transfers

(a) No rights can be acquired by the transferee under a forged transfer as it is *void*.
(b) The rights and liabilities of the company on a forged transfer are as follows.

(i) It must restore the 'transferor' (i.e. the true owner) to the register and compensate him for dividends due to him.

(ii) It must remove the transferee's name from the register, and recover from him any dividends he may have received as the result of the forgery.

(iii) It must compensate a second transferee (if any) who has received a share certificate and has been entered in the Register of Members.

NOTE: In this case the company is estopped from denying the title of a second transferee, *if* he had relied on the share certificate and had acted in good faith.

(*iv*) It may claim compensation for all losses suffered as a result of the forgery from the person who lodged the transfer.

NOTE: That person, by lodging the transfer for registration, gave an implied warranty that it was genuine and that he would compensate the company if the transfer should prove to be a forgery.

(c) The rights of the *'transferor'*, i.e. the true owner, are as follows.

(*i*) He can compel the company to restore his name to the Register of Members and make good any dividends he may have lost as the result of the forgery.

(*ii*) His right of action lies *only* against the company.

(d) The *transferee*, even though he may have acted innocently:

(*i*) obtains no title to the shares included in the transfer;

(*ii*) is liable to repay any dividends he may have received, as the result of the forgery, to the company; and

(*iii*) is liable to indemnify the company for any loss it may have suffered.

The transferee will, of course, have a claim against the forger.

(e) A *second* transferee, acting in good faith, who has relied upon the share certificate:

(*i*) is entitled to compensation from the company, as the company is estopped from denying his title to the shares; or

(*ii*) as an alternative, the company may procure an equivalent number of shares and have them transferred into his name, and so replace those which must be restored to the true owner.

11. Forged Transfers Acts 1891 and 1892

(a) A company may, by its Articles or by *special* resolution, adopt these Acts, which prescribe methods for providing compensation for persons who suffer loss as the result of forged transfers, or forged powers of attorney.

NOTE: There is no compulsion to adopt these Acts.

(b) The methods prescribed are as follows:

(*i*) The company may charge an additional fee on each transfer, but not exceeding 5p per £100 transferred.

(*ii*) Creating a fund by reservation of capital, accumulation of income or any other method which the company may decide upon.

(*iii*) Covering the risk by taking out a forged transfers insurance policy — the method which is most commonly adopted.

> NOTE: It is more usual for companies to have a forged transfers insurance policy, either with an insurance company or with Lloyd's, to cover this risk. Such policies generally cover documents lodged for registration, dividend warrants, etc., the forgery of which could involve the company in liabilities.

Transmission of shares

12. Transmission

Transmission signifies a change in ownership of securities otherwise than by ordinary transfer; that is, either:

(a) by death; or
(b) by operation of law, as in bankruptcy.

13. Member's death

(a) The following provisions are of assistance to the legal representatives of a deceased member.

(*i*) Section 183(1) CA 1985 provides that a transfer of shares or debentures must not be registered except on production of an instrument of transfer, but it is made clear that the section does not prevent a company from registering as shareholder or debenture holder a person to whom the shares or debentures are transmitted by operation of law.

(*ii*) Section 183(3) CA 1985 states that a transfer of the shares of a deceased member made by a personal representative shall, although the personal representative is not himself a member, be as valid as if he were.

(*iii*) Section 187 CA 1985 provides that the production to a company of any document which is by law sufficient evidence of probate or letters of administration shall be accepted by the company as sufficient evidence of the grant.

(b) The courses open to a personal representative in dealing with the shares (or debentures) of a deceased member of a company will be determined by various considerations, namely:

(*i*) whether the deceased had held the shares solely or jointly;

(*ii*) whether he died testate or intestate; and

(*iii*) whether, having died testate, he appointed an executor who was able and willing to act as his executor.

(c) Assuming that the deceased had held the shares *solely:*

(*i*) if he left a will, and appointed an executor, his executor must produce probate of the will to the company;

(*ii*) if he left a will, without naming an executor, or

(1) appointed an executor who refused to act, or

(2) appointed an executor who predeceased him,

his legal representative will be an administrator who must produce letters of administration with the will annexed to the company as evidence of his appointment as administrator of the deceased;

(*iii*) if he died intestate, i.e. without leaving a will, his next of kin (or other person or persons so entitled) may apply to the Court for, and produce to the company, General Letters of Administration, as evidence of his appointment as administrator of the deceased.

NOTE: If the deceased had *no* next of kin, the Crown, any creditor, or a Consul (in the case of a foreigner) may apply for Letters of Administration.

(d) After production of the appropriate document(s) by the legal representative of the deceased in the above cases, the procedure is as follows.

(*i*) The documents must be accepted by the company as sufficient evidence, despite anything in the Articles to the contrary: s. 187 CA 1985.

(*ii*) The executor or administrator cannot be treated automatically as holder of the shares, and the name of the deceased must be allowed to remain in the Register of Members.

(*iii*) If, however, the Articles permit, the executor or administrator may request the company to place his name on the register. In that case, if his request is approved, he will be treated as a shareholder in his own right and responsible for any liability attaching to the shares.

(*iv*) The company's Articles will decide the method to be adopted for registering the legal representative; that is:

(1) whether a formal transfer is required, to transfer from (say) the executor of X to the executor in his own private capacity; or

(2) whether a Letter of Request will suffice.

(*v*) In some cases the Articles permit the directors to compel the legal representative either:

(1) to have the shares registered in his own name, or

(2) to transfer the shares within a stipulated period, failing which, dividends, bonuses or other moneys payable in respect of the shares may be withheld until the legal representative complies with the company's requirements.

(e) Assuming that the deceased had held the shares *jointly:*

(*i*) the shares vest in the survivor or survivors of the joint holding;

(*ii*) the company will require evidence of death, in the form of a death certificate; if probate of the will or letters of administration is accepted instead, the document produced should be endorsed in such a way as to make it quite clear that it was accepted as evidence of death only.

NOTE: The Articles usually provide that the estate of the deceased joint holder is not released from any liability remaining on the shares which had been jointly held by him with other persons.

(f) Where the estate of a deceased shareholder does not exceed £5000 the deceased's representatives may take advantage of the provisions of the Administration of Estates (Small Payments) Act 1965 and adopt a less formal course of action than that outlined above. In such circumstances it is usual to call for:

(*i*) a death certificate;

(*ii*) a letter from the Capital Taxes Office agreeing that, on the information furnished to it, no liability to inheritance tax arises;

(*iii*) the share certificate;

(*iv*) a statutory declaration to the effect that the person claiming to deal with the shareholding is entitled to do so;

(*v*) a letter of indemnity from the same person, indemnifying the company against any loss or liability it may incur as a result of dealing with the shareholding informally, and undertaking to obtain formal probate or administration if called upon by the company to do so.

14. Member's bankruptcy

(a) On becoming bankrupt, a member's shares vest in his trustee in bankruptcy.

(b) The trustee must, however, prove to the company that he is entitled to deal with the bankrupt's shares, by producing:

(*i*) an office copy of the Court's order by which he was appointed, *or* the company may accept a copy of the *Gazette* advertising his appointment; and

(*ii*) an authenticated copy of his signature.

(c) Production of the above documents permits the trustees to deal with the bankrupt's shares in the course of realizing his property. He may elect to deal with the shares in any of the following ways.

(*i*) He may transfer the shares, as the Insolvency Act 1986 gives him the same right of transfer as the bankrupt himself has formerly possessed.

(*ii*) He may have the shares registered in his own name, where the Articles permit or require him to do so; if, however, there is any liability on the shares, he is unlikely to do so as he would then become personally liable, and, moreover, he would also lose his right to disclaim the shares.

(*iii*) He may disclaim the shares if they are onerous and so long as he had not had them registered in his own name; in which case, the company will be entitled to prove in the bankruptcy for any loss suffered as a result of the disclaimer.

(d) If the bankrupt is a joint holder, the above procedure still applies; that is, the shares pass to the trustee in bankruptcy and *not* to the surviving joint holder(s).

15. Unsoundness of mind of a member

(a) The Court may appoint a Receiver to administer the affairs of a shareholder who is of unsound mind.
(b) The Receiver must produce to the company the court order, or an office copy of it, confirming his appointment, and this must be accepted by the company as sufficient evidence of the appointment.
(c) The Receiver is then able to deal with the shares concerned, in accordance with the authority given in the order, e.g. to transfer the shares, or merely to receive dividends due to the insane member.
(d) If the member concerned is a joint holder, his interest does *not* pass to the surviving joint holder(s) but to the Receiver.

16. Liquidation of a corporate member

(a) When a corporate member is wound up, the liquidator must produce evidence of his appointment before he becomes entitled to deal with the shares concerned. The evidence required depends upon the mode of winding up adopted, i.e. whether it is a compulsory liquidation or a voluntary liquidation.
(b) In a *compulsory* liquidation, the liquidator will be required to produce the court order by which he was appointed, or a copy of the *Gazette* in which it was advertised.
(c) In a *voluntary* liquidation, the liquidator must produce certified copies of the resolutions for winding up and authorizing his appointment.
(d) A liquidator has a power to disclaim onerous property akin to that of a trustee in bankruptcy.

17. Chain of transmission

(a) If the sole legal representative of a deceased member, i.e. executor or administrator, has the shares of the deceased registered in his own name, then in the event of his own death *his* personal representative (whether executor or administrator) can deal with the shares as part of his estate.

(b) If, however, the sole legal representative of a deceased member had allowed the shares to remain in the name of the deceased, a chain of transmission (or chain of representation) may be formed, and from that point:

(*i*) there will be an unbroken chain of transmission, provided the legal representative dies testate; that is, his right of representation will pass by operation of law to his executor, and so on from executor to executor, until one of them dies intestate;

(*ii*) the chain of transmission might also be broken if an executor in the 'chain' died testate, but failed to appoint an executor, or appointed one who refused to act or had predeceased him.

(c) It is important to note that the chain of transmission cannot be continued by an administrator, as he is not a person appointed by the deceased executor as being capable of administering the estate of the original deceased shareholder.

NOTE: As already explained earlier in this chapter, most companies require legal representatives either to transfer the shares of the deceased shareholder or to have them registered in their own names; therefore, the chain of transmission and the legal complications which it might entail are usually avoided.

Progress test 8

1. What are the statutory provisions affecting a shareholder's right to transfer his shares and the form of the transfer instrument? **(1, 2)**

2. Describe an office procedure for dealing with transfers lodged with a company for registration, paying particular attention to the points which should be borne in mind when scrutinising the transfer forms and accompanying documents. **(3, 6)**

3. Explain what is meant by certification of transfers? *ICSA* **(7)**

4. Discuss the merits and disadvantages of the adoption by a company of a system of non-returnable transfer receipts and balance receipts. **(6)**

5. A holds 1,000 shares in a public company. He instructs a broker to sell 400 of the shares. They are sold through the Stock Exchange as to 300 to a broker acting for B and as to 100 to a broker acting for C. Describe the documents you, as Company Secretary, should receive as a result of these sales, and from whom; and the action to be taken in the Registration department to complete the transactions. *ICSA* **(3, 6)**

6. Outline the procedure involved in a market transaction utilizing the TALISMAN settlement system. **(4)**

7. Describe the following and explain in what circumstances they are used:

(a) an offer for sale;
(b) broker's transfer forms or (in countries outside the United Kingdom) transfer deeds;

(c) consolidated listing forms.
ICSA (2: **4**, 3: **22**, 8: **3**)

8. Explain the purpose and legal effect of certification of transfer. Discuss the legal effect where certification is carried out on the Stock Exchange. (**7, 8**)

9. You are the registrar of a listed public company. Would you accept the following documents for registration? If not, give your reasons for rejection:

(a) a probate granted overseas;
(b) a transfer not previously certified of 500 ordinary shares accompanied by a certificate for 750 ordinary shares;
(c) a transfer with a material alteration thereon. (8: **3**, 9: **4, 10**)

10. What do you understand by a 'blank' transfer? For what purpose(s) might it be used? (**9**)

11. Describe the various ways in which ownership of shares in a company may change, outlining the procedure to be followed in each case, including any necessary action by directors. (**3, 12**)

12. What courses are open to a personal representative in dealing with the shares of a deceased member of a company? In what respect (if any) would the position be altered if the deceased member had held his shares jointly with another? (**13**)

13. What do you understand by 'transmission' of shares? Which provisions of the Act are of assistance to the legal representatives of a deceased member? (**12**)

14. Distinguish between (*a*) transfer and transmission; (*b*) executor and administrator; (*c*) probate and letters of administration. (8: **12**, 9: **4, 5**)

15. Explain (*a*) 'chain of transmission', (*b*) letter of request. Prepare a specimen letter of request. **(13, 17)**

16. In connection with the death of a shareholder explain how as Secretary you would deal with:

(a) a small estate;
(b) letter of request;
(c) joint ownership. *ICSA* **(13)**

17. (*a*) What do you understand by certification of transfer?
(*b*) In what circumstances may the need for certification arise?
(*c*) Explain fully the certification procedure. *ICSA* **(7)**

9

Registration of documents

Documents received for registration

1. The registration department

The registration department of a large company is usually in the charge of the company registrar, who is directly responsible to the company secretary. Many large companies now use the Registrar Departments of banks to carry out the functions of a registration department.

2. The work of the registration department

(a) Registration of transfers of shares and debentures.

(b) Preparing and filing returns with the Registrar of Companies.

(c) Payment of dividend and, where applicable, debenture interest.

(d) Registration of miscellaneous documents, other than those received in connection with certification and registration of transfers.

(e) Maintaining, and keeping up to date, various registers, including the Register of Members, Register of Directors' Interests, Register of Charges, Register of Directors and Secretaries, Register of Interests in Shares, Register of Debenture Holders (if any), and various non-statutory registers kept for the purpose of registering miscellaneous documents referred to in **(d)** above.

3. Miscellaneous documents

Miscellaneous documents requiring registration, other than those concerned with transfer procedure:

(a) probates;
(b) Letters of Administration;
(c) powers of attorney;
(d) court orders, e.g. appointments of trustee in bankruptcy, receiver in case of insanity, liquidator;
(e) certificates, e.g. of death, marriage, etc.;
(f) statutory declaration, e.g. of identity.

4. Probate

(a) The probate of a will is an official copy of the will, sealed by the Court of Probate after it has been proved.
(b) It is one of the first duties of the executor appointed in the will to obtain probate to enable him to administer the estate of the deceased.
(c) When he presents the probate (or a photostat copy of it) to a company, the company is bound to accept it as evidence of the executor's right to deal with the property of the deceased, including his shares and debentures: s. 187 CA 1985.
(d) It is, however, important to ensure that the probate bears the seal of the appropriate Court.

5. Letters of Administration

(a) This is the Court's official appointment of an administrator, giving him authority to administer the estate of a deceased person, usually because the deceased died without leaving a will or, having left a will, failed to appoint an executor.
(b) Letters of Administration are usually granted to a person (or persons) interested in the real or personal estate of the deceased, e.g. the next of kin, or a legatee if there was a will but no executor appointed. If there are no next of kin, the grant may be made to:

(i) the Crown,
(ii) a creditor, or
(iii) a consul, in the case of a foreigner.

(c) Having been granted Letters of Administration and produced the document (or a photostat copy of it) to the company, the administrator is then entitled to deal with the property of the deceased, including his shares and debentures; the company is, in fact, bound to accept the document as evidence of his authority: s. 187 CA 1985.

NOTE: This document, like the probate, must be sealed by the appropriate Court; if not, it must be re-sealed or a fresh grant (an ancillary grant) taken out.

(d) Letters of Administration may take various forms, the form being determined by the circumstances in each case.

(i) A general grant of administration is made where the deceased died intestate. This is, of course, the commonest form of grant.

(ii) Letters of Administration with the will annexed are granted where the deceased died testate but failed to appoint an executor, or where the executor appointed refuses to act or pre-deceased him.

(iii) Letters of Administration *de bonis non*, granted where an administrator is appointed to take over the administration of an estate because the original executor or administrator had died without completing the administration of the estate.

(iv) Letters of Administration pending suit, granted to an administrator appointed to act pending the result of litigation concerning validity of the will.

(v) Letters of Administration during mental incapacity, granted to an administrator appointed to carry on the administration of the estate during insanity of an executor or administrator.

(vi) Letters of Administration for the use and benefit of a minor, granted where an administrator is appointed to take over administration of an estate during infancy of a sole executor named in the will.

6. Power of attorney

(a) A power of attorney is the actual authority or instrument embodying an authorization to one person, the attorney (grantee or donee), or to two or more persons either jointly, or jointly and severally, to act on behalf of the principal (grantor or donor).

(b) Section 1 of the Powers of Attorney Act 1971 provides that such an instrument shall be signed and sealed by or by direction of and in the presence of the donor, and that where it is not signed by the donor himself but by some other person on his behalf in his presence and at his direction, two other persons shall be present as witnesses and shall attest the instrument. This confirms the view that the term 'power of attorney' is properly restricted to an authority given under seal.

(c) A power of attorney may be general, giving the attorney wide power as regards the grantor's business, or it may be special, specifying a limited number of actions or even the execution of a single document.

(d) A photocopy of a power of attorney, certified by the donor or by a solicitor or stockbroker, and any copy of a photocopy, similarly certified, shall be sufficient proof of the existence and contents of the power: Powers of Attorney Act 1971, s. 3.

(e) By s. 4 of the Powers of Attorney Act 1971 a power of attorney whenever created, which is created to secure a proprietary interest of the donee, or the performance of an obligation owed to the donee, shall not be revoked, so long as the donee has that interest or the obligation remains undischarged, either by the donor without the donee's consent, or by the reason of death, incapacity, or bankruptcy of the donor or, if the donor is a body corporate, by reason of its dissolution.

(f) Where the donee of a power of attorney acts in pursuance of the power at a time when it has been revoked he shall not incur any liability (either to the donor or to any other person) if at that time he did not know of the revocation; and where a person, without knowledge of the revocation, deals with the donee the transaction shall be valid as if the power had then been in existence: s. 5 Powers of Attorney Act 1971.

(g) Section 7 of the Powers of Attorney Act 1971 provides that the donee of a power of attorney may execute any instrument with his own signature and, where sealing is required, with his own seal, and do any other thing in his own name, by the authority of the donor of the power; any document so executed or thing so done has the same effect as if executed or done by the donee with the signature or seal, or in the name of the donor.

(h) Under the Enduring Powers of Attorney Act 1985 individuals may give a power of attorney in the form prescribed in the Regulations made under the Act which will continue in force even if the donor should become mentally incapable, subject to the power being registered with the Court of Protection.

7. Registration of miscellaneous documents

(a) In large companies, where requests for alteration of the Register of Members for various reasons (apart from transfers) are numerous, it may be found convenient and time-saving to have a separate register in which to record the receipt of the more important documents. Thus, separate registers may be kept for, say:

(*i*) probates and Letters of Administration;
(*ii*) powers of attorney;
(*iii*) court orders, notices and certificates.

(b) Specimen rulings for two of these registers are illustrated below:

Register of probates and letters of administration

No.	Date regd.	*Particulars of deceased*		Date of death	*Executor/Administrator*		Folio in Register	Remarks
		Name	Shares held		Name	Address		

Register of powers of attorney

No.	Date regd.	*Shareholder*		*Particulars of power of attorney*		*Attorney*		By whom presented	Folio in register
		Name	Address	Date	Description	Name	Address		

(c) It may, however, be sufficient in many cases to keep a single register, which might be named 'Register of Important Documents' and either ruled to record every type of document received for registration, or divided into sections, such as (1) Probates and Letters of Administration, (2) Powers of attorney, (3) Death certificates, (4) Marriage certificates, (5) Notices and orders, (6) Miscellaneous.

(d) Some companies have already dispensed with 'registers' in book form, and many will now favour the use of computers. This they are entitled to do under s. 723 CA 1985, so long as their computerized recordings are capable of being reproduced in a legible form.

(e) On receiving documents for registration, it is advisable to have them checked and endorsed (usually by means of a rubber stamp) after which the endorsement is signed by the secretary, registrar or other responsible official. Where a registration fee is charged, the endorsement will serve as an acknowledgment of the document and as a receipt for the registration fee.

The usual registration stamp is as follows:

Registered

For and on behalf of

EXCHANGE TRADING CO. LTD.

.... Registrar

Received fee .... Date ....

(f) On receipt of probate or Letters of Administration for registration, the relevant share certificate should be endorsed with the following particulars:

Probate/Letters of administration

of the Will of .... who died on ... 19 ....
has this day been presented by the persons undermentioned,
and registered in the Company's books.

Name(s) .... Executor/Administrator
Addresses ....
....

Dated this ....day of ....19...

For and on behalf of
EXCHANGE TRADING CO. LTD.

Secretary

.... Registrar

8. Photographic copies of documents

(a) Photographic copies of documents are presented for registration as common practice. In many cases such copies are generally acceptable; in other cases, the secretary (or registrar) must use his discretion, and in any doubtful case it is always advisable to insist on production of the original document.

(b) Present practice regarding the acceptance of photographic copies of documents for registration may be summarized as follows.

(*i*) *Probates and Letters of Administration.* A photostatic copy may be accepted with safety if it bears the impressed seal of the probate office. A privately produced copy, photographic or otherwise, should *not* be accepted.

(*ii*) *Powers of attorney.* A photocopy of a power of attorney, certified by the donor or by a solicitor or stockbroker, and any copy of a photocopy, similarly certified, shall be sufficient proof of the existence and contents of the power.

(*iii*) *Death and marriage certificates.* Certified copies issued by the appropriate registrar are generally acceptable. Privately photographed copies should not be accepted unless fully authenticated by a responsible person.

(*iv*) *Court orders.* Court orders appointing a liquidator, Receiver under the Mental Health Act 1983, trustee in bankruptcy, etc., are commonly presented as 'office copies'.

These are quite acceptable, so long as they bear the seal of the appropriate Court. Copies in any other form should not be accepted.

(*v*) *Certified copies of resolutions,* such as the resolution appointing a liquidator in a voluntary winding-up, are acceptable, so long as they are fully authenticated in manner provided in s. 41 CA 1985, i.e. actually signed by a director, Secretary or other authorized officer of the company. The same may be said of certified extracts from a company's Articles, minutes, etc.

9. Circumstances in which documents are submitted for registration

Apart from alterations due to transfer of shares, the following are some of the circumstances in which documents are presented to a company for registration.

(a) *Member's death,* where deceased had held shares:

(*i*) solely,

(*ii*) jointly.

(b) *Registering power of attorney,* where the attorney wishes to establish his authority to deal with shares, etc.

(c) *Member's bankruptcy,* where the trustee in bankruptcy produces evidence of his appointment.

(d) *Member's unsoundness of mind,* the Receiver appointed by the Court proving his appointment and entitlement to deal with the estate of the insane member.

(e) *Liquidation of a corporate member,* the liquidator producing evidence of his appointment.

(f) *Change of name,* from various causes, e.g.

(*i*) marriage of a female shareholder;

(*ii*) shareholder's elevation to the peerage;

(*iii*) corporate member changing name by special resolution;

(*iv*) change by deed poll;

(*v*) combination of various accounts under one name.

(g) *Change of address,* either by letter or on any standard form for the purpose.

Procedure on receipt

10. Procedure on receipt of documents for registration

Circumstances	*Document(s) produced or required to be produced*	*Procedure*
1. Member's death	Probate/Letters of Administration (or acceptable copy) and share certificate.	(1) Ensure probate (or letters of administration) is correctly sealed by English Court of Probate. (2) Enter in Register of Probates. (3) Endorse probate/letters of administration with 'registration stamp' (*see* illustration in **7**). (4) Endorse share certificate with the general 'registration stamp' (also illustrated in **7**). (5) Record member's death in Register of Members; e.g.: '*Probate of the will of John Blank (deceased) registered at Company's office*....................19...... *Executor/Administrator:* *Name*......................*Address*.................................' (6) Return share certificate and any other document not to be retained. If equipment is available, the latter may be photocopied before return. (7) Carefully file any copies retained. (8) Prepare new address plate in favour of legal representatives.

2. Registering power of attorney	Power of attorney (or acceptable copy).	(1) Carefully examine the power, to ensure that it is: **(a)** correct in form; **(b)** still in force; and **(c)** correctly signed and sealed by appointer. (2) Enter in Register of Powers of Attorney. (3) Particulars of the power of attorney should not, as such, be recorded in the Register of Members for they are essentially the private concern of the grantor and grantee. However, the existence of the power could be noted as an *aide-mémoire* through the use of some code indication against the appropriate entry in the register. (4) Carefully note exact power given to the attorney and/or copy document; file copy. (5) If in doubt as to power being still in force, obtain statutory declaration of non-revocation. (6) Endorse the power with registration stamp, and return. (7) Prepare new address plate in favour of attorney.

Circumstances	*Document(s) produced or required to be produced*	*Procedure*
3. Member's bankruptcy	Bankruptcy Order (or acceptable copy). NOTE: A copy of the *Gazette* containing notice of appointment is sometimes accepted.	(1) Record receipt of document in Register of Important Documents or special register (if any). (2) Record particulars of appointment in Register of Members, e.g.: *'Notice of appointment of Trustee in Bankruptcy, dated......................registered Company's office (date)..............Trustee's name/address....................* *..',* (3) Endorse the order (or copy) with 'registration' stamp. (4) Return the order (or copy) to trustee, usually after taking a copy. (5) Prepare new address plate in favour of the trustee.
4. Member's unsoundness of mind	Protection Order (or acceptable copy). NOTE: The order may give only limited power to the Receiver.	(1) Record receipt of document in Register of Important Documents or special register (if any). (2) Record particulars of appointment in Register of Members, e.g.: *'Order appointing Receiver dated.........................* *registered at Company's office................ (date)..........* *........................Receiver.......................name/address'*

4. Member's unsoundness of mind (*cont.*)		(3) Endorse the order (or copy) with 'registration' stamp. (4) Return the order (or copy) to Receiver, usually after taking a copy. (5) Prepare new address plate in favour of the Receiver.
5. Liquidation of corporate member	In *compulsory* winding-up: Court order (or acceptable copy) appointing liquidator. In *voluntary* winding-up: certified copies of the resolutions: **(a)** for winding up **(b)** appointing the liquidator.	(1) Record receipt of document(s) in Register of Important Documents or special register (if any). (2) Record particulars of appointment in Register of Members, e.g.: *'Order of Court for compulsory winding-up dated........ registered at Company's office..... (date) .... Liquidator(s)..................and ....'* (3) Return document(s), usually after taking copy. (4) Prepare new address plate in favour of liquidator.

	Circumstances	*Document(s) produced or required to be produced*	*Procedure*
6.	Change of name due to marriage of female shareholder	Marriage certificate (or acceptable copy) and share certificate.	(1) Send member a special request form (if any) for completion in her new name. (2) Record request in Register of Important Documents, or any special register. (3) Amend entry in Register of Members. (4) Prepare new share certificate or endorse the old certificate. (5) Endorse marriage certificate (or copy) with 'registration' stamp. (6) Return marriage certificate (or copy) and new share certificate (or old one, suitably endorsed). (7) File the request form. (8) Prepare new address plate.
7.	Change of name due to shareholder's elevation to the peerage	Copy of *Gazette* notifying change of name and share certificate usually accepted.	(1) Record in Register of Important Documents or any special register. (2) Amend Register of Members, e.g.: '*Copy of* Gazette, *dated*...................... *registered at Company's office (date)*.........' followed by detail of the change. (3) Prepare new share certificate or endorse the old one. (4) File copy of the *Gazette*. (5) Prepare new address plate.

8.	Change of name by corporate members	Certified copy of special resolution authorizing the change. Share certificate. If the company has a seal, impression of the company's new seal. Certified extract of company's Articles as to use of seal.	(1) Record receipt of documents in Register of Important Documents, or any special register. (2) Amend Register of Members, i.e. alter name of the company, and note production of documents. (3) Prepare new share certificate, or endorse the old one with the change of name. (4) Return any documents whose return is requested (after photocopying) together with amended (or new) share certificate. (5) File copies of any documents retained and (if applicable) cancelled share certificate. (6) Prepare new address plate.
9.	Change of name by deed poll	Deed of poll, or copy of *Gazette* notifying the change of name and share certificate.	(1) Send member a special request form (if any) for completion in new name. (2) Record receipt of documents in Register of Important Documents, or special register. (3) Amend entry in Register of Members, e.g. '*Deed of Poll dated............registered at Company office ....date.............*'

	Circumstances	Document(s) produced or required to be produced	Procedure
9.	Change of name by deed poll (cont.)		(4) Prepare new share certificate, or endorse the old one, showing change of name. (5) Return the deed of poll (after taking a copy) together with either new share certificate or the old one suitably endorsed. (6) File letter of request and, where applicable, cancelled share certificate and copy of *Gazette*. (7) Prepare new address plate.
10.	Shareholder's request to have shares in various names combined under his true name	Statutory Declaration of Identity and share certificates.	(1) Record receipt of documents in Register of Important Documents. (2) Make necessary amendments in the Register of Members, transferring from accounts in fictitious names into true name of the member. (3) Prepare new share certificate in shareholder's true name. (4) Send new share certificate to member, after cancelling and filing old certificates. (5) File the Statutory Declaration. (6) Prepare new address plate.

11. Change of address	Notice of change of address. NOTE: It is not usually necessary to produce share certificate.	(1) If a standard form is provided, ensure that it bears signature of shareholder. (2) Acknowledge the notice, to both old and new addresses, if in doubt. (3) Amend the Register of Members. (4) File the shareholder's notice. (5) Prepare new address plate.

11. The document service

(a) Introduced by the Stock Exchange in liaison with the Institute's Registrars' Group, this service facilitates the registration of the following documents:

(*i*) English probates;
(*ii*) Letters of Administration;
(*iii*) Powers of attorney;
(*iv*) Death certificates;
(*v*) Deed polls;
(*vi*) Marriage certificates;
(*vii*) Certificates of incorporation on change of name;
(*viii*) Memorandum and Articles of Association.

(b) Under the service, certified copies of these documents are prepared for dispatch to companies or their registrars. The broker concerned submits to the Stock Exchange Centre:

(*i*) the original or a Court-sealed copy of the document;
(*ii*) a correctly completed Document Advice form for each company registrar to whom a copy of the document is to be sent; and
(*iii*) the relevant certificates and transfers.

The Centre checks the authenticity of the documents and produces photocopies of them which are certified as true copies and dispatched to companies or registrars for registration. The company acts upon the document received from the Centre in the same way as if they had had an original or certified true copy of the document lodged with them direct.

(c) The broker putting forward the document to the Centre undertakes to indemnify the company and registrar against any loss or liability that may arise from the information provided in the Document Advice.

Progress test 9

1. Give specimen rulings for the following:

(a) Register of probates and letters of administration;
(b) Register of powers of attorney.

To enable your company to dispense with these and other registers of this type, what alternative measures would you suggest? **(7)**

2. Discuss the growth of documentary photography in so far as it concerns documents presented to a company for registration. Summarize the type of documents of which photographs might be presented, and state which of these, in your opinion, should be accepted, giving reasons for your answer. **(8)**

3. How would you deal with the following documents submitted to you for registration:

(*a*) Bankruptcy order; (*b*) deed poll; (*c*) notification of member's elevation to the peerage; (*d*) notice of change of name of corporate member; (*e*) court order appointing liquidator of corporate member. **(10)**

4. (a) X is a shareholder in the public company of which you are secretary. Probate is lodged by the executors of X. What alterations would you make in the company's register of members? You return the probate to the executors enclosing the usual 'letter of request' for completion by them but, before this is returned to the company, the executors sell part of the holding and the necessary documents of transfer are lodged. Detail the action you would take.
(b) What action would you take on receipt of probate of the will of a deceased member whose shares were held by him jointly with his wife? *ICSA* **(4, 9, 10)**

5. What action should be taken by the secretary of a public company upon receipt of the following documents:

(a) letters of administration granted by Bermuda;
(b) death certificate of A, who holds shares jointly with B;
(c) letter from a solicitor advising that a shareholder has died and asking for a valuation of the company's shares on the date of his death. The company does not have an official quotation. *ICSA* **(5, 9, 10)**

6. Some months ago a power of attorney was submitted to you, as secretary, and after examination was registered in the usual manner. Subsequently several transfers of shares took place, the attorney signed on behalf of the transferor. A further transfer, similarly signed, is now submitted, but on this occasion the attorney is named as transferee. What action would you take and what advice would you give to the board in reference to this transfer? **(6, 10)**

7. As secretary of a public company you receive the following letters. You are required to draft appropriate letters in reply:

(a) A shareholder, Miss C. Dee, writes to tell you that she has married and her name is now Wye. You reply in the usual form requesting a sight of the marriage certificate. You receive an indignant reply, refusing to send the certificate as she considers that you should accept her written advice.
(b) The widow of a shareholder, A. Bee, writes enclosing the death certificate of her husband who had 15 shares in your company having a market value of £27. In a covering letter Mrs Bee explains that the total value of her husband's estate is only £180 and, to save the cost of a grant of administration she asks if you will transfer the shares to her name. *ICSA* **(5, 10)**

8. Outline the circumstances in which the following documents may be lodged with the secretary of a company;

(a) letters of administration *de bonis non*;
(b) a garnishee order absolute;
(c) a stop notice.

What action should the secretary take on each document? (6: **12;** 9: **5, 9, 10)**

9. Explain:

(a) the difference between a stock transfer form and a broker's transfer form;
(b) the action you would take on receiving advice of a change of address from a shareholder;

(c) what the Stock Exchange requires to be shown on the face of a share certificate;
(d) how would you deal with a probate lodged for registration.
ICSA (7: **1**; 8: **6**; 9: **4, 10**)

10. You receive from Watson and Brown, Solicitors, a photostat copy of a Power of Attorney granted by your shareholder, Mr William Forbes in favour of Mrs Alison Hammond. Explain fully the registration procedure. *ICSA* **(6)**

10

Dividends and employees' share schemes

General rules — profits available for distribution

1. Definition

A dividend is that part of a company's net profit which is distributed to its shareholders in proportion to their respective shareholdings.

2. The chief rules relating to declaration and payment of dividends

(a) *Power to declare dividends.* In most cases the power to declare a dividend and other provisions relating to declaration and payment of dividends are set out in a company's Articles.
(b) *Provisions of Table A* relating to dividends are as follows.

(i) Power to declare dividends is given to the company in general meeting, but the dividend must not exceed the amount recommended by the directors: Article 102.

(ii) Interim dividends. The directors have power to pay interim dividends, where it is justified by the profits: Article 103.

(iii) Source of dividend. The power of the company to pay a dividend is subject to the provisions of the Companies Act 1985 (*see* **3** *below*).

(iv) Calculation of dividend. Unless shares have special rights, dividends are to be calculated on the amounts paid, or credited as paid, on the shares: Article 105.

(v) Permitted forms of payment. Dividend may be paid wholly or partly in the form of specific assets, such as shares or debenture stock of another company, and the issue of fractional

certificates is permitted in regard to such distribution: Article 104.

(*vi*) *Method of payment.* Dividend, interest or other moneys payable in cash may be paid by cheque sent through the post to a shareholder's registered address: Article 106.

(*vii*) *Dividend, etc., due to joint holders* will be sent to the address of the joint holder first named in the register, unless the joint holders direct otherwise in writing: Article 106.

(*viii*) *Delay in payment of dividend* does not entitle a shareholder to claim for interest against the company: Article 107.

(*ix*) Any dividend which has remained unclaimed for 12 years from the date when it became due for payment shall, if the directors so resolve, be forfeited and cease to remain owing by the company: Article 108.

(c) *If, however, Table A is expressly excluded* and the Articles make no provision to the contrary, dividend will be calculable on the *nominal* value of the shares concerned, i.e. irrespective of the amount paid up: *Re Bridgewater Navigation Co.* (1891).

(d) *Unclaimed dividends.* In order to deal with this matter the Articles may empower the company to sell shares of untraceable shareholders, the company retaining the net proceeds of the shares pending the possible receipt of claims from the shareholders concerned. The Articles of listed companies if they provide for such must stipulate that power will not be exercised until 12 years or more after the date of the declaration of the dividend.

NOTE: It must be realized, however, that the appearance of 'unclaimed dividends' in a company's balance sheet may constitute sufficient acknowledgment of the debt to permit its revival: *Jones* v. *Bellgrove Properties* (1949).

3. Profits available for distribution

In order to ensure that a company's capital fund was not reduced by payments of capital masquerading as payments of dividend the courts declared that 'dividends could only be paid out of profits and not out of capital'. This rule, simple enough to state in the abstract, in practice became clouded and subject to potential abuse as the judiciary sought to establish what for this purpose was to be regarded as profit and what was to be regarded as capital.

Happily, however, the Companies Act 1980 in implementation of the EEC Second Directive on the Harmonization of Company Law, while continuing and giving statutory effect to the basic principle established by the judges, laid down specific detailed rules to give effect to that principle and in so doing overrode the decisions of the courts in so far as they were inconsistent with the legislation.

The law as established by the Companies Act 1980 and now set out in the Companies Act 1985 may be summarized as follows:

(a) A company must not make a distribution except out of profits available for the purpose, which, broadly interpreted, means its accumulated realized profits so far as not previously utilized by distribution or capitalization less its accumulated realized losses, in so far as they have not previously been written off in a reduction or reorganization of capital duly made: s. 263 CA 1985.

(b) In the case of a *public* company, it may only make a distribution at any time:

(*i*) if at that time the amount of its net assets is not less than the aggregate of the company's called-up share capital and its undistributable reserves; and

(*ii*) if, and to the extent that, the distribution does not reduce the amount of those assets to less than that aggregate.

NOTE: For this purpose 'undistributable reserves' include the share premium account, capital redemption reserve, a revaluation reserve and any other reserve which the company is prohibited from distributing by any enactment, or by its Articles or Memorandum: s. 264 CA 1985.

(c) The right to make, and the amount of, any distribution is, however, dependent upon the company being able to produce 'relevant accounts', and this applies to an interim as well as to a final distribution; i.e., in all cases, a distribution must be demonstrably justified by the accounts.

NOTE: The 'relevant accounts' in the case of a particular distribution are the last annual accounts which were laid or filed in respect of the last preceding accounting reference period; or such interim accounts as are necessary to enable a proper judgment to be made as to the amounts of any of the relevant items: ss. 271–275 CA 1985.

(d) The consequences of making an unlawful distribution are stated but do not impose any criminal sanction. If, however, a member knows (or has reasonable grounds for believing) that a distribution to him was in contravention of the Act, he will be liable to repay to the company a sum equal to the value of any distribution unlawfully made to him: s. 277 CA 1985.

NOTE: The above sections do not refer to investment companies. Provisions relating to distributions made by such companies are dealt with separately in ss. 265–267. CA 1985.

Dividend procedure and documents

4. Procedure on declaration and payment of dividends

(a) *Consult the Articles.* When profit available for dividend has been determined, it may be necessary to consult the company's Articles so as to ensure that the dividend rights of the various classes of shareholders are understood and that the distribution will be properly made.

(b) *A board meeting is convened* at which the directors decide what dividend (if any) they recommend for each of the various classes of shares, and a resolution is passed, recommending the payment of dividend(s) and stating the rate(s) and date of payment.

(c) *Further resolutions may be passed at the same meeting,* on the assumption that the directors' recommendation concerning the payment of dividends will be approved, namely:

(*i*) that the Register of Members (and Transfer Register, if any) be closed and the fact advertised;

NOTE: In practice, many companies do not close the books but announce payment of dividends to all persons appearing in the Register of Members on a specified date prior to the date fixed for payment.

(*ii*) that the bank be authorized to deal with the payment of dividends, and to open a special dividend account or accounts;

(*iii*) that the draft of the directors' report be approved;

(*iv*) that copies of the directors' report and accounts, together with auditors' report and the balance sheet, be distributed to those so entitled;

(*v*) that the annual general meeting be convened, the notices to be accompanied by companies of the report and accounts, and sent not less than 21 days before the meeting.

(d) *Convene the annual general meeting*, ensuring that the notices are accompanied by copies of the directors' report and accounts, and that adequate notice is given.

NOTE: Notice should also be sent to the company's auditors and, where applicable, copies of the report and accounts *only* should be sent to any members who are not entitled to attend the meeting, and to debenture holders.

(e) *Give notice in the press* as to the closing of the Register of Members, if that is intended.

(f) *The Register of Members is brought up to date.* Transfers received on or before the date fixed for closing the register (and Transfer Register, if any) will be the subject of another board meeting (or meeting of the transfer committee), at which a resolution will be passed authorizing transfers.

(g) *The dividend lists can be prepared* from the register, once the Register of Members has been brought up to date. These lists are usually on loose sheets to facilitate distribution of the work. A specimen ruling is shown.

Dividend list

Shareholder							
Name	Address	No. of shares	Gross dividend	*Less* tax	Net amount	Warrant no.	Remarks dividend mandates, etc.
			£	£	£		

(h) *At the annual general meeting*, it may be assumed that the dividend(s) recommended by the directors are approved by the shareholders.

(i) *Dividend warrants*, having already been printed and serially numbered, are now prepared from the dividend lists (in practice this work is often done even before the holding of the annual general meeting).

(j) *Check dividend warrants* and reconcile them back to the dividend list total(s), after which the bank may be supplied with a dividend list and instructed to transfer the list total to a special dividend account or accounts.

(k) *The secretary may now sign the warrants* or, alternatively, in a large company, either of the following methods may be employed:

(*i*) by resolution of the board, the signing may be delegated to several responsible officials; or

(*ii*) if permitted by the Articles, mechanical signatures may be used.

NOTE: If this method is used, the bank must be notified and special precautions must be taken to minimize error or fraud.

(l) *Dividend warrants can now be made ready for posting.* After they have been folded, inserted in addressed envelopes (or window envelopes), sealed and franked, they should be given a final check and the total number of envelopes agreed with the dividend lists.

NOTE: At this stage, it may be necessary to prepare vouchers and 'strip lists', ready for despatch to 'listed' (or 'bulk') banks, referred to in **(m)** below.

(m) *Finally, the dividend warrants are posted.* At the same time, where applicable, post vouchers and 'strip lists' to the 'listed' banks.

(n) Subsequently, the bank will return the 'cheque' portion of the warrants as they are presented for payment by the shareholders. After checking them against the bank statement they should be securely filed and retained for at least 12 years, as should dividend lists, to satisfy the Limitations Act 1980.

NOTE: If the company concerned was listed, the procedure outlined above would have to be modified and the documentation drafted to take account of the Continuing Obligations imposed upon such a company by the Stock Exchange. The Continuing Obligations are set out in Chapter 2 and reference should be made thereto.

5. Dividend warrants

(a) A dividend warrant is an important document, as it serves two main purposes.

(*i*) The 'notice' or 'counterfoil' portion informs the shareholder of the gross amount of the dividend, the rate and amount of tax deducted, and the net amount of dividend to which he is entitled. It also states that tax has been or will be paid. This must be carefully preserved as evidence of the tax deducted.

(*ii*) The 'warrant' or 'cheque' portion must be presented to the bank upon which it is drawn — usually within a specified period of, say, six months — otherwise it becomes 'stale'.

(*iii*) There is a standard form of dividend/interest warrant and related tax voucher. It is Standard 32 'Dividend and Interest Warrants and Related Tax Voucher' published by the Committee of the London and Scottish Clearing Bankers.

The Stock Exchange requires that, in the case of listed securities, the full identifying code should be printed in the box 'Securities code' to be located as close as possible to the top right-hand corner of the tax voucher. These security code numbers are published against the names of companies in the Stock Exchange Daily Official Listing.

(b) To prevent fraud during the preparation of dividend warrants:

(*i*) there must be strict control, by a responsible official, on the issue of blank warrants to the staff engaged in completing them;

(*ii*) only the exact number of blank warrants should be issued by him, and spoilt warrants must be returned to him for replacement and cancellation.

(c) Even stricter security measures are necessary when facsimile signatures are used on the dividend warrants, whether the 'signing' is done by machine in the company's own offices or by the printers who were responsible for the printing of the warrants. In the latter case, the measures suggested are as follows.

(*i*) Notify the company's bankers that it is intended to use facsimile signatures on dividend warrants, and provide them with specimens of the signatories (if, as is usual in most cases, the warrants are to be initialled for the purpose of identification, the bank will also require specimens of the initials of persons so authorized).

(*ii*) Instruct the printers to supply a specified number of warrants bearing facsimile signatures. The number specified should include a small number of spares, to allow for spoilt warrants.

NOTE: It is usually necessary to order a small supply of warrants *without* signature, to replace any which may be lost after using up all of those bearing facsimile signatures. These must be signed manually as and when they are needed.

(*iii*) When the warrants are received from the printers they must be strictly controlled by a responsible official as regards issue, replacement in exchange for spoilt warrants, and cancellation of the latter.

(*iv*) After completion of the warrants, they should be thoroughly checked, and then initialled in the space provided. The checking must be carried out by members of the staff who had no part in preparing the warrants, or by the company's auditors.

(*v*) Notify the bank of the number of warrants to be issued and serial numbers of the warrants.

(*vi*) Any 'signed' warrants in excess of requirements must be cancelled as soon as ever possible. If any replacements are subsequently required, the unsigned warrants (already referred to) must be used, after hand signature.

(*vii*) The printers' 'blocks' of facsimile signatures should be returned, and carefully stored in safe or strong room.

(*viii*) Obtain a certificate from the printers confirming:

(1) the number of warrants printed by them;

(2) that they have 'broken type' and cancelled or destroyed any warrants used by them in trial prints.

6. Dividend mandates

(a) *Definition.* A dividend mandate is an instruction, given to a company by one of its shareholders, to pay any dividend to which he is entitled to his bank, broker or other person. The instruction may, of course, refer to the payment of interest on, say, debentures.

(b) *Forms.* A shareholder is usually entitled to this facility, and most large companies provide printed forms for the purpose; if not, the official mandate form (or Dividend Request Form, as it is called) recommended by the Committee of the London Clearing Bankers is obtainable from banks in the clearing house system.

(c) *Joint holders.* A mandate in respect of dividend payable to a joint holding must be signed by *all* the joint holders, and the death of any one of them automatically revokes the instructions. A fresh mandate should then be obtained from the surviving joint holder(s).

(d) *'Listed' banks.*

(*i*) Where, as often happens, a bank is named in a large number of mandates, labour and stationery can be saved if only one warrant is prepared for the total dividend payable to all the shareholders who have mandated in favour of that particular bank.

(*ii*) This one 'cheque' portion of the warrant is then sent to the head office of the bank concerned, together with a list of the shareholders affected, showing the dividend due to each and the branches at which they have their respective accounts. A 'counterfoil' portion is also sent for each shareholder included in the list.

7. Outstanding dividends

(a) These are a source of trouble and expense. It may surprise many to learn that there should be any difficulty in getting shareholders to claim the dividend to which they are entitled. Nevertheless it is a fact that many large public companies regard this as a serious problem, as a great deal of time is taken in marking off paid warrants as they are received from the company's bank and, in the last resort, recording those warrants which remain outstanding.

(b) To ensure that the number of outstanding warrants is kept to a minimum, companies introduce all manner of devices, on the principle that 'prevention is better than cure'; of these, the following are typical.

(*i*) The attention of shareholders is drawn to the many advantages, to themselves as well as to the company, of completing a dividend mandate. This may be done by circular letter to the shareholders.

(*ii*) As an alternative to the sending of circular letters, some companies print a memorandum on the back of their dividend warrant counterfoils, in which they bring to the shareholders' notice the advantages of dividend mandates, and provide a form of mandate on each warrant.

(*iii*) In the case of new members, a letter of welcome might be sent which would include a recommendation to make use of a dividend mandate (enclosed with the letter).

(*iv*) As warrants frequently become outstanding following a shareholder's death, it is often a good plan to draw the attention of the legal representative(s) to the current dividend position and, where applicable, to any outstanding dividends as soon as possible after probate or letters of administration have been presented.

(*v*) A footnote printed on all dividend warrants, reminding shareholders that the warrant becomes 'stale' after (say) six months, is another method employed by many companies, but it is doubtful whether it has the desired effect with the more troublesome cases.

(c) If, despite all the above preventive measures, the number of unclaimed dividends continues to mount, then some system of recording the unclaimed sums must be devised, for example as follows.

(*i*) Mark off paid warrants against the dividend list as the warrants are received from the bank after payment. Check also against the bank statement concerned with the dividend account.

(*ii*) Prepare a list of outstanding warrants (i.e. those which had not been marked off against the dividend list) giving brief particulars, including warrant numbers and their respective amounts.

(*iii*) Amend the list if, during (say) the next six months, any of the outstanding warrants are cashed and the paid warrants received from the bank.

(*iv*) At the end of the period of (say) six months, outstanding warrants having become 'stale', they require re-dating, and shareholders are usually required to present them at the company's office for re-dating and verification. A footnote on the warrant usually emphasizes this, If, however, a large number of warrants are still outstanding, a letter to the shareholders concerned along the following lines might serve a useful purpose.

Dear Sir (or Madam),

We note from the Company's dividend account that the dividend warrant(s) described below, issued to you on .... 19..... do(es) not appear to have been presented for payment.

As the warrant is now out of date, we should be obliged if you would return it to us for verification and re-dating. It will be returned to you as soon as possible, after which you may present it to your bank for early payment.

If you have lost or destroyed your warrant, please let us know by return. We shall then provide you with the necessary form for completion, to enable us to supply you with a duplicate warrant.

Please return this letter with your reply.

Yours faithfully,

Date........................ ....Secretary.

Particulars of outstanding warrant(s)

Date payable	Dividend No	Warrant No.	Amount	
			£	p

(*v*) The dividend account is closed at the end of the (say) six-month period and any balance transferred to an Outstanding Dividends Account.

(*vi*) An 'Outstanding Dividend Register' may be prepared, if warranted by the number of unclaimed dividends. It is usually advisable to use a loose-leaf register for this purpose.

(*vii*) A separate account is kept in the register for each dividend, in which a record will be made whenever unclaimed dividends are transferred to the Outstanding Dividends Account. As outstanding dividends are cashed from time to time and the paid warrants received from the bank, an entry will be made in the appropriate account or accounts and, where applicable, any 'closed' account will be removed from the register.

(*viii*) A Summary Account is kept in the register. If this is kept up to date, the running total of this account ought to agree, or be reconcilable with, the Outstanding Dividends Account at the bank.

(d) In the case of listed companies, companies may take power in their Articles to cease sending dividend warrants by post because warrants have been returned or left uncashed on two consecutive occasions.

8. Loss or destruction of dividend warrants

A large company often receives letters from its shareholders stating that a dividend warrant has been lost, mislaid or destroyed. In such cases, it is obviously necessary to safeguard the company against false statements and against the fraudulent conversion of the original warrant if the company issues a duplicate. A typical procedure on receipt of a shareholder's request for a duplicate warrant is as follows.

(a) Notify the bank at once and give instructions to stop payment on the original warrant (if the shareholder has delayed his request, it may be found that someone has already fraudulently cashed the warrant!).

(b) Acknowledge the shareholder's letter and send him a form of indemnity, requesting him to return the completed form and (if permitted by the Articles) a nominal replacement fee.

(c) On receipt of the completed form of indemnity and

remittance of the replacement fee (where applicable), supply a copy of the warrant, taking care to mark it DUPLICATE.

(d) If the counterfoil portion of the warrant is also to be replaced, the copy must also be marked DUPLICATE, as this is a requirement of the Inland Revenue authorities.

(e) Authorize the bank to honour only the *duplicate* warrant.

(f) Record the issue of the duplicate warrant on the dividend list.

> NOTE: Some companies demand a banker's counter-indemnity in addition to the shareholder's own indemnity. If the amount of the warrant is large, such a demand may be justifiable.

9. Power of the Secretary of State under s. 445 CA 1985

The Secretary of State can impose restrictions, including (*inter alia*) the withholding of payment of dividend, as follows.

(a) where the Secretary of State is having difficulty in finding out the relevant facts concerning shares which are the subject of an investigation owing to the unwillingness of the persons concerned to assist the investigation, he has power to direct that no payment shall be made on any sums due from the company on those shares, whether in respect of capital or otherwise.

(b) An aggrieved person may, however, apply to the Court to remove the restriction imposed by the Secretary of State.

(c) In order to obtain information from a person on whom a notice is served under s. 212 CA 1985 (power of company to require information with respect to interests in its voting shares), s. 216 CA 1985 gives the company rights to apply to the court for an order directing that the shares in question shall be subject to the restrictions imposed by s. 445 CA 1985 relating to the transfer, voting or dividend rights in respect of such shares.

(d) Under s. 135 CA 1989 the Secretary of State is given power by statutory instrument to amend the above provisions relating to restrictions on shares.

Employees' share schemes

10. Definition

For the purposes of the Companies Act 1985 the term

'employees' share scheme' is defined by s. 743 of the Act as 'a scheme for encouraging or facilitating the holding of shares or debentures in a company by or for the benefit of:

(a) the bona fide employees or former employees of the company, the company's subsidiary or holding company or a subsidiary of the company's holding company, or
(b) the wives, husbands, widows, widowers or children or stepchildren under the age of 18 of such employees or former employees'.

The establishment and maintenance of such a scheme constitutes an exception to the prohibition on a company's providing financial assistance for the purpose of purchasing its own shares.

In the case of listed companies and their subsidiaries the adoption of such a scheme requires approval by an ordinary resolution of the shareholders and the scheme must contain provisions relating to various specified matters.

11. Background

(a) Share schemes have been operated by companies in favour of their employees for many years. Legislation in 1972 and 1974, which subjected capital profits to income tax, made the schemes unfashionable, but in 1978, 1980 and 1984 the respective Finance Acts offered taxation concessions for approved schemes set up for employees.
(b) Three types of Revenue-approved share scheme avoid the tax pitfalls which can arise in the operation of an employees' share scheme. These comprise a form of share incentive scheme, the profit-sharing scheme, and two share option schemes, the savings-related share option scheme and the approved share option scheme. The latter scheme has proved very popular as, unlike the others, it can be operated on a selective basis.

12. Revenue-approved schemes

(a) Such a scheme may extend to employees or directors of the company establishing the scheme or of all or any of the companies which it controls. Such a scheme is referred to as a 'group scheme', and the companies over which it extends are 'participating companies'.

(b) In relation to all such schemes the Revenue will only give approval if certain conditions are met. These relate to the proper use of the scheme and the prevention of what the Revenue see as excessive relief being given to individuals by manipulation of the circumstances in which the scheme is to operate. The principal requirements therefore relate to:

(*i*) persons having a 'material interest' in relation to the scheme; and

(*ii*) the shares to which directors or employees become or may become entitled.

(c) *'Material interest'.* An employee cannot participate in the share scheme if, together with his 'associates', he has or at any time within the preceding 12 months he has had a 'material interest' in a 'close company' which is either the company whose shares are to be obtained or appropriated, or a company which has 'control' of that company or is a 'member of a consortium which owns that company'.

'Material interest' refers to beneficial ownership or direct/indirect control of more than 10 per cent of 'ordinary share capital' (25 per cent for the profit-sharing scheme and savings-related share option scheme) or entitlement on an apportionment of the whole distributable income to the same percentage thereof.

(d) *Scheme shares.* Scheme shares are shares a director or employee has rights to acquire under the scheme or shares to be acquired by the trustees as appropriate.

Scheme shares must satisfy various conditions as follows.

(*i*) They must form part of the ordinary share capital of

(1) the grantor; or

(2) a company which controls the grantor; or

(3) a company which either is or has control of a company which:

(*A*) is a member of a consortium owning either the grantor or a company having control of the grantor; and

(*B*) beneficially owns not less than three-twentieths of the ordinary share capital of the company so owned.

(*ii*) They must be

(1) shares of a class quoted on a recognized stock exchange; or

(2) shares of a company which is not under the control of another company; or

(3) shares in a company which is under the control of another company (other than a close company, or one which would be a close company if resident in the UK) whose shares are quoted on a recognized stock exchange.

(*iii*) They must be fully paid up and not redeemable and not subject to any restrictions other than authorized restrictions.

(*iv*) Except where the scheme shares are in a company with only one class of shares, the majority of the issued shares of the same class must either be 'employee-control' shares, or must be held by persons other than:

(1) persons who acquired them in pursuance of a right conferred on them or an opportunity afforded to them as director or employee of the acquiring company or any other company and not in pursuance of an offer to the public;

(2) trustees holding shares for those who acquired them as in (1) above;

(3) companies which have control of the company whose shares are in question or of which that company is an associated company (where the shares are not of a class quoted on a recognized stock exchange but fall within (*ii*)(3) above).

Employee-control shares are shares by virtue of which the persons holding them are together able to control the company; where those persons are or have been employees or directors of the company, or of another company which is under the control of the company.

(e) *Approval of schemes generally.* To obtain approval, a written application must be made to the board and must contain such particulars and be supported by such evidence as the board may require.

The board must approve a scheme if the necessary conditions for that particular type of scheme are satisfied, unless they decide that there are features of the scheme which are neither essential nor reasonably incidental to the purpose of providing for employees and directors benefits in the nature of rights to acquire shares or of interests in shares, as appropriate.

If an approved scheme is altered, the approval is ineffective thereafter, unless the Board approves the alteration: Sch. 9 Para.4 Income and Corporation Taxes Act 1988.

13. Approved profit-sharing schemes

The Finance Act 1978, ss. 53–61 introduced provisions to give relief from income tax for employees participating in approved profit-sharing schemes. These provisions are now largely contained in ss. 186, 187, Sch. 9 and Sch. 10 ICTA 1988. These schemes involve a company in setting up a trust fund with trustees acquiring shares in the company which are then appropriated to individual employees. The shares can be acquired through purchase from existing shareholders; or through a gift; or by subscription for newly issued shares; or by way of a rights or bonus issue in respect of shares which they already beneficially hold. The trustees receive the necessary funds from the company; in practice the amount set aside by a company may vary according to the company's profitability. All full-time working directors and employees must be given the right to participate in the scheme. The main criteria to be satisfied for approval of the scheme are that:

(a) the market value of shares appropriated to an employee in any one year must not be less than £1250 or 10 per cent of his salary, whichever is the greater, subject to a maximum of £5000. This applies for the tax year in question or the preceding tax year.

(b) the shares appropriated must be retained by the trustees for at least two years or until the earlier death or retirement of the employee.

No tax charge arises on the appropriation or on any subsequent increase in value of the shares. After the appropriation any dividends belong to the employee.

Once the two-year period has expired, the employee can direct the trustees to sell the shares. No income tax liability arises if the shares are disposed of five or more years after the appropriation date. If sold within five years, income tax is payable on the lower of the actual sale proceeds and an appropriate percentage of the original market value of the shares. This percentage is 100 per cent if the shares concerned were disposed of within four years of allocation and 75 per cent if disposal occurs after four years but less than five.

Where the employment ceases or the employee reaches retirement age within the five-year period, the percentage of the original market value charged is 50 per cent. Approved profit-sharing schemes are tax-free for employers, who can deduct sums paid to such a scheme as a business expense for corporation tax, provided that the sums are spent on acquiring the shares within the following nine months or are used to pay the trustees' expenses.

14. Approved savings-related share option schemes

A share option scheme which is open to all employees may be approved under s. 185(1)–3(A) ICTA 1988. Ordinary shares have to be acquired from the proceeds of Save-As-You-Earn (SAYE) savings contracts in which the maximum permitted monthly contribution by an employee is currently £100.

The price of the shares must be fixed at the time when the employee is granted the option and must not be less than 90 per cent in value of the shares at that time. Provided that the option is not exercisable or not exercised within three years of its acquisition the employee is exempt from any charge to income tax on the grant or exercise of the option. If such a scheme is to be an approved scheme the option rights given thereby cannot be transferred.

15. Approved share option schemes

If the scheme comes within the scope of s. 185(2) ICTA 1988, no income tax is charged on the exercise of an option to acquire ordinary shares in the employer company when that option is granted after 5th April 1984. The only charge is to Capital Gains Tax — if and when the shares are sold. Approval will be granted if:

(a) the price charged for the shares is not less than their market value at the date the option is granted;
(b) the scheme must be restricted to employees and full-time working directors, though employees who exercise the option after they have left full-time employment, and their personal

representatives who exercise the option within one year of the employee's death, may be included;
(c) the option must be exercisable after three but within ten years of its grant;
(d) the aggregate market value of the total shares available per employee must not exceed the greater of £100,000 and four times his current or previous year's salary (or in the absence of a preceding-year salary, his annual salary).

Progress test 10

1. Define the term 'dividend' and state the chief rules to be applied by a company as regards the payment of dividends to its shareholders. (1, 2)

2. Outline the procedure for paying a dividend on ordinary shares, commencing with the board's decision to recommend a distribution. (4)

3. Prepare a programme covering the procedure for paying a dividend to a large number of shareholders. The programme should be set out in chronological order so that each item can be marked off as it is completed. *ICSA* (4)

4. Owing to a large increase in the number of shareholders of the public company of which you are secretary, it is intended to print future dividend warrants with a facsimile signature. Detail the precautions which should be taken in connection with the issue of these warrants and draft a form to be used to ensure that every warrant printed is accounted for. *ICSA* (5)

5. Write brief notes on (a) dividend warrant, (b) dividend mandate, (c) interim dividend, (d) listed banks. (2–6)

6. On being appointed secretary of a public company incorporated thirty years ago, you find that a considerable number of dividend warrants have remained unclaimed from time to time. The company has regularly paid two dividends annually, but no composite record of the outstanding dividends

has been maintained. Discuss the advantages and disadvantages of endeavouring to trace and pay the persons entitled to the outstanding dividends and state how you would keep a record of the unclaimed sums so that a continual reference to individual dividend sheets could be avoided. Assuming that the directors instructed you to make every effort to pay the outstanding dividends, how would you deal with the matter? **(7)**

7. As secretary of a company, you are informed in writing by a shareholder that a dividend warrant for £50 recently received by him has been accidentally destroyed. Explain in detail the office procedure involved in connection with the lost warrant and also write a letter in reply to the shareholder. **(8)**

8. In certain circumstances the Secretary of State is empowered by s. 445 of the Companies Act 1985 to subject shares or debentures to certain restrictions. You are asked to assume that this power has been exercised in regard to a holding which is registered in your company's books and you are required to write to the member concerned explaining why you are unable to pay him a dividend which has been declared. **(9)**

9. What is an 'employees' share scheme'? **(10)**

10. Outline the various approved employee share schemes. **(11–15)**

11. Your directors are considering the introduction of a savings-related share option scheme. Draft a memorandum briefly indicating what is involved and explain how approval of the scheme by the taxation authorities is obtained. *ICSA* **(10–15)**

12. Explain the following and discuss with reference to the practical elements:

(a) alternative directors;
(b) unclaimed dividends;
(c) directors who reach the age of 70 years; and
(d) directors' qualification shares. *ICSA* **(10; 14: 3, 4, 15)**

13. As Secretary of a company, you are informed in writing by a shareholder that a dividend warrant for £150 recently received by him has been accidentally destroyed. Explain in detail the office procedure involved in connection with the lost warrant and also write a letter in reply to the shareholder. *ICSA* (8)

11 Alterations of share capital

Alteration of capital under s. 121 CA 1985

1. Permitted forms of alteration

For various reasons a company may find it necessary to alter its share capital, and s. 121 CA 1985 provides that a company limited by shares, or a company limited by guarantee and having a share capital, may, *if its Articles permit,* alter the conditions of its Memorandum in order to effect any of the following alterations.

(a) *Increase* the share capital by new shares of such amount as the company thinks necessary.
(b) *Consolidate and divide* all or part of the share capital into shares of larger amount.
(c) *Convert* all or any of its paid-up shares into stock.
(d) *Re-convert* stock into paid-up shares of any amount.
(e) *Subdivide* all or part of its shares into shares of smaller denomination, but maintaining the proportion between the amount paid and the amount (if any) unpaid on each reduced share.
(f) *Cancel* shares which have not been taken up, and thus reduce the whole or part of the company's unissued authorized capital.

NOTE: This form of cancellation must not be confused with a reduction of capital under s. 135 CA 1985.

2. Consent of general meeting

The above alterations can be effected only by the company

in general meeting; that is, the power to make the alteration *cannot* be delegated to the directors.

3. Form of resolution required

(a) *An ordinary* resolution is adequate, unless the company's Articles demand another form of resolution.
(b) Where the Articles give no power to alter the capital, *one* special resolution is sufficient both to alter the Articles for the purpose and to alter the share capital: *Campbell's Case* (1873).

4. Notice to the Registrar

Notice must be given to the Registrar of the passing of the resolution to give effect to any of the above resolutions:

(a) *within 15 days* after passing the resolution to *increase* the capital: s. 123 CA 1985;
(b) *within one month* after passing the resolution in all other forms of alteration of capital permitted under s. 121 CA 1985.

5. Increase of capital

(a) *The need for increased capital* is usually the result of expanding business. If, for example, the whole of a company's authorized capital has been issued and paid up, further capital may be needed for purposes of development, and the directors may prefer to increase the authorized capital and, assuming there to be authority under s. 80 CA 1985, issue further shares rather than issue debentures or apply to the bank for an overdraft.
(b) *Procedure.*

(*i*) Convene a general meeting of the company, giving notice required by the Articles — but not less than 14 days' notice of an extraordinary general meeting.

NOTE: If the Articles require a special resolution to increase capital, not less than 21 days' notice is required.

(*ii*) The necessary resolution is passed, e.g.:

RESOLVED: THAT the capital of the Company be and is hereby increased from £50,000 in shares of £1 each to £100,000 by the addition to the authorized capital of 25,000 £1 shares, to rank *pari passu* in all respects with the aforementioned £1 shares, and 25,000 6 per cent preference shares of £1 each.

(*iii*) Within 15 days of the passing of the resolution, file with the Registrar of Companies:

(1) *notice of Increase in Nominal Capital* on the prescribed form (Form G123);

(2) *a copy of the resolution* authorizing the increase of capital;

(3) a copy of the Memorandum as amended.

(*iv*) Amend all copies of the Memorandum to ensure that every copy subsequently issued shows the increase of capital. Failure to comply renders the company, and every officer of the company, in default, liable to fines for each occasion on which copies are issued after the date of the alteration.

NOTE: If the company concerned was listed, the procedure outlined above, would have to be modified and the documentation drafted to take account of the Continuing Obligations imposed upon such a company by the Stock Exchange. The Continuing Obligations are set out in Chapter 2 and reference should be made thereto.

6. Consolidation and division into shares of larger denomination

(a) *When desirable.* Although consolidation alone is now a comparatively rare occurrence, when used in conjunction with a division it enables a company to even out shares of odd nominal values; where, for example, a company has on some previous occasion created shares of 7½p each as the result of a repayment of capital under s. 135 CA 1985, ten 7½p shares may be consolidated into one 75p share and the latter be subdivided into three 25p shares.

(b) *Procedure.*

(*i*) Convene a general meeting of the company, giving notice appropriate to the form of resolution required by the articles.

(*ii*) The necessary resolution is passed, i.e. an *ordinary* resolution (unless the Articles provide to the contrary), for example:

RESOLVED: THAT the 300,000 fully paid ordinary shares of 7½p each be consolidated into 30,000 fully paid ordinary shares of 75p each, and that the said 30,000 fully paid ordinary shares of 75p each be divided into 90,000 fully paid ordinary shares of 25p each.

(*iii*) Within one month of the passing of the resolution, file with the Registrar of Companies a Notice of Consolidation on the prescribed form (Form G123) accompanied by an amended copy of the Memorandum.

NOTE: If an ordinary resolution is adequate to authorize the consolidation, it will *not* be necessary to file a copy with the Registrar; if, however, a special resolution is required by the Articles, it will be necessary to file a copy of it within 15 days.

(*iv*) Amend all copies of the Memorandum in stock, so that the effect of the consolidation is clearly shown: s. 20 CA 1985.

NOTE: If the company concerned was listed, the procedure outlined above would have to be modified and the documentation drafted to take account of the Continuing Obligations imposed upon such a company by the Stock Exchange. The Continuing Obligations are set out in Chapter 2 and reference should be made thereto.

7. Conversion of fully paid shares into stock, and re-conversion

(a) *The advantages claimed* for conversion of shares into stock — namely, that it enables a company to dispense with distinguishing numbering of its shares and permits transfer in irregular amounts or fractions — are now less apparent, if they exist at all. This may be judged from a consideration of the following points.

(*i*) Section 182(2) CA 1985 permits a company to dispense with the numbering of its shares, subject to conditions laid down in that section.

(*ii*) The Articles of most companies require stock to be transferred in fixed multiples.

(*iii*) Where Stock Exchange regulations apply, transfer is restricted to multiples of £1.

(b) *Procedure.*

(*i*) As a preliminary, ensure that the Articles give the necessary power to effect the conversion, and that the shares *are* fully paid.

(*ii*) Convene a general meeting of the company, giving notice appropriate to the form of resolution required.

(*iii*) The necessary resolution is passed — an ordinary resolution, unless the Articles require any other form of resolution; for example:

> RESOLVED: THAT the 2,000,000 ordinary shares of 25p each forming part of the Company's capital, already issued and fully paid, be and are hereby converted into stock, to be known as Ordinary Stock.

(*iv*) Within one month of the passing of the resolution, file with the Registrar of Companies a Notice of Conversion (or, where applicable, of re-conversion) accompanied by an amended copy of the memorandum.

> NOTE: If an ordinary resolution is adequate to authorize the conversion (or re-conversion), it will *not* be necessary to file a copy with the Registrar; if, however, the Articles require a special resolution, it will be necessary to file a copy of it within 15 days.

(*v*) Amend all copies of the Memorandum in stock, so that the effect of the conversion is clearly shown: s. 20 CA 1985.

> NOTE: If the company concerned was listed, the procedure outlined above would have to be modified and the documentation drafted to take account of the Continuing Obligations imposed upon such a company by the Stock Exchange. The Continuing Obligations are set out in Chapter 2 and reference should be made thereto.

8. Subdivision of shares into shares of smaller denomination, e.g. £1 shares subdivided into 20 5p shares

(a) *When desirable.* This is usually done because of the

increasing popularity of shares of small denomination and the wider section of the public they appear to attract.

(b) *Procedure.*

(*i*) Convene a general meeting of the company, giving notice appropriate to the form of resolution required.

(*ii*) The necessary resolution is passed — an ordinary resolution, unless the Articles require any other form of resolution; for example:

> RESOLVED: THAT the capital of the Company, comprising 100,000 ordinary shares of £1 each fully paid up, be subdivided into 2,000,000 ordinary shares of 5p each fully paid up.

(*iii*) Within one month of the passing of the resolution, file Notice of Subdivision on the prescribed form (Form G122) accompanied by an amended copy of the Memorandum.

(*iv*) Amend all copies of the Memorandum in stock, so that the effect of the subdivision is clearly shown: s. 20 CA 1985.

> NOTE: If the company concerned was listed, the procedure outlined above would have to be modified and the documentation drafted to take account of the Continuing Obligations imposed upon such a company by the Stock Exchange. The Continuing Obligations are set out in Chapter 2 and reference should be made thereto.

9. Cancellation of shares

Cancellation of shares which have not been taken up; e.g. a company with authorized capital of £1,00,000 and issued capital of £50,000 may cancel (say) £30,000 of its *unissued* authorized capital, thereby reducing the authorized capital to £70,000.

(a) *The effect* is to reduce the capital which the company is by its Memorandum authorized to issue, and can only be effected under s. 121 CA 1985 where the authorized capital exceeds the issued capital.

(b) *Not a reduction of issued capital.* It is not to be confused with a reduction of capital such as can be effected under the provisions of s. 135 CA 1985 (*see* **11–14**).

(c) *Procedure.*

(*i*) Convene a general meeting of the company, giving notice appropriate to the form of resolution required.

(*ii*) The necessary resolution is passed, i.e. an ordinary resolution unless the Articles require any other form of resolution; for example:

> RESOLVED: THAT the unissued 50,000 deferred shares of £1 each forming part of the Company's authorized capital, be and they are hereby cancelled.

(*iii*) Within one month of the passing of the resolution, file Notice of Cancellation on the prescribed form (Form G122), such to be accompanied by an amended copy of the Memorandum.

> NOTE: If the cancellation is effected simultaneously with an increase of capital, so long as there is no increase beyond the registered capital of the company, it will *not* be necessary to file any other documents.

(*iv*) Amend all copies of the Memorandum in stock, so that the effect of the cancellation (and simultaneous increase, where applicable) is clearly shown: s. 20 CA 1985.

> NOTE: If the company concerned was listed, the procedure outlined above would have to be modified and the documentation drafted to take account of the Continuing Obligations imposed upon such a company by the Stock Exchange. The Continuing Obligations are set out in Chapter 2 and reference should be made thereto.

10. Additional work entailed in connection with the above procedures

According to the form of alteration, some or all of the following matters may have to be dealt with by the secretary and/or registrar:

(a) preparation of new share certificates;
(b) closing the Register of Members if it is intended to call in share (or stock) certificates;

> NOTE: In practice the certificates are *not* usually called in, i.e. they continue to be accepted on the Stock Exchange as

good delivery, and the exchange of a new certificate for the old one is effected if or when a transfer is subsequently lodged for registration..

(c) alteration of the Register of members, e.g. in cases of consolidation or subdivision;

(d) transfer from Share Register to Stock Register, in case of a conversion to stock.

Reduction of capital under s. 135 CA 1985

11. When reduction is allowed

Section 135 CA 1985 permits a company limited by shares, or a company limited by guarantee and having a share capital, to reduce its share capital in any way:

(a) if the Articles permit,
(b) by special resolution, and
(c) with Court sanction.

NOTE: Power given in the Memorandum alone is *not* sufficient: *Re Dexine Patent Packing Co.* (1903).

12. Statutory methods

The Companies Act 1985 mentions the following particular methods of capital reduction, but these are not to be regarded as exhaustive and do not affect the generality of the power.

(a) Extinguishing or reducing the unpaid liability on any of the company's shares; for example:

(*i*) a £1 share with 75p paid up to rank as a 75p share fully paid, i.e. *extinguishing* the liability of 25p per share; or

(*ii*) a £1 share with 37½p paid up to rank as a 50p share with 37½p paid up, i.e. *reducing* the liability.

(b) With or without extinguishing or reducing liability on any of the company's shares, cancelling any paid-up share capital which is lost or unrepresented by available assets; for example:

(*i*) a fully paid £1 share to rank as a fully paid 50p share, i.e. *without reducing liability*; or (*ii*) a £1 share with 75p paid up to rank as a 50p share fully paid, i.e. *extinguishing* liability.

(c) With or without extinguishing or reducing liability on any of the company's shares, paying off any paid-up share capital which is in excess of the wants of the company; for example:

(*i*) each holder of £1 fully paid shares to be repaid 25p per share, and the shares then to rank as 75p fully paid shares, i.e. *without extinguishing or reducing* liability;

(*ii*) each holder of £1 shares with 87½p paid up to be repaid 37½p per share, and the shares then to rank as 50p shares fully paid, i.e. *extinguishing* the liability.

13. Possible reasons for reduction of capital

(a) A company's paid-up capital may not be adequately represented by available assets, owing, for example, to losses on fixed assets or on investments, and the assets concerned are to be written down.

(b) A company's capital may be in excess of requirements, in which case a return of capital might be advisable.

Thus, over-capitalization may be the result of closing down part of the business, and it is being found that capital invested outside the business at low rates of interest is resulting in an overall reduction of dividends.

(c) A company with a considerable adverse balance on profit and loss account, the result of an accumulation of previous losses, may wish to write off the balance.

14. Procedure

(a) Preliminary discussion of an informal character will take place at a board meeting. Subsequently, the directors will probably consult the company's solicitors and accountants. Together they will plan a scheme of reduction.

(b) It is often advisable to do some preliminary research on the reaction of those who are most likely to be affected by the reduction.

(*i*) It might be well to ascertain the views of some of the largest shareholders, particularly those with voting power. If their support is not forthcoming there is a poor chance of passing a special resolution for reduction of capital.

(*ii*) It might also be advisable to invite some of the largest creditors (including debenture holders, if any) to a board meeting, with the object of explaining the scheme and how, if at all, it is likely to affect them and to solicit their support. This might forestall their later objections to the Court when the company petitions the Court for sanction.

(c) Convene a general meeting of the company, bearing in mind that the notice requires special attention:

(*i*) at least 21 days' notice is required;

(*ii*) it must set out the exact wording of the resolution to be passed, and state that it is to be a special resolution;

(*iii*) it is usually accompanied by a circular, setting out the reasons for the proposed reduction of capital.

(d) At the meeting, the special resolution is passed authorizing the reduction of capital; for example:

RESOLVED: THAT the capital of the company be reduced from £500,000 divided into 400,000 ordinary shares of £1 each and 100,000 6 per cent preference shares of £1 each, all of which are issued and fully paid into £200,000 divided into 400,000 shares of 50p each fully paid up; the reduction to be effected:

(*i*) by repaying to the holders of the 400,000 £1 ordinary shares the sum of 50p per share, and by reducing the nominal amount of all the said 400,000 ordinary shares from £1 to 50p per share.

(*ii*) by cancellation of the 100,000 6 per cent preference shares of £1 each, to be effected by repayment to the holders of the said 100,000 6 per cent preference shares the sum of 105p per share, which sum includes a premium of 5p per share.

NOTE: If the Articles require alteration, i.e. where they do not already permit reduction of capital, this must also be done by special resolution, preferably at an earlier meeting. In this case, one special resolution will not serve the double purpose of both altering the Articles and authorizing reduction of capital: *Re Patent Invert Sugar Co.* (1885).

(e) File a copy of the resolution with the Registrar of Companies, within 15 days of the passing of the resolution.

(f) Application can be made to the Court as soon as desired after the passing of the special resolution. It is presented in the form of a petition for confirmation of the reduction.
(g) The Court may then take such steps as it considers necessary to safeguard creditors (including debenture-holders) and to ensure that rights as between different classes of shareholders are maintained. Using its powers under s. 137 CA 1985 it may:

(*i*) settle a list of creditors entitled to object to the reduction, and permit such creditors to submit their objections;

(*ii*) ascertain the wishes of the creditors;

(*iii*) decide that any class or classes of creditors are not entitled to object, where the circumstances justify that course;

(*iv*) dispense with the consent of any dissenting creditor, if the company secures payment of his debt in manner directed by the Court.

(h) The Court may then confirm the reduction of capital, but on such terms or conditions as it thinks fit. Thus the court order may:

(*i*) direct the company that the words 'and reduced' be added to its name for a specified period;

NOTE: The Act does not indicate any particular reason for making such an order, which is now rarely made.

(*ii*) direct the company to publish the reasons for the reduction of capital, and in some cases, the causes that led to the reduction: s. 137 CA 1985.

NOTE: Under s. 139 CA 1985 if the court reduces the share capital of a public company to below £50,000 (the current authorized minimum capital) it must re-register as a private company. The court may authorize re-registration without the company having to follow the procedure specified under s. 53 CA 1985 and the court order may specify and make the necessary changes in the company's constitution, e.g. in its name (*see* **15** *below*).

(i) Deliver to the Registrar of Companies, in accordance with the requirements of s. 138 CA 1985:

(*i*) the court order confirming the reduction of capital and a copy of the order;

(*ii*) copy of a minute in form approved by the Court, showing:

(1) amount of the reduced share capital;
(2) number of shares into which the capital is divided;
(3) amount of each share, and
(4) amount, if any, deemed to be paid up on each share.

NOTE: This minute is deemed to be substituted for the corresponding part of the Memorandum.

(j) The Registrar having registered the court order and copy of the minute, the resolution for reduction of capital becomes effective, and not before. His certificate as to the registration of the order and minute is conclusive evidence that all requirements of the Act have been complied with and that the share capital of the company is correctly stated in the minute: s. 138(4) CA 1985.

(k) Publish notice of the registration of the order and minute, in manner directed by the Court; also, if applicable, add the words 'and reduced' to the company's name on all stationery, and on the common seal.

(l) Ensure that all future copies of the Memorandum issued by the company include the minute, which now replaces the capital clause of the Memorandum: ss. 20 and 138 CA 1985. The Registrar must be forwarded an amended copy of the Memorandum.

NOTE: It should also be borne in mind that every copy of the Articles issued in future must have a copy of the special resolution for reduction embodied in or annexed to it: s. 380 CA 1985.

(m) Finally, deal with any or all of the following matters, according to the form of reduction.

(*i*) Where capital is being returned to shareholders, issue cheques to them direct or instruct the company's bankers to handle the payment out of a special banking account opened for the purpose.

(*ii*) Call in the old share certificates, and issue new ones in return.

NOTE: In practice, companies often prefer *not* to call in the old share certificates, and either replace or endorse them if and when they are received for registration of transfer.

(*iii*) Make any alterations which may be necessary in the Register of Members and in the financial books.

NOTE: If the company concerned was listed, the procedure outlined above would have to be modified and the documentation drafted to take account of the Continuing Obligations imposed upon such a company by the Stock Exchange. The Continuing Obligations are set out in Chapter 2 and reference should be made thereto.

15. Reduction below public company's authorized minimum

(a) Where the Court makes an order confirming a reduction of capital of a public company which would reduce the nominal value of its allotted share capital below the authorized minimum, the Registrar will not register the order unless the court directs otherwise, or the company is first re-registered as a *private* company.

(b) The Court making such an order may authorize the company to re-register as a private company without passing a special resolution and, if so, the court order must also specify the alterations to be made in the company's Memorandum and Articles: s. 139 CA 1985.

Progress test 11

1. You are secretary of a public company which has a Stock Exchange listing. An extraordinary general meeting of your company passes resolutions which:

(a) increase the authorized capital from £500,000 to £600,000 by the creation of 100,000 ordinary shares of £1 each which upon issue and becoming fully paid, will rank *pari passu* with the existing ordinary shares; and

(b) authorize the directors to offer these shares, at par, to the present holders of ordinary shares in proportion to their holdings.

You are required to prepare a programme, in numbered paragraphs, which will give effect to these decisions. *ICSA* (3:33; 5)

2. The former £1 shares of a public company have been reduced to shares of 75p each, fully paid, by paying off capital in excess of the wants of the company. The shares are listed on a stock exchange and do not bear distinguishing numbers. The directors are of opinion that it would be advantageous for the share capital now represented by the 75p shares to be consolidated and divided into shares of £1 each, fully paid. In numbered paragraphs, give details of the complete office procedure necessary to effect a consolidation and division. (6)

3. The directors of a company, the shares of which are listed on a stock exchange, are of opinion that the shares should be converted into stock. In numbered paragraphs, give details of the procedure necessary to effect the conversion. What are the practical advantages to be gained by converting shares into stock? (7)

4. In what ways may a company alter its share capital by ordinary resolution, if so authorized by its articles? State in every case the circumstances in which a company might desire to effect such alterations, and draft the resolutions necessary to carry out any TWO of the alterations you mention. (1, 5–9)

5. In what ways may a company alter its share capital by ordinary resolution? State in each case the circumstances in which a company might wish to effect such alterations. (1, 5, 6–9)

6. In what circumstances, and by what means, may a company reduce its capital? Are the debenture holders entitled to object to the reduction? In what circumstances, if any, is a company entitled to pay off shares without recourse to the Court? **(11, 12)**

7. Set out in numbered paragraphs the procedure necessary to effect a reduction of capital. *ICSA* **(14)**

8. Only 32½p has been called up on each of the £1 ordinary shares of A.B.C. Ltd. It is proposed to pay up a further 12½p per share by transfer from reserve, and to cancel the liability for the balance. Outline the procedure to be followed, enumerating any resolutions required, and indicating any steps you would take to meet objections. **(14)**

9. Outline the procedure required to effect:

(a) a reduction of capital;
(b) a capital distribution or 'bonus'. **(3: 33; 14)**

10. 'A company cannot legally reduce its capital without Court sanction.' Discuss, and qualify the statement if you think it is necessary to do so. **(15)**

11. Write brief notes on the procedure relating to (*a*) reduction of capital, (*b*) return of capital. **(11–15)**

12. State the procedures necessary to:

(a) increase the authorized share capital; and
(b) alter the objects clause of the Memorandum of Association. *ICSA* **(5; 1: 33)**

12

Voluntary arrangements; reconstruction; amalgamation; schemes of arrangement; the City Code; Register of Interests in Shares

Survey of schemes available

1. Circumstances that justify reorganization of capital

(a) Various forms of reorganization of capital have already been dealt with in the preceding chapter, where the comparatively straight-forward procedures under ss. 121 and 135 CA 1985 for altering and reducing capital, respectively, were explained.
(b) In this chapter, it is intended to deal with voluntary arrangements, scheme of reconstruction, amalgamation and arrangement, which are usually more complicated than a mere alteration or reduction of capital, although many such schemes include alteration, reduction, or both.
(c) Schemes involving voluntary arrangements, reconstruction, amalgamation, arrangements with creditors, and other forms of reorganization are carried out for a variety of reasons, for example:

(*i*) to overcome the company's financial difficulties;

(*ii*) to make compromise or other arrangements with creditors;

(iii) to reorganize the company's capital structure and, at the same time, rid it of shares with exceptionally heavy voting power; or

(iv) to extend the company's objects, where its Memorandum states that the objects are unalterable.

2. Methods

The following methods are available, according to the purpose and circumstances.

(a) *Voluntary arrangements under ss. 1–7 Insolvency Act 1986.* The procedures provided by these provisions apply to any composition in satisfaction of debts (i.e. all creditors agree to take a proportion of what is owed to them) or to a scheme of arrangement of the company's affairs. The purpose of the provision is to enable such arrangements to be effected with minimal involvement by the Court. In this respect they contrast with the schemes of arrangement provided for by ss. 425–7 CA 1985 and to which they constitute an alternative.

(b) *Scheme of arrangement under s. 425 CA 1985,* probably with the assistance of s. 427 CA 1985. The principal features are that:

(i) it requires the approval of a specified majority of creditors and/or members;

(ii) the sanction of the Court must be obtained;

(iii) winding up is not necessary.

(c) *Reconstruction under s. 110 IA 1986.* The principal features are that:

(i) it involves the winding up of the company;

(ii) Court sanction is not necessary.

(d) *Company's sale of its undertaking to a new company,* the sale being effected under powers contained in the vendor company's Memorandum. As will be explained later in this chapter, such a scheme has many complications.

(e) *Acquisition of, or amalgamation with, another company,* which may entail compulsory acquisition of shares under ss. 428–30F CA 1985.

(f) *Reconstruction by special Act of Parliament,* a method which is likely to be too slow and costly to be undertaken except in the most unusual circumstances.

Company voluntary arrangements

3. The proposal: s. 1 IA 1986

(a) Under S. 1 IA 1986 a proposal for a voluntary arrangement may be made by:

(*i*) the liquidator if the company is in liquidation;
(*ii*) the administrator if an administration order is in force;
(*iii*) the directors in any other case.

(b) A voluntary arrangement for these purposes includes a composition in satisfaction of debts or a scheme of arrangement of the company's affairs.

(c) The proposal must provide that a qualified insolvency practitioner will supervise the implementation of the scheme, either as trustee or otherwise. This person is termed 'the nominee'.

4. Procedure: ss. 2–3 IA 1986

(a) The nominee will need to summon meetings of the company and the creditors to decide whether to approve the proposal.

(b) If the nominee is the liquidator or administrator he may summon the required meetings at the time, date and place he thinks fit.

(c) If the nominee is not the liquidator or administrator he must submit a report to the Court, stating whether in his opinion meetings of the company and creditors need to be summoned. The report must be submitted within 28 days after he is given notice of the proposal. Notice of the creditors' meeting must be sent to every creditor whose claim and address are known to the nominee. So that the nominee is able to prepare his report for the Court the person who proposed the scheme must supply him with written details of the proposal and a statement of the company's affairs.

5. Consideration of the proposal: s. 4 IA 1986

(a) The meetings may approve the proposal as submitted to them, or subject to slight modifications. However, they cannot approve any proposal that affects the priority of any secured or preferential creditors, but the modifications may include the replacement of the nominee by another qualified insolvency practitioner.

(b) On conclusion of the meetings the chairman must report to the court and to such other persons specified the decisions of the meetings.

6. Challenge of decisions: s. 6 IA 1986

(a) Within 28 days of the chairman's report to the Court an application to challenge the decision may be made by:

(*i*) a person entitled to vote at either the company meeting or the creditors' meeting;

(*ii*) the nominee or any person who has replaced him;

(*iii*) the liquidator or administrator (where appropriate).

(b) The challenge may be on the ground(s) that:

(*i*) the proposal approved at the meeting is unfairly prejudicial to the interests of a creditor, member or contributory of the company; and/or

(*ii*) there has been a material irregularity at or in relation to either of the meetings.

(c) Where the Court is satisfied that there is a valid challenge on the ground that the proposal is unfairly prejudicial it may revoke or suspend approval of the proposal, or direct any person to summon a further meeting to consider a revised proposal from the original proposer. If the challenge is considered valid on the ground of material irregularity at or in relation to the meetings the Court may revoke or suspend the approval given by the meeting and may direct that the meeting be re-convened to reconsider the original proposal.

7. Effect of the proposal: s. 5 IA 1986

If the proposal is approved at the meetings and, at the time, the company is being wound up or is subject to an administration order, the court may stay all the proceedings in the winding-up, or discharge the administration order, or give directions that assist the implementation of the proposal. However, the Court may not stay winding-up or discharge the administration order before the end of 28 days after the chairman's reports on the results of the meetings have been made to the Court, not can it do so when an application to challenge the decision has been made (*see* **6** *above*).

8. Implementation of the proposal: s. 7 IA 1986

(a) If the proposal is approved without challenge, the voluntary arrangement arising from the proposal is implemented by its supervisor. He acts under the supervision of the Court and may apply to the court for directions. He may also apply to the Court to have the company wound up or made subject to an administration order.
(b) If a creditor or any other person is dissatisfied with an act, omission or decision of the supervisor he can apply to the Court and the Court may confirm, modify or reverse the act or decision. The Court may also give any directions or make such other order as it thinks fit.
(c) The Court has power to appoint a supervisor in the event of a vacancy occurring in the office of supervisor; and to appoint an additional supervisor if it feels such an appointment to be necessary.

Schemes of arrangement under s. 425 CA 1985

9. Form of arrangement

An arrangement or reconstruction under this section may take *any* form, provided it is:

(a) approved by a majority in number, representing at least three-quarters in value of the creditors (or class of creditors) or members (or class of members), as the case may be, who are present and voting in person or by proxy; and
(b) sanctioned by the Court.

10. Principal uses

The procedure for carrying out schemes under s. 425 CA 1985 is usually complicated, and it is advisable to take legal advice at the outset; nevertheless, it is more widely used than other forms of reconstruction. Companies experiencing financial difficulties frequently make use of s. 425 schemes for the following purposes.

(a) To make a compromise or arrangement with its creditors, or any class of creditors, for example:

(*i*) agreement by secured creditors to relinquish their security, or to permit the creation of a prior charge;

(*ii*) agreement by debenture-holders and/or trade creditors to take shares, or part shares and part cash, in satisfaction of their debts.

(b) To vary the rights of its members, or any class of members, usually by way of restricting their rights, for example:

(*i*) agreement by ordinary shareholders to surrender part of their holding to the preference shareholders, who have agreed to accept ordinary shares in lieu of dividend arrears;

(*ii*) agreement by preference shareholders to cancellation of dividend arrears and reduction of the fixed rate of dividend.

11. Schemes sanctioned

The Court has, however, sanctioned a wide variety of schemes under s. 425 CA 1985, in addition to those which are mainly concerned with compromise and arrangement. The following are only examples.

(a) Reorganization of capital structure, involving:

(*i*) reduction of share capital, perhaps with modification of shareholders' rights;

(*ii*) cancellation of (say) deferred shares with exceptionally burdensome dividend and/or voting rights;

(*iii*) alteration of share capital by subdivision of partly paid shares.

(b) Amalgamation with another company, including reorganization of the capital structure of one or both companies.

(c) Formation of a new company for the purpose of replacing another company whose objects are wider. The Court may facilitate such a scheme by using powers under s. 427 CA 1985 to dissolve the 'transferor' company without the usual winding-up procedure (*see* **12** *below*).

12. Advantages of conducting schemes under s. 425 CA 1985

(a) The company need not be wound up in order to carry out any scheme under this section; in that respect it differs from schemes under s. 110 IA 1986.

(b) The facilities available under s. 427 CA 1985 for schemes of reconstruction and amalgamation are applicable only to schemes under s. 425 CA 1985. Section 427 enables the Court to make provision for all or any of the following:

(*i*) the transfer to the transferee company of the whole or any part of the undertaking and of the property or liabilities of any transferor company;

(*ii*) the allotting or appropriation by the transferee company of any shares, debentures, policies or other like interests in that company which under the compromise or arrangement are to be allotted or appropriated by that company to or for any person;

(*iii*) the continuation by or against the transferee company of any legal proceedings pending by or against any transferor company;

(*iv*) the dissolution, without winding up, of any transferor company;

(*v*) the provision to be made for any persons, who within such time and in such manner as the Court directs, dissent from the compromise or arrangement;

(*vi*) such incidental, consequential and supplemental matters as are necessary to secure that the reconstruction or amalgamation shall be fully and effectively carried out.

(c) The decision of the specified majority will overrule the minority in any scheme of arrangement, unless the Court directs otherwise. Thus, it will be unnecessary to purchase the interests of dissenting members and/or creditors. In this respect it has the advantage over schemes under s. 110 IA 1986.

(d) Section 425 CA 1985 schemes can be applied in many cases where s. 110 IA 1986 procedure is not available; that is, where more is involved than in a typical s. 110 IA 1986 procedure.

13. Procedure

(a) *Draft scheme.* The directors prepare a draft scheme, usually in consultation with legal and financial experts.

(b) *Canvassing support.* The attitudes of the various parties affected are tested, e.g. by inviting some of the largest debenture holders (or their trustees), creditors, and shareholders to separate board meetings, and soliciting their support.

(c) *Final form of scheme.* After these consultations, the final form of the proposed scheme is settled by the directors.

(d) *An explanatory statement* is then prepared, to explain to all interested parties the proposed scheme, and to recommend its acceptance.

> NOTE: At this stage, a draft of the scheme should be submitted to the Controller of Stamps, Inland Revenue, to decide what capital duty (if any) is payable. Where under a scheme or arrangement a company allots shares to the holders of shares in another company in consideration of the surrender or cancellation of their shares in that company, the surrendered or cancelled shares are treated as assets contributed to them by the first company. Accordingly, capital duty becomes chargeable, unless the transaction qualifies as an exempt transaction.

(e) *Accompanying documents.* According to the requirements of the scheme to be undertaken, some or all of the following documents are drawn up to accompany the explanatory statement, these being settled as regards form by counsel and finally approved by the board.

(*i*) *Scheme of Arrangement:* the form in which are set out details of the proposed scheme, and how it will affect creditors and shareholders.

(*ii*) *Notice convening the scheme meetings:* the same notice usually serves for all classes of creditor and shareholder, but the respective dates and times are stated for each meeting.

(*iii*) *Voting slips for use at scheme meetings:* usually on paper of a different colour for each class of creditor and/or shareholder. In some cases they are also made to serve as admission tickets.

(*iv*) *Forms of proxy for use at scheme meetings:* in standard form approved by the Court, with space provided for voting 'for' or 'against'; usually printed on paper of different colours to make them readily distinguishable.

(*v*) *Notice convening an extraordinary general meeting:* where applicable, i.e. if the scheme involves *reduction* of capital, a special resolution is necessary under s. 135 CA 1985, and this cannot be passed at the scheme meeting.

(*vi*) *Voting slips for use at the extraordinary general meeting:* no special form is required, but columns are usually provided so that holdings of different classes of shares can be stated.

(vii) Form of proxy for use at the extraordinary general meeting: this must be in the form demanded by the company's Articles. It must be made clear in a footnote that the person appointed as proxy need not be a member: s. 372 CA 1985.

(f) *Application to the Court.* The company's solicitors usually apply to the Court on the company's behalf. The application is by way of an originating summons in the Chancery Division of the High Court. It is supported by affidavit, giving a brief history of the company, the events which led up to the proposed scheme, and any other matters of which the Court may require notice.

NOTE: Application may be made to the Court by any creditor or member of the company or, in the case of a company being wound up, by the liquidator: s. 425(1) CA 1985.

(g) *Documents to be produced to the Court.* When the application is made, certain documents will be exhibited to the Court, namely:

(i) Certificate of Incorporation;
(ii) Memorandum of Association;
(iii) Articles of Association;
(iv) copy of the company's last balance sheet;
(v) copy of the Scheme of Arrangement;
(vi) draft notice convening scheme meetings;
(vii) form of proxy for use at scheme meetings;
(viii) names of proposed chairmen for the scheme meetings.

NOTE: Documents *(vi)* and *(vii)* are submitted for the Court's approval.

(h) *At the hearing,* company's counsel asks the Court to make an order directing the holding of the scheme meetings.

(i) *Court orders the convening of scheme meetings,* i.e

(i) a meeting of the creditors, or class of creditor;

(ii) a meeting of members, or class of member, and gives any other directions it may consider necessary.

NOTE: The extraordinary general meeting (if required in order to pass a special resolution for reduction of capital) will *not* be subject to the directions of the Court.

(j) *Board meeting.* In order to carry out the Court's directions, a board meeting is held and a resolution passed, authorizing the secretary to convene scheme and, where applicable, extraordinary general meetings, and to send the various documents (already referred to) with the notices.

(k) *Secretary's procedure.* Before sending out notices and documents, the secretary should take the following steps.

(*i*) Ensure that scheme documents are in the exact form approved by the Court.

(*ii*) If practicable, arrange to have proxy forms and voting slips completed as to name, address, holding, etc., in order to simplify and expedite the meeting procedure.

(*iii*) In a very large company, where this may not be practicable, the holders of proxies and voting slips should be instructed to fill in their names in block capitals.

(*iv*) Obtain a certificate of posting from the post office at the time of posting notices and documents.

(l) *Prepare a list of persons entitled to attend the meetings.* After posting the notices, but before the holding of the various meetings, it is advisable to prepare lists of persons entitled to attend the respective meetings, showing against each person's name his shareholding, debenture holding or, in the case of a creditor, the extent of the debt to him.

(m) *At the scheme meeting* the following points ought to be borne in mind.

(*i*) The quorum will be that fixed by the Court, and *not* that specified in the company's Articles.

(*ii*) Voting by show of hands is pointless, and the result will finally depend on the results shown on completed voting slips and proxy forms.

(*iii*) Great care must be taken to ensure that the resolution is properly carried, i.e. by a majority in number, representing three-quarters in value of those of the class who are present and voting, either in person or by proxy.

(*iv*) At each scheme meeting, the chairman should be provided with an audited statement of the number and value of votes cast 'for' and 'against' the scheme on valid proxy forms, and the completed proxy forms should be available for reference.

(n) *At the extraordinary general meeting*, if required:

(*i*) the quorum must be in accordance with the company's Articles.

(*ii*) the majority required to pass a special resolution for reduction of capital (where applicable) will be that required by s. 378 CA 1985, namely a three-quarters majority, and not that required for the scheme meetings.

(o) *Petition is presented to the Court.* Assuming that the scheme is approved by all parties at their respective meetings, a petition is presented to the Court for approval of the scheme and, where applicable, to sanction reduction of capital.

The petition sets out the terms of the scheme, a brief history of the company and circumstances which have made the scheme necessary. It must be accompanied by affidavits to prove that the necessary meetings have been held, that notices in proper form were sent out, and that the resolutions were passed by the requisite majorities.

(p) *Date for the hearing.* A date is fixed by the Court for hearing the petition. If the Court so directs, the presentation of the petition and the date for the hearing are advertised in the press to enable any dissenters to state their views.

(q) *The Court's powers.* At the hearing, the Court has power to sanction the scheme, to modify it or reject it, provided that:

(*i*) the scheme is reasonable;

(*ii*) it complies with the Act;

(*iii*) it has the approval of the necessary majorities, acting in good faith; and

(*iv*) it imposes no injustice on any of the parties concerned.

(r) *Court order.* Assuming that the scheme is approved, the Court makes an order sanctioning it. If the scheme involves the transfer of the whole or part of the company's undertaking to another company, the Court may, under s. 427 CA 1985 (*see* **12(b)** *above*), order the transfer of property and otherwise facilitate the scheme, without a winding-up and without making any provision for dissentients.

(s) *Registration of the court order.* As soon as possible after receipt of it, the Court's order sanctioning the scheme must be produced to the Registrar of Companies. At the same time an office copy of the order must be filed with him for registration.

NOTE: If the Court has also made an order under s. 427 CA 1985 an office copy of it must also be filed within seven days.

(t) *Putting the scheme into effect.* Once the office copy of the court order sanctioning the scheme has been filed, the scheme can be put into effect, but not before.
(u) *All subsequent issues of the Memorandum and Articles* must include, or have annexed, a copy of the Court's order. If the scheme has effected any alteration in the company's incorporating documents, amended copies of such must be delivered to the Registrar.
(v) *Within 15 days* of its being passed, file with the Registrar a copy of any special or extraordinary resolution passed in regard to the scheme.
(w) *Subsequent procedure* to put the scheme into effect will, of course, vary according to the nature and aims of the scheme, but will almost certainly involve a great deal of work for the secretary of the company; in particular:

(*i*) convening and attending board meetings for the purpose of passing resolutions to authorize the calling-in of old share certificates, stock certificates, debenture and/or debenture stock certificates;

(*ii*) endorsement of old certificates, or preparation of new certificates;

(*iii*) preparation of Allotment Sheets, and convening and attending board meeting(s) to authorize the various allotments;

(*iv*) filing a Return of Allotments with the Registrar;

(*v*) handling correspondence, e.g. relating to lost certificates, and obtaining letters of indemnity in such cases;

(*vi*) answering queries from shareholders and debenture holders;

(*vii*) issuing new share and/or debenture certificates, or returning the old certificates after suitable endorsement;

(*viii*) writing up the Register of Members and/or Register of Debenture Holders;

(*ix*) preparation of cheques and issuing them to shareholders, if the reorganization involves a return of capital;

(*x*) writing up the minute books and, where applicable, the Register of Sealed Documents.

NOTE: If the company concerned was listed, the procedure outlined above would have to be modified and the documentation drafted to take account of the Continuing Obligations imposed upon such a company by the Stock Exchange. The Continuing Obligations are set out in Chapter 2 and reference should be made thereto.

Reconstruction under s. 110 IA 1986

14. Purposes

(a) *Working capital.* This form of reconstruction is often used when additional working capital is needed and other means of raising it are not available.
(b) *Other purposes.* It has, however, also been used for a variety of other purposes, including:
(*i*) alteration of the company's objects; if, for example, an attempt to alter them under ss. 4–6 CA 1985 has been ruled out by the Court's upholding objections of the requisite proportion of shareholders or debenture holders;
(*ii*) variation of shareholders' rights, where these are set out in the Memorandum and stated to be unalterable;
(*iii*) effecting a compromise with creditors, or with any class of creditor, e.g. debenture holders.

15. Method

The method generally adopted is broadly as follows.

(a) A new company is formed (i.e. the 'transferee' company), to acquire the undertaking of an existing company.
(b) The existing company (i.e. the 'transferor' company) is wound up voluntarily.
(c) The assets of the old company are sold to the new company.
(d) The consideration given by the new company usually consists of shares in its undertaking, and the taking over of the old company's debts.
(e) The shares in the new company are distributed to

shareholders of the old company either directly or through the liquidator.

16. Advantages

The advantages of reconstruction under s. 110 IA 1986 are that:

(a) procedure is comparatively simple;
(b) sanction of the Court is not necessary, unless it is desired to make the scheme immediately binding on the creditors.

NOTE: If sanction to bind creditors is applied for but refused:
(*i*) shareholders will be bound at once; but
(*ii*) creditors will not be bound until one year has elapsed after date of execution of the scheme.

17. Procedure

(a) *Agreement for sale.* Prepare, or instruct the company's solicitors to prepare, an agreement for sale to the transferee company of the assets and undertaking of the transferor company containing details of the proposed scheme.
(b) *Board meeting.* A board meeting is held to prepare a statutory declaration of solvency under s. 89 IA 1986 and, after it has been prepared, to authorize its subsequent filing with the Registrar.

NOTE: For the purpose of the Act, such a declaration is of no effect unless made not more than five weeks before the date of the resolution to wind up, or on that date but before the passing of the resolution, and shall be delivered to the Registrar before the expiry of the period of 15 days immediately following the date on which the resolution for winding-up is made. If a declaration of solvency cannot be made, it will be necessary to wind up the company in a creditors' voluntary winding-up and *not* as a members' voluntary winding-up.

(c) *Creditors.* To obviate opposition from creditors at a later date, suitable arrangements should be made with the old company's creditors, for example:

(*i*) debenture holders may be persuaded to take debentures in the new company in exchange for their existing debentures;

(*ii*) unsecured creditors will be asked to accept the new company as their debtor;

(*iii*) unsecured creditors who do not agree to accept the new company as their debtor must either be paid off or secured, e.g. they may be prepared to accept debentures in full or part settlement of their debts.

(d) *Extraordinary general meeting.* It will be necessary to convene an extraordinary general meeting (the notice being accompanied by a circular describing the scheme) for a date within five weeks of making the Declaration of Solvency.

> NOTE: In preparing the circular, no doubt the scheme will be made as attractive as possible; nevertheless, care must be taken to avoid misrepresentation.

(e) *Resolutions.* At the extraordinary general meeting, *two* special resolutions are passed:

(*i*) winding up the company and appointing a liquidator;

(*ii*) authorizing the liquidator to enter into an agreement for sale with the new company, when formed.

(f) *Publication.* Notice of the resolution for winding up (and of the liquidator's appointment) must be inserted in the *Gazette* within 14 days: s. 85 IA 1986.

(g) *File a copy of each resolution* with the Registrar within 15 days of the passing of the resolutions: s. 380 CA 1985, such to be accompanied by the Declaration of Solvency which must at the latest be filed within 15 days of the passing of the resolution for winding up.

(h) *Incorporation of the new company.* Steps can now be taken to incorporate the new company and, when this has been done, to put into effect the agreement for sale.

(i) *Shares in the new company are distributed* to the old company's shareholders, either directly or through the liquidator.

> NOTE: If the shares are allotted directly, transfer fees and stamp duties are avoided and, if partly paid shares are involved, it also saves the liquidator from incurring personal liability.

(j) *File a Return of Allotments* with the Registrar within one month of allotment: s. 88 CA 1985.

(k) *Completion of winding-up.* Finally, the winding-up of the old company is completed; that is, either:

(*i*) as a *members'* voluntary winding-up, if a Declaration of Solvency was filed; or

(*ii*) as a *creditors'* voluntary winding-up, if no Declaration was filed.

(l) *Final general meeting of the company.* In either case, as soon as the old company's affairs are fully wound up, the liquidator prepares his accounts, calls the final general meeting, by advertisement in the *Gazette* at least one month before the meeting, and lays his accounts before the meeting.

(m) *Liquidator's return to the Registrar.* Within one week after the final general meeting, the liquidator must send to the Registrar:

(*i*) a return of the meeting and of its date; and

(*ii*) a copy of his account of the winding-up.

(n) *Dissolution.* On the expiration of three months from the registration of the return, the company is deemed to be dissolved: s. 201 IA 1986.

NOTE: If the company concerned was listed, the procedure outlined above would have to be modified and the documentation drafted to take account of the Continuing Obligations imposed upon such a company by the Stock Exchange. The Continuing Obligations are set out in Chapter 2 and reference should be made thereto.

18. Important points to be noted in schemes under s. 110 IA 1986

(a) *Treatment of dissentient shareholders.*

(*i*) As they have important rights, the utmost care is necessary in dealing with dissentient shareholders.

(*ii*) If considerable opposition is expected, they should be circularized before the meeting, to ascertain their views beforehand.

(*iii*) The passing of a special resolution to approve the scheme is not in itself an indication that there will necessarily be few dissentients, as the meeting might not have been truly representative.

(*iv*) If there are many dissentients, the scheme may have to be revised or abandoned altogether.

(*v*) If, on the other hand, the amount of dissent is unlikely to prevent the scheme going through, provisions must be made for dealing with dissentients.

(b) *Dissentients.*

(*i*) A dissentient is any shareholder who did *not* vote in favour of the scheme.

(*ii*) Within seven days of the passing of the resolution, a dissentient may serve written notice at the company's registered office, stating that he dissents and requires the liquidator either to refrain from proceeding with the scheme, or to acquire his shares.

(*iii*) The fact that such a notice is deposited out of time, or at some place other than the registered office, may not invalidate the notice, if accepted by the liquidator: *Brailey* v. *Rhodesia Consolidated* (1910).

(*iv*) The notice may, however, be invalidated if it fails to specify the alternative courses which are open to the liquidator: *Re Demerara Rubber Co.* (1913).

(c) *Fund for purchase of dissentients' interests.* The scheme ought to provide for creating a separate fund out of which to purchase the interests of any dissentient shareholders. In order to create such a fund, certain of the old company's assets may be excluded from the agreement for sale; alternatively, the agreement may provide that the new company is to set up the necessary fund.

(d) *Distribution of the new company's shares* to shareholders of the old company.

(*i*) Distribution is usually in accordance with powers given in the old company's Memorandum or Articles.

(*ii*) If, however, distribution rights are fixed by the Articles, they may be altered by special resolution if the rights fixed are not in keeping with the requirements of the scheme.

(e) *Failure to claim new shares.* Arrangements for shareholders who fail to claim their new shares are as follows.

(*i*) Although legally such shareholders lose their rights in the new company, in practice provision is usually made for them in the agreement for sale; for example, a shareholder may be entitled to the proceeds of the sale of the shares to which he would have been entitled.

(*ii*) In such cases, the liquidator may have authority to sell any unclaimed shares in the new company by tender, and to distribute the proceeds of the sale (less advertising and other expenses) to shareholders so entitled, in accordance with the provisions of the agreement for sale.

Other schemes of reconstruction

19. Sale by a company of its undertaking to a new company under powers in its Memorandum

(a) It has been held that a sale under powers given in a company's Memorandum is legal if liquidation is neither contemplated nor in progress: *Bisgood* v. *Henderson's Transvaal Estate* (1908), i.e. if it genuinely intended to retain the proceeds of the sale in the business without winding up, then the power given by the Memorandum may be used.
(b) It is, however, doubtful whether such a scheme is now practicable, for the following reasons.

(*i*) To put it into effect does usually involve liquidation and the Court's power to transfer a company's assets without a winding up, under s. 427 CA 1985, is intended only for schemes under s. 425 CA 1985.

(*ii*) Provision must be made for dissentients; otherwise the scheme might justifiably be regarded as an evasion of s. 110 IA 1986.

(c) Therefore, unless there is complete unanimity among the shareholders, so that there is no likelihood of a dissentient shareholder taking the matter to the Courts, it is usually considered to be safer to carry out such a scheme under s. 110 IA 1986 in which adequate provision is made for dissentients.

20. Acquisition of another company, or of controlling interest in another company

(a) This method amounts to an amalgamation and can be effected either:

(*i*) by purchasing *all* the shares of another company; or

(*ii*) by purchasing sufficient shares of another company to acquire a majority of the voting power.

(b) In some cases, it may be possible to purchase sufficient shares on the open market to acquire a controlling interest — but this may prove to be a costly method unless the buying is spread over a long period, as the demand created might well cause the price of the shares to rise excessively.

(c) Nowadays, the 'take-over bid' technique, which amounts to amalgamation or acquisition by share purchase, is usually effected in the following stages.

(*i*) An agreement may be reached between the directors of the 'transferor' and 'transferee' companies respectively, the agreement, of course, being subject to ratification by a sufficient majority of the 'transferor' company's shareholders (or class of shareholders) affected, within a fixed period.

(*ii*) The 'transferor' company's directors then circularize their shareholders, explaining the scheme, setting out its advantages and recommending acceptance.

> NOTE: If the directors of the 'transferor' company are not in agreement with the 'transferee' company's offer, they will no doubt consider it is their duty to circularize their shareholders, explaining the scheme, pointing out its disadvantages and recommending rejection of the offer.

(*iii*) If the scheme is ratified within the time specified and by the requisite majority, it then becomes effective, though still subject to the right of dissenting shareholders to appeal to the Court.

(d) Thus, a 'transferee' company which has already acquired 90 per cent of the 'transferor' company's shares in a scheme of the sort described above is given power under s. 429 CA 1985 to acquire the remaining 10 per cent if the following conditions are fulfilled.

(*i*) The scheme has been approved within four months of the offer being made, i.e. by the holders of not less than nine-tenths in value of the shares concerned.

(*ii*) Notice has been given in the prescribed form and manner by the 'transferee' company to any dissenting shareholder within two months (after expiration of the four-month period referred to above) that it desires to acquire his shares.

(e) The 'transferee' company is then entitled and bound to acquire the shares of a dissenting shareholder on the same terms as those offered to the approving shareholders, unless the Court, on application of the dissenting shareholder within six weeks of the date of the notice, thinks fit to order otherwise.

(f) An alternative is supplied by s. 430A CA 1985 which provides that, where the transferee company holds nine-tenths in value of the shares affected:

(*i*) the transferee company must, within one month, give notice in the prescribed form and manner to that effect to holders of the remaining shares who have not assented to the scheme;

(*ii*) any such holder may within three months of the notice serve counter notice on the transferee company, requiring it to acquire his shares; and

(*iii*) the transferee company is then entitled and bound to acquire the shares on the same terms as were offered to the approving shareholders, or on such other terms as may be agreed, or as the Court thinks fit to order.

(g) This method of amalgamation or acquisition by purchase of shares is now frequently used, because it has advantages over other forms of reconstruction; in particular

(*i*) it can be used to acquire control of one or a number of companies;

(*ii*) the company (or companies) acquired may be allowed to retain their separate identities, continue to trade under their own names and preserve any goodwill they have built up; and

(*iii*) it may prove less costly than other forms of reconstruction, as a controlling interest may be acquired without purchasing the whole of the undertaking.

The City Code

21. The background to the Code

The Code arose as a result of adverse criticism concerning the methods used in some takeovers and mergers in the 1950s and 1960s. In particular, there was concern regarding:

(a) the inequality of terms offered to investors;

(b) the manoeuvres adopted by the boards of companies in order to force through or fight off a bid;
(c) the quality of disclosure made to the market in respect of takeover deals;
(d) the secrecy surrounding the purchase of shares in bid for companies during the course of bids, either by the bidding company itself, or by its associates.

The City Code on Takeovers and Mergers, to give it its full title, first appeared in its present form in March 1968 and revised editions of the Code have been issued in 1969, 1972, 1976, 1981, 1985 and 1988.

In 1986 the Code was amended to incorporate 'The Rules Governing Substantial Acquisitions of Shares'. These regulate acquisitions which would result in holdings or rights over shares amounting to between 15 per cent and 30 per cent of the company's voting rights. Administered by the executive of the Panel on Takeovers and Mergers, the object of these rules is to restrict the speed by which a person (or group of persons acting in concert) will increase their holdings or rights in shares amounting to an aggregate between 15 per cent and 30 per cent of the company's voting rights. They do not apply, however, in the case where a company has announced a firm intention to make an offer for the shares of another company, in which case the rules of the Code apply. The Code also deals with acquisitions amounting to 30 per cent or more of the voting rights.

22. The nature of the Code

The Code represents the collective opinion of those professionally concerned in the field of takeovers and mergers on a range of business standards. It is not concerned with the evaluation of the financial or commercial advantages or disadvantages of a takeover or merger. These are considered to be the concern of the company and its shareholders and in certain circumstances of the Government, advised by the Monopolies and Mergers Commission.

The Code has not, and does not seek to have, the force of the law, though it operates within the legal framework of, and is complementary to, the existing statute and case law on takeovers and mergers. Its observance is purely voluntary though backed by the disciplinary sanctions administered by the City institutions over their members.

23. The scope of the Code

The Code has been drafted with listed public companies particularly in mind. It also applies, nevertheless, to takeovers of unlisted companies and to certain private companies.

24. Operation and enforcement of the Code

The Code is administered and enforced by the Panel on Takeovers and Mergers (the Panel), body representative of those using the securities markets and concerned with the observance of good business practice, not the enforcement of the law.

The Panel's chairman and deputy chairman are nominees of the Bank of England and the rest of the Panel includes, *inter alia*, the Chairman or senior nominees of the Stock Exchange, the Accepting Houses Committee, the Association of Investment Trust Companies, the Committee of London and Scottish Bankers, the Confederation of British Industry, the Institute of Chartered Accountants in England and Wales and the Issuing Houses Association.

The Panel works on a day-to-day basis through its executive, headed by the Director General, but there is a right of appeal against his rulings as to the interpretation and enforcement of the Code to the Panel. Further, he may refer such questions to the Panel, as well as all allegations that the provisions of the Code have been broken.

If the Panel finds that there has been a breach of the Code it may administer a private reprimand or a public censure, or in more serious cases take steps to ensure that the offender is prevented from availing himself of the facilities of the securities market.

Appeal lies to the Appeal Committee of the Panel.

25. Structure of the Code

In addition to an introductory section, the Code, as published in its fifth edition, consists of four sections:

(a) *Introduction.* This sets out the constitution of the Panel, the nature and purpose of the Code and the companies and transactions subject to it. In particular it makes it clear that the boards of companies involved and their advisers have a primary duty to act in the best interests of their respective shareholders. It also requires persons engaged in takeovers to be aware of and observe the spirit as well as the precise words of the Code.
(b) *General Principles.* The General Principles, of which there are 10, are a codification of good standards of commercial behaviour as such relate to takeover and merger situations.
(c) *Rules.* These lay down certain precise procedures and requirements which must be observed in takeover and merger situations. Some are examples of the application of the general principles whilst others are rules of procedure designed to govern specific forms of takeover and merger transactions practised in the United Kingdom. There are 37 such rules.
(d) *Practice Notes.* These are rulings on specific matters usually based on decided cases. They are set out immediately after the Rule to which they apply.

26. General Principles of the Code

These are mainly concerned with the provision of information to shareholders and the responsibilities of the directors of the companies concerned. They are as follows:

Rule 1 All shareholders of the same class of an offeree company must be treated similarly by an offeror.
Rule 2 During the course of a takeover, or when such is in contemplation, neither the offeror, nor the offeree company, nor any of their respective advisers may furnish information to some shareholders which is not made available to all shareholders. This principle does not apply to the furnishing of information in confidence by an offeree company to a bona fide potential offeror or vice versa.
Rule 3 An offeror should only announce an offer after the most careful and responsible consideration. Such an announcement should be made only when the offeror has every reason to believe that it can and will continue to be able to implement the

offer: responsibility in this connection also rests on the financial adviser to the offeror.

Rule 4 Shareholders must be given sufficient information and advice to enable them to reach a properly informed decision and must have sufficient time to do so. No relevant information should be withheld from them.

Rule 5 Any document or advertisement addressed to shareholders containing information or advice from an offeror or the board of an offeree company or their respective advisers must, as in the case with a prospectus or equivalent document, be prepared with the highest standards of care and accuracy.

Rule 6 All parties to a takeover transaction must use every endeavour to prevent the creation of a false market in the securities of an offeror or offeree company. Parties involved in such transactions must take care that statements are not made which may mislead shareholders or the market.

Rule 7 At no time after a bona fide offer has been communicated to the board of an offeree company, or after the board of an offeree company has reason to believe that a bona fide offer might be imminent, may any action be taken by the board of the offeree company in relation to the affairs of the company, without the approval of the shareholders in general meeting, which could effectively result in any bona fide offer being frustrated or in the shareholders being denied an opportunity to decide on its merits.

Rule 8 Rights of control must be exercised in good faith and the oppression of a minority is wholly unacceptable.

Rule 9 Directors of an offeror or an offeree company must always, in advising their shareholders, act only in their capacity as directors and not have regard to their personal or family shareholdings or to their personal relationships with the companies. It is the shareholders' interests taken as a whole, together with those of employees and creditors, which should be considered when the directors are giving advice to shareholders.

Rule 10 Where control of a company is acquired by a person, or persons acting in concert, a general offer to all other shareholders is normally required; a similar obligation may arise if control is consolidated. Where an acquisition is contemplated as a result of which a person may incur such an obligation, he must, before making the acquisition, ensure that he can and will continue to be able to implement such an offer.

27. Rules of the Code

(a) The rules of the Code give more precise content to its General Principles but in no way restrict the latter's applications to situations which are analogous to, or slightly different from, those covered specifically by the rules.
(b) The rules are concerned with:
(*i*) the approach;
(*ii*) consideration of an offer;
(*iii*) documentation;
(*iv*) mechanics of the formal offer;
(*v*) restrictions on dealings; and
(*vi*) registration of transfers.
(c) A few of the important areas specifically covered are outlined below.

(*i*) *Secrecy.* The vital importance of absolute secrecy before an announcement must be emphasized.

(*ii*) *Restrictions on acquisitions.* Except with the consent of the Panel, when:

(1) any person acquires, whether by a series of transactions over a period of time or not, shares which (taken together with shares held or acquired by persons acting in concert with him) carry 30 per cent or more of the voting rights of a company; or

(2) any person who, together with persons acting in concert with him, holds not less than 30 per cent but not more than 50 per cent of the voting rights and such person, or any person acting in concert with him, acquires in any period of 12 months additional shares carrying more than 2 per cent of the voting rights,

such person shall extend offers, on the basis set out in the rules, to the holders of any class of equity share capital whether voting or non-voting and also to the holders of any class of voting non-equity share capital in which such person or persons acting in concert with him hold shares. Offers for different classes of equity capital must be comparable; the Panel should be consulted in advance in such cases.

(iii) The offer price. If, while the offer is open, the offeror purchases shares at above the offer price, the offer must be increased to that price.

(iv) Mandatory offers. Any acquisitions which are contrary to (b) above result in the offeror being obliged to launch a full bid.

(v) Conditions. The only condition to an offer that is usually permissible is one that states that the offer will only progress if acceptances in respect of more than 50 per cent of the voting rights are received.

(vi) Timing. The offer must be open for at least 21 days and this time can be extended (but usually not beyond the 60th day).

(vii) Subsequent offers. If an offer fails, the offeror is generally forbidden from making another offer within 21 months.

(viii) Partial offers. The Panel's consent is required for any offer designed to create a holding of between 30 per cent and 50 per cent.

28. Stock Exchange Regulations

The Stock Exchange's Admission of Securities to Listing contains a series of provisions about take-overs, the first being that the Council of the Stock Exchange attaches great importance to the observance of the City Code. In addition the Exchange requires, *inter alia*, that:

(a) listed companies must submit drafts of all documents intended to be issued in connection with take-overs and take-over offers to the Quotations Department of the Stock Exchange, and it is requested that drafts of circulars proposed to be issued to holders of the securities of a listed company by or on behalf of other organizations should also be submitted to the Department for approval. All offer documents must contain as a heading the words 'If you are in doubt about this offer you should consult your stockbroker, bank manager, solicitor, accountant or other professional adviser' or similar wording;

(b) where any document or circular issued in connection with an offer by either party includes expressly or by implication a recommendation or an opinion by a financial adviser or other

expert for or against acceptance of the offer, the Committee on Quotations may require the document, unless issued by the expert in question, to include a statement that the expert has given and not withdrawn his written consent to the issue of the document and the inclusion therein of his written recommendation in the form and context in which it is included;
(c) where listing particulars are required in relation to a take-over, specific requirements regarding the form, contents and issue of such particulars be adhered to; and
(d) where it is proposed to increase the authorized capital of a company in order to satisfy the terms of an offer, the Committee will require the resolution to be drawn in such a way that it becomes effective only if the offer is declared unconditional.

Register of Interests in Shares

29. Register of Interests in Shares

(a) Section 211 CA 1985 requires every public company to keep a register and to enter into it against the name of the person concerned any information it receives from a person in consequence of the fulfilment of an obligation imposed on him by ss. 198–202 CA 1985. The date of the entry must also be recorded in the register.
(b) Entries in the register must be in chronological order and have to be made within three days of receipt of the information.
(c) The register has to be kept at the same place as the Register of Members and is open to public inspection.

30. Obligation of disclosure for the purpose of the register

(a) Section 198 CA 1985 requires a person who knows or becomes aware that he has acquired or ceased to have an interest in 3 per cent of a public company's issued capital carrying unrestricted voting rights or, if already interested in 3 per cent or more of such share capital of a public company, he increases or reduces the extent of his interest, to notify the company thereof in writing within five days.
(b) Such notice must specify the share capital to which it relates and either the number of shares in which the person concerned has or still has an interest if he has or retains more than 3 per

cent of the company's relevant share capital or that he has ceased to hold more that 3 per cent where such is the case. Further, by s. 202 CA 1985, except in the case of a notification as regards cessation of a notifiable holding, the notification must state

(*i*) the identity of each registered shareholder to which it relates and the number of shares held by that holder, and

(*ii*) the number of such shares in which the interest of the person giving notification is such an interest as is mentioned in s. 208(5) CA 1985;

i.e. if, otherwise than by virtue of having an interest under a trust, he has a right to call for delivery of the shares to himself or to his order, or he has a right to acquire an interest in shares or is under an obligation to take an interest in shares, whether in any case the right or obligation is conditional or absolute, so far as known to the person making the notification.

(c) Sections 203–205 CA 1985 specify what constitutes an interest for the purposes of ss. 198–202 CA 1985 and ss. 204–205 CA 1985 specifically extend the provisions to accommodate the concert-party arrangement and the consequential dawn raid.

(d) Section 208 CA 1985 lays down rules for determining whether a person has a notifiable interest for the purposes of ss. 198–202 CA 1985 and s. 209 CA 1985 establishes those interests that might be disregarded for those purposes.

31. Investigation by a company of interests in shares

(a) Section 212 CA 1985 enables any public company by notice in writing to require any person whom the company knows or has reasonable cause to believe to be, or, at any time during the three years immediately preceding the date on which the notice is issued, to have been interested in shares forming part of the company's issued capital carrying unrestricted voting rights, to confirm that fact or (as the case may be) to indicate whether or not it is the case, and, whether he holds, or has during that time held, any interest in shares so compromised.

(b) Where information is received under s. 212 CA 1985 the company must enter against the name of the registered holder of those shares in a separate part of the company's Register of Interests in Shares:

(*i*) the fact that the requirement was imposed and the date on which it was imposed; and

(*ii*) any information received in response to such a request.

(c) The powers made available to a company by s. 212 CA 1985 (*see* **(a)** *above*) may under s. 214 CA 1985 be required to be exercised on the requisition of the holders of not less than one-tenth of the company's share capital carrying the right to vote.

(d) In order to obtain information from a person on whom a notice is served under s. 212 CA 1985, s. 216 CA 1985 gives the company rights to apply to the Court for an order directing that the shares in question shall be subject to the restrictions imposed by Part XV of the Act relating to the transfer, voting or dividend rights in respect of such shares (*see* 10:9).

Progress test 12

1. In what circumstances would a 'reorganization of capital' be recommended by you to your board, and what statutory duties would follow the adoption of such a scheme? **(1, 2)**

2. You are asked to prepare a scheme for the amalgamation of two companies known as A Ltd. and B Ltd. Both have share capitals which consist entirely of ordinary shares of £1 each fully paid. The capital of A Ltd. is £1,200,000 and of B Ltd. £800,000. Agreement has been reached on the valuation of the shares: A Ltd. at £3 and B Ltd. at £1.50 per share. Outline in numbered paragraphs the procedure you consider should be followed to effect the amalgamation. *ICSA* **(11, 13)**

3. You are secretary of a company which has just adopted a reconstruction scheme. The holders of the company's debenture stock have agreed to surrender it in return for £60 of a new debenture stock plus 40 ordinary shares of £1, fully paid, in exchange for each £100 of the old debenture stock. All the necessary resolutions have been passed and you are required to prepare, in numbered paragraphs, a programme showing in detail the procedure required to make this conversion. *ICSA* **(13)**.

4. PQR Plc. has made trading losses for many years. Today its assets comprise office furniture valued at £4500, a bank balance of £5000 and a patent which it is unable to work itself, but which, in conjunction with the goodwill associated with the name of the company, earns about £30,000 per annum in licence fees. It has issued to the public £20,000 5 per cent debentures secured by a floating charge, £5000 6% preference stock and £60,000 ordinary stock. Draft a report suggesting how the company may be reconstructed, making such assumptions as you may feel necessary (income tax aspects may be ignored). **(14, 17)**

5. Your company is solvent but has accumulated losses. Set out in the form of a memorandum to your board your suggestions as to how a reconstruction may be effected. *ICSA* **(17)**

6. What are the rights of a shareholder who objects to the transfer, during a winding up, of the company's property to another company, and how does he exercise them? **(18)**

7. How can the amalgamation of companies be effected where it is desired to preserve the goodwill of the separate companies concerned? Can shareholders validly object? **(20)**

8. Your company is considering making an offer to acquire the shares of another company. Summarize the procedure from the aspects of both companies, and explain how complete control may be achieved should not all shareholders in the offeree company accept. *ICSA* **(20)**

9. Examine fully the functions served by the City Code on Takeovers and Mergers and the role of the Panel on Takeovers and Mergers in relation to the Code. **(21–27)**

10. Explain how a public company may ascertain who is interested in its voting share capital. **(28–30)**

11. Describe the procedure under a scheme whereby arrears of dividends on cumulative preference shares are to be cancelled. *ICSA* (13)

12. What is the City Code on Mergers and Takeovers? How did it arise and what do you consider to be its underlying principles? *ICSA* (21–27)

13. In connection with the liquidation of a company, explain the procedure regarding the sale of the company's business for shares in a new company. *ICSA* (17)

13
Winding-up

Introduction

1. Definition

The winding-up or liquidation of a company is a legal process whereby it is dissolved and its property administered for the benefit of its creditors and members.

NOTE: A company cannot be made bankrupt.

2. Methods of winding-up

According to s. 73 IA 1986, a company may be wound up:

(a) by the court; that is a compulsory winding-up;
(b) voluntarily, either as (*i*) a *members'* voluntary winding-up; or (*ii*) a *creditors'* voluntary winding-up.

Winding-up by the Court

3. A company may be wound up by the Court (under s. 122(1) IA 1986) in the following circumstances

(a) *Special resolution.* Where the company has, by special resolution, resolved that the company be wound up by the Court.
(b) In the case of a public company which was registered as such on its original incorporation, the company has not been issued with a certificate under s. 117 CA 1985 and more than a year has elapsed since it was so registered.

(c) It is an old public company, within the meaning of the Companies Consolidation (Consequential Provisions) Act 1985.
(d) *Failure to commence business.* Where the company does not commence business within a year of its incorporation, or suspends its business for a year.

> NOTE: The court will not, as a rule, wind up a company under these circumstances unless it appears that the company has no intention of commencing business or of continuing its business.

(e) *Number of members.* Where the number of members of the company is reduced below two.
(f) *Inability to pay its debts.* Where the company is unable to pay its debts, i.e.

(*i*) if a creditor whose debt exceeds £750 serves notice requiring payment and is not paid within three weeks; or

(*ii*) if execution in favour of a creditor of the company is returned unsatisfied, in whole or in part; or

(*iii*) if the Court is satisfied that the company cannot pay its debts as they fall due; or

(*iv*) it is proved to the satisfaction of the Court that, taking the company's contingent and prospective liabilities into account, the value of its assets is less than the amount of its liabilities: s. 123 IA 1986.

> NOTE: In practice the Court applies the same minimum of £750 in case (*ii*) and (*iii*) as is prescribed by (*i*).

(g) *The just and equitable ground.* Where the Court is of the opinion that it is just and equitable that the company should be wound up, for example:

(*i*) where the substratum (main object) of the company has ceased to exist: *Re German Date Coffee Co.* (1882);

(*ii*) where the company is in substitute a partnership between the persons owning its share capital and there are grounds for dissolving a partnership: *Re Yenidje Tobacco Co. Ltd.* (1916);

(*iii*) where the company never had a business to carry on; that is, it was merely a 'bubble' company: *Re London County Coal Co.* (1866);

(*iv*) where in the case of a domestic and family company there has been mismanagement by the directors who hold a majority of the voting shares: *Loch* v. *John Blackwood Ltd.* (1924);

(*v*) where the company has been formed to carry out a fraud or to carry on an illegal business: *Re International Securities Corporation* (1908).

> NOTE: In the case of a petition on the just and equitable ground by a contributory, if the court considers that the petitioner has some other remedy, but that otherwise it would be just and equitable to order a winding-up, the court is bound to make the order, unless it considers the petitioner is acting unreasonably in asking for a winding-up instead of pursuing his other remedy: s. 125(2) IA 1986.

4. The winding-up petition

(a) *Appropriate Court.* Under s. 117 IA 1986 a winding-up petition must be presented to the Court having the necessary jurisdiction:

(*i*) the *High Court,* which has jurisdiction to wind up *any* company registered in England;

(*ii*) the *County Court of the district* in which the company's registered office is situated, if the paid-up capital does not exceed £120,000.

(b) *The petition.* The petition must be supported by affidavit, setting out:

(*i*) date of incorporation of the company;
(*ii*) address of its registered office;
(*iii*) capital;
(*iv*) objects;
(*v*) grounds for presenting the petition.

(c) *Time and place for hearing.* After the presentation of the petition, the Registrar will fix the time and place for the hearing of the petition.

(d) *Hearing advertised.* Seven days prior to the hearing, it must be advertised, as an invitation to creditors and contributories to support or oppose the petition:

(*i*) in the *Gazette*; and

(*ii*) in a newspaper circulating in the district in which the company's registered office is situated.

(e) *Provisional liquidator.* After a petition has been presented, the Court has power, under s. 135 IA 1986, even before the hearing of the petition, to appoint the Official Receiver, or any other person, to be provisional liquidator (usually because the assets are in jeopardy). The provisional liquidator shall carry out such functions as the Court may confer on him. An appointment is made if the assets are in jeopardy, or to avoid possible prejudices.

(f) *Court power to stay proceedings.* At any time after the presentation of the petition, and before making the winding-up order, the Court (on application of the company or any creditor or contributory) may also stay or restrain any legal proceedings against the company: s. 126 IA 1986.

5. Hearing of the petition

(a) *Entitlement to attend the hearing.* On the date fixed for the hearing, the company, creditor and any contributory may attend, provided that:

(*i*) any creditor or contributory gives notice to the petitioner that he intends to appeal and states whether he will support or oppose the petition;

NOTE: A 'contributory' is defined as every person liable to contribute to the assets of a company in the event of its being wound up and, in the course of winding-up proceedings, includes any person alleged to be a contributory: s. 74 IA 1986.

(*ii*) if he is opposing the petition, his opposition must be supported by affidavit, and this must be filed within seven days of the date on which the affidavit supporting the petition was filed;

(*iii*) the petitioner can file affidavit in reply to the opposition within three days, and the deponent is liable to be called for cross-examination on his affidavit.

(b) *Result of the hearing.* When the hearing takes place, the Court has power to:

(*i*) dismiss the petition, with or without costs;

(*ii*) adjourn the hearing, conditionally or unconditionally;

(*iii*) make an interim order, or any other order that it thinks fit;

(*iv*) order the petition to stand over for a time, as in *Re Brighton Hotel Co.* (1868);

(*v*) make a compulsory order for winding-up of the company.

(c) *If the petition is successful,* i.e. where the Court makes a compulsory order for winding up the company:

(*i*) an appeal can be made against the winding-up order, if brought within 14 days;

(*ii*) *petitioner's costs:* the Court will usually order that the petitioner's costs shall be a first charge on the assets of the company available for ordinary creditors, but not on property securing debentures.

6. Commencement of the winding-up

(a) It is important to fix the date on which the winding-up commenced.

(b) In a winding-up by the Court, i.e. a compulsory liquidation, the commencement of winding-up is:

(*i*) the time of presentation of the petition for winding up; or

(*ii*) the date of the resolution for winding up, i.e. if the company is already in *voluntary* liquidation, the effect is to make the order retrospective to the date of the resolution for voluntary winding up: s. 129 IA 1986.

7. Consequences of the winding-up

(a) A copy of the winding-up order must be filed with the Registrar of Companies: s. 130(1) IA 1986.

(b) Any disposition of the company's property, any transfer of its shares, or alteration in status of its members, made after commencement of the winding-up are, unless the Court orders otherwise, void: s. 127 IA 1986.

> NOTE: This prevents the dissipation of the company's assets and the shedding of liability, which might otherwise take place between presentation and hearing of the petition.

(c) Any attachment, sequestration, distress or execution put in force against the estate or effects of the company after the commencement of the winding-up is void: s. 138 IA 1986.

(d) No actions can be commenced or proceeded with against the company, without leave of the Court: s. 130(2) IA 1986.

(e) The Official Receiver becomes liquidator under s. 136 IA 1986 and continues to act until another liquidator is appointed.

(f) Most of the powers of the directors cease, and are assumed by the liquidator: *Fowler* v. *Broad's Patent Night Light Co.* (1893).
(g) Liquidator or provisional liquidator, as appropriate, may apply to the Court for the appointment of a special manager of the company's business or property if the nature of that business or property or the interests of the creditors, members or contributories require it: s. 177 IA 1986.
(h) Servants of the company are *ipso facto* dismissed: *Chapman's Case* (1866).
(i) The Official Receiver takes control of all books and papers of the company immediately the winding-up order is made.
(j) Every invoice, order for goods or business letter issued by or on behalf of the company or the liquidator, on which the company's name appears, must contain a statement that the company is being wound up: s. 188 IA 1986.
(k) A statement of affairs must be submitted to the Official Receiver. The Official Receiver serves notice on the directors and Secretary who were in office at the date of the winding-up, ordering them to submit to him a statement of the company's affairs (*see* **8** *below*).

8. The Statement of Affairs: s. 131 IA 1986

(a) When the court has made a winding-up order or appointed a provisional liquidator, the Official Receiver may require some or all of the persons specified (in s. 131(3) IA 1986) to make out or submit to him a statement in the prescribed form as to the affairs of the company.
(b) The statement has to be verified by affidavit by the person required to submit it and must state:

(*i*) particulars of the company's assets, debts and liabilities;
(*ii*) the names and addresses of the company's creditors;
(*iii*) the securities held by them respectively; and
(*iv*) such further or other information as may be prescribed or as the Official Receiver may require.

(c) The persons referred to in **(a)** are:

(*i*) those who are or have been officers of the company;
(*ii*) those who have taken part in the formation of the company at any time within one year before the relevant date;
(*iii*) those who are in the company's employment or have

been in the Official Receiver's opinion capable of giving the information required;

(iv) those who are or have been within that year officers of, or in the employment of, a company which is, or within that year was, an officer of the company: s. 131(3) IA 1986.

(d) The statement, if required, must be submitted to the Official Receiver within 21 days of being requested.

9. Investigation by the Official Receiver: s. 132 IA 1986

It is the duty of the official receiver to investigate:

(a) if the company has failed, the causes of the failure; and

(b) generally, the promotion, formation, business, dealings and affairs of the company,

and to make such report (if any) to the court as he thinks fit.

The report is, in any proceedings, *prima facie* evidence of the facts stated in it.

10. Public examinations of officers: s. 133 IA 1986

(a) In a compulsory liquidation, the Official Receiver may at any time before the dissolution of the company apply to the court for the public examination of any person who:

(i) is or has been an officer of the company; or

(ii) has acted as liquidator or administrator for the company or as receiver or manager; or

(iii) not being a person falling within *(i)* or *(ii)* is or has been concerned, or has taken part, in the promotion, formation or management of the company.

(b) Unless the Court otherwise orders, the Official Receiver must make an application to the court for the public examination of any person if he is requested to do so by:

(i) one-half, in value, of the company creditors; or

(ii) three-quarters, in value, of the company's contributories.

(c) The person to whom the application relates must attend on the day appointed by the Court and be publicly examined as to the promotion, formation or management of the company or as to the conduct of its business and affairs, or his conduct or dealings in relation to the company.

11. The first meetings of creditors and contributories

(a) By s. 136 IA 1986 within 12 weeks of the winding-up order the Official Receiver must decide whether to summon meetings of creditors and contributories. If he decides not to do so he must inform the Court, the creditors and the contributories. However, he must summon meetings of both creditors and contributories if required to do so by one-quarter in value of the creditors.

(b) The primary purpose of these first meetings is to choose a liquidator. If each meeting nominates a different person, the creditors' nominee shall be the liquidator, but any creditor or contributory may within seven days apply to the court for some other person (including the contributories' nominee) to be appointed, either instead of, or in addition to the creditors' nominee.

If the meetings do not appoint a liquidator the Official Receiver must decide whether to refer the need for an appointment to the Secretary of State, who may make an appointment, or decline to make one, in which case the Official Receiver will continue as liquidator. If a vacancy occurs in the office of liquidator, it is filled by the Official Receiver: ss. 137 and 139 IA 1986.

(c) The meetings may also establish a committee ('the liquidation committee') to act with the liquidator. The function of the committee is to assist the liquidator and act as a link between the creditors and contributories and the liquidator. It also has statutory power to sanction some of the liquidator's actions. Where the Official Receiver is the liquidator any committee that may have been established shall have no authority to act; instead the functions of the committee will be vested in the Secretary of State. If the Official Receiver is not the liquidator and no committee has been established the functions assigned to the committee are vested in the Secretary of State: s. 141 IA 1986.

NOTE: In addition to appointment by the first meetings the committee can be appointed at the instigation of the liquidator. He (provided he is not the Official Receiver) can call general meetings of the company's creditors and contributories to decide whether there should be a committee and, if so, who should be its members. The liquidator must call these meetings if required to do so by one-tenth in value of the company's creditors. If the meetings do not agree on whether the committee should be appointed then a committee must be established unless the court orders otherwise.

12. The liquidator

(a) *Appointment.* The provisions governing appointment of the liquidator in a compulsory liquidation have been outlined in **11(b)** above.

(b) *Qualifications.* With the exception of the Official Receiver, only a qualified insolvency practitioner may act as liquidator.

An insolvency practitioner is an individual who acts as liquidator, administrator, administrative receiver or supervisor of a voluntary arrangement under Part 1 IA 1986. An individual will only be able to act as an insolvency practitioner if he is authorized to do so by a recognized professional body or the relevant authority set up by the Secretary of State. Further there must be some security in force at the time the individual acts. A person cannot act as an insolvency practitioner if he is an undischarged bankrupt, subject to a disqualification order under the C.D.D.A. 1986 or is a patient within terms of the Mental Health Act 1983.

(c) *Disqualification.* There are various people disqualified from acting as insolvency practitioners.

(d) *Functions.* The basic function of the liquidator is to secure that the assets of the company are got in, realized and distributed to the company's creditors and, if there is a surplus, to the persons entitled to it: s. 143(1) IA 1986.

(e) *Duty.* If he is not the Official Receiver, the liquidator must furnish such information, produce and permit inspection of such books, papers and other records, and give such other assistance as, and to, the Official Receiver as the Official Receiver may reasonably require for the purpose of carrying out his functions in relation to the winding up: s. 143(2) IA 1986.

(f) Custody of property. The liquidator (or provisional liquidator) must take into his custody or under his control all the property and things in action to which the company is or appears to be entitled: s. 144(1) IA 1986. The company's property only vests in the liquidator if he applies for and obtains a court order to that effect: s. 145(1) IA 1986.

(g) Summoning of final meeting. If the liquidator is someone other than the Official Receiver he must call a general meeting of creditors when he is satisfied that the winding-up is complete. He reports to the meeting and it decides whether he should be released from office: s. 146 IA 1986.

If the Official Receiver is the liquidator there is no final meeting of creditors; the Official Receiver merely informs the Registrar that the winding-up is complete.

13. Dissolution

When the Registrar receives notice from the Official Receiver that the winding-up is complete, or receives notice that the final meeting of creditors has been held, he notes this fact on the company's file and three months later the company is dissolved: s. 205 IA 1986.

NOTE: Under s. 202 IA 1986 if the Official Receiver is the liquidator and it appears to him that the assets are insufficient to cover the expenses of the winding-up and that the company's affairs do not require further investigation, he can apply to the Registrar of Companies for early dissolution. Before doing so the Official Receiver must give 28 days' notice to creditors, contributories and the administrative receiver (if there is one). Any creditor, contributory or the administrative receiver then has three months from the date of the application to apply to the Secretary of State for directions on the following grounds:

(a) that the assets are sufficient to cover the expenses of the winding-up;
(b) that the affairs of the company do require further investigation;
(c) that for any other reason early dissolution is inappropriate.

Unless directions are given the company is automatically dissolved three months after the date of the Official Receiver's application. If directions are given they will be that the winding-up proceeds as if no notice had been given by the Official Receiver.

Voluntary winding-up

14. A voluntary winding-up

A voluntary winding-up enables the company concerned and its creditors to settle their affairs without many of the formalities already described in a winding-up by the Court. It is the method most commonly adopted.

15. When appropriate

A company may be wound up voluntarily in the following circumstances, as provided in s. 84 IA 1986.

(a) When the period (if any) fixed for the duration of the company by the Articles expires, or the event (if any) occurs on the occurrence of which the Articles provide that the company shall be dissolved, and the company in general meeting has passed a resolution requiring the company to be wound up voluntarily.

NOTE: An *ordinary* resolution is sufficient, unless another form of resolution is required by the Articles.

(b) If the company resolves by *special* resolution to be wound up voluntarily.

(c) If the company resolves by *extraordinary* resolution that it cannot, by reason of its liabilities, continue its business and that it is advisable to wind up.

16. Notice of the resolution

Notice of the resolution to wind up voluntarily must be advertised in the *Gazette* within 14 days after the passing of the resolution: s. 85 IA 1986.

NOTE: Failure to give such notice renders the company and every officer in default liable to fines: s. 85(2) IA 1986.

17. Commencement of the winding-up: s. 86 IA 1986

A voluntary winding-up dates from the passing of the resolution which authorized it.

18. Consequences of the winding-up

(a) *Business and status of the company.* As from the commencement

of the winding-up, the company must cease to carry on its business, except so far as may be required for its beneficial winding-up. However, the corporate state and corporate powers of the company, notwithstanding anything to the contrary in its Articles, continue until the company is dissolved: s. 87 IA 1986.
(b) *Avoidance of share transfers, etc.* Any transfer of shares, not being a transfer made to or with the sanction of the liquidator, and any alteration in the status of the company's members, made after the commencement of a voluntary winding-up, is void: s. 88 IA 1986.
(c) On the appointment of a liquidator the powers of the directors cease except so far as the company in general meeting or the liquidator (in a members' voluntary winding-up), or the liquidation committee or, if there is no such committee, the creditors sanction their continuance: s. 103 IA 1986.
(d) A *statement* that the company is being wound up must be made on every invoice, order for goods or business letter issued by or on behalf of the company or the liquidator on which the company's name appears: s. 188 IA 1986.

> NOTE: This section applies in *all* forms of winding up, and the company and any person wilfully authorizing or permitting the default are liable to a fine.

(e) *Company's servants.* The winding-up may operate as a dismissal of the company's servants; if, for example, the company is insolvent, it will act as a dismissal: *Fowler* v. *Commercial Timber Co. Ltd* (1930), but if for the purpose of amalgamation, it will not operate as a discharge: *Midland Counties Bank* v. *Attwood* (1905). In any case, the liquidator may continue to employ the company's servants to wind up the company under a new contract of employment. In doing so he is acting as manager of the company: *Smith* v. *Lord Advocate* (1978).
(f) *Stay of proceedings.* There is *no* provision for the stay of proceedings (such as applies in a winding-up by the Court), but the Court may stay proceedings if the liquidator can show the need to do so: s. 112 IA 1986.

19. Forms of voluntary winding-up

(a) A voluntary winding-up may be either
(*i*) a members' voluntary winding-up; or

(*ii*) a creditors' voluntary winding-up: s. 90 IA 1986.

(b) A members' voluntary winding-up takes place only when the company is solvent. It is entirely managed by the members, and the liquidator is appointed by them. No meeting of creditors is held and no liquidation committee is appointed. To obtain the benefit of this form of winding-up, a declaration of solvency must be filed under s. 89 IA 1986.

(c) If no declaration of solvency is filed with the Registrar, a voluntary winding-up is a creditors' voluntary winding-up.

Proceedings in a members' voluntary winding-up

20. Statutory Declaration of Solvency

The directors of the company (or, if there are more than two, a majority of them) may, at a board meeting, make a statutory Declaration of Solvency which, under s. 89 IA 1986:

(a) must contain a declaration by the directors that, having made full enquiry into the company's affairs, they are of the opinion that the company will be able to pay its debts in full within 12 months of the commencement of the winding-up;

(b) must be made not more than five weeks before the date of the resolution to wind up or on that date, but before the passing of that resolution;

(c) must be filed with the Registrar of Companies before the expiry of the period of 15 days immediately following the date on which the resolution for winding-up is made;

(d) must contain a statement of the company's assets and liabilities as at the last practicable date before making the Declaration of Solvency.

> NOTE: Unless the above provisions are complied with, the declaration is of no effect, and there are heavy penalties for making the declaration without sufficient grounds, the onus being upon the directors to show they had reasonable grounds for their opinion: s. 89(4) IA 1986.

21. Resolution for winding-up

Assuming that a Declaration of Solvency can be made and will subsequently be filed in accordance with the above provisions:

(a) the company in general meeting passes the appropriate resolution for winding up, i.e.

(*i*) an ordinary resolution, if the duration of the company fixed by the Articles has expired; or

(*ii*) a special resolution, if no reason is stated;

(b) one or more liquidators are appointed to wind up the company's affairs and distribute its assets: s. 91 IA 1986;

(c) the remuneration of the liquidator(s) may be fixed.

22. Effect and notice of liquidator's appointment

(a) *Effect of liquidator's appointment.* On appointment of the liquidator(s) all powers of the directors cease, unless the company in general meeting, or the liquidator himself, sanctions their continuance: s. 91(2) IA 1986.

(b) *Notice of liquidator's appointment.* Within 14 days after his appointment, the liquidator must publish in the *Gazette* and deliver to the Registrar a notice of his appointment. Failure to do so renders him liable to a fine during the continuance of the default.

23. Liquidator's duty in case of insolvency: s. 95 IA 1986

If the liquidator is of the opinion that the company will not be able to pay its debts in full within the period stated in the statutory Declaration of Solvency, he must:

(a) summon a meeting of the creditors for a day not later than 28 days after the day on which he formed the opinion;

(b) lay before the meeting a statement of the assets and liabilities of the company.

The requirements as regards notice of this meeting and the contents of the statement of affairs are as for the first meeting of creditors in a creditors' voluntary winding-up (*see* **28** *below*).

NOTE: If this occurs, the winding-up becomes, in effect, a creditors' voluntary winding-up.

24. Liquidator's normal duties

Assuming that the winding-up continues as a *members'* voluntary winding-up, these are:

(a) to wind up the company's affairs and distribute its assets;
(b) to obtain the sanction of an extraordinary resolution of the company when he wishes to pay any class of creditors in full; to make a compromise or arrangement with creditors; to compromise calls, debts and other liabilities between the company and its members, or to take any security for the discharge of such debts and to give a complete discharge for them;

NOTE: For similar purposes in a creditors' voluntary winding up, he must obtain the sanction of the Court or of the liquidation committee or, if there is no such committee, of the creditors at a meeting of the creditors.

(c) to summon a general meeting of the company at the end of the first and each succeeding year of the liquidation, or within three months after the end of the year, or any longer period permitted by the Secretary of State, and to lay before the meeting an account of his acts and dealings, and of the conduct of the winding up, during the preceding year: s. 93 IA 1986.

25. The conclusion of the winding-up

As soon as the affairs of the company are fully wound up the liquidator must:

(a) summon a general meeting of the company, by notice in the *Gazette*, the notice to be given at least one month before the meeting, specifying the time, place and object of the meeting;
(b) prepare an account of the winding-up, lay it before the meeting and give any explanations required;
(c) send to the Registrar, within one week after the meeting, a copy of his account and a return of the holding of the meeting: s. 94 IA 1986.

NOTE: If there was less than a quorum present at the final meeting his return to the Registrar must state that the meeting had been called and that no quorum was present. This is then deemed to comply with the Act as to the making of the return. Failure to summon the meeting renders the liquidator liable to a fine.

26. Dissolution of the company

On receipt of the relevant return as to the holding of the final meeting, it is then the duty of the Registrar to enter it in his register; on the expiration of three months from the date of registration of the return, the company is deemed to be dissolved and its name is struck off the register: s. 201(1) and (2) IA 1986.

NOTE: It is provided, however, that the Court has power to defer the date of dissolution, on the application of the liquidator or any interested persons under s. 201(3) IA 1986.

Proceedings in a creditors' voluntary winding-up

In any case where a Declaration of Solvency is not filed with the Registrar, the winding-up is a creditors' voluntary winding-up to which the following provisions apply.

27. The company must summon two meetings

(a) *A general meeting of the company*, for the purpose of passing a resolution for winding up, under s. 84 IA 1986. an extraordinary resolution will be required in this case, as the company is to be wound up because it cannot continue its business by reason of its liabilities.
(b) *A creditors' meeting*, to be held within 14 days of the general meeting of the company.

28. Creditors' meetings

(a) Notices of the creditors' meetings must be sent by post to the creditors not less than seven days before the day on which that meeting is to be held and, in addition, must be advertised in the *Gazette* and two local newspapers circulating in the district where the registered office of the company is situate: IA 1986.
(b) At the meeting of creditors:

(*i*) a director of the company, appointed by the other directors, must preside;

(*ii*) a full statement of the company's affairs, showing particulars of the company's assets, debts and liabilities, the names and addresses of the company's creditors, the securities held by them, the dates when the securities were given and such further or other information as may be prescribed must be laid before the creditors by the directors of the company: s. 99 IA 1986;

(*iii*) a liquidator may be nominated: s. 100 IA 1986 (*see* **29** *below*);

(*iv*) a liquidation committee may be appointed, consisting of not more than five persons: s. 101 IA 1986.

29. Appointment of liquidator

(a) Both the creditors and the company, at their respective meetings, have power to nominate a liquidator: s. 100 IA 1986.

(b) If different persons are nominated by creditors and company respectively, the person nominated by the creditors shall be liquidator; but

(*i*) if the creditors make no nomination, the person nominated by the company shall be liquidator; or

(*ii*) any director, member or creditor may apply to the Court, within seven days of the nomination, to uphold the company's nomination or to appoint some other person: s. 100 IA 1986.

(c) After his appointment, all powers of the directors cease, unless the committee of inspection (or the creditors, if there is no committee) sanction otherwise: s. 103 IA 1986.

(d) Any vacancy in the office of liquidator caused by his death, resignation or otherwise, may be filled by the creditors, unless he was a liquidator appointed by the Court: s. 104 IA 1986.

30. Liquidator's powers and duties

(a) With the sanction of the Court, or the liquidation committee or (if no committee is appointed) a meeting of the creditors, he may exercise the powers specified in Part 1 Sch. 4 IA 1986, namely to:

(*i*) pay any classes of creditors in full;

(*ii*) make compromises or arrangements with creditors; or

(*iii*) compromise all calls and liabilities to calls, debts and liabilities capable of resulting in debts.

(b) Without sanction, he may exercise the powers specified in Part II Sch. 4 IA 1986, namely to:

(*i*) bring or defend any action or other legal proceeding in the name and on behalf of the company;

(*ii*) carry on the business of the company so far as may be necessary for its beneficial winding up.

31. Appointment of a liquidation committee: s. 101 IA 1986

(a) The creditors have power to appoint not more than five persons as members of a liquidation committee. This appointment may be made either at the first or subsequent meeting of the creditors.
(b) If the creditors make such an appointment, the company may also appoint not more than five persons to act as members of the committee, along with those appointed by the creditors. This appointment may be made either at the first or subsequent general meeting of the company.
(c) The creditors may, however, reject the company's nominees, unless the Court otherwise directs and (on receiving application) appoint other persons to act as members of the committee.

32. If the winding-up continues for more than one year
It is the duty of the liquidator:

(a) to summon a general meeting of the company and a meeting of creditors at the end of the first and each succeeding year of the winding-up, or within three months after the end of the year, or such longer period as the Secretary of State may allow;
(b) to lay before the respective meetings an account of his acts and dealings, and of the conduct of the winding-up during the preceding year: s. 105 IA 1986.

33. The conclusion of the winding-up
As soon as the company's affairs are fully wound up, the liquidator must:

(a) make up an account of the winding up, showing how it has been conducted and the company's property has been disposed of;
(b) call a general meeting of the company and a meeting of creditors, by notice in the *Gazette* at least one month before the meeting, specifying the time, place and object of the meeting;
(c) lay his account before the meetings and give any explanations required;
(d) send to the Registrar, within one week after the date of the

meetings (or after the date of the later meeting, if not held on the same day), a copy of his account, and a return of the holding of the meetings: s. 106 IA 1986.

NOTE: If there was less than a quorum present at either meeting, his return to the Registrar must state that the meeting was called but no quorum was present. This is then deemed to comply with the Act as to the making of the return. Failure to summon the meeting renders the liquidator liable to a fine.

34. Dissolution of the company

On the expiration of three months from the date of registration of the return, the company is deemed to be dissolved: s. 201(2) IA 1986.

The Court may defer the date of dissolution, on the application of the liquidator or any other interested party under s. 201 IA 1986.

Progress test 13

1. Upon what grounds might a company be wound up compulsorily? When is a company deemed to be unable to pay its debts? **(3)**

2. **(a)** Describe the various ways in which a company may be liquidated, indicating how each method is initiated.
(b) How is a liquidation committee formed and what are its functions?
(c) Who are the contributories in the liquidation of a company and what are their liabilities? *ICSA* **(2, 3)**

3. What is the meaning of the following terms used in connection with the winding-up of companies:

(a) statement of affairs;
(b) public examination;
(c) first meetings of creditors and contributories;
(d) liquidation committee?
(8, 10, 11)

4. When does a voluntary winding-up commence, and what are the immediate effects of such commencement? *ICSA* (15, 17)

5. You have been appointed liquidator in a voluntary winding-up. Explain how your appointment affects:
(a) the continuance of the company's trade;
(b) the transfer of its shares;
(c) the employment of its servants;
(d) the company's existence.
ICSA (18)

6. The reason for which your company was originally formed having ceased to exist, it has been decided to wind-up the company and distribute the considerable surplus to the shareholders. The necessary meetings have been held and you have been appointed liquidator. Detail all the steps you would take from the time of your appointment until the winding-up is complete, assuming that this takes more than a year. *Corporation of Secretaries* (20–25, 32)

7. Describe how a members' voluntary winding-up is initiated and the proceedings thereunder. *ICSA* (20–26)

8. Set out the procedure for members' winding-up. What would you do as a liquidator if it became apparent during the course of the liquidation that the company would not in fact be able to pay its debts in full? *ICSA* (20–26)

9. You have been appointed liquidator of a company whose shares are partly paid. It is expected that it will be necessary to call up the amounts unpaid. Set out the procedure you would adopt. *ICSA* (27–30)

10. What meetings are required to be called by a liquidator? What are his duties when the affairs of the company are fully wound up? *ICSA* (28, 31–34)

11. You are secretary of a small manufacturing company. There are only two shareholders who are also the only directors. They concern themselves with the manufacturing and sales aspects of the business and rely on you for guidance on accountancy and finance. The company has had a succession of adverse trading years and you reach the conclusion that the company is only just solvent but that it is unlikely that even this can be held for more than one or two months unless business improves. Prepare a memorandum on the situation, for consideration by your two directors, covering the following points:

(a) the present financial position, explaining what is meant by 'solvent';
(b) the possible courses of action with an outline of the probable consequences of each;
(c) your recommended course of action, giving reasons.
ICSA **(14, 27–34)**

12. Explain fully the meaning of each of the following terms used in connection with the winding up of a company:

(a) declaration of solvency;
(b) proof of claim;
(c) statement of affairs;
(d) dissolution.
ICSA **(8, 20, 26, 34)**

13. Explain in detail the procedure for a members' voluntary winding up. *ICSA* **(10–26)**

14. You have been appointed liquidator in a voluntary winding-up. Explain how your appointment affects:

(a) the continuance of the company's trade;
(b) the transfer of its shares;
(c) the status of its members;
(d) the employment of its servants.
ICSA **(18)**

15. Set out the initial procedure on putting a company into voluntary liquidation and the further procedure to be carried out by the liquidator. *ICSA* **(14–34)**

14

Directors, secretaries and auditors; directors' report

Directors

1. Definition and status of directors

(a) *Definition.* A director is defined in s. 741 CA 1985 as 'any person occupying the position of director, by whatever name called'.
(b) *As trustees.*

(*i*) A director *is*, to some extent, a trustee for the company; that is, of its money and property, and of the powers entrusted to him.

(*ii*) He *is not*, however, a trustee for the individual shareholder: *Percival* v. *Wright* (1902).
(c) *As agents.* He *is* an agent for the company, and contracts made by him will bind the company so long as he acts within the scope of his authority.
(d) *As managers.*

(*i*) *Functions.* It is the principal function of the directors, acting as a board, to manage the company, and this function may be divided roughly into three basic activities: forecasting, planning and control.

(*ii*) *Responsibilities.* In carrying out their function of management, the directors are in a fiduciary position in relation to the shareholders who appointed them to manage the company. They have a duty to, and are expected by, the shareholders to maximise profits and give them a reasonable return on their capital investment.

But they also have responsibilities to the company's employees and, in the performance of their managerial functions, they must have regard to the interests of employees as well as the interests of the company's members: s. 309 CA 1985.

(e) *As officers.* A director is an officer of the company, a term defined as including a director, manager or secretary.

(f) *As employees.*

(*i*) Directors are not, as such, employees of the company or employed by the company: *Hampson* v. *Prices Patent Candle Co.* (1876); nor are they servants of the company or members of its staff: *Hutton* v. *West Cork Railways* (1883).

(*ii*) A director may, however, hold a salaried employment or an office in addition to his directorship which may, for these purposes, make him an employee or servant and in such a case he would enjoy any rights given to employees as such: *Re Beeton & Co. Ltd* (1913).

(*iii*) Whether a director is an employee for the purposes of employment protection legislation is a question of fact in each case: *Parsons* v. *Parsons (Albert J.) & Sons Ltd.* (1979). On the other hand a director is generally regarded as an employee for tax purposes.

2. Appointment

(a) *The first directors.*

(*i*) Section 10 CA 1985 provides that a Memorandum delivered for registration must be accompanied by a statement in prescribed form, signed by the subscribers to the Memorandum, giving particulars of the first directors and containing a consent signed by each person named.

(*ii*) On incorporation, the persons named shall be deemed to have been appointed as first directors of the company.

(*iii*) An appointment by any Articles delivered with the Memorandum of a person as director of the company is void unless he is named as a director in the statement.

(b) *Subsequent appointments.* The appointment of any subsequent directors will be governed by the Articles of Association. It is usual for the Articles to provide as follows:

(*i*) The board of directors is formally empowered to fill casual vacancies or to appoint additional directors up to any maximum set by the Articles. Where the Articles give the directors exclusive power to appoint additional or new directors, the company in general meeting will have no power of appointment as this would usurp the powers delegated to the directors.

(*ii*) Any person appointed by the directors as an additional director will normally hold office only until the next annual general meeting when an ordinary resolution must be proposed for his re-appointment: Regulation 79 Table A.

(*iii*) The company is normally empowered by the Articles to appoint, by ordinary resolution, a person to fill a vacancy or as an additional director.

(c) *All appointments.*

(*i*) When directors of a public company are elected in general meeting the appointment of each director must be voted on separately unless the meeting previously agrees without dissent to waive the rule: s. 292 CA 1985.

(*ii*) A procedural defect in the appointment of a director does not usually invalidate the acts of that director: s. 285 CA 1985. This section provides that the acts of a director or manager are valid notwithstanding any defect that may afterwards be discovered in his appointment or qualification. Further, the Articles, as in the case of Table A, may provide that all acts done by any meeting of the directors or of a committee of directors or by any person acting as a director shall, notwithstanding that it be afterwards discovered that there was some defect in the appointment of any such director or person acting as aforesaid, or that they or any of them were disqualified, be as valid as if every such person had been duly appointed and was qualified and had continued to be a director (Article 92).

(d) *Procedure for appointing a director.*

(*i*) Check the Articles of Association for the mode of appointment. Ensure that the additional appointment will not cause the number of directors to exceed any maximum prescribed by the Articles.

(*ii*) Obtain approval of the appointment at a board meeting or at a general meeting, as appropriate. It should be noted that a composite resolution to appoint two or more directors, proposed at a general meeting of a public company, is void: s. 292 CA 1985. Accordingly, all resolutions at a general meeting to appoint or re-appoint directors to a public company must be voted upon individually.

(iii) Supply a Form G288 to the new director for completion. In particular, the appointee must sign a form of consent to act.

(iv) Submit Form G288 to the Registrar within 14 days of the date of appointment.

(v) Enter details of the appointee in the Register of Directors of the company. The particulars to be inserted are his name, any former name, usual residential address, nationality, business occupation (if any), particulars of past and present directorships and date of birth (s. 289 CA 1985; Para. 2 Sch. 19 CA 1989).

(vi) Remind the director of any share qualification required by the Articles. Where a qualification is required, the Articles will often provide a maximum period not to exceed two months (s. 291 CA 1985).

(vii) Invite the director to make disclosure of any interest in shares and debentures of the company and also to give general notice of any interest in contracts. He should also be reminded of his obligation to keep the company informed, from time to time, of any changes in interests in shares, debentures or contracts and he should be provided with pro-formas on which to make such disclosure.

(viii) Notify the company's bankers of the appointment and, if the appointee is to be a bank signatory, amend the bank mandate.

(ix) Remind the director of his responsibility to notify the company of any change in address or personal details, and any changes in other UK directorships.

> NOTE: If the company concerned was listed, the procedure outlined above would have to be modified and the documentation drafted to take account to the Continuing Obligations imposed upon such a company by the Stock Exchange. The Continuing Obligations are set out in Chapter 2 and reference should be made thereto.

3. Share qualifications

(a) *When required.* A share qualification is not essential, unless the Articles so provide.

(b) *If a share qualification is required* it is only satisfied by the director being the registered holder of the required number of shares; hence the holding of share warrants to bearer is not sufficient: s. 291 CA 1985. To hold shares as nominee of the owner or jointly with another will, however, suffice. If the Articles require a holding in his own right this merely excludes a case where the company is aware that someone else is entitled to have the shares transferred out of his name, e.g. his trustee in bankruptcy.

(c) *Obtaining share qualification.* Where a share qualification *is* required by the company's Articles, each director must take up his qualification shares within two months after his appointment, or within any shorter period determined by the Articles: s. 291 CA 1985. A director vacates office immediately if he ceases to hold the required qualification shares.

4. Age limit

(a) Section 293 CA 1985 establishes an upper age limit for directors. This section, however, only applies to public companies or to private companies which are subsidiaries of public companies (s. 293(1) CA 1985). Even as regards these companies, the section has effect subject to the company's articles and, in any case, the age limit does not apply if the director's appointment is approved by a resolution of the general meeting of which special notice (within s. 379 CA 1985 stating the age of the director has been given: s. 293(5) CA 1985).

(b) Where s. 293 CA 1985 does apply, sub-sections (2) and (3) provide that a person may not be appointed a director once he has attained the age of 70, and if already a director he must vacate his office at the conclusion of the next annual general meeting following his 70th birthday.

(c) A person appointed or to his knowledge proposed to be appointed as a director of a company subject to s. 293 CA 1985 is under an obligation to inform the company of his age if he has attained the retiring age: s. 294 CA 1985. This does not apply to re-appointments since the director's date of birth will be already contained in the company's Register of Directors pursuant to s. 289 CA 1985.

(d) On the resignation or retirement of a director, notice must be given to the Registrar of Companies on Form 288.

5. Retirement

(a) There is no requirement in the Companies Act for directors to retire by rotation or otherwise. It is, however, common for the Articles of a company to make some such provision.

(b) Under Table A, for example, all directors retire at the first annual general meeting and one-third of them retire at each subsequent annual general meeting (Article 73). A managing director and a director holding any other executive office are not subject to retirement by rotation (Article 84) and any director who was appointed to fill a casual vacancy is disregarded in arriving at the numbers to retire (Article 79). Those longest in office since their last election shall retire first (Article 74). The chairman, unless also a managing director, is subject to normal retirement by rotation.

(c) As stated in Chapter 1, the Stock Exchange requires that the Articles of all listed companies include provision for the retirement of directors appointed by the board during the year, but there is no similar requirement for retirement by rotation.

6. Disqualification of directors

(a) The law regarding disqualification of directors is now consolidated in the Company Directors Disqualification Act 1986.

(b) Sections 2–5 CDDA 1986 provides that in the circumstances listed below the Court may make against a person a disqualification order, i.e. an order that he shall not, for a specified period beginning with the date of the order, without leave of the Court:

(*i*) be a director of a company, or

(*ii*) be a liquidator or administrator of a company, or

(*iii*) be a receiver or manager of a company's property, or

(*iv*) in any way, whether directly or indirectly, be concerned or take part in the promotion, formation or management of a company.

The circumstances concerned are:

(*i*) On conviction of an indictable offence in connection with the promotion, formation, management or liquidation of a company or with the receivership or management of a company's property.

(*ii*) For persistent breaches of the companies legislation requiring any return, account or other document to be filed with, delivered or sent, or notice of any matter to be given, to the Registrar of Companies.

(*iii*) If, in the course of the winding-up of a company, it appears a person has been guilty of an offence for which he is liable (whether he has been convicted or not) under s. 458 (Fraudulent Trading CA 1985) or has otherwise been guilty, while an officer or liquidator of the company or Receiver or manager of its property, of any fraud in relation to the company or of any breach of his duty as such officer, liquidator, Receiver or manager.

(*iv*) On conviction in consequence of a contravention of, or failure to comply with, any provisions of the companies legislation requiring a return, account or other document to be filed with, delivered or sent, or notice of any matter to be given to the Registrar of Companies.

(c) Further, under s. 6 CDDA 1986 the Court must make a disqualification order against a person in any case where it is satisfied:

(*i*) that he is or has been a director of a company which has at any time become insolvent (whether while he was a director or subsequently) and

(*ii*) that his conduct as a director of that company (either taken alone or taken together with his conduct as a director of any other company or companies) makes him unfit to be concerned in the management of a company.

(d) Under s. 8 CDDA 1986 if it appears to the Secretary of State from a report made by his inspectors under s. 437 CA 1985 or s. 94 or 177 FSA 1986 or from information or documents obtained under s. 447 or 448 CA 1985 or s. 105 FSA 1986 or s. 2 of the Criminal Justice Act 1987 or s. 52 of the Criminal Justice (Scotland) Act 1987 or s. 83 CA 1989 that it is expedient in the public interest that a disqualification order should be made against any person who is or has been a director or shadow director of any company, he may apply to the Court for such an order to be made against that person.

(e) Section 10 CDDA 1986 provides that a disqualification order may be made against a person required to make a contribution to a company's assets under s. 213 (Fraudulent Trading) or s. 214 (Wrongful Trading) IA 1986.

(f) Section 11 CDDA 1986 makes it an offence for an undischarged bankrupt to act as director of, or directly or indirectly to take part in or be concerned in the promotion, formation or management of a company except with the leave of the Court.

(g) Finally, s. 12 CDDA 1986 provides that a person who fails to pay under a County Court administration order he shall not, except with the leave of the Court, act as director or liquidator of, or directly or indirectly take part or be concerned in the promotion or management of a company.

7. Removal of directors

(a) The members have a statutory power of removal by passing an ordinary resolution in general meeting to remove any director from office, notwithstanding the provisions of the Articles or any other agreement: s. 303 CA 1985.

(b) Special notice is required of a resolution to remove a director under s. 303 CA 1985 or to appoint somebody instead of a director so removed at the meeting at which he is removed.

(c) The requirement of 'special notice' is defined by s. 379 CA 1985. This provides that the resolution concerned is not effective unless notice of the intention to move it has been given the company at least 28 days before the meeting at which it is moved.

The company shall give its members notice of any such resolution at the same time and in the same manner as it gives notice of the meeting or, if that is not practicable, shall give them notice either by advertisement in a newspaper having an appropriate circulation or in any other mode allowed by the company's Articles, at least 21 days before the meeting.

(d) By s. 304 CA 1985 the company must send a copy of the special notice received to the director concerned. Such a director has a right to speak on the resolution at the meeting at which it is proposed and also has the right to make written representations to the company. At the request of the director, and if time allows, the company must send a copy of the written representations to every member to whom notice has been given.

If the representations are received too late to circulate to members prior to the meeting, the director concerned may require that they be read out at the meeting.

(e) Removal under the provisions of s. 303 CA 1985 does not deprive the director concerned of compensation or damages payable to him in respect of the termination of his appointment as director or of any appointment terminating with that as director.

(f) Section 303 CA 1985 does not derogate from any power to remove a director which may exist apart from the section.

(g) The Articles may give a director's shares special voting rights on a resolution to remove him: *Bushell* v. *Faith* (1970)(though the ratio of the case seems to limit the application of such Articles to private companies).

(h) Section 379 CA 1985 does not confer any rights on a shareholder to have a resolution to which it applies circulated if he cannot fulfil the requirements of s. 376 CA 1985, i.e. that he holds or has the support of members holding not less than one-twentieth of the voting rights of the members entitled to vote at the relevant meeting, or of 100 members on whose shares there has been paid up an average sum of not less than £100 a member.

8. Vacation of office

The office of director is personal to the appointee and is therefore vacated upon death. Termination of a director's appointment may also occur in the following circumstances:

(a) resignation;
(b) removal from office (see below);
(c) disqualification by court order, e.g. for offences under the Companies Acts;
(d) upon bankruptcy (unless permitted by the Court to continue);
(e) failure to obtain any share qualification required by the Articles within two months of appointment (s. 291 CA 1985);
(f) at the annual general meeting next following his 70th birthday (for those companies to which such age restriction applies).

In addition the Articles of Association will normally provide certain additional circumstances in which the office of director will be vacated. Regulation 81 of Table A, for example, provides that a director shall cease to act if:

(a) he is suffering from mental disorder and is admitted to hospital pursuant to the Mental Health Act 1984 or a court order is made on the grounds of his mental disorder;

(b) he is absent without permission of the directors from meetings of directors for more than six consecutive months and the directors resolve that he shall vacate office;
(c) he has a receiving order made against him or if he compounds with his creditors generally.

On every occasion of vacation of office, notice of that fact must be submitted to the Registrar of Companies on Form G288 and the fact must be recorded in the Register of Directors.

9. Assignment of office

(a) A director may only assign his office provided such is either authorized by the Articles, or there is an agreement to that effect between the company and the director concerned and in either case is approved by a special resolution of the company: s. 308 CA 1985.
(b) Assignment of office is absolute, i.e. the assignor no longer holds the office and, in this respect, should be contrasted with the appointment of an alternate director (*see* **10** *below*).

10. Alternate (or substitute) directors

(a) A director has no power to delegate his authority to an alternate (or substitute) director, e.g. during his temporary incapacity or absence abroad, unless:
(*i*) this is sanctioned by the *Articles*; or
(*ii*) power to do so is included in the terms of his appointment.
(b) Table A Articles 65–69 provide for the appointment of alternate directors. They provide that:

(*i*) Any director (other than an alternate director) may appoint any other director, or any other person approved by the directors and willing to act, to be an alternate director and may remove from office an alternate director so appointed by him: Article 65.

(*ii*) An alternate director shall be entitled to receive notice of all meetings of directors and of all meetings of committees of directors of which his appointor is a member, to attend and vote at any such meeting at which the director appointing him is not personally present, and generally to perform all the functions of his appointor as director in his absence, but shall not be entitled to receive any remuneration from the company for his services as an alternate director. But it shall not be necessary to give notice of such to an alternative director who is absent from the United Kingdom: Article 66.

(*iii*) An alternate director shall cease to be an alternate director if his appointor ceases to be a director: but, if a director retires by rotation or otherwise but is re-appointed or deemed to have been re-appointed at the meeting at which he retires, any appointment of an alternate director made by him which was in force immediately prior to his retirement shall continue after his re-appointment: Article 67.

(*iv*) Any appointment or removal of an alternate director shall be by notice to the company signed by the director making or revoking the appointment or in any other manner approved by the directors: Article 68.

(*v*) Save as otherwise provided in the Articles, an alternate director shall be deemed for all purposes to be a director and shall alone be responsible for his own acts and defaults and he shall not be deemed to be the agent of the director appointing him.

(c) Particulars of the appointment of an alternate director must be filed with the Registrar on Form G288 within 14 days of the appointment.

(d) The appointment will also entail alterations in:

(*i*) the Register of Directors and Secretaries: s. 288 CA 1985;

(*ii*) The Register of Directors' Interests: s. 325 CA 1985; and

(*iii*) where applicable, letter heads, trade circulars, etc.: s. 305 CA 1985.

(e) Further provisions of CA 1985 which apply equally to alternate directors are as follows:

(*i*) section 293 relating to the director's age limit;

(*ii*) section 317 requiring disclosure of interests in contracts.

(f) The Stock Exchange should be notified of the appointment of an alternative director, if the company's shares are listed.

(g) Vacation of office. An alternate director may vacate office, and his powers cease:

(*i*) *by revocation*, i.e. where the appointing director revokes his appointment;

(*ii*) *by death*, i.e. if the appointing director dies or himself ceases to be a director, in which case revocation is automatic;

(*iii*) *on expiration of the term fixed* for the appointment;

(*iv*) *by his own act*, for example, retirement, resignation, etc.;

(*v*) *by disqualification*, i.e. for any cause that would disqualify the appointor himself.

11. Remuneration

(a) *Not a right.* A director has no implied right to remuneration; he is only entitled to remuneration where:

(*i*) it is provided for in the company's Articles; or

(*ii*) fixed by the company in general meeting, e.g. by a lump sum *ex gratia* payment, to be divided amongst all the directors.

As regards the former possibility, Table A Article 82 provides that directors shall be entitled to such remuneration as the company may by ordinary resolution decide.

(b) *Provisions of Articles.* When the director's remuneration is fixed by the Articles:

(*i*) it cannot be amended, except by special resolution;

(*ii*) a director can sue for it, even if there are no profits: *Re Lundy Granite Co. Ltd.; Lewis's Case* (1872);

(*iii*) he may prove for his remuneration, with other creditors, in a winding-up;

(*iv*) his remuneration is deemed to cover his expenses, unless the Articles (or the company in general meeting) authorize an additional sum for expenses.

Table A Article 83 permits payment of travelling, hotel and other expenses properly incurred by directors in connection with their attendance at meetings or otherwise in connection with the discharge of their duties.

(c) *Wording of Articles.* The right to a proportionate part of a director's remuneration may depend upon the wording of the Articles.

(*i*) The Articles usually state that his remuneration shall be 'at the rate of £...... per annum', which gives a resigning or disqualified director the right to receive a proportionate part of the yearly fee if he vacates office during the course of a year.

(*ii*) If, however, the Articles state that his remuneration shall be (say) 'a yearly sum of £......' or '£...... per annum', there is some doubt whether the director is entitled to an apportionment of the yearly fee: *Inman* v. *Ackroyd Best Ltd.* (1901).

NOTE: The Apportionment Act 1870 provides that all salaries and other periodical payments of income shall be considered as accruing from day to day, and apportionable in respect of time accordingly. This is considered to be applicable to directors' remuneration; nevertheless, the wording of the Articles ought to be explicit.

(*iii*) Table A (Article 82) expressly states that the remuneration of directors shall be deemed to accrue from day to day.

(d) *Tax-free remuneration.* The payment of tax-free remuneration to a director is unlawful: s. 311 CA 1985. This applies equally to the payment of remuneration varying with the amount of his income tax, or with the current rate of income tax.

Any payments that are made gross will be treated by the Inland Revenue as net payments and the company will be liable to account to the Revenue for tax payable thereon.

(e) *Disclosure in accounts.* The Act requires that emoluments of directors (including emoluments waived), pensions of directors and past directors and compensation for loss of office to directors and past directors must be shown in a note to the accounts prepared under s. 226 CA 1985; s. 232 and Sch. 6 Part I CA 1985.

12. Compensation for loss of office: ss. 312–315 CA 1985

(a) It is illegal to pay a director compensation for loss of office — for example, on retirement or on amalgamation with another company — unless:

(*i*) particulars, including the amount of compensation, are disclosed to the members;

(*ii*) approval is granted by the company in general meeting.

(b) If loss of office is due to transfer of the whole or part of the company's undertaking, any payment of compensation made illegally to a director is deemed to be held in trust for the transferee company.

NOTE: The *aggregate* amount of any compensation paid to directors or past directors for loss of office must be shown in a note to the accounts prepared under s. 226 CA 1985; s. 232 and Sch. 6 Part I CA 1985.

13. Loans to directors and connected persons

Section 330 CA 1985 provides as follows, subject to various exceptions (*see* **14**).

(a) A company must not make a loan to a director of the company or of its holding company, nor enter into any guarantee or provide any security in connection with a loan made by any person to such a director.

(b) A 'relevant company' (*see* **15**) must not:

(*i*) make a 'quasi-loan' (*see* **15**) to a director of the company or of its holding company; or

(*ii*) make a loan or a quasi-loan to a person connected with such a director; or

(*iii*) enter into a guarantee or provide any security in connection with a loan or quasi-loan by any other person for such a director or a person so connected; or

(*iv*) enter into a credit transaction as creditor for such a director or a person so connected; or

(*v*) enter into any guarantee or provide any security in connection with a credit transaction made by any other person for such a director or a person so connected.

(c) A company must not arrange for the assignment to it or the assumption by it of any rights, obligations or liabilities under a transaction which, if entered into by the company, would contravene any of the above prohibitions.

(d) A company must not take part in any arrangement whereby another person enters into a transaction which, if it had been entered into by the company, would have been in contravention of any of the above prohibitions, and where that other person has obtained or is about to obtain, any benefit from the company or its holding company.

14. Exceptions

The following are the principal exceptions provided by ss. 332–338 CA 1985.

(a) Where a relevant company is a member of a group of companies (a holding company and its subsidiaries) the prohibitions preventing a relevant company making a loan or a quasi-loan to a person connected with a director of the company or its holding company, or entering into a guarantee or providing any security in connection with a loan or quasi-loan made by any other person for such a director or a person so connected, shall not prohibit the relevant company from making a loan or quasi-loan to another member of that group or entering into a guarantee or providing any security in connection with a loan or quasi-loan made by any person to another member of the group, by reason only that a director of one member of the group is associated with another.

(b) A relevant company ('the creditor') is not prohibited from making a quasi-loan to one of its directors, or to a director of its holding company, if the terms of the loan require the director (or a person on his behalf) to reimburse the creditor within two months of the debt being incurred, and the aggregate amount of that quasi-loan and of the amount outstanding under each relevant quasi-loan does not exceed £5000.

(c) A company is not prohibited from making a loan to a director of the company or of its holding company if the aggregate of the relevant amount does not exceed £5000.

(d) A company is not prohibited from entering into any transaction for any person if the aggregate of the relevant amount does not exceed £5000, or any transaction which is in the ordinary course of business; and the value of the transaction is not greater, and the terms on which it is entered into are no more favourable, than it would be reasonable to expect the company to offer to any person unconnected with the company.

(e) Subject to various conditions, the following are also excepted from the prohibitions of s. 330 CA 1985.

(*i*) A loan or quasi-loan by a company to its holding company.

(*ii*) A company's entering into a guarantee or providing any security in connection with a loan or quasi-loan made by any person to its holding company.

(*iii*) A company's entering into a credit transaction as creditor for its holding company, or entering into a guarantee or providing any security in connection with any such credit transaction.

(*iv*) A company's doing anything to provide any of its directors with funds to meet expenditure incurred, or to be incurred, by him to enable him to perform his duties as an officer of the company.

(*v*) A loan or quasi-loan made by a money-lending company to any person, or a money-lending company's entering into a guarantee in connection with any other loan or quasi-loan.

NOTE: The exception in **(e)**(*iv*) applies only if prior approval of the company is given at a general meeting or, if not approved at or before the next following annual general meeting, the loan must be repaid within six months after the meeting. In any event, however, the exception in **(e)**(*iv*) does not apply if the aggregate of the relevant amounts exceeds £10,000.

The exception in **(e)**(*v*) does not authorize a relevant company (unless it is a banking company) to enter into any transaction if the aggregate of the relevant amount exceeds £100,000.

15. Definitions for s. 330 CA 1985

(a) 'Relevant company' is defined in s. 331(6) CA 1985 but might be more simply interpreted as meaning a public company or its subsidiary.

(b) 'Quasi-loan', expansively defined in s. 331(3) CA 1985, might be more briefly defined as payment by a creditor on behalf of the debtor — to a third party — where there is provision made for reimbursement.

(c) 'Connected persons', fully defined in s. 346 CA 1985, include a director's spouse or child, a company or partner with which he is associated, and any person acting as trustee in any trust (other than in relation to an employees' share scheme or a pension scheme), the beneficiaries of which include the director himself or any of the connected persons already mentioned.

16. Penalties

(a) Where a company enters into a transaction or arrangement which contravenes s. 330 CA 1985, it is *voidable* at the instance of the company, but subject to third party rights: s. 341 CA 1985.

(b) A director of a relevant company and a relevant company acting in contravention of s. 330 CA 1985 provisions are guilty of an offence and liable to a fine and/or imprisonment. The same also applies to any person who procures a relevant company to enter into a transaction or arrangement knowing or having reasonable cause to believe that the company was thereby contravening s. 330 CA 1985: s. 342 CA 1985.

17. Disclosure

Subject to certain exceptions, the group accounts of a parent company must contain specified particulars of any of the loan transactions or arrangements described above: s. 231 and Sch. 5 Part II CA 1985.

18. Directors' interests in contracts with the company

(a) At common law, a director of a company cannot himself contract with that company or have an interest in contracts between third parties and the company: *Aberdeen Ry. Co.* v. *Blaikie Bros.* (1854).

(b) Table A removes this prohibition to some extent by permitting a director:

(*i*) to be a director or other officer of another company with which it is contracting;

(*ii*) to have an interest in contracts with that company;

(*iii*) to retain remuneration or other benefits derived as a result, unless the company direct otherwise: Article 85.

(c) Section 317 CA 1985 imposes upon a director who is directly or indirectly interested in a contract, or proposed contract, an obligation to declare the nature of his interest, either:

(*i*) at a board meeting, when the contract is first considered; or

(*ii*) at the first board meeting held after he acquired an interest in the contract.

(d) A general notice to the directors to the effect that:

(*i*) he is a member of a specified company or firm and is to be regarded as interested in any contract which may, after the date of the notice, be made with that company or firm; or

(*ii*) he is to be regarded as interested in any contract which may, after the date of notice, be made with a specified person who is connected with him;

shall be deemed to be sufficient declaration of interest in relation to any such contract, provided that no such notice shall be effective unless either it is given at a meeting of the directors, or the director takes reasonable steps to ensure that it is brought up and read at the next meeting of the directors after it is given.

(e) Where Stock Exchange regulations apply, a director is not permitted to vote on contracts in which he has an interest or, if he does vote, his vote shall not be counted.

(f) At general meetings, however, there is nothing to prevent a director from being included in the quorum and actually voting on matters affecting any contract in which he has a personal interest. In that case, he attends and votes merely as a member: *North-west Transportation Co.* v. *Beatty* (1887).

NOTE: Schedule 7 CA 1985 also requires disclosure in the directors' report of certain contracts in which a director of the company has, or during the year had, an interest.

19. Contracts of employment of directors

Under s. 319 CA 1985, subject to certain exceptions, any service agreement between a company and one of its directors which provides for continuance of the agreement beyond a period of five years and is terminable only in specific circumstances, or not at all, is *void* unless:

(a) the term of the contract is first approved by resolution of the company in general meeting; and

(b) a written memorandum setting out the proposed agreement and incorporating the term is available for inspection by members:

(*i*) at the registered office of the company for not less than the period of 15 days ending with the date of the meeting; and

(*ii*) at the meeting itself.

If, at the general meeting, no resolution is passed, the original agreement will be deemed to contain a term entitling the company to terminate it at any time by giving reasonable notice.

Copies of all directors' service contracts must be available for inspection at a company's registered office, or at the place where its Register of Members is kept or at its principal place of business. Notice of the location must be given to the Registrar of Companies where the copies are kept at a place other than the registered office: s. 318 CA 1985.

20. Substantial property transactions involving directors, etc.: ss. 320–322 CA 1985

(a) Subject to certain exceptions a company must not enter into any arrangement:

(*i*) in which a director of the company (or of its holding company), or a person connected with him, is to acquire non-cash assets of the requisite value from the company; or

(*ii*) in which the company is to acquire non-cash assets of the requisite value from such director, or from a person so connected; unless the arrangement is first approved by resolution of the company in general meeting.

(b) *A non-cash asset* is of requisite value if, at the time of the arrangement, its value is not less than £2,000 but, subject to that, exceeds £100,000 or 10 per cent of the amount of the company's relevant assets.

(c) *Relevant assets* for this purpose are the value of the company's *net* assets, determined by reference to the accounts prepared and laid in respect of the last preceding accounting reference period, or, where no accounts have been prepared and laid before that time, the amount of its called-up share capital.

(d) Any arrangement made in contravention, and any transaction entered into in connection with such arrangement, is *voidable* at the instance of the company. The arrangement or transaction cannot, however, be avoided if:

(*i*) restitution cannot be made of the money or any other asset which is the subject-matter of the arrangement or transaction;

(*ii*) the rights of a third party would be affected by the avoidance; or

(*iii*) the arrangement is affirmed by the company within a reasonable period.

(e) *Disclosure:* subject to certain exceptions, notes to the group accounts prepared by a parent company must contain particulars of any of the transactions or arrangements described above: s. 227 Sch. 6 Part II

21. Register of Directors and Secretaries: s. 288 CA 1985

(a) *Location*. Section 288 CA 1985 provides that every company must keep this register at its registered office.

(b) *Contents with respect to each director.* The following particulars must be included:

(*i*) present name;

NOTE: The corporate name only is required in the case of a corporate director.

(*ii*) any former name;

NOTE: Essentially 'name' means a person's Christian name (or other forename) and surname.

(*iii*) nationality;

(*iv*) usual residential address, or the address of the registered or principal office, in the case of a corporate director;

(*v*) business occupation (if any);

(*vi*) particulars of any other directorships held by the director or which have been held by the director;

NOTE: However, it is not necessary for the register to contain on any day particulars of any directorship:

(a) which has not been held by a director at any time during the five years preceding that day;

(b) which is held by a director

(*i*) in any company which is dormant or, in relation to the company keeping the register, is a relevant company; and

(*ii*) if he also held that directorship for any period during the five years immediately preceding that day, and was for the whole of that period either dormant or such a relevant company;

(c) which was held by a director for any period during the five years preceding that day in a company which for the whole of that period was either dormant or, in relation to the company keeping the register, a relevant company.

For these purposes a 'dormant company' is one falling within s. 250 CA 1985 (*see* **39**), and a 'relevant company' is a wholly owned subsidiary of that other company or of another company of which that other is or was a wholly owned subsidiary.

(*vii*) date of birth;

(c) *Contents with respect to the secretary* (or, where applicable, of each joint secretary). The following particulars are required:

(*i*) present name;

NOTE: The corporate name only is required in the case of a corporate secretary.

(*ii*) any former name;
(*iii*) usual residential address, or the address of the registered or principal office in the case of a corporate secretary.

NOTE: If there are *joint* secretaries, particulars must be given for each of them, except where all the partners of a firm act as joint secretaries, when the firm's name and the firm's principal office may be stated.

(d) *Registration of particulars.*
(*i*) Particulars of directors and secretaries, similar to those set out in the register, must be filed with the Registrar within 14 days from the appointment of the first directors of the company.
(*ii*) The nature and date of any changes affecting the register, in respect of either directors or secretaries, must be filed with the Registrar within 14 days of the change.
(e) *Inspection.* The register must be open for inspection:
(*i*) free of charge to members;
(*ii*) at such fee as may be prescribed to others;
The Court has power to compel an immediate inspection of the register.

22. Register of Directors' Interests

(a) *Contents.* Section 325 CA 1985 requires every company to keep a register for the purposes of s. 324 CA 1985 and to record in it all information received from its directors under that section so that the entries against each name shall appear in chronological order.
(b) *Form.* The ruling below will satisfy statutory requirements.
(c) *Location.* The register must be kept at the company's registered office or at any other office at which the company's register of members is kept.

Except where the register is kept at the registered office, the company must notify the Registrar of Companies where it is kept.
(d) *Purpose of the register.* The register is intended to reveal

information concerning the interests of a person who is a director of a company in:

(*i*) shares in or debentures of the company; or

(*ii*) any other body corporate being the company's subsidiary or holding company; or

(*iii*) a subsidiary of the company's holding company,

and of any rights he, or his wife, or infant children, may have to subscribe for shares in or debentures of the company.

For this purpose it is the duty of directors to notify the company within *five days* of the acquisition of such securities by him, his wife or infant children, and the company must (if the securities are 'listed') notify a recognized investment exchange other than an overseas investment exchange within the meaning of the FSA 1986 before the end of the following day: s. 328, Sch. 13 Part II and s. 329 CA 1985.

Register of Directors' Interests

Entry		Name of Company	Class of shares or debentures	Date or event	Date of Notification	No. or amount	Consideration	
No.	Date						Paid	Received

Grant of right to subscribe					Nature of event and remarks
Period during which exercisable	Consideration paid for grant	Consideration received for assignment	Subscription price	Name(s) in which registered	

(e) *Record of directors' interests.*

(*i*) The nature and extent of an interest recorded in the register of a director in any shares or debentures shall, if he requires, be recorded in the register.

(*ii*) The company shall not, by virtue of anything done for the purposes of s. 325 CA 1985, be affected with notice of, or put upon inquiry as to the rights of, any person in relation to any shares or debentures.

(f) *Inspection.*

(*i*) The register must be open for inspection:

(1) free of charge to members;

(2) at such fee as may be prescribed to others.

(*ii*) It must also be produced at the commencement of the annual general meeting of the company and remain open and accessible during the meeting to any person attending.

(*iii*) Anyone may require a copy of the register or any part of it on payment of such fee as may be prescribed; any copy so required must be sent within 10 days of the request.

(*iv*) In the case of refusal of an inspection of the register, or to supply a copy, the Court may, by order, compel compliance.

(*v*) If it appears to the Secretary of State that there are circumstances suggesting that contraventions have occurred in relation to (*inter alia*) disclosures of directors' interests the directors may appoint one or more inspectors to carry out any necessary investigations and report thereon: s. 446 CA 1985

(g) *Penalties for default.* The company and every officer in default shall be liable to default fines.

NOTE: Whenever a company whose shares or debentures are listed on a recognized investment exchange (*see* **22(d)** *above*) is notified of any matter by a director in consequence of the fulfilment of an obligation imposed by s. 324 or 328 CA 1985, and that matter relates to shares or debentures so listed, the company is under no obligation to notify that investment exchange of that matter; and the investment exchange may publish, in such manner as it may determine, any information so furnished to it. The obligation so imposed must be fulfilled before the end of the day next following that on which it arises: s. 329 CA 1985.

(h) *The Stock Exchange's Model Code for Securities Transactions by Directors of Listed Companies.* The Stock Exchange's Continuing Obligations require listed companies to adopt rules governing dealing by directors in the listed securities of a company no less exacting than those of the Model Code issued by the Stock Exchange. This Code provides that directors must not deal in the securities of the company concerned on considerations of a short-term nature and, in particular, provides that directors may not generally deal in the securities of the company in the two-month period preceding the announcement of the annual results and half-year results. The Code also provides that dealings should not take place prior to the announcement of matters of an exceptional nature which are likely to affect the share price in the stock market. Further, the Code provides that a director shall not deal in the securities of the company at any time without first notifying the chairman (or other director(s) appointed for the purpose) and receiving an acknowledgment. The chairman himself should first notify the board at a board meeting or the other director(s) appointed for the purpose and receive acknowledgment.

23. Particulars of directors in business letters, etc.: s. 305 CA 1985

(a) A company to which this section applies shall not state, in any form, the name of any of its directors (otherwise in the text or as a signatory) on any business letter on which the company's name appears unless it states on the letter in legible characters the name of every director of the company who is an individual and the corporate name of every corporate director.

For the purposes of s. 305 the term 'director' includes a shadow director.

(b) The companies to which s. 305 applies are those registered, and foreign companies which have established a place of business, in Great Britain, on or after 23rd November 1916.

> NOTE: Section 351 CA 1985 imposes an obligation on companies to show, on all business letters and order forms, the place of registration, the company's registration number, the address of its registered office and, if, in the case of a company having a share capital, there is a reference to share capital on its business letters or order forms, the reference must be to *paid-up* share capital. Further, in the case of an investment company (as defined in s. 266 CA 1985) all business letters and order forms of the company must state the fact that it is an investment company.

24. Managing director

(a) Appointment of a managing director. The directors of a company have no power to appoint one of their number as a managing director, unless they are permitted to do so by the company's Articles.

(b) Table A, Article 84, gives directors the power, *inter alia,* to

appoint one or more of their body as managing director, to delegate any of their powers to him, and fix his remuneration.
(c) If the Articles make no provision for the appointment of a managing director, it can, of course, be made by the company in general meeting.

25. Executive and non-executive directors

These terms are commonly used to describe a full-time, working director (executive) and a person who devotes only part of his time to the business and affairs of the company (non-executive director). Neither term is recognized by the Companies Acts and if a non-executive director qualifies as a director in terms of s. 741 CA 1985, he is subject to the same statutory obligations and liabilities as any other director.

26. Special directors

(a) *Purpose of appointing 'special' directors.* In recent years, a number of companies have appointed quasi-directors bearing such titles as 'special' director, 'executive' director, 'assistant' director and the like, usually for their senior executives. The purposes of such appointments are usually as follows:

(*i*) to provide a training ground for top management;

(*ii*) to improve the status of senior executives without, however, giving them the full stature of a director, principally to enable them to deal with customers and others on a 'director' level.
(b) *Limited powers of 'special' directors.* Companies making such appointments usually include in their Articles the power to appoint 'special' directors 'who will not become directors within the meaning of the expression "director" as defined in s. 741 CA 1985'. As a rule, the Articles place severe restrictions upon the powers and rights of the 'special' director.

(*i*) He is not to be a member of the board of directors or of any committee appointed by the board.

(*ii*) He is entitled to attend board or committee meetings only at the request of the board of directors.

(*iii*) The board has power to define and limit his powers, and to disqualify him.

(*iv*) His remuneration and duties are to be fixed and determined by the board.

(c) *Recording and filing particulars of 'special' directors.* As 'special' directors are not deemed to be 'directors' within the meaning of s. 741 CA 1985, it is *not* usually considered necessary:

(*i*) to insert particulars concerning them in the Register of Directors and Secretaries; or

(*ii*) to give notice to the Registrar of their appointment or removal from office.

27. Shadow directors

(a) A 'shadow director' is 'a person in accordance with whose directions or instructions the directors of a company are accustomed to act': s. 741 CA 1985.

(b) If, however, the directors act on that person's directions or instructions only because his advice is given in a professional capacity, he will *not* be a director for the purpose of s. 741. Nor will a holding company be a shadow director of any of its subsidiaries by reason only of this section.

(c) A shadow director who complies with the above requirements will be treated as a director of the company, and subject to provisions requiring disclosure of interests.

The secretary

28. Every company must have a secretary: s. 283 CA 1985

There may, however, be *joint* secretaries.

29. Director as secretary

(a) In general, there is nothing to prevent a director acting also as secretary of a company. However, under s. 283 CA 1985:

(*i*) a sole director cannot also act as secretary; and

(*ii*) no company can

(1) have as secretary to the company a corporation the sole director of which is a sole director of the company;

(2) have as sole director of the company a corporation the sole director of which is secretary to the company.

(b) Further, by s. 284 CA 1985 a provision requiring or authorizing a thing to be done by or to a director and the secretary, is not satisfied by its being done by or to the same person acting both as director and as, or in place of, the secretary.

30. Appointment

(a) A Memorandum delivered for registration must be accompanied by a statement in prescribed form (Form G288), signed by the subscribers to the Memorandum, giving particulars of the first secretary, and containing a consent signed by that person. On incorporation, the person named shall be deemed to have been appointed as first secretary of the company: s. 10 CA 1985.

(b) Subsequent appointments must be made in accordance with the Articles, which usually permit the directors to appoint (and remove) the secretary and fix remuneration.

A new secretary should complete Form G288 for delivery to the Registrar of Companies within 14 days of the date of appointment. Notification of removal or resignation must also be given to the Registrar on Form G288 within 14 days of the event. Details of any appointment should be entered in the Register of Directors and Secretaries.

31. The secretary's status

(a) He is a servant of the company.

(b) He is also an 'officer' of the company, according to s. 744 CA 1985, and, therefore, liable to penalties in that capacity.

(c) The traditional view was that a company secretary was 'a mere servant; his position is that he is to do what he is told, and no person can assume that he has any authority to represent anything at all' *per* Lord Esher, M.R., in *Barnett, Hoares & Co.* v. *South London Tramways Co.* (1887). However, in *Panorama Developments (Guildford) Ltd.* v. *Fidelis Furnishing Fabrics Ltd.* (1971) it was recognized that a company secretary is the company's chief administrative officer and, as such, has apparent authority to act on behalf of the company.

32. The secretary's capacity to act

(a) As stated above, where the Act requires anything to be done or authorized by a director and the secretary, the same person cannot act in dual capacity as both director and secretary: s. 284 CA 1985.

(b) If the office of secretary is vacant or if, for any other reason, there is no secretary capable of acting, e.g. due to illness, his functions and responsibilities may be undertaken by:

(*i*) an assistant or deputy secretary; or

(*ii*) any officer of the company, authorized generally or specially for the purpose by the directors, if there is no assistant or deputy secretary capable of acting: s. 283(3) CA 1985.

33. The secretary's signature

(a) The secretary's signature is an important feature on many documents, and in the case of the annual return he is one of the recognized signatories: s. 363(2) CA 1985.

(b) When signing any document on behalf of the company, he should take care to negative his own personal liability, by ensuring that he signs in a representative capacity; for example

'For and on behalf of ....Co.Ltd.,

[signed] ....

Secretary'.

(c) He should also ensure that the company is correctly described by name, as a slight variation in the name, or even the omission of the word 'Limited' from the name, may render him, as any signatory, personally liable: s. 349(4) CA 1985 and *Penrose* v. *Martyr* (1858).

34. Qualifications

Section 286 CA 1985 gives statutory recognition to the post of company secretary, although its provisions apply only to *public* companies.

It is the duty of the directors of a public company to ensure that the secretary (or each joint secretary) of the company is a person who appears to them to have the knowledge and experience to discharge the functions of secretary of the company. Such a person must be:

(a) one who on 22nd December 1980 held the office of secretary (or assistant or deputy secretary) of the company; or

(b) one who for at least three years of the five years immediately

preceding his appointment as secretary held the office of secretary of a company other than a private company; or
(c) a member of specified professional bodies, *viz.* Chartered Secretaries, Chartered Accountants, Certified Accountants, Management Accountants, and Public and Financial Accountants; or
(d) a barrister, advocate or solicitor called or admitted in the United Kingdom; or
(e) a person who appears to the directors to be capable of discharging those functions by reason of his holding, or having held, any other position, or his being a member of any other body.

35. Duties

(a) It is difficult to specify precisely the duties of a company secretary for such vary with the size and nature of the company and the terms of arrangement made with him.
(b) Many of his statutory obligations have been referred to in the text; however, the following may be proffered as a general summary of his obligations.

(*i*) He is present at all meetings of the company and of the directors, and is responsible for the taking of minutes thereof.

(*ii*) He issues, under the direction of the board, all necessary notices to members and others.

(*iii*) He conducts all correspondence with shareholders as regards calls, transfers, forfeiture and otherwise.

(*iv*) He is responsible for keeping the statutory books and administrative records of the company.

(*v*) He makes all necessary returns to the Registrar.

Auditors

36. Eligibility for appointment

(a) Section 25 CA 1989 provides that a person is eligible for appointment as a company auditor only if he

(*i*) is a member of a recognized supervisory body, and

(*ii*) is eligible for the appointment under the rules of that body.

(b) An individual or a firm (a term defined as meaning a body corporate or a partnership: s. 53(1) CA 1989) may be appointed a company auditor. This accordingly removes the prohibition against auditors being incorporated.

(c) Further, by s. 27 CA 1989 a person even though eligible under s. 25 CA 1985 to act as a company auditor, will be ineligible to so act if he lacks independence, i.e. if he is

(*i*) an officer or an employee of the company, or

(*ii*) a partner or employee of such a person, or a partnership of which such a person is a partner,

or if he is ineligible by virtue of (*i*) or (*ii*) above for appointment as company auditor of any associated undertaking of the company.

A person is also ineligible for appointment as company auditor of a company under s. 27 if there exists between him or any associate of his and the company or any associated undertaking a connection of any such description as may be specified by regulations made by the Secretary of State. For this purpose an 'associated undertaking' means a parent undertaking or subsidiary undertaking of the company or a subsidiary undertaking of any parent undertaking of the company.

(d) No person shall act as a company auditor if he is ineligible for appointment to the office; and if during his term of office he becomes ineligible, he must thereupon vacate office and forthwith give notice in writing to the company concerned that he has vacated it by reason of ineligibility: s. 28 CA 1989.

(e) If an audit is carried out by an auditor who is not independent, then the Secretary of State may order another audit to take place: s. 29 CA 1989.

37. Appointment of the first auditors

(a) The first auditors may be appointed by the directors at any time before the first general meeting of the company, and auditors so appointed shall hold office until the conclusion of that meeting: s. 385(3) CA 1985.

NOTE: Assuming the company not to be a private company which has elected to dispense with the laying of accounts, the general meeting referred to is one at which the directors must lay before the company a copy of every document required to be comprised in the accounts of the company in respect of the appropriate accounting reference period: s. 384 CA 1985.

(b) If the directors fail to exercise their powers to appoint the first auditors, those powers may be exercised by the company in general meeting: s. 385(4) CA 1985.

38. Subsequent appointments

(a) Subsequently, at each general meeting (as defined above) the company shall appoint an auditor (or auditors) to hold office from the conclusion of that meeting until the conclusion of the next such general meeting of the company: s. 385(2) CA 1985.
(b) Where at any general meeting satisfying the above requirements, no auditors are appointed or reappointed, the Secretary of State may appoint a person to fill the vacancy; and the company shall, within one week of the Secretary of State's powers becoming exercisable, give him notice of that fact: s. 387 CA 1985.
(c) The directors, or the company in general meeting, may fill any casual vacancy in the office of auditor, but, while any such vacancy continues, the surviving or continuing auditor (or auditors), if any, may act.

Special notice is required for a resolution at a general meeting of a company

(*i*) filling a casual vacancy in the office of auditor, or

(*ii*) re-appointing as auditor a retiring auditor who was appointed by the directors to fill a casual vacancy.

On receipt of notice of such an intended resolution the company shall forthwith send a copy of it

(*i*) to the person proposed to be appointed, and

(*ii*) if the casual vacancy was caused by the resignation of an auditor, to the auditor who resigned.

39. Dormant companies

(a) Section 250 CA 1985 provides that where a company is one that is small for the purpose of the accounting exemptions provided by that Act, and has had no significant accounting transactions in the period concerned, it can relieve itself of the obligation to appoint auditors and deliver an auditors' report by passing a special resolution.
(b) A company is classified as small for the purposes of the

accounting exemptions referred to above if it satisfies any two or more of the qualifying conditions, e.g.:

(*i*) the amount of its turnover must not exceed £2,000,000;

(*ii*) its balance sheet total must not exceed £975,000; and

(*iii*) the average number of persons employed by the company in the financial year in question (determined on a weekly basis) must not exceed 50.

(c) A significant accounting transaction is one required to be entered in a company's accounting records though there is an exception for shares taken under a undertaking in the company's Memorandum by a subscriber thereto, thus enabling a newly formed company to be considered dormant from its formation: s. 250(3) CA 1985.

(d) If and when the exemption ceases then if the company has not dispensed with the requirement to lay accounts, the directors may appoint auditors at any time before the next meeting at which accounts are to be laid and auditors so appointed hold office until the end of that meeting.

Where the company has dispensed with the requirement to lay accounts the directors may appoint auditors:

(*i*) at any time before the end of a period of 28 days beginning with the day on which copies of the company's annual accounts are next sent to the members; or

(*ii*) if notice has been given, for example, by a member requiring the laying of accounts, at any time before the beginning of the requested meeting.

Auditors so appointed hold office until the end of the period or the end of the meeting as the case may be.

If the directors fail to exercise the above powers the members in general meeting may do so.

40. Private companies

(a) *Appointment by private company which is not obliged to lay accounts: s. 385(A) CA 1985*. Where a private company has dispensed with the laying of accounts before a general meeting, auditors must be appointed by the members in general meeting before the end of the period of 28 days beginning with the day on which copies of the company's accounts for the previous financial year are sent to the members.

(b) *Appointment without resolution: ss. 385(A) and 386 CA 1985.* Under CA 1989 it is possible for private company shareholders to elect not to re-elect auditors at the annual general meeting each year.

(c) *Election by private company to dispense with annual appointment: s. 386 CA 1985.* A private company may elect, by means of an elective resolution, to dispense with the requirement to appoint auditors annually.

41. Resignation

(a) An auditor of a company may resign his office by depositing notice in writing to that effect at the registered office of the company: s. 392 CA 1985; but the notice shall not be effective unless it contains either:

(*i*) a statement that there are no circumstances connected with his resignation which he considers should be brought to the notice of the members or creditors of the company; or

(*ii*) a statement of any such circumstances: s. 394 CA 1985.

(b) Where a notice of resignation is deposited at the company's registered office, the company must, within 14 days, send a copy of the notice to the Registrar of Companies.

If the statement is of circumstances which the auditor considers should be brought to the attention of the members or creditors of the company, the company must within 14 days of the deposit of the statement either:

(*i*) send a copy of it to every person who under s. 238 CA 1985 is entitled to be sent copies of the accounts, or

(*ii*) apply to the court on the grounds that the statement is being used to secure needless publicity for defamatory matter.

In the latter case the company must notify the auditor of the application. However, unless the auditor receives notice of such an application before the end of the period of 21 days beginning with the day on which he deposited the statement, he must within a further seven days send a copy of the statement to the Registrar.

(c) Where an auditor's notice of resignation contains a statement of the kind defined above, provisions are made in s. 392(A) CA 1985 which enable him:

(*i*) to require the directors to convene an extraordinary

general meeting for the purpose of explaining the circumstances connected with his resignation; and

(*ii*) to request the company to circulate to the company's members a statement in writing of reasonable length before the general meeting at which his term of office would otherwise have expired, or before any general meeting at which it is proposed to fill the vacancy caused by his resignation, or convened on his requisition.

(d) The company shall (unless the statement is received too late for it to comply):

(*i*) in any notice of the meeting given to members of the company state the fact of the statement having been made, and

(*ii*) send a copy of the statement to every member of the company to whom notice of the meeting is or has been sent.

Directors must within 21 days of the deposit of the requisition proceed duly to convene the meeting and that meeting must be held more than 28 days after the date on which the notice convening it is given: s. 392(A)(4) and (5) CA 1985.

42. Removal of auditors

(a) A company may, by ordinary resolution, remove an auditor before the expiration of his term of office, notwithstanding anything in any agreement between it and him.

(b) Where a resolution removing an auditor is passed at a general meeting of the company, the company must, within 14 days, give notice of that fact in prescribed form to the Registrar of Companies.

(c) *Special notice* shall be required for a resolution at a general meeting of a company to remove an auditor before the expiration of his term of office or to appoint as auditor a person other than a retiring auditor.

(d) On receipt of the special notice of an intended resolution to *remove* an auditor, the company must forthwith send a copy of it to the auditor it is proposed to remove or, as the case may be, to the person proposed to be appointed, and to the retiring auditor.

(e) He may then make representations in writing, of reasonable length, to the company. At the same time, he is entitled to request the company to notify members of his representations; or if his representations are not received in time by the company, that they be read out at the meeting.

(f) He is also entitled to receive notices of and to attend the general meeting at which his term of office would otherwise have expired, and at any general meeting at which it is proposed to fill the vacancy caused by his removal. At such meetings he is entitled to be heard on business which concerns him as former auditor of the company.

(g) Where an auditor ceases for any reason to hold office (including removal) the statement relating to circumstances connected with ceasing to hold office must be deposited with the company and the procedures under s. 394 CA 1985 (*above*) followed.

43. Remuneration: s.s. 390(A) and (B) CA 1985

(a) In the case of an auditor appointed by the directors or by the Secretary of State his remuneration may be fixed by the directors or by the Secretary of State, as the case may be.

(b) In other cases it will be fixed by the company in general meeting, or in manner determined by the company in general meeting.

(c) The amount of the remuneration relating to audit work must appear in a note to the accounts.

(d) Remuneration includes expenses and the provisions set out immediately above apply to benefits in kind which must be shown at the estimated money value.

(e) By s. 390(B) the Secretary of State is given power to make regulations to secure the disclosure of the amounts of any remuneration received or receivable by the auditors or their associates for services other than the audit. The regulations may require disclosure in the auditors' report or by way of a note to the accounts and in the latter case the auditors will be required to supply the directors with information necessary to make the disclosure.

44. Auditors' rights

The rights of the auditors may be summarized as follows:

(a) to have free access to books, accounts and vouchers at all times;

(b) to require from officers of the company any information and explanations they think necessary in the performance of their duties;
(c) to receive the same notices as members are entitled to of all general meetings of the company;
(d) to attend and be heard at general meetings of the company on any business with which they are concerned; and
(e) as regards a written solution proposed to be agreed to by a private company in accordance with s. 381A CA 1985,

(*i*) to receive all such communications relating to the resolution as, by virtue of any provision of Sch. 15A CA 1985, are required to be supplied to a member of the company;

(*ii*) to give notice in accordance with s. 381(B) CA 1985 of their opinion that the resolution concerns them as auditors and should be considered by the company in general meeting or, as the case may be, by a meeting of the relevant class of members of the company;

(*iii*) to attend any such meeting; and

(*iv*) to be heard at any such meeting which they attend on any part of the business of the meeting which concerns them as auditors.

NOTE: An auditor's right to attend or be heard at a meeting is exercised, in the case of the body corporate or partnership which are auditors, by an individual authorized by it in writing to act as its representative at the meeting.

45. Auditors' duties

(a) To familiarize themselves with their duties under the Articles and the Acts.
(b) To examine the company's books and accounts.
(c) To make a report to the members on the accounts examined by them and on every balance sheet, every profit and loss account and all group accounts laid before the company in general meeting during their tenure of office.
(d) To report on particulars of assets and liabilities, profits and dividends included in any listing particulars or prospectus issued by the company.
(e) To act honestly, and with reasonable care and skill.

46. The auditors' report: ss. 235–237 CA 1985

(a) The auditors must report to the company's members on all annual accounts of the company of which copies are to be laid before the company in general meeting during their tenure of office.

(b) The report must state whether in the auditors' opinion the annual accounts have been properly prepared in accordance with the Act, and in particular whether a true and fair view is given:

(*i*) in the case of an individual balance sheet, of the state of the company's affairs as at the end of its financial year;

(*ii*) in the case of an individual profit and loss account (if it is not framed as a consolidated profit and loss account), of the company's profit or loss for its financial year;

(*iii*) in the case of group accounts, of the state of affairs as at the end of the financial year, and the profit or loss for the financial year, of the undertakings included in the consolidation as a whole, so far as concerns members of the company.

(c) The auditors must consider whether the information given in the directors' report for the financial year for which the annual accounts are prepared is consistent with those accounts; and if they are of opinion that it is not, they must state that fact in their report.

(d) In preparing their report the auditors must carry out such investigations as will enable them to form an opinion as to whether:

(*i*) proper accounting records have been kept by the company and proper returns adequate for their audit have been received from branches not visited by them; and

(*ii*) whether the company's individual accounts are in agreement with the accounting records and returns.

If the auditors are of the opinion that either of these requirements has not been satisfied or if they fail to obtain the information and explanations which, to the best of their knowledge and belief, they consider necessary for the purpose of the audit, they must state any such conclusion in their report.

(e) The report must give particulars of directors' emoluments or loans if these are not adequately or correctly disclosed in the accounts.

(f) In preparing their report the auditors must carry out the investigations specified in **(d)** above; they may require information from any subsidiary undertaking and its auditors; and it is a criminal offence for any officer of a company knowingly or recklessly to supply false or misleading information to auditors.

(g) The auditors' report must state the names of auditors and be signed by them. Every copy of the auditors' report which is laid before the company in general meeting, or which is otherwise circulated, published or issued must state the names of the auditors. The copy of the auditors' report which is delivered to the Registrar must state the names of the auditors and be signed by them.

(h) The report drawn up by the auditors must be attached to the accounts when sent to those entitled to receive them under s. 238 CA 1985 and must be laid before the company in general meeting under s. 241 CA 1985. A copy must also be sent to the Registrar.

Under s. 239 CA 1985 members and debenture-holders of a company are entitled to be furnished, on demand and without charge, with a copy of the company's last annual accounts and directors' report and a copy of the auditors' report on those accounts.

(i) If a company publishes any of its statutory accounts, they must be accompanied by the relevant auditors' report; and if a company publishes non-statutory accounts, it must publish with them a statement indicating, *inter alia,* whether the company's auditors have made a report on the statutory accounts for any such financial year and whether any report so made was qualified or contained a statement to the effect that the accounting records or returns were inadequate, that the accounts did not agree with the records or returns or that there was a failure to obtain necessary information and explanations. Further, the company must not publish with non-statutory accounts any auditors' report relating to the company's statutory accounts.

Directors' report

47. The directors' report: s. 234 CA 1985

(a) A directors' report must be prepared for each financial year. It must be approved by the board of directors and signed on behalf of the board by a director or the secretary. The copy of the report delivered to the Registrar must be signed on behalf of the board by a director or the secretary of the company. Every copy of the directors' report which is laid before the company in general meeting or which is otherwise circulated, published or issued must state the name of the person who signed it on behalf of the board.

(b) The directors' report must contain the following information required by s. 234 and Sch. 7 CA 1985. The information to be given for an individual company is as follows:

(*i*) A fair review of the development of the business of the company and its subsidiary undertakings (if any) during the financial year and of their position at the end of it.

(*ii*) The amount (if any) which the directors recommend should be paid as dividend and the amount (if any) which they propose to carry to reserves.

(*iii*) The names of the persons who at any time during the financial year were directors of the company.

(*iv*) The principal activities of the company and of its subsidiary undertakings in the course of the year and any significant changes in those activities during the year.

(*v*) Details of any significant changes in fixed assets of the company or any of its subsidiary undertakings during the year.

(*vi*) Any difference in the market value of interests in land over the value disclosed in the balance sheet, if the difference is, in the directors' opinion, of such significance as to require that the attention of members or debenture-holders should be drawn to it.

(*vii*) Interests of directors in shares or debentures of the company or any other body corporate in the same group at the beginning and end of the financial year. The information to be given must be extracted from the Register of Directors' Interests maintained by the company. Details of directors' interests may be included in the notes to the accounts rather than in the directors' report.

(*viii*) Particulars of contributions made for political or charitable purposes if the total exceeds £200.

(*ix*) Particulars of any important events affecting the company or any of its subsidiary undertakings which have occurred since the end of the financial year.

(*x*) An indication of likely future developments in the business of the company and its subsidiary undertakings.

(*xi*) An indication of the activities (if any) of the company and its subsidiary undertakings in the field of research and development.

(*xii*) Details of any acquisition of its own shares during the year.

(*xiii*) Where the average numbers of employees of the company exceeds 250:

(1) a statement describing the company's policy towards disabled persons;

(2) a statement concerning employee involvement; and

(3) a statement of the company's policy for securing the health and safety and welfare at work of employees of the company and its subsidiary undertakings and for protecting other persons against risks to health or safety arising out of or in connection with the activities at work of those employees.

(c) A copy of the directors' report must accompany a copy of the company's annual accounts when such is sent to those entitled to receive the accounts under s. 238 CA 1985. It must also be laid before the company in general meeting along with the accounts.

48. Stock Exchange requirements

Companies subject to Stock Exchange regulations are required to include in the report of their directors various matters additional to those specified by the Act. These have been outlined in Chapter 2 and constitute an element of the Continuing Obligations imposed by the Stock Exchange upon listed companies. Reference should be made to Chapter 2.

Insider trading

49. Prohibition on stock exchange deals by insiders: s. 1 Company Securities (Insider Dealing) Act 1985

(a) *Individuals affected.* The following 'insiders' are prohibited under s. 1 CS(ID)A 1985 from dealing on a recognized stock exchange in listed securities of a company:

(*i*) a person who is, or at any time in the preceding six months has been, knowingly connected with that company, and has, or would reasonably be expected to have, unpublished price-sensitive information relating to that company's securities;

(*ii*) a person who is contemplating, or has contemplated making, a take-over offer for a company, in a particular capacity, knowing that he is in possession of unpublished price-sensitive information concerning that company's securities;

(*iii*) a person who has knowingly obtained, either directly or indirectly, information from an 'insider' in either of the above categories concerning price-sensitive securities of a company.

(b) *Exceptions*. The above provisions do not apply to the following.

(*i*) A person in any of the above categories who possesses price-sensitive information concerning securities is not prohibited from dealing with them if his object in so doing is not to make a profit or avoid a loss (whether for himself or for another person) by the use of that information.

(*ii*) A person acting in the capacity of liquidator, receiver, or trustee in bankruptcy is not prohibited under s. 1 CS(ID)A 1985 from entering into a transaction where he exercises his function in good faith.

(*iii*) A person engaged as a market maker is not prohibited from using information obtained in the course of his business, so long as he uses it in good faith in the course of that business.

> NOTE: A 'market-maker' is defined as a person (whether an individual, partnership or company) who holds himself out at all normal times in compliance with the rules of a recognized stock exchange as willing to buy and sell securities at prices specified by him and is recognized as doing so by that recognized stock exchange.

(*iv*) A trustee, a personal representative (or a person who acts on behalf of a corporate trustee or personal representative) is also excepted from the prohibitions of s. 68 CS(ID)A 1985 if he either deals in securities or counsels or procures another person to deal in them. He is, in such circumstances, presumed to have acted otherwise than with a view to making a profit or avoiding a loss by using any unpublished price-sensitive information, if he acted on the advice of a person who appeared to him to be an appropriate person from whom to seek such advice, and who did not appear to him to be prohibited from dealing in listed securities.

(*v*) An individual will not be prohibited as an 'insider' by reason only of his having information relating to any particular transaction from dealing on a recognized stock exchange in any securities, or from doing any other thing in relation to securities, which he is prohibited from dealing in by s. 1 CS(ID)A 1985, if he does that thing in order to facilitate the completion, or carrying out of, that transaction.

50. Prohibition on the abuse of information

Prohibition on the abuse of information obtained in official capacity: s. 2 CS(ID)A 1985:

(a) *Individuals affected.* The prohibitions laid down in s. 2 CS(ID)A 1985 apply to any information which is held by:

(*i*) a public servant (or former public servant) by virtue of his position (or former position as a public servant); or

(*ii*) any individual who knowingly obtained such information directly or indirectly, from a public servant (or from a former public servant), knowing, or having reasonable cause to believe, that the latter held the information by virtue of his position.

(b) *Prohibitions.* An individual in either of the above categories is prohibited from:

(*i*) dealing on a recognized stock exchange in any relevant securities;

(*ii*) counselling or procuring any other person to deal in any such securities, knowing, or having reasonable cause to believe, that that other person would deal in them on a recognized stock exchange; and

(*iii*) communicating to any other person the information held by or obtained by him, if he knows, or has reasonable cause to believe, that that person or some other person will make use of the information for the purpose of dealing, or of counselling or procuring any other person to deal, on a recognized stock exchange in such securities.

(c) *Exceptions.* The exceptions listed above in **49(b)** also apply to s. 2 CS(ID)A 1985 prohibitions.

51. Off-market deals

(a) *Prohibitions.* The prohibitions of ss. 1 and 2 CS(ID)A 1985 are applicable also to 'off-market deals'.

(b) *Definitions*

(i) Off-market deals. These are defined in s. 4 CS(ID)A 1985 as dealings otherwise than on a recognized stock exchange in the advertised securities of any company through an off-market dealer, or as an off-market dealer who is making a market in those securities, or as an officer, employee or agent of such a dealer acting in the course of the dealer's business. The market in which such deals take place might be described as an 'over-the-counter market'.

NOTE: The prohibitions of ss. 1 and 2 CS(ID)A 1985 relating to counselling, procuring and communicating information are also applicable in relation to off-market deals.

(ii) Off-market dealer means a person who is an authorized person within the meaning of the FSA 1986.

(iii) Advertised securities, in relation to a particular occurrence, means listed securities, or securities in respect of which, not more than six months before that occurrence, information indicating the prices at which persons have dealt, or were willing to deal, in those securities has been published for the purpose of facilitating deals in those securities.

(c) *Exceptions.* The exceptions listed above in **49(b)** also apply to s. 4 CS(ID)A 1985 prohibitions.

52. International bonds: s. 6 CS(ID)A 1985

(a) *Definition.* An international bond issue (or Eurobond issue) means an issue of debentures of a company all of which are offered, or to be offered, by an off-market dealer to persons (whether principals or agents) whose business includes the buying or selling of debentures.

If, however, the debentures are denominated in sterling, the issue will not be classified as an international bond issue unless not less than 50 per cent (nominal value) of the debentures are offered to persons who are neither citizens of the United Kingdom and Colonies nor companies incorporated or otherwise formed under the law of any part of the United Kingdom.

(b) *Protection for managers of international bond issues.* Section 6 CS(ID)A 1985 provides that no provision of ss. 1, 2, 4 or 5 of that Act prohibits an individual from doing anything for the purpose of stabilizing the price of securities if it is done in conformity with rules made under s. 48 of the FSA 1986 and

(*i*) in respect of securities which fall within any of Paras. 1–5 of Schedule 1 to the FSA 1986 and are specified by the rules; and

(*ii*) during such period before or after the issue of those securities as is specified by the rules.

53. Contravention of ss. 1 and 2 CS(ID)A 1985

(a) *Penalty.* The penalty for contravening ss. 1 and 2 CS(ID)A 1985 is laid down in s. 8 CS(ID)A 1985 as follows:

(*i*) on conviction on indictment, to imprisonment for a term not exceeding two years, or a fine, or both; and

(*ii*) on summary conviction, to imprisonment for a term not exceeding six months, or a fine not exceeding the statutory maximum, or both.

(b) *Proceedings* for an offence under this section in England and Wales can be instituted only by, or with the consent of, the Secretary of State or the Director of Public Prosecutions.

(c) *Legal effect.* No transaction will be void or voidable by reason only of its contravening ss. 1 and 2 CS(ID)A 1985.

54. The Financial Services Act 1986

This Act as amended by the Companies Act 1989 contains provisions extending the law regarding insider trading and the mechanisms to regulate such. In particular s. 177 of the FSA 1986 enables the Secretary of State to appoint inspectors to investigate circumstances suggesting contravention of s. 1, 2, 4 or 5 CS(ID)A 1985.

Progress test 14

1. (a) The Companies Act 1985 prohibits the appointment of directors who attain the age of 70. Can this requirement be excluded or modified?

(b) You are asked by a newly appointed director what action he has to take regarding acquiring qualification shares in the company. Advise him. *ICSA* **(3, 4)**

2. **(a)** How may a director be removed from office?
(b) In what circumstances may he be disqualified from office? *ICSA* **(5–7)**

3. Comment on the appointment of an alternate director, indicating circumstances in which you consider this desirable. **(10)**

4. Explain fully how and by whom a change in the constitution of a board of directors may be effected and who should be notified of such a change. **(5–9)**

5. Draft a form for circulation to directors to ensure that they are aware of and fully comply with the requirements of s. 231 of the Companies Act 1985, relating to disclosure of directors' emoluments. **(11)**

6. What approval is required for the payment of compensation for loss of office to a director? *ICSA* **(12)**

7. **(a)** The directors (who are also the shareholders) of a private company are proposing that the company lends them money (to avoid drawing profits as salaries and paying tax). Ignoring the tax consequences, explain whether this may be done.
(b) The directors (all of whom hold executive office) wish to know if there are any restrictions regarding their remuneration. Advise them. *ICSA* **(11, 12)**

8. Advise the directors of your company regarding the disclosure of their interests in any contracts entered into by the company. Consider also whether they can vote on any such contracts. *ICSA* **(18)**

9. Are directors allowed to be interested in contracts with the company? *ICSA* **(18)**

10. Set out in the form of a letter to the directors the requirements regarding disclosure of their interests in shares in the company. *ICSA* **(22)**

11. The directors of your company ask you what is meant by special (or associate) directors. Write (*a*) a brief memorandum explaining the significance of such appointments, and (*b*) set out in numbered paragraphs the points to be covered in the Articles of Association providing for such appointments. *ICSA* **(26)**

12. Summarize the matters to be attended to upon the appointment of a new director. *ICSA* **(3, 4, 9, 10, 23)**

13. A director has just been appointed to the board of a private company of which you are secretary. Write to him requesting from him the matters he is liable to disclose in order for you to file the notice of appointment and to comply with other statutory requirements. *ICSA* **(3, 6, 18, 22)**

14. Who may be appointed auditors of a company? How is an auditor removed? *ICSA* **(36, 37, 42)**

15. Some members of the company of which you are secretary have given notice at the forthcoming annual general meeting they intend to nominate for election as auditor a person other than the retiring auditor. What are your duties on receiving this intimation, and what further duties might follow? **(42)**

16. Apart from account books and vouchers, what documents and records are likely to be required by auditors, and how can the secretary of a company facilitate the auditor's work? **(44–46)**

17. In relation to auditors state (*a*) how they are appointed, (*b*) who may be appointed, (*c*) the action required when an auditor becomes aware of his disqualification. *ICSA* **(36–41)**

18. List the contents of the directors' report. **(47–48)**

19. How does the Companies Act 1985 seek to curb the abuse of insider trading? **(49–54)**

20. Draft a memorandum to your Board advising them as to the extent, if any, to which directors are allowed to be interested in contracts with the company. *ICSA* **(18)**

21. In relation to auditors state:

(a) how they are appointed;
(b) who may be appointed;
(c) the action required when an auditor becomes aware of his disqualification.
ICSA **(36–41)**

22. At a recent board meeting, Mr Robin Smyth, a director of your company, tendered his resignation which was accepted. Explain in detail what action you, as company secretary, would take as a result of this resignation. *ICSA* **(8)**

15
Borrowing powers; trust deeds; receiverships; administration

Methods of borrowing

1. Borrowing as an alternative to further share issue

When a company requires further capital to develop its business, it must decide whether to issue further shares or to borrow. If it has the necessary borrowing power, it may be considered advantageous to make use of it, but the questions then arise: what form of borrowing is best suited for the purpose, having regard to the amount required and the period for which it is to be borrowed, and what security can be offered?

2. Methods of borrowing

(a) *A bank loan or overdraft.* These methods would not normally meet the company's long-term loan requirements, as banks are usually averse to the making of long-term loans for the purpose of capital developments. Moreover, the bank would almost certainly require some form of security.

(b) *An issue of debentures* would probably meet requirements more adequately where a large loan is required for an extended period — where, for example, it is required for extensive capital development.

3. Shares or debentures?

When deciding between shares and debentures, the following factors ought to be considered.

(a) *Redemption.* If the company would prefer to have the opportunity to clear off the debt within a given period, debentures would obviously meet this requirement, as redeemability is an important feature of that type of security.

Against this, it might be argued that the advantage of redeemability can be gained by the issue of redeemable shares, but the rather stringent conditions laid down by statute for their issue and redemption frequently rules them out.

(b) *Interest.* Another way of making debentures more attractive than shares is to offer interest at a fixed rate and payable (usually half-yearly) irrespective of the company's trading results.

Preference shares might be considered as an alternative, but the fixed dividend on such shares is dependent upon the company's trading results and may be passed over or carried forward.

(c) *Security.* If the company is in a position to offer adequate security to prospective debenture-holders, that would be yet another way of making debentures more attractive than shares.

On the other hand, the directors might regard the creation of a charge upon the company's assets as a disadvantage in that it is likely to be restrictive as regards the assets so charged. If, however, the security is in the form of a 'floating' charge, this objection can be put aside.

(d) *Economy.* Because the above advantages can be offered along with debentures, they can usually be issued at a lower rate of interest — that is, as compared with the rate of dividend that it would be necessary to offer to prospective preference shareholders.

(e) *Membership.* As debenture holders are merely 'loan creditors' of the company, the raising of funds by way of debentures does not extend the membership and therefore by the same token there is no further spread of voting power.

Against this, it must be accepted that the preference shares of many companies carry no voting power. Furthermore, in recent years an increasing number of companies have appeared to favour the issue of non-voting ordinary shares.

(f) *Convertibility.* A debenture is available which might prove attractive to the investor who is undecided between debentures and shares. This is the convertible debenture, referred to later in 6(h) below.

(g) *Taxation.* Debenture interest is chargeable against profits, whereas dividend on shares is regarded as a distribution of profits — a very important consideration as regards taxation.

(h) *Capital duty.* If the company has already issued the whole of its authorized capital, the issue of debentures, as an alternative to an issue of shares, would save the company the trouble and expense of increasing its authorized capital and paying capital duty on the increased amount. It is not suggested that this would be a weighty consideration; nevertheless, it could entail a considerable saving where the increase in the capital was substantial.

Debentures

4. Definition

(a) Section 744 CA 1985 states that the term 'debenture' includes debenture stock, bonds and any other securities given by the company, whether constituting a charge on the assets of the company or not.

(b) In legal terms a debenture is a document which either creates a debt or acknowledges it, and any document which fulfils either of these conditions is a debenture.

(c) In commercial wage it is commonly understood that the term debenture refers to a document evidencing some secured obligation. This is reflected in the rules of the Stock Exchange which require that any issue of unsecured debentures be denominated 'unsecured' and indeed it is more common for the word to be avoided altogether in this situation and a term such as 'loan stock' or 'loan note' to be used instead.

(d) Debentures as a group may have some or all of the following features, according to the type.

(i) Form. Debentures are almost invariably under seal, although this is not a statutory requirement.

(ii) Redeemability. All debentures are redeemable, the company undertaking to repay the loan within a specified period, or upon the happening of various specified contingencies.

(iii) Security. Most debentures are secured on the property or undertaking of the company, by way of a fixed or 'floating' charge. Evidence of the charge is usually set out in the form of a trust deed.

(iv) Interest. In most cases, the company undertakes payment

of interest at a fixed rate (usually half-yearly) irrespective of trading results.

5. The power to borrow

Before issuing debentures or adopting any other method of borrowing, it is necessary to ensure that the company has power and, if so, within what limits. In this connection, the following points are relevant.

(a) A trading company has an implied power to borrow: *General Auction Estate Co.* v. *Smith* (1891).
(b) The implied power of a trading company may be limited, or even excluded, by its Memorandum or Articles.
(c) A non-trading company has no implied borrowing power, but such may be conferred by its Memorandum.
(d) *Power to give security.* A company with express or implied power to borrow is also entitled to mortgage or charge its assets as security, unless restricted by its Memorandum or Articles: *Re Patent File Co., ex parte Birmingham Co.* (1870).

6. Types of debenture

(a) *Mortgage debentures.* The name applied in a general way to all debentures which are secured on the property or undertaking of the company, i.e. in the form of:
   (*i*) a 'floating' charge;
   (*ii*) a fixed (or specific) charge; or
   (*iii*) both floating and fixed charges.
(b) *Simple (or naked) debentures.* A comparatively rare form of debenture, issued without security. On the winding-up of the company, the holders of these debentures would rank with the unsecured creditors.
(c) *Redeemable debentures.* These are issued subject to the condition that the company shall redeem them on or before a fixed date, or within a specified period.

The company usually reserves the right to redeem at an earlier date, in which case it may be able to buy up some or all of its debentures on the open market before the redemption date.
(d) *Irredeemable (or perpetual) debentures*: s. 193 CA 1985. These are

issued without fixing any specific date or period for redemption. The fact that they are described as 'irredeemable' or 'perpetual' simply means that the debenture holders can demand repayment only on the happening of one of a number of specified contingencies, such as default in payment of interest, or winding-up of the company.

> NOTE: It is, in fact, illegal to issue debentures which are never to be redeemed, but s. 193 CA 1985 sanctions the issue of irredeemable or perpetual debentures such as are described above.

(e) *Registered debentures.* Certificates are issued to the holders of these debentures and their names and addresses recorded in the Register of Debenture Holders (*see* **12** *below*).

Interest is paid to the registered holder, or to his order, in the same manner as applies to the payment of dividend on shares.

Transfer and transmission procedure is basically the same as that used for shares, e.g. as regards form of transfer and registration.

(f) *Bearer debentures.*

(*i*) *Transfer* is by simple delivery. The document is a negotiable instrument and can, therefore, be handed over without the formality of a transfer instrument or payment of transfer duty. Furthermore, the transferee acquires a good title, so long as he acted in good faith and gave value for the debentures.

(*ii*) *Interest* is usually payable against the presentation of coupons attached to the debenture.

(g) *Income debentures.* The holders of these securities usually have the right to a fixed rate of interest, but only out of the current year's profits. If no profits are earned, no interest may be payable, or it may be reduced in a poor financial year.

Debentures of this type are not popular with investors, and are comparatively rare nowadays

(h) *Convertible debentures.* These give the holder the option to convert his debentures into ordinary or preference shares, so long as he exercises his option within the period stated in the conditions of issue.

(i) *Debenture stock.* This differs from debentures as stock differs from shares; that is — in theory at least — debenture stock is divisible and transferable in factional amounts, whereas debentures are indivisible and can be transferred only in complete units. For the sake of convenience, the conditions of issue usually provide that the stock must be transferred in multiples of fixed amount.

Debenture stock differs from stock created out of shares in that it *can* be issued originally as debenture stock.

7. Floating charge

Earlier in this chapter, reference was made to floating and fixed (or specific) charges in connection with mortgage debentures. The main characteristics of a floating charge are as follows:

(a) It is an equitable charge on assets for the time being of the company.

(b) It does not become fixed on any specific assets, unless or until an event occurs upon the happening of which the charge is said to 'crystallize', for example:

(*i*) on the company's default in payment of interest on the debentures concerned; or any other 'event' specified in the conditions of issue;

(*ii*) on liquidation of the company.

(c) The company can deal with the property charged in the ordinary course of business, and for that reason the floating charge is a popular form of security.

8. Fixed (or specific) charge

(a) This creates a charge on one or more specific assets of the company which are clearly identifiable, such as (say) leasehold or freehold property.

(b) The company is unable to deal freely with the assets charged; it must not, for example, create any prior charge on the assets affected, nor dispose of any of them without the agreement of the debenture holders.

Procedure on issue of debentures

9. Issue procedure

This is similar in many respects to that for the issue of shares.

Where important difference occur, attention has been drawn to them in the following itemized procedure.

(a) *Preparation of issuing documents.* On the assumption that debentures are being offered to the public, issue documents must be prepared, bearing in mind that the requirements of the FSA 1986 apply equally to an issue of debentures. It is, of course, possible that both shares *and* debentures are being included in the same issue.

(b) *Arrangements for underwriting the issue.* There is, of course, no restriction on the amount or rate payable, as s. 97 CA 1985 does not apply to debentures.

(c) *Board meeting.* Convene a board meeting for the purpose of authorizing the issue of relevant issue documents.

(d) *Issue of issue documents.* This will probably be done through advertising agents and by the distribution of issue document forms through the company's bankers, etc., and to the Stock Exchange.

(e) *Application and allotment.* Procedure is similar to that for an issue of shares, except that it will be unnecessary to make a return of allotments to the Registrar.

(f) *Registration of Charges.* Where applicable, i.e. if a charge is created for the purpose of securing the debentures, particulars of the charge must be filed with the Registrar within 21 days after the date of its creation, i.e. the date on which the charge is executed: *see* **11** *below*.

(g) *Register entries.* The company's Register of Charges must then be written up, giving particulars of any specific and/or floating charge, in accordance with s. 411 CA 1985.

(h) *Register of Debenture Holders.* On the assumption that the debentures issued are registered debentures, the Register of Debenture Holders is now written up.

> NOTE: The Register of Debenture Holders is not one of the statutory books but a company is often required to have one to comply with the conditions of issue of their debentures, in which case it must conform to the requirements of the Act: ss. 190 and 191 CA 1985. These are referred to in **12** below.

(i) *Certificate of registration.* Request a certificate of registration from the Registrar (*see* (f) *above* and **11** *below*) and endorse a copy of the certificate on every debenture or debenture stock certificate before issue.

(j) *Copies of instruments creating charges* are required to be kept at the company's registered office: s. 411 CA 1985. If applicable, therefore, a copy of one debenture in a series must be kept, and also a copy of any trust deed creating a charge.

> NOTE: If the company concerned was listed, the procedure outlined above would have to be modified and the documentation drafted to take account of the Continuing Obligations imposed upon such a company by the Stock Exchange. The Continuing Obligations are set out in Chapter 2 and reference should be made thereto.

10. The Register of Charges

Section 411 CA 1985 requires every company to keep a Register of Charges and sets out the following provisions as to its contents, location, inspection, etc.

(a) *Contents.* It must contain the following particulars concerning all charges created by the company:

(*i*) amount of the charge;

(*ii*) short description of the property charged;

(*iii*) names of the persons secured — except in the case of bearer securities.

(b) *Location.* The register must be kept at the company's registered office, together with a copy of every instrument creating a charge; but a copy of *one* debenture in a series will be adequate: s. 411 CA 1985.

> NOTE: The Act does *not*, in this case, provide for any alternative location.

(c) *Inspection etc.* s. 412 CA 1985.

(*i*) The register and any copies of instruments creating charges must be open for inspection of creditors and members, free of charge.

(*ii*) Any other person may inspect the register on payment of a fee.

(*iii*) Any person may request the company to provide him with a copy of any instrument creating or evidencing a charge over the company's property, or any entry in the Register of Charges kept by the company, on payment of such fee as may be prescribed. The copy must be sent to the person requesting it within ten days of his request being received or, if later, on which payment is received.

(*iv*) The Court has power to compel immediate inspection etc. of the register and documents.

(d) *Effects of non-compliance*, i.e. as to keeping a Register of Charges or failing to make an entry:

(*i*) the security itself is *not* prejudiced;

(*ii*) every officer of the company knowingly or wilfully authorizing the omission is liable to a fine: s. 411 CA 1985.

11. Registrar's Register of Charges: s. 397 CA 1985

(a) The Registrar of Companies is obliged to maintain a Register of Charges for every company: s. 397 CA 1985.

(b) The register must include, amongst other things, details of all particulars of charges delivered to the Registrar, any memoranda of satisfaction or release received, details of the issue of debentures of a series, the appointment of receivers or managers and the crystallization or attachment of a floating charge and other matters.

As regards the particulars of charges, the specified particulars are:

(*i*) if it is a charge created by the company, the date of its creation, and if it is a charge which was existing on property acquired by the company, the date of the acquisition of the property;

(*ii*) the amount secured by the charge;

(*iii*) short particulars of the property charged; and

(*iv*) the persons entitled to the charge.

The register is available for inspection by the public and a person taking a charge over a company's property shall be taken to have notice of any matter requiring registration and disclosed on the register at the time of the charge is created. Further, a person may require the Registrar to provide a certificate stating the date on which any specified particulars of a charge, or other information relating thereto, were delivered to him. The certificate is conclusive evidence that the particulars or other information were duly delivered to the Registrar.

(c) The charges of which particulars must be registered with the Registrar are:

(*i*) a charge on land or any interest in land, other than

(1) in England and Wales, a charge for rent or any other periodical sum issuing out of the land,

(2) in Scotland, a charge for any rent, ground annual or other periodical sum payable in respect of the land;

(*ii*) a charge on goods or any interest in goods, other than a charge under which the chargee is entitled to possession either of the goods or of a document of title to them;

(*iii*) a charge on intangible moveable property (in Scotland, incorporeal moveable property) of any of the following descriptions —

(1) goodwill,

(2) intellectual property,

(3) book debts (whether book debts of the company or assigned to the company),

(4) uncalled share capital of the company or calls made but not paid;

(*iv*) a charge for securing an issue of debentures; or

(*v*) a floating charge on the whole or part of the company's property.

(d) It is the duty of a company which creates a charge or acquires property subject to an existing charge, to notify the Registrar in the prescribed form: s. 395 CA 1985. Such notification must be made within 21 days of the date of the creation of the charge, or the date on which property was acquired subject to an existing charge, as the case may be. The duty of the company does not prevent any other person interested in the charge from delivering particulars to the Registrar and that person is entitled to recover from the company the amount of any fees paid by him to the Registrar in connection with the registration. It is standard practice for the holder of the charge to register it with the Registrar.

(e) Upon receipt of the prescribed form, details are noted on the company's register by the Registrar who will send a copy of the particulars filed by him and a note of the date on which they were delivered to the company, the chargee and, if the particulars were delivered by another person interested in the charge, to that person: s. 398(5) CA 1985.

(f) Failure to deliver particulars in the prescribed form to the Registrar shall render the charge void against an administrator or liquidator of the company and any person who for value acquires an interest in or right over property subject to the charge: s. 399 CA 1985.

(g) Where particulars of a charge in the prescribed form are delivered to the Registrar after the 21-day period, the following provisions apply:

(*i*) If a 'relevant event' occurs after the particulars are delivered, the charge will not be void: s. 400(1) CA 1985. A relevant event includes the presentation of an administration or winding-up order, a resolution for voluntary winding up or the acquisition of an interest in or right over property subject to a charge: s. 399(2) CA 1985.

(*ii*) If the company is, at the date of delivery of the particulars, unable to pay its debts in terms of the IA 1986 or, subsequently becomes unable to pay its debts in consequence of the transaction under which the charge is created, the charge may be void as against the administrator or liquidator if insolvency proceedings begin before the end of:

(1) two years in the case of a floating charge created in favour of a 'connected person' of the company,

(2) one year in the case of the floating charge created in favour of the person not so connected, and

(3) six months in any other case: s. 400(3) CA 1985.

(h) It is open to the company and the chargee to file further particulars of a charge with the Registrar, where the particulars previously delivered, omitted or mis-stated information or the particulars given are no longer accurate: s. 401(1) CA 1985.

The further particulars must be given on the prescribed form and be signed by or on behalf of both the company and the chargee.

On noting further particulars in the register, the Registrar will send to the company, the chargee or, where a person other than the company delivered the particulars, that other person, a copy of the particulars so filed and a note of the date on which they were delivered.

(i) A Memorandum of Satisfaction or Release, given on the prescribed form, may be delivered to the Registrar when a particular charge no longer affects the company's property or the debt for which a charge was given is paid or otherwise satisfied: s. 403 CA 1985.

The Memorandum must be signed by or on behalf of both the company and the chargee. Upon receipt of the Memorandum the Registrar will file the Memorandum in the register, note the date upon which it was delivered to him and send to the company, the chargee, and if the Memorandum was delivered by a person other than the company, that person, a copy of the Memorandum filed by him and a note made by him as to the date upon which it was delivered.

(j) In addition to the delivery for registration of particulars of a charge securing a series of debentures, a company must also deliver particulars in the prescribed form, giving the date and amount of each issue of debentures of the series within the period of 21 days after the date of each issue: s. 408 CA 1985.

(k) Any person obtaining an order for the appointment of a receiver or a manager of a company's property, or any person who appoints such receiver or manager under powers contained in an instrument must, within seven days of the order or of the appointment, give notice of that fact to the Registrar. Thereupon the Registrar will file notice in the register of the company: s. 409 CA 1985. Notice must also be given to the Registrar of any person ceasing to act as receiver or manager.

12. Register of Debenture Holders

As already indicated in 9(h) above this is *not* one of the statutory books. If however, a company keeps a Register of Debenture Holders in compliance with the conditions of issue of its debentures, the register must conform to the following provisions.

(a) *Location.* The register must be kept at the company's registered office, or at any office where it is written up, within the company's domicile.

(b) *Notice of location.* Notice must be given to the Registrar of the place where the register is kept, and of any change, unless it has always been kept at the company's registered office: s. 190 CA 1985.

(c) *Inspection.* The register must be open for inspection:

(*i*) to debenture holders and shareholders without fee;

(ii) to other persons on payment of such fee as may be prescribed.

(d) *Copies.* Any person may require a copy of the register or any part of it, on payment of such fee as may be prescribed.

(e) *Closing the register.* The company may close the register for a period or periods not exceeding 30 days on the whole in any year, in accordance with its Articles or as provided in the conditions of issue of its debentures.

(f) *Inspection refused.* If inspection of a copy of the register is refused:

(i) the Court may compel the company to afford immediate inspection and direct that the copies required be sent;

(ii) the company and every officer in default are liable to default fines.

13. Re-issue of debentures

(a) Section 194 CA 1985 permits the re-issue of debentures which have been redeemed, or the issue of other debentures in their place, unless:

(i) the Articles provide to the contrary, expressly or by implication; or

(ii) any contract entered into by the company contains express or implied provisions to the contrary; or

(iii) the company has done some act, by resolution or otherwise, manifesting or implying intention to cancel the debentures.

(b) Debentures re-issued by the company will rank *pari passu,* i.e. as to rights and priorities, with the debentures which they replace.

14. Sinking fund (or debenture redemption fund)

(a) *Purpose.* A sinking fund may be created by a company for the purpose of redeeming its debentures.

(b) *Annual investment.* The most satisfactory method is to provide the fund by making an annual investment outside the business in, say, guilt-edged securities.

(c) *The amount invested* is based upon tables which show the amount which, with compound interest for a given number of years, will produce the sum required on the date of redemption.

15. Alternative methods used for redeeming debentures

(a) *A service fund.* This is sometimes created by setting aside fixed annual sums to cover both debenture interest and the sum required for redemption of the debentures.
(b) *Purchase on the open market.* If the conditions of issue of the debentures permit, the company may purchase them on the Stock Exchange before the date for redemption. Money accumulated in the sinking fund may be used for this purpose.
(c) *Tender by debenture holders.* Debenture holders may be permitted to tender their debentures, stating the price at which they are prepared to sell them back to the company for cancellation.
(d) *Annual drawings.* The company may have power under the conditions of issue to redeem annually a stipulated number of debentures by drawings, i.e. the debentures are 'drawn' from a container in which the number of all unredeemed debentures have been deposited.

Trust deeds

16. Trust deeds

(a) *Nature.* Debentures and debenture stock are often secured by trust or covering deed conveying property of the company to trustees in favour of the debenture holders, charging other property and containing a number of ancillary provisions regulating the respective rights of the company and the debenture holders.
(b) *Advantages.* The existence of a trust or covering deed improves and strengthens the security. It constitutes trustees charged with the duty of looking after the rights and interests of the debenture holders. The debenture holders can by these trustees enter and sell the property comprised in the security; the trustees will have a legal mortgage over the company's land, so that persons who subsequently lend money to the company cannot gain priority over the debenture holders secured through the trust deed.
(c) *Contents.* The trust deed will usually provide for the following:
(*i*) the appointment of the trustee;

(*ii*) the amount of the issue, the rate of interest and the date of payment, terms of redemption, conversion rights, if any, etc.;

(*iii*) the creation of a charge over some or all of the company's assets as security;

> NOTE: This will usually consist of a legal mortgage of the freehold and leasehold property of the company, and a general charge by way of floating security on the rest of the assets and undertaking. Such gives the trustees a fixed and not merely a floating charge so that the freeholds and leaseholds cannot be sold or dealt with without the trustees' consent. This, as stated, strengthens the security of the debenture holders.

(*iv*) the various events on the happening of which the security is to become enforceable;

(*v*) the powers and duties of the trustees in particular with regard to the enforcement of the security;

(*vi*) the imposition on the company of additional obligations, regarding the submission of information and similar matters;

(*vii*) the holding of meetings of the debenture holders.

(d) *Listed companies.* Where the trust deed relates to debentures issued by a listed company, the regulations of the Stock Exchange require it to contain specific provisions relating to:

(*i*) redemption;
(*ii*) conversion rights;
(*iii*) meetings and voting rights;
(*iv*) transfer;
(*v*) definitive certificates;
(*vi*) security; and
(*vii*) unclaimed interest.

Receiverships

17. Remedies of debenture holders

(a) The remedies of a debenture holder vary according to whether he is unsecured or secured.

(b) If the debenture holder is unsecured he has the same remedies as any other creditor, and may enforce payment of principal or interest by an action for debt or through taking steps to have the company wound up.

Where there is a trust deed, the trustees are the only persons who can exercise these remedies, and if they refuse, the debenture holders may bring an action against the trustees requiring them to exercise the remedies available. The company must also be joined as co-defendant so that judgment may be given against it in the same action.

(c) Where, however, the debenture-holder is secured, he has in addition to the remedies available to an unsecured debenture holder the following methods of enforcing his security:

(*i*) if the debenture is issued under the common seal of the company he has under s. 101(1) of the Law of Property Act 1925 a power to sell the property or to appoint a receiver of its income in specified circumstances of default;

(*ii*) utilization of any express power given by the debenture to be exercised on the occurrence of any one of the specified happenings or defaults of the company;

(*iii*) application to the Court for an order for:

(1) sale;

(2) delivery of possession;

(3) foreclosure;

(4) appointment of a receiver of the property subject to the charge.

NOTE: The Court will only order a sale or appoint a receiver when the principal or interest is in arrears, when the company has gone into liquidation and when the security is in jeopardy.

18. Receivers, receivers and managers, and administrative receivers

The term 'receiver' is a general one and applies to any person administering any type of receivership. The powers of a receiver may include the power to manage the business, in which case the person is called a receiver and manager. The term 'administrative receiver' essentially means a person appointed as a receiver or manager under a floating charge over all or most of the company's assets: s. 29 IA 1986.

19. Appointment of a receiver

(a) An administrative receiver must be a qualified insolvency practitioner. In other cases any fit person may be appointed except a corporation (s. 30 IA 1986), an undischarged bankrupt (s. 31 IA 1986) or a person disqualified by the Court under CDDA 1986. If the company is being wound up the official receiver may be appointed: s. 32 IA 1986.

(b) If appointed by the Court the receiver's remuneration will be fixed by the court. Where appointed by the debenture holders the debenture holders will fix his remuneration. Under s. 36 IA 1986 if the company goes into liquidation the liquidator may apply to the Court to fix the remuneration of the receiver or manager.

(c) A receiver appointed by the Court is an officer of the court. A receiver appointed out of court under powers given by the debenture would be an agent of the debenture-holders, but the terms of the debenture will generally provide that he is to be an agent of the company and thus establish that it is the company rather than the debenture-holders which is liable for his actions. An administrative receiver is deemed to be the agent of the company unless and until it goes into liquidation: s. 44 IA 1986.

Where a receiver is appointed out of court the appointment will not be effective unless accepted by the receiver by the end of the business day following the day on which he received the instrument of appointment: s. 33 IA 1986. If an appointment is discovered to be invalid the Court may order the person who made the appointment to indemnify the appointee against any liability arising from the invalid appointment: s. 34 IA 1986.

(d) When a receiver or manager of the property of a company has been appointed, every invoice, order for goods or business letter issued by or on behalf of the company or receiver or manager or the liquidator of the company or in which the company's name appears must contain a statement that a receiver or manager has been appointed: s. 39 IA 1986.

(e) The appointment of a receiver will bring about the crystallization of all floating charges. Further, where appointed by the Court, all servants of the company are automatically dismissed, though the receiver may re-employ them. Where the receiver is appointed out of court and the receiver is the agent of the company, contracts of employment are not determined: *Re Mack Trucks (Britain) Ltd* (1967). Both receivers appointed by the Court and out of court are liable on any contracts entered into in the performance of their functions, including any contract of employment adopted in order to perform those functions. For this purpose a receiver is not taken to have adopted a contract of employment by reason of anything done within 14 days of his appointment: s. 37 IA 1986. Similar rules also apply to administrative receivers: s. 44 IA 1986. During the continuation of the receivership the powers of the directors are suspended, though the directors may exercise them in so far as the receiver does not wish to do so and provided the receiver is not prejudiced thereby: *Newhart Developments Ltd* v. *Commercial Co-operative Bank Ltd* (1978).

(f) A floating charge holder is able to block the appointment of an administrator: s. 9 IA 1986.

20. Receivers' powers

(a) A receiver will have the power conferred on him by the trust deed under which he was appointed. By s. 42 IA 1986 an administrative receiver is in addition deemed to have the powers specified in Sch. 1 of that Act (*see* **30** *below*) although references in the schedule to 'property of the company' must be construed as references to that part of the property subject to the charge.

(b) By s. 43 IA 1986 an administrative receiver has powers akin to those of an administrator to apply to the court for an order allowing him to dispose of property subject to a security as if it were uncharged provided:

(*i*) the security is not held by the person who appointed the administrative receiver; or

(*ii*) the security does not rank after the security over which the administrative receiver has authority.

The court will not authorize the disposal unless it will promote a more advantageous realization of the company's assets than would otherwise be the case. The proceeds of the disposal must be applied to pay off the sum secured by the charge. The administrative receiver must send to the Registrar, within 14 days, a copy of the court order authorizing the sale.

(c) A receiver may repudiate existing contracts, but he may not do this if such would adversely affect the subsequent realization of the company's assets or if it would injure its goodwill if it were to trade again: *Re Newdigate Colliery Ltd.* (1912).

21. Receivers' general duties

(a) The person who obtains an order for the appointment of a receiver or manager of a company's property, or appoints such a receiver or manager under powers contained in an instrument, must within seven days give notice of the fact to the Registrar: s. 409 CA 1985.

(b) Every document issued by or on behalf of the company or the receiver must show his appointment (*see* **19(d)** *above*).

(c) The receiver should familiarize himself with the terms of his appointment. He should also ensure that the charge under which he has been appointed was valid, since he may be held personally liable if he acts under an invalid charge.

(d) He should collect in the assets charged, collect rents and profits, exercise the debenture holders' powers of realization, and pay the net proceeds to them. If a receiver is appointed in respect of a debenture secured by a floating charge, by s. 175 IA 1986 the preferential debts must be paid as soon as the receiver has assets in his hands and before any payment is made to the debenture holders.

(e) Where the receiver is also appointed as manager he should ensure that nothing is done without his authority. In particular he should:

(*i*) contact the company's bank and arrange for the bank account to be transferred into his name as receiver and manager;

(*ii*) notify managers of branch offices of his appointment and instruct them that no goods are to be ordered or payments made except with his consent;

(*iii*) obtain a list of principal officers and employees, since it may be necessary in some cases to terminate their contracts of employment;

(*iv*) take an inventory of plant etc.;

(*v*) prepare a list of debts due to the company, noting the period of credit which has been allowed.

22. Duties of an administrative receiver

(a) By s. 46 IA 1986 where an administrative receiver is appointed he must:

(*i*) immediately send to the company and publish in the prescribed manner a notice of his appointment, and

(*ii*) within 28 days after his appointment, unless the court otherwise directs, send such a notice to all the creditors of the company.

(b) He must immediately require a statement of affairs: s. 47 IA 1986. This must be submitted within 21 days. The persons responsible and the contents are the same as when an administrator is appointed (*see below*).

(c) By s. 48 IA 1986 within three months he must send a report to the Registrar, secured creditors and trustees for secured creditors, containing information as to the following matters:

(*i*) the events leading up to his appointment, so far as he is aware of such;

(*ii*) his disposal or proposed disposal of any of the company's property;

(*iii*) his plans for carrying on the business;

(*iv*) the amounts of principal and interest payable to the debenture holders by whom he was appointed and the amounts payable to preferential creditors;

(*v*) the amount, if any, likely to be available to pay other creditors;

(*vi*) a summary of the statement of affairs and his comments, if any, on it.

The administrative receiver does not have to include any information that would seriously prejudice the carrying out of his functions. He must also send a copy of the report to unsecured creditors or publish in the prescribed manner a notice giving an address to which the creditors can write for a free copy of the report. In either case he must lay a copy of the report before a meeting of unsecured creditors summoned for the purpose on not less than 14 days' notice. The meeting of creditors may establish a committee. Like the committee of creditors in administration it may summon the administrative receiver on seven days' notice and require reasonable information concerning the performance of his functions, but it cannot give him any directions nor is its consent required for any of his acts.

If the company has gone or goes into liquidation the administrative receiver must also send a copy of the report to the liquidator. If the report is sent to the liquidator within three months of the administrative receiver's appointment, the receiver is released from his obligation to call a meeting of unsecured creditors and send his report to them or publish it.

23. Vacation of office by the receiver

(a) By s. 45 IA 1986 an administrative receiver vacates office:
(*i*) on order of the Court;
(*ii*) by resignation in the prescribed manner;
(*iii*) if he ceases to be a qualified insolvency practitioner.
He must inform the Registrar within 14 days.

(b) A receiver appointed by the court may only be discharged by a court order, obtained when his duties have been completed.

(c) A receiver appointed out of court must inform the Registrar of companies when his duties have been completed: s. 409(2) CA 1985. He should also give formal notice to the company and to the persons who appointed him.

Administration orders

24. Introduction

Administration is a new procedure introduced on the recommendation of the Cork Committee (The Review Committee on Insolvency Law and Practice) as an alternative to receivership. The basic aim of the procedure is to freeze the debts of a company in financial difficulties to assist an administrator to save the company or at least achieve the better realization of its assets. The relevant legislation is to be found in Part II IA 1986 (ss. 8–27).

25. Power of the Court to make an order: s. 8 IA 1986

Before making an order the Court must be satisfied that the company is, or is likely to become, unable to pay its debts (as defined in s. 123 IA 1986) and that the order would be likely to achieve one or more of the following purposes:

(a) The survival of the whole or part of the business as a going concern;

(b) The approval by the creditors of a composition in satisfaction of debts, or by the members of a scheme of arrangement of the company's affairs — a company voluntary arrangement;

(c) The sanctioning under s. 425 of a compromise or arrangement;
(d) A more advantageous realization of the assets than would be effected on a winding-up.

An administration order cannot be made after the company has gone into liquidation.

26. Application for an order: s. 9 IA 1986

(a) Application is by petition presented by the company, the directors, a creditor or creditors, or a combination of these persons.
(b) Notice of presentation of the petition must be given to any person who has appointed or is entitled to appoint a receiver.
(c) The Court may dismiss the application, adjourn the proceedings, make an interim order (restricting the power of the directors) or any other order it thinks fit.
(d) Where there is an administrative receiver in office (*see* **18** *above*) the Court must dismiss the petition unless it is satisfied that:

(*i*) the person who appointed the receiver consents to the making of an administration order, or

(*ii*) if an order were made any security by virtue of which the receiver was appointed would be liable to be avoided under ss. 238–240 (transactions at an undervalue and preferences) or s. 245 (avoidance of floating charges) IA 1986.

27. Effect of an application: s. 10 IA 1986

During the period beginning with the presentation of a petition for an administration order and ending with the making of such an order or the dismissal of the petition:

(a) The company cannot be wound up.
(b) No charge, hire purchase or retention of title clause can be enforced against the company without the consent of the Court.
(c) No other proceedings can be commenced or proceeded with against the company without the consent of the Court.

28. The nature and effect of the order

An administration order is an order directing that during the period for which the order is in force the affairs, business and property of the company shall be managed by a person termed an administrator appointed for the purpose by the Court: s. 8(2) IA 1986.

The effect of the making of such an order is that:

(a) the restrictions on winding up and legal proceedings continue;
(b) any administrative receiver vacates office;
(c) any receiver of part of the company's property must vacate office if required to do so by the liquidator: s. 11 IA 1986.

Further, under s. 12 IA 1986 all company documents must indicate that an administration order is in force and must name the administrator.

29. Appointment of the administrator: s. 13 IA 1986

An administrator may be appointed:

(a) by an administration order;
(b) by order of the court to fill a vacancy caused by death, resignation or any other event. In the latter case the application may be made:

(*i*) by any continuing administrator of the company; or
(*ii*) where there is no such administrator, by a creditors' committee (*see* **34** *below*), or
(*iii*) where there is no such administrator and no such committee, by the company or the directors or by any creditor or creditors of the company.

30. Administrator's powers: ss. 14–15 IA 1986

(a) Under s. 14 the administrator is given general power to do all such things as may be necessary to manage the affairs, business and property of the company. Without prejudice to the generality of this power Sch. 1 IA 1986 gives some 23 examples of such powers. These include powers:

(*i*) to carry on the business;
(*ii*) to deal with and dispose of assets;
(*iii*) to borrow money and grant security;
(*iv*) to bring and defend legal proceedings on the company's behalf;
(*v*) to establish subsidiaries and transfer to them the whole or part of the company's business;

(*vi*) to employ and dismiss employees.

Further, under s. 14 IA 1986 the administrator also has power:

(*i*) to remove any director of the company and to appoint any person to be a director of it, whether to fill a vacancy or otherwise, and

(*ii*) to call any meeting of the members or creditors of the company.

In exercising his powers the administrator is deemed to act as the agent of the company; and a person dealing with him in good faith for value is not concerned to inquire whether he is acting within his powers.

(b) Under s. 15 IA 1986 the administrator has specific powers on application to the Court to dispose of charged property.

31. Administrator's duties: s. 17 IA 1986

The primary duty of an administrator is, on his appointment, to take into his custody or under his control all the property to which the company is or appears to be entitled.

32. Ascertainment and investigation of company's affairs: ss. 21–22 IA 1986.

(a) By s. 21 IA 1986 the administrator must send notice of his appointment:

(*i*) to the company immediately;
(*ii*) to the Registrar of Companies — within 14 days;
(*iii*) to the creditors — within 28 days.

(b) He must require, within 21 days, a statement of affairs, verified by affidavit, giving details of:

(*i*) assets, debts and liabilities;
(*ii*) names and addresses of creditors;
(*iii*) securities held by creditors with the dates when given;
(*iv*) such further or other information as may be prescribed.

The statement of affairs must be made and submitted by some or all of the following:

(*i*) persons who are or have been officers of the company;

(*ii*) Persons who took part in the company's formation within one year before the administration order;

(*iii*) Employees, or persons employed within the past year

who are, in the administrator's opinion, capable of giving the information;

(*iv*) officers or employees (within the past year) of another company which is (or was within the past year) itself an officer of the company.

33. Administrator's proposals: ss. 23–25 IA 1986

Within three months of the administration order (or such longer period as the Court may allow) the administrator must send to the Registrar of Companies, the creditors and the members a statement of his proposals for achieving the purpose of the administration. He must lay this statement before a meeting of creditors summoned for this purpose on not less than 14 days' notice. The purpose of this meeting is to approve the proposals, with modifications if the administrator agrees. If, subsequently, the administrator wishes to make substantial modifications he must notify the members and call another meeting of creditors.

If the creditors' meeting does not approve the proposals the Court may discharge the administration order, or make any other order it thinks fit.

34. Protection of members and creditors: ss. 26–27 IA 1986

(a) If the meeting of creditors approves the proposals (with or without modifications) it may appoint a committee of creditors. This committee may on seven days' notice require the administrator to attend before it and give such information as it may reasonably require.

(b) Any creditor or member of the company may apply to the Court for an order on the ground that the company is or has been managed by the administrator in a manner unfairly prejudicial to the creditors or members or that any act or omission of the administrator is or would be so prejudicial. On such an application the Court may make such order as it thinks fit.

35. Discharge or variation of the administration order: s. 18 IA 1986

(a) The administrator may make an application to the Court at any time to discharge or vary the order:

(*i*) if it appears to him that the purpose of the administration order has been achieved or is incapable of achievement; or

(*ii*) if he has been instructed to apply to the Court by the meeting of creditors.

(b) The Court may discharge or vary the order or make any other order it thinks fit. If the order is discharged or varied the administrator must within 14 days send a copy of the order of discharge or variation to the Registrar of Companies.

36. Vacation of office and release of the administrator: ss. 19–20 IA 1986

(a) The administrator vacates office if:

(*i*) he is removed by the Court;

(*ii*) he resigns having given notice of such resignation to the court;

(*iii*) he ceases to be a qualified insolvency practitioner;

(*iv*) the administration order is discharged.

(b) The date of release of the administrator is determined by the court. As from that date the administrator is discharged from liability for acts or omissions in relation to his conduct as administrator, but if he has broken any duty the Court may order him to restore property or contribute to the company's assets, even after he has been released.

(c) When an administrator is released his remuneration and expenses shall be paid in priority to secured creditors, but after liabilities incurred under contracts entered into or contracts of employment adopted while he, or any predecessor, was administrator. For this purpose, this administrator is not taken to have adopted a contract of employment by reason of anything done within 14 days of his appointment.

Progress test 15

1. Write explanatory notes to distinguish between:

(a) certification of a transfer and registration thereof;

(b) retirement of a director by rotation and vacation of office;

(c) a call and an instalment;

(d) redeemable and convertible debenture stock.

ICSA (4: 3; 8:1, 6; 14: 5, 8; 15: 6)

2. What do you understand by the term '5 per cent Debenture Stock, 1963/67'? What is a trust deed and what provision would you expect such a document to contain with respect to the aforementioned stock? (4, 6)

3. Your company is proposing to take an interest in another company by way of taking up Convertible Debenture Stock. Outline the main provisions you would expect to find in the Trust Deed. *ICSA* (4, 6)

4. What are the respective advantages of debentures secured by fixed and floating charges? *ICSA* (6, 7, 8)

5. In what ways does the register of charges kept by the Registrar of Companies with respect to every company differ from the register of charges required to be kept at the registered office of every limited company? Give (*a*) two examples of charges which must be registered with the Registrar, and (*b*) one example of a charge which needs to be recorded only in a company's own register. (10–11)

6. Explain what is meant by registration of charges secured on the property of a company. *ICSA* (10, 11)

7. A company has issued £500,000 of debenture stock in units of £1. The debenture trust deed requires that, each year, 500 lots of 100 units each must be redeemed by drawing. Outline, in numbered paragraphs, the procedure to be followed. *ICSA* (17)

8. (a) What information has to be recorded by a company in respect of any debentures which it has issued?
(b) What are the usual methods by which debentures are redeemed? *ICSA* (10–15)

9. Discuss the ways in which debenture stock may be redeemed. What is a Memorandum of Satisfaction? *ICSA* (15–17)

10. Your directors are proposing the repayment of debentures and a new issue at a lower rate of interest. How would such a scheme be carried out? (9, 13)

11. What is a debenture trust deed? what are the advantages of utilizing a debenture trust deed? **(16)**

12. Explain the terms receiver, receiver and manager, and administrative receiver when used in relation to secured debentures. **(18)**

13. Examine the legal position of a receiver. **(19)**

14. Outline the powers and duties of a receiver. **(20–21)**

15. What are the duties of an administrative receiver? **(22)**

16. When may the court make an administration order? **(25)**

17. What is the effect of an application for an administration order? **(26)**

18. Examine the nature and effect of an administration order. **(28)**

19. In what circumstances may an administration order be discharged or varied? **(35)**

20. How does the law protect members and creditors of a company involved in administration proceedings? **(34)**

21. Set out the procedure on the appointment and termination of appointment of a receiver. *ICSA* **(19, 23)**

22. Explain how a receiver is appointed and what is the effect of such appointment. *ICSA* **(19, 21)**

Index

abuse of information obtained in official capacity, 353
account day, 181
accounting reference date, 63
accounts, relevant, 226–7
acquisition of a company, 277
acquisition by a company of its own shares, 49
acquisition of shares in a company by company's nominees, 50
Administration of Estates (Small Payments) Act 1965, 197
administration orders, 381–6
  application for, 380
  discharge or vacation of, 383
  effect of application for, 380
  nature and effect of, 380
  power of court to make, 379
administrative receiver, 376
  duties of, 379
administrator,
  appointment, 381
  duties, 382
  powers, 381
  proposals, 383
  vacation of and release of, 384
age limit of directors, 316
allotment, 64
  of bonus shares, 123
  fully-paid letter of, 125
  letter of, 107, 108
  non-returnable letter of, 80
  procedure on, 105
  renouncing, 113
  resolution of, 107
  returns of, 110
  splitting, 113
  voidable, 112
  where issue not fully subscribed, 112
allotment of securities by directors, 108
allotment of shares, 105
  effects of irregular, 112
  to existing members, 117
  restrictions on, 112
alteration,
  of articles of association, 40
  of memorandum of association, 28
  of share capital, 245–52
alterations in register of members, 150
alternate directors, 321
amalgamation of companies, 260
annual return, 158–61
  contents, 159–61
  delivery, 158
  free, 161
application and allotment, 105
  procedure on, 105
  sheets, 105
arrangement,
  scheme under s. 425, 264
articles of association, 11, 37
  alteration of, 40
  form of, 36
  legal effects of, 34
  purpose and contents, 34
  stock exchange requirements *re*, 36
assignment of office by director, 321
association clause, 27
auditors, 340–9
  appointment, 63, 341
  duties, 347
  eligibility for appointment, 340

private companies, 343
removal of, 345
remuneration, 346
report, 348
resignation, 344
rights, 346
subsequent appointment, 342
authorized capital, 27
authorized minimum capital, 3

bankers, appointment of, 63
bankruptcy of member, 198
bearer debentures, 363
blank transfer, 193
board meeting, first, 62
bonds, international, 354
bonus shares, 123
books of account, 66
books, statutory, 66
borrowing powers, 359–61
brokerage, 99
brokers, appointment, 63
broker's transfer form, 183, 190
business, commencement of, 3, 15

call letters, preparation of, 132
call list, specimen of, 133
improperly made, 129
payment in advance of, 130
call, procedure on making, 131–4
calls and instalments, 128–9
Table A, *re*, 129
capital,
alteration of, 245
authorized, 42
clause in memorandum, 8, 27
gearing, 47
increase of, 246
maintenance of, 48
nominal, 42
reduction of, 252
requirements, 8
serious loss of, 48
structure, 42, 47
capital duty on allotment, 111
capital redemption reserve, 145
casual vacancies,
of auditors, 342
of directors, 313
certificate to commence business, 3, 15
certificate of incorporation, 13
issue and effects of, 13

re limited company re-registered as unlimited company, 20
re private company re-registered as public company, 18
re public company re-registered as private company, 19
re unlimited company re-registered as limited company, 20
re unlimited company re-registered as public company, 18
certificates,
of death, 212
of marriage, 216
certification of registration of charge, 365
certification of transfer, 189, 192
effects of, 192
chain of transmission, 199
chairman, appointment of, 63
change of address, 219
change of name,
by corporate member, 217
by deed poll, 217
due to marriage, 216
elevation to peerage, 216
charges, registration of, 366–70
charges taken by public company on its own shares, 52
City Code, 279–86
background, 280
general principles, 282
nature, 281
operation and enforcement, 281
rules, 284
scope, 281
structure, 281
classification of companies, 2
closing of register of members, 151
commencement of business, 3
commencement of winding up, 295, 301
common seal, 63, 142
adopting design for, 142
custody of, 142
Table A provisions, 142
when required, 143
companies, types compared, 3
company contracts, form of, 142
Company Registry, The, 13
company secretary, necessary qualifications, 339
company voluntary arrangements, 262–4

compensation, directors', 324
compulsory winding up, 291–300
computers, permitted use for company records, 148
conflict of interests, 328
connected persons, 327
consequences of winding up, 295, 301
consolidation listing form, 116
consolidation of capital and division, 191
continuing obligations, 74
re annual accounts, 76
re communications with holders of listed securities, 83
re directors, 85
re general, 74
re half-yearly reports and preliminary statements for the full year, 83
re public announcements, 74
re settlements, 83
contracts of employment of directors, 329
conversion of shares into stock, 248
coupons attached to share warrants, 171, 172
creditors' voluntary winding-up, 306–9
Crown, application for letters of administration to, 154
cumulative preference shares, 43

death certificates, 212
debenture defined, 47
debenture holders, remedies of, 373
debenture stock, 363
debentures, 361–4
definition, 361
issue procedure, 364
or shares, 359
types of, 362
declaration of solvency, 303
deferred shares, 144
dematerialization, 184
designated accounts, 155
destruction of dividend warrants, 235
directors, 316
age limit, 316
alternate, 321
appointment of, 313–15
assignment of office, 321
compensation for loss of office, 324
conflict of interests, 328
and connected persons' loans, 325–8
contracts of employment, 329
definition, 312
disqualification of, 317
executive and non-executive, 336
first directors, appointment of, 62, 313
interests in contracts with the company, 328
interests, register of, 332
loans to, 325–8
managing, 335
names of, 11
particulars in business letters of, 335–51
removal, 319
remuneration of, 323
reports, 349–51
retirement of, 316
and secretaries, register of, 330
shadow, 337
share qualification of, 315
special, 336
status of, 312
substantial property transactions involving, 330
vacation of office, 320
disapplication of pre-emption rights, 122
discount, issue of shares at, 99
dissenting shareholders,
rights under ss. 428–430F, 266
rights under s. 110 Insolvency Act 1986, 275
dissolution of a company, 300, 306, 309
dividend, 224
definition, 224
lists, 228
mandates, 232
restrictions by Secretary of State upon payment, 236
warrant, loss of, 235
warrants, 230
dividends, 224–36
chief rules, 224
delay in payment of, 225
due to joint holders, 225
interim, 224
outstanding, 232
payment of, 224–5

procedure and documents, 227–36
profits available for, 225
unclaimed, 232
document service, 220
documents,
examination of, 13
execution of, 141
form, 12, 14
received for registration, 204
registration of, 9
signing of, 10
domicile of registered office, 9, 25
dormant companies, 342

employees, directors to have regard to interests of, 313
employees' share schemes, 236–42
approved profit-sharing schemes, 240
approved savings-related share option scheme, 241
approved share option schemes, 241
background, 237
definition, 236
Revenue approved schemes, 237
Enduring Powers of Attorney Act 1985, 208
executors, 205

Finance Act 1989, 185
Finance Act 1990, 185
financial assistance for acquisition of shares, 53
firm underwriting, 97
first board meeting, 62
first directors, 313
first meeting of creditors and contributories, 298
fixed charge, 364
floating charge, 364
forfeited shares,
re-issue of, 138
treatment of, 138
forfeiture of shares,
legal effects, 135
limits on, 135
nature, 135
notice of, 137
under Table A, 135
forged transfers, 193
Forged Transfers Acts 1891–2, 194
form of company contracts, 142
general letters of administration, 206
group reconstructions, 101
guarantee companies, 2
guarantee, limitation by, 2
income debentures, 363
increase of capital, 190
index of company names, Registrar's, 23
index of register of members, 148
insider dealing, prohibition on stock exchange deals by insiders, 351–3
insider trading, 351–5
contravention of, 355
insolvency practitioner, 241
inspection,
of register of charges, 366
of register of debenture holders, 370
of register of directors and secretaries, 330
of register of directors' interests, 331
of register of members, 147
of register of substantial individual interests, 286
instalment distinguished from a call, 128–9
insurance against forged transfer, 194
interest on calls, 134
interests in contracts etc., director's duty to disclose, 328
international bond issue, 354
investigation by a company of interests in shares, 287
investigation of official receiver, 297
irredeemable debentures, 362
irregular allotment, 70, 71

joint holders, 152

Law of Property Act 1925, s. 101(1), 374
legal representative of shareholder, 195
letter,
allotment, 107, 108
call, 133
of administration, 196, 205–6
of indemnity, 121, 183
of regret, 107, 108

of renunciation, 110, 113
of request, 197
of rights, 118, 120
limitation of liability clause, 27
limited, exemption from use of word, 24
liquidation, 291–300
compulsory, 291
of corporate member, 199
voluntary, 291, 300–9
liquidation committee, 298, 308
liquidator,
appointment of, 299, 304,306
duties of, 299, 304, 307
powers of, 307
provisional, 296
qualifications, 299
listing rules, 71
particulars, 72, 86
loans to directors and connected persons, prohibition of, 325–8
looseleaf books, 149
loss of limitation of liability, 27
loss of office, directors' compensation for, 324
lost dividend warrant, 235
lost share certificate, 169

maintenance of capital, 48
managing director, 335
market maker, defined, 352
marriage certificate produced by female shareholder, 216
member,
bankruptcy of, 198
death of, 195
unsoundness of mind of, 199
members' voluntary winding-up, 301–6
membership of a company, 153
memorandum of association, 11, 21
alteration of, 28
contents, 22
main purpose, 21
memorandum of satisfaction, 369
merger relief, 101
mortgage debentures, 362

name of company, 9, 23
directions to change, 31
procedure on change of, 30
name of company, publication of, 32
restriction on choice of, 23
name, trading under misleading, 25, 32
non-cumulative preference shares, 43
non-voting shares, 44
notice,
of forfeiture, 136
of location of register of members, 152
of refusal to register a transfer, 180
of situation of registered office, 111
of trust, 153
number, company's registered, 13

objects clause, 8, 26
alteration of, 33
general commercial company, 26
offer for sale, 67
offer for subscription, 67
offers of unlisted securities, 90
official listing,
basic conditions for, 72
securities of, 71
official notification, 14
official seal, 143–4
'off-market dealer', meaning of, 354
off-market deals, 353
ordinary shares, 44
outstanding dividends, 232
overriding commission, 96
overseas branch register, 156
advantages of operating, 157
provisions *re*, 156
transfer of shares to, 157
what companies may keep, 156
oversea companies, 21

participating preference shares, 43
partly-paid shares, transfer of, 187
perpetual debentures, 362
personal estate, shares as, 179
personal representatives, 195
photographic copies of documents, acceptability of, 210
placings, 68
power of attorney, 206
pre-emption rights, 122
preference shares, 43
cumulative, 43
non-cumulative, 43
participating, 43
Power of Attorney Act 1971, 207
premium, issue of shares at, 100

primary offers, 70
private companies, 2
  deregulation, 5
  differences, *re* public companies, 3
  elective resolutions, 7
  written resolutions, 6
probate(s), 205
procedures,
  after incorporation, 44
profits available for distribution, 225
prohibition on abuse of information obtained in an official capacity, 353
prohibition on issue of shares at a discount, 99
prohibition of loans, etc. to directors and connected persons, 325–8
proper instrument of transfer, 179
prospectus, 90
provisional allotment letter, 118
proxy forms, 212, 213
public companies, 2
public examination of officers, 297
public issue,
  arrangements for, 101
public offers, regulation of, 69
public servant,
  abuse of information, *re*, 353
publication of company's name, 32
puchase agreement, execution of, 64
purchase by a company of its own shares, 56

qualification shares, 315
qualifications of company secretary, 339
quasi-loan, 327

raising capital, 67
receiver,
  and managers, 374
  appointment of, 374
  general duties, 376
  general powers, 376
receiverships, 373–9
reconstruction, 260–1
  example of, 220
  under s. 110 Insolvency Act 1986, 272–7
reconversion of stock into shares, 248
redeemable debentures, 362
  re-issue of, 371
redeemable shares, 45
redemption of debentures, methods used for, 371–2
redemption or purchase of own shares out of capital, 57
reduction below authorized minimum of allotted share capital of public company, 257
reduction of capital, 252–7
refusal to register a transfer, 138
register,
  of charges, 366
  of debenture holders, 66, 365, 370
  of directors' interests, 66, 332
  of directors and secretaries, 66, 330
  of documents sealed, 66, 143–61
  of important documents, 67
  of interests in shares, 66
  of members, 66, 147
    alteration, 150
    contents, 147
    form, 147–9
    inspection, 150
    location, 150
    rectification, 151
  of powers of attorney, 208
  of probates and letters of administration, 208
  of transfers, 66, 187
register of substantial individual interests in shares, 286
  contents of, 286
  inspection of, 286
  location of, 286
  obligation of disclosure, 286
registered company,
  nature, 1
  types, 1
registered debentures, 363
registered office, 8
  domicile of, 25
  notice of situation of, 11
Registrar of Companies, documents filed with on formation, 9
  form of, 12, 14
  notices to, 106
Registrar's Register of Charges, 367–70
registration,
  of company, preliminary considerations, 8
  signing of documents, 10
  of documents, 204, 212–19

registration department, 204
registration fees, 11
  on annual return, 161
'relevant accounts', meaning, 174
'relevant company', meaning, 325
renunciation, letters of, 110, 114
  split letters of, 110
  stock exchange requirements, 113
reports of directors, 349–52
representation, chain of, 199
request, letter of, 197
re-registration,
  of companies, 16
  of limited company as unlimited, 20
  of private company as public, 16
  of public company as private, 18
  of unlimited company as limited, 19
  of unlimited company as public, 18
resolution(s),
  re allotment of shares, 107
  re cancellation of shares, 251
  re consolidation and division, 248
  re conversion shares into stock, 249
  elective, 7
  re increase of capital, 246
  re reduction of capital, 254
  re sub-division of shares, 250
  re winding-up, 303
  written, 6
restrictions on allotment, 70–1
retirement of directors, 316
return of allotments, 110
rights issue, 118–21

sale of undertaking under powers in memorandum, 277
scheme meetings, 269
schemes of arrangement, under s. 425, 264–72
seal, common, 147
seals register, 66, 143
secondary offers, defined, 70
secretary,
  appointment of, 63, 274, 338
  capacity to act as, 338
  director as, 337
  duties, 340
  qualifications of, 339
  requirement, 337
  signature of, 339
  status of, 338
securities seal, 145
SEPON, 180, 182
shadow directors, 337
share certificates, 163–77
  damaged, worn or mutilated, 170
  exemption from obligation to prepare, 166
  issue, 166
  legal effects, 163
  lost, 169
  preparation and issue, 110
share premium, 100
share qualification, 315
share warrants, 171–7
  authority to issue, 171
  effects of issuing, 175
  issue, 173
  lost, 176
  surrender of, 176
shareholder, death of, 212
shares,
  acquisition of a company's shares by the company, 49
  acquisition of a company's shares by the company's nominees, 50
  cancellation of, 194
  charges taken by public company on its own shares, 52
  or debentures, 359
  deferred, 44
  financial assistance for acquisition of shares, 53
  held by or on behalf of a public company, treatment of, 51
  issued at a premium, 100
  limitation of liability by, 1
  non-voting, 44
  ordinary, 44
  preference, 43
  redeemable, 45
  transfer of, 179–95
  transmission of, 195
  when payable, 128
signature, mechanical, 119, 178
sinking fund, 371
solicitors,
  appointment of, 63
  role of on formation, 8
solvency, declaration of, 303
special directors, 336
split letters of renunciation, 110, 114
statement of affairs, 296
statutory books, 66
statutory declaration,

of compliance, 11
of solvency, 303
stock, 46
Stock Exchange,
continuing obligation of, 74
Model Code for Securities Transactions by Directors, 332
requirements of articles, 36
requirements of directors' report, 351
Settlement Centre, 183
Stock Exchange (Completion of Bargains) Act 1976, 179, 182
Stock Transfer Act 1963, 179
stock transfer form, 182
'stop notice', 154
subscribers to memorandum, 27
subscription clause, 27
substantial property transactions involving directors, 330
sub-underwriting, 96
surrender of shares, 138

Table A, 35
TALISMAN settlement system, 179, 182–4
talon on share warrant, 126
TAURUS, 184
tender offer, 67
transfer,
advice, 187
blank, 193
duties of secretary, 185
fees, 186
forged, 193
form of, 179
procedure, 181
receipt, 187
register, 66, 187
right of, 180
transfer of shares, 179–95
notice of refusal to register, 180, 189
re private companies, 180
procedure on, 181
transferor's signature, 186
transmission of shares, 195–200
treatment of shares held by or on behalf of a public company, 51
trust deeds, 372
trust, notice of, 153
trustee in bankruptcy, 198

ultra vires, basic nature, 26
statutory modification, 26
underwriter, 94
underwriting, 10, 94, 118
advantages of, 95
commission, 95
contract, 10, 94
of debentures, 95
examples of, 96–9
'firm', 97
in 'rights' issue, 118
re statutory provisions, 95
undistributable reserves, 226
unlimited company, 1
Unlisted Securities Market, 93
unlisted securities,
offer of, 90–3

voluntary winding up, 291, 301–9

Wales, registration of company in, 25
Welsh, language, 22, 25
winding up,
appointment of liquidator, 299, 304, 306
commencement of, 295, 301
conclusion of, 300, 305, 308
consequences of, 295, 301
definition, 291
hearing of a petition, 294
members', 234, 244–8
methods, 291
petition, 293
statement of affairs, 296
voluntary, 234, 243–51

Yellow Book, 72